DIGITAL ASSETS IN ENFORCEMENT AND INSOLVENCY

This book offers the first comprehensive analysis of the national and international legal issues surrounding digital assets in enforcement and insolvency.

Its primary aim is to ensure that the economic value of digital assets can be fully realised by creditors and other stakeholders through the legal processes and remedies available to them, and that holders of digital assets receive adequate protection. These legal issues are considered in diverse commercial and technical contexts, ranging from native cryptocurrencies to tokens, whether held directly or with custodians and other intermediaries.

The book offers analysis on different levels: firstly, it scrutinises the existing legal frameworks for enforcement and insolvency in various countries and evaluates the extent to which they can accommodate digital forms of value; secondly, it compares the approaches taken in different jurisdictions and addresses the cross-border issues of jurisdiction and conflict of laws issues that may arise; and thirdly, it focuses on international texts, such as the UNIDROIT Principles on Digital Assets and Private Law, as well as the Global Code of Digital Enforcement, and suggested avenues for further harmonisation and unification of the law.

The book provides much-needed responses to the increasing significance of digital assets in modern insolvency and enforcement proceedings. It takes a unique global approach to a wide range of legal perspectives, drawing upon the contributors' experience as leading practitioners, representatives of international organisations, and academics, in common law and civil law jurisdictions around the world. The book identifies the most pressing areas for law reform, and proposes solutions that are both legally robust as well as fit for practical purpose.

Hart Studies in Commercial and Financial Law: Volume 17

Hart Studies in Commercial and Financial Law
Series Editors: John Linarelli and Teresa Rodríguez de las Heras Ballell

This series offers a venue for publishing works on commercial law as well as on the regulation of banking and finance, and the law on insolvency and bankruptcy. It publishes works on the law on secured credit, the regulatory and transactional aspects of banking and finance, the transactional and regulatory institutions for financial markets, legal and policy aspects associated with access to commercial and consumer credit, new generation subjects having to do with the institutional architecture associated with innovation and the digital economy including works on blockchain technology, works on the relationship of law to economic growth, the harmonisation or unification of commercial law, transnational commercial law, and the global financial order. The series promotes interdisciplinary work. It publishes research on the law using the methods of empirical legal studies, behavioural economics, political economy, normative welfare economics, law and society inquiry, socio-legal studies, political theory, and historical methods. Its coverage includes international and comparative investigations of areas of law within its remit.

Volume 1: The Financialisation of the Citizen: Social and Financial Inclusion through European Private Law
Guido Comparato

Volume 2: MiFID II and Private Law: Enforcing EU Conduct of Business Rules
Federico Della Negra

Volume 3: Reforming Corporate Retail Investor Protection: Regulating to Avert Mis-Selling
Diane Bugeja

Volume 4: The Future of Commercial Law: Ways Forward for Change and Reform
Edited by Orkun Akseli and John Linarelli

Volume 5: The Cape Town Convention: A Documentary History
Anton Didenko

Volume 6: Regulating the Crypto Economy: Business Transformations and Financialisation
Iris H-Y Chiu

Volume 7: The Future of High-Cost Credit: Rethinking Payday Lending
Jodi Gardner

Volume 8: The Enforcement of EU Financial Law
Edited by Jan Crijns, Matthias Haentjens and Rijnhard Haentjens

Volume 9: International Bank Crisis Management: A Transatlantic Perspective
Marco Bodellini

Volume 10: Creditor Priority in European Bank Insolvency Law: Financial Stability and the Hierarchy of Claims
Sjur Swensen Ellingsæter

Volume 11: Chinese and Global Financial Integration through Stock Connect: A Legal Analysis
Flora Huang

Volume 12: The Governance of Macroprudential Policy: How to Build Regulatory Legitimacy Through a Social Justice Approach
Tracy C Maguze

Volume 13: A Socio-Legal Theory of Money for the Digital Commercial Society: A New Analytical Framework to Understand Cryptoassets
Israel Cedillo Lazcano

Volume 14: Venture Capital Investment and Government Incentives: Law, Regulation and Policy Design
Tamara Wilkinson

Volume 15: Regulating Primary Markets in the Capital Markets Union: Between Uniformity and Differentiation
Konstantinos Serdaris

Volume 16: Regulating Innovation in the Digital Age: A Demand-Centred Toolbox for the Data-Driven Economy
Nikita Divissenko

Volume 17: Digital Assets in Enforcement and Insolvency: Securing Creditor Access and Protecting Customer Interests in the Crypto World
Edited by Christian Koller and Matthias Lehmann

Digital Assets in Enforcement and Insolvency

Securing Creditor Access and Protecting Customer Interests in the Crypto World

Edited by
Christian Koller
and
Matthias Lehmann

•HART•
OXFORD • LONDON • NEW YORK • NEW DELHI • SYDNEY

HART PUBLISHING

Bloomsbury Publishing Plc

Kemp House, Chawley Park, Cumnor Hill, Oxford, OX2 9PH, UK

1385 Broadway, New York, NY 10018, USA

Bloomsbury Publishing Ireland Limited, 29 Earlsfort Terrace, Dublin 2, D02 AY28, Ireland

HART PUBLISHING, the Hart/Stag logo, BLOOMSBURY and the Diana logo are trademarks of Bloomsbury Publishing Plc

First published in Great Britain 2025

A catalogue record for this book is available from the British Library.

A catalogue record for this book is available from the Library of Congress.

Library of Congress Control Number: 2024950740

ISBN: HB: 978-1-50997-675-1
ePDF: 978-1-50997-677-5
ePub: 978-1-50997-676-8

Typeset by Compuscript Ltd, Shannon

For product safety related questions contact productsafety@bloomsbury.com

To find out more about our authors and books visit www.hartpublishing.co.uk. Here you will find extracts, author information, details of forthcoming events and the option to sign up for our newsletters.

FOREWORD

Digital assets have permeated the traditional flows of economic value and penetrated into the spaces for the circulation of wealth in the contemporary global economy. They are amply held by companies and individuals in their investment portfolios, intensively traded in global markets, and used as backing for fundraising and access to finance. Despite periods of instability and the cyclical evolution of the market ('crypto winters'), the use of digital assets is increasingly widespread in most domestic economies, enthusiastically accepted by individuals and businesses alike, and has an undeniable economic relevance. The emergence of burgeoning markets for various sub-types of digital assets, in the international scene, has also led to the progressive consolidation of a growing network of intermediaries and specialised service providers, from custodians, crypto lenders, and wallet service providers, to crypto exchanges and trading venues. As a result, digital assets have created new business opportunities, new intermediaries, new markets, new forms of economic value, and new vehicles for the transfer of wealth in modern economies.

Concurrently, the pervasive, rapid, and relatively silent penetration of the economy by digital assets has also raised worries and stoked concerns about their risks and uncertainties. Their ascent has been met with concerns, scepticism, and distrust by public authorities, regulators, and supervisors. They are concerned, above all, about the implications and consequences of the new phenomena for investors' rights and the market's stability. The worries of public authorities had been fuelled and partly proven right by an increasing number of disquieting and troubling cases that have surfaced in the last years. A series of responses have been tried. Some of them are regulatory in nature, prohibiting or curtailing a certain activity or product; others are exploratory, aiming at prudently understanding the phenomenon and unveiling the risks. Some are, in line with the global character of the market, substantially supranational; while, others, rooted in fundamentally domestic worries and sovereignty sensitiveness, are purely national. In sum, a variety of answers have been attempted. Nevertheless, the conversation about the best solution, both from a global as well as a domestic viewpoint, is still ongoing.

This book is a major contribution to this ongoing conversation. It puts two questions into the spotlight that are often under-researched: enforcement and insolvency. It tries to answer where, when, and how digital assets can be enforced, tracked, recovered or realised. In doing so, this book builds on the more fundamental question whether digital assets can be the object of proprietary rights. Without answering this question in the affirmative, the conversation on insolvency and enforcement could hardly continue, because it would then turn into a complex conversation about personal rights.

Two consequences follow from the fundamental decision to accept digital assets as being proper objects of proprietary rights. First, the conversation on digital assets in enforcement and insolvency is primarily approached from a property-law framework. Second, the conversation on digital assets sharply departs from a general narrative on the value of data and data transactions in today's economy. The stance adopted over digital assets, approached as 'assets', has a profound and decisive conceptualising effect. It looks at what 'digital assets' are and what they are not by drawing a clear line between digital assets and data or pure information. How to solve the question of the concept (and the definition) of digital assets pervades the current, multifaceted legal and policy discussion of whether the notion should be uniform and internationally harmonised, or is better left to domestic law. Conceptualising the new phenomena as 'digital assets' may be a way of justifying the analogous application of the rules governing other assets, or of stressing their differences to these assets, which would call for a different treatment. It also raises the question whether, and if so, to what extent, the regulatory concepts and rules should influence the rules of private law, including private procedural law.

The thematic choice – enforcement and insolvency – is doubly pertinent and commendable. On the one hand, after an initial stage of emergence, growth, and assimilation by the market of these new classes of assets, the increasing use of digital assets for trade, investment and finance has led to a wave of private litigation and situations of financial distress. Courts, with different intensity and frequency depending upon the jurisdiction, have started to hear disputes that highlight how the distinctive characteristics of digital assets – their functional, structural, and operational features – pose challenges in enforcement. Courts and parties have started to confront a variety of complexities, from conflicts of laws to contractual and tort law issues. Besides these legal issues, there are also others of a more practical nature. Both types of issues potentially distort and hamper effective enforcement proceedings in the frequent cross-border context. Doubts about the competent court or enforcement agent and about the applicable law are compounded by uncertainties over the effective application of existing enforcement rules, procedures, and measures. To these are added practical difficulties in identifying the debtor or the relevant holder, in tracing and recovering the relevant digital assets, and in realising the value with the traditional pricing formulae, the classical methods of valuation, or in-place trading mechanisms. Hence, as the market grows and expands, litigation increases, and enforcement-related issues grow and expand as well.

In parallel, market volatility and periods of substantial decline in value – as seen in the 'crypto winter' – have triggered situations of financial distress for major intermediaries and providers in the crypto market. As a consequence, we have witnessed a chain of crypto-related insolvencies, some of them with high visibility in the media and significant global impact. They have unveiled certain difficulties and possible limitations of existing insolvency laws. In the spotlight is the very relation between the customer and the intermediary, yet even the seemingly simple issue of whether digital assets are part of the debtor's estate is consistently raising novel legal issues in insolvency proceedings.

Hence, reality calls for a closer look at the issues arising in enforcement and insolvency, which have recently gained in visibility, factual relevance, and practical interest. This book acknowledges this and rightly puts the multiple facets of this thread of the conversation into the spotlight.

The issues dealt with in this book have also received increasing attention by international harmonising organisations and formulating agencies, as well as by domestic lawmakers and regulators. Thus, UNIDROIT, the organisation for the unification of private law, has addressed questions relating to enforcement and insolvency in its landmark instrument on digital assets, the Principles on Digital Assets and Private Law. In addition, UNIDROIT is also looking closer at digital assets in enforcement as part of its ongoing project on Best Practices on Effective Enforcement. Likewise, the United Nations Commission on International Trade and Development Law (UNCITRAL) has prepared a toolkit for civil asset tracing and recovery in insolvency proceedings (ATR), which includes digital assets. The European Law Institute (ELI) is continuing its project 'Access to Digital Assets' with a special sub-group aiming at the elaboration of principles and recommendations on enforcement. This increasing 'normative' attention deserves a profound study of various questions.

This book is exemplary in this respect by bringing together analyses of international legal harmonisation and comparative law, of private law and international private law, of a practical and a theoretical nature, and of empirical and doctrinal research. It explores a string of relevant and important questions raised by digital assets in enforcement and insolvency proceedings. It does so from different perspectives, sometimes from a domestic viewpoint, sometimes from an international harmonisation viewpoint, sometimes through thoughtful doctrinal analysis, sometimes emphasising practical problems and experience.

Indeed, to grapple with the essence of a problem, the right questions need to be asked. The first question is whether a global response to digital assets is necessary, possible, and desirable. In delving into the fields of enforcement and insolvency, we immediately realise that multiple legal and policy considerations interweave: domestic conceptions of property; primary goals of insolvency law; the role of enforcement agents; the tension between judicial and extrajudicial enforcement; the position on creditor protection vis-à-vis debtors' interests; considerations related to monetary and macroeconomic policies; the extent of cooperation duties in enforcement proceedings, and many others. The intangible nature of digital assets, the inherent global scope of the crypto market, and the irrelevance (or disconcerting weakness) of the notion of situs support the case for international harmonisation. But this cannot conceal the fact that such strategy is fraught with complexities, limitations, and difficulties, and must be reconciled with sovereign sensitivities and domestic concerns. While there are strong arguments for harmonisation, a balance with these concerns must be struck. How this can be achieved is still an unsettled question.

Even if it is accepted that a certain level of harmonisation is vital for a sustainable, reliable, and efficient 'crypto economy', it must be discussed how intense and extensive the harmonisation effort should be. That leads to the problem of the types of international legal harmonisation instruments to be promoted. Considering the domestic concerns, and the national components of some legal aspects influenced by digital assets, the harmonisation intensity is a key success factor. Do we need only principles, or should we adopt binding rules? Are best practices effective to promote a silent, progressive, and smooth harmonisation trend? Which kind of harmonisation would discourage regulatory arbitrage or forum shopping? And should substantive law be harmonised, or could uniform international private law rules provide a good, and sufficient, solution?

Underneath these questions lies an even more profound issue that influences any conversation about digital assets. It is the common uneasiness about how the new and disruptive assets should be dealt with. Do the existing rules and practices suffice, or should new and special rules and practices be created? This is the second question to pose. While everyone will readily agree that this is a problem, opinions on the appropriate solution vary. Domestic legislators and courts have given different responses. Some jurisdictions try to accommodate the 'novelties' of digital assets by using their 'old' concepts, solutions, and legal rules, on the basis of functional equivalences or substantial similarities, without reforming their law. Others, in turn, address the phenomenon with an overhaul of their rules and practices, spurred by the conviction that 'new realities require new laws'. The divergence between the domestic responses makes the international response to digital assets more complicated but also more decisive. Bespoke international rules for digital assets would reinforce the perception of their novelty and the necessity to fill gaps in the legal system. Best practices rather stress the adaptability of the existing rules and their ability to capture everything from the 'old to the new'. The book weaves together an enlightening thread of illustrations, reasoning, and rationale for both approaches.

Yet, there is still a third question to put forward. As in many other areas of international trade, the issues raised by digital assets reveal an intimate and increasingly inseparable interplay between regulation and private law. Due to their (partial) intersection with regulated markets, transactions in digital assets have consistently given rise to this tension. This leads to several questions: How relevant should regulatory characterisation and taxonomy be for the private-law discourse? Might regulation solve all, or part of, the questions that enforcement and insolvency in digital assets pose? Should the interplay between regulation and private law differ in this particular industry for any reason? In this regard, the relation between regulation and private law in the realm of digital assets may perhaps become a model or blueprint for other areas of the economy.

This book helps in correctly formulating and thoughtfully answering all of the three questions raised. It contributes to the ongoing polyhedric global conversation, which it enriches with sound arguments, complementary views, and well-reasoned analysis. For anyone interested in this conversation, the following pages will be instructive.

Teresa Rodríguez de las Heras Ballell
Sancti Petri, Cádiz, August 2024

CONTENTS

PART III
INSOLVENCY AND DIGITAL ASSETS

CONTRIBUTORS

Benjamin Geva

LL.B. (cum laude) (1970), Jerusalem; LL.M. and S.J.D Harvard Law School; Member of the Ontario Bar Research Fellow, University of Vienna specializing in banking, negotiable instruments, funds transfers, digital currencies, payment and settlement systems, and documents of title. Professor of Law, Osgoode Hall Law School of York University, Toronto, Canada (faculty member since 1977); Counsel (part-time), payments and cards group in Torys LLP, Toronto (since 2012); founding Editor of the *Banking and Finance Law Review*; and author of *Financing Consumer Sales and Product Defences*, *The Law of Electronic Funds Transfers*, *Bank Collections and Payment Transactions: Comparative Study of Legal Aspects*, and *The Payment Order of Antiquity and the Middle Ages: A Legal History*. Co-author of *International negotiable Instruments*. Under the IMF technical assistance program he advised and drafted key financial sector legislation, particularly payment laws, in several developing and post-conflict countries (particularly in the former Yugoslavia, Cambodia, Sri Lanka, and Timor-Leste).

Louise Gullifer

Professor Louise Gullifer KC (hon) FBA is Rouse Ball Professor of English Law at the University of Cambridge, and a fellow of Gonville and Caius College, Cambridge, UK. She is an associate member of 3VB, where she practised for a number of years, and a Bencher of Gray's Inn. She teaches and writes extensively in all areas of commercial and financial law. She is the editor of *Goode and Gullifer on Legal Problems of Credit and Security* and has co-authored a number of books on commercial law, debt financing, and the law of Intermediated Securities. She was the UK delegate to UNCITRAL working group VI during its work on secured transactions, and is a member of several UNIDROIT working groups, including chairing the drafting group for the Principles on Digital Assets and Private Law and, now, as senior adviser to UNIDROIT on the project on Verified Carbon Credits.

Amy Held

Amy Held was called to the Bar of England and Wales in 2019 and is an Affiliate Academic in the Common Law at the University of Vienna. She has maintained an academic specialisation in the private law aspects of cryptoassets and DLT from national English law, comparative law, and private international law perspectives since 2017, with a particular focus on property law. Amy is actively involved in law reform initiatives at the Law Commission of England and Wales, as well as international initiatives at the HCCH and UNIDROIT relating to digital and other modern assets. She continues to publish and lecture widely on these and related legal issues in both the academic and practitioner contexts.

Christian Koller

Christian Koller is a Full Professor of European and International Civil Procedure Law at the University of Vienna. His research focuses on cross-border dispute resolution, international insolvency law, and issues of cross-border enforcement. He is frequently invited as a guest professor at leading European universities, including Panthéon-Sorbonne University in France, where he teaches international arbitration

Matthias Lehmann

Matthias Lehmann is a full professor for private law, private international and comparative law at the University of Vienna, as well as professor for European and comparative business law at Radboud University Nijmegen. His main interest lies in international and comparative aspects of financial law as well as cross-border dispute resolution. He has been visiting academic at the London School of Economics and Political Science, at Oxford University and at Stanford University, and is regularly invited as a guest professor at various European Universities, including Sorbonne University (France), where he teaches a class on the law and regulation of crypto markets. Matthias is a member of the European Law Institute, the American Law Institute, the Academia Europaea and the European Banking Institute. He has participated in the European Commission's Expert Group on Conflict of Laws Regarding Securities and Claims, and in various working groups of the UK Financial Markets Law Committee, UNIDROIT and HCCH, inter alia on digital assets and digital tokens.

Tetsuo Morishita

Tetsuo Morishita is a Professor of law, Sophia University, Tokyo Japan, where he teaches international business law, banking & finance law and negotiation. B.A. in Law, University of Tokyo (1989), M.A. in Law, University of Tokyo (1994). He formerly worked for The Sumitomo Bank, Limited (Japan) from 1989 to 1999. He has served on various governmental committees at the Financial Services Agency and the Ministry of Justice of Japan.

Hossein Nabilou

Hossein Nabilou is an Assistant Professor of Law & Finance at the University of Amsterdam (UvA) Law School. Prior to joining UvA, Hossein was UNIDROIT-Bank of Italy Chair at the International Institute for the Unification of Private Law (UNIDROIT). His research focuses on monetary and banking law, shadow banking, financial market infrastructures, financial contracting, alternative investment funds, and legal issues of fintech, payments, and crypto-assets. He teaches European Banking Law, Financial Contracting, Fintech: Law & Policy, and Law & Economics.

Thomas Nägele

Thomas Nägele is Managing Partner of NÄGELE Attorneys at Law LLC. He advised international finance, technology, and industrial enterprises, thereby carrying out projects in the fields of blockchain/DLT technology ever since. He builds the bridge between the technical and legal world through his 10-year experience within different roles at two Liechtenstein technology companies. He has been a member of the government workgroup drafting the Liechtenstein Blockchain Act (TVTG), Liechtenstein CCA Crypto Country Association founder and president, founding member of the thinkBLOCKtank in Luxembourg, Chair of the board of INATBA.org and founding member of the House of Blockchain Vaduz.

Michael Ng

Michael Ng holds a Bachelor of Laws (summa cum laude) from Singapore Management University and a Master of Laws (Distinction) from the London School of Economics. He is currently a Senior Lecturer with the Singapore University of Social Sciences School of Law with a research focus on private international law, trust law and the intersection between blockchain and commercial law. He is also a qualified lawyer in Singapore and Of Counsel with Beyond Legal LLC, where he advises on various commercial disputes.

Areti Nikolakopoulou

Areti Nikolakopoulou is a Doctoral Researcher at the ADA Chair in Financial Law (Inclusive Finance) at the University of Luxembourg. She holds a Bachelor of Laws (J.D. equivalent) from the National & Kapodistrian University of Athens and an LLM in European Banking and Financial Law from the University of Luxembourg. She has published in leading journals on financial regulation and FinTech. Her current research focuses on Investment Funds, Sustainable Finance and FinTech. Some of her publications are available at ssrn.com/author=6465494.

Teresa Rodríguez de las Heras Ballell

Full Professor of Commercial Law at University Carlos III of Madrid, Spain. She was Sir Roy Goode Scholar at Unidroit 2021–22. She is member of the Unidroit Project on BPEE; a delegate of Spain at UNCITRAL for WGs VI, IV and I, and an Expert for UNCITRAL and Unidroit on digital economy projects. Arbitrator. Member of the Austrian Academy of Sciences. Member of the European Commission Expert Groups on Liability and New Technologies, for the Observatory on Online Platform Economy, and on B2B Data Sharing and Cloud Computing. Member of the ELI Executive Committee and Council.

Dominik Skauradszun

Judge of Appeal Professor Dr. Dominik Skauradszun, LL.M. is a full Professor of civil law, civil procedure and company law at Fulda University, Germany, judge at the Higher Regional Court of Frankfurt, and an Honorary Professor of insolvency law and the law of crypto-assets at the Nottingham Trent University, England. He has published extensively and participated in hearings of parliaments and ministries on crypto-assets and has written several legal opinions on crypto-assets in enforcement and insolvency.

Jos Uitdehaag

Enforcement agent in the Netherlands since 1995. First Vice-President of the International Union of Judicial Officers (UIHJ), treasurer of the International Institute for Justice Excellence. For 25 years, he has been active as a legal reform and legal drafting expert in numerous countries both within and outside Europe, mainly in the field of enforcement law. Lecturer at the Dutch University of Applied Sciences in Utrecht, the Netherlands, Prishtina State University, Kosovo and as a guest lecturer at different universities and judicial academies. Co-reporter of the Project Fiduciary Access to Digital Assets of the European Law Institute and observer member of the Unidroit project on principles for effective enforcement.

Hubert de Vauplane

Hubert de Vauplane is a partner at Kramer Levin LLP in Paris, where he is in charge of the Regulatory/Fintech practice. Prior to joining this firm, he was Group General Counsel at Crédit Agricole Group, Head of CIB Legal Affairs at BNPP, after spending several years at ODDO BHF as a derivatives trader. He completed his university studies at the Université Panthéon – Assas Paris II and obtained a doctorate in law. He taught banking and finance law as an associate professor at the same university for 18 years before joining the Sciences Po Law School, where he teaches international banking law. He is or has been a member of the following organizations: European Financial Lawyer Group; Financial Law Market Committee. He is or has been appointed as an expert to the Autorité des marchés financiers, the World Bank and the European Commission. He is and was a member of the French delegations to UNIDROIT and the Hague Conference on financial securities law and cryptoassets. One of his books was awarded a prize by the Académie de Sciences Morales et Politques.

Anna Veneziano

Anna Veneziano (LL.M. Yale Law School, PhD University of Florence, Italy) is Deputy Secretary-General of UNIDROIT and Professor of Comparative Private Law at Teramo University, with previous roles as Director of the Department of Private Law and a tenured position as Professor of European Property Law at the University of Amsterdam, as well as visiting professorships in several other academic institutions. Her fields of expertise and publication include international and comparative contract law and international and comparative secured transactions law. At UNIDROIT she is involved, among other projects, in the development of Best Practices for Effective Enforcement.

Oliver Völkel

Oliver Völkel is a founding partner of STADLER VÖLKEL, a leading full-service law firm based in Vienna, Austria. His expertise includes banking, capital market and crypto-asset law. Oliver regularly publishes articles on legal aspects of blockchain and crypto-assets and gives lectures at multiple Austrian universities. His clients include renowned international corporations and banks. Oliver studied law at the University of Vienna and at Columbia Law School in New York. In the past, he has worked in international corporate law firms.

Anna K Wilke

Dr. Anna K. Wilke, LL.M. oec. has been an associate of Prof. Dr. Lucas F. Flöther at the law firm FLÖTHER & WISSING Insolvenzverwaltung GbR since 2018. She is a lawyer in the field of insolvency and restructuring court and is active both in classic insolvency proceedings as well as in self-administration and (pre-insolvency) restructuring advice. Prior to this, she graduated with a Master of Business Law and Economic Law and she completed a doctorate under Prof. Madaus on the subject of insolvency and restructuring of municipalities.

Nik Yeo

Nik Yeo is a barrister at Fountain Court Chambers in London who focuses on complex finance, fintech and professional negligence matters. He has litigated some of the world's most significant finance and fintech disputes, including acting for Lehman Bros Inc in certain of its cases against other Lehman entities after the bank's collapse, and assisting the UK Government in the GBP½ trillion bank bail-out during the GFC. He has an extensive crypto litigation practice, representing the Bahamian liquidators of FTX, and acting for many crypto intermediaries, such exchanges and blockchain bridges. Previously, Nik was a transactional solicitor at Slaughter and May, and has taught law at Melbourne and Oxford Universities.

Dirk Zetzsche

Professor Zetzsche holds the ADA Chair in Financial Law (inclusive finance) at the University of Luxembourg's Faculty of Law, Economics and Finance and co-leads Luxembourg's FinTech National Centre of Excellence in Research. His more than 400 publications focus on FinTech, Inclusive and Sustainable Finance, investment funds, and corporate governance. Professor Zetzsche functions, inter alia, as co-chair of the EBI FinTech committee, and member of the ESRB's task force on crypto-assets as well as ESMA Investment Management Steering Committee's Consultative Working Group.

PART I

Overarching Issues

1

Introduction

CHRISTIAN KOLLER AND MATTHIAS LEHMANN

Technological innovation has the power to reshape traditional law, eg, by transforming existing assets, by enhancing their capabilities, or by creating entirely new categories of assets. Distributed ledger technologies (DLTs), in particular the blockchain, provide a prime example in this respect. The blockchain has generated a broad variety of digital assets, from cryptocurrencies and non-fungible tokens (NFTs) to utility tokens, stablecoins and beyond.[1] Their rise has put traditional law to the test and triggered an intense debate about the need for introducing specific legal instruments tailored to these new phenomena.

Most of the legal discussion surrounding the blockchain focuses on regulatory rules.[2] However, it also raises a plethora of private-law problems. Among the most urgent is how crypto assets shall be treated in enforcement and insolvency law. For instance, how can claims be enforced against intangible assets in a pseudonymous and distributed environment? Which rights do customers have in the insolvency of a crypto exchange? These are just two of the many problems raised by digital assets. The debate about them in academic, regulatory and legislative circles is still in its early days. This book aims to make a significant contribution to its advancement. It unites experts from around the world, who analyse the issue from a wide range of perspectives. Almost all of the contributions have been presented on 3 and 4 May 2023 at a conference at the University of Vienna, which was jointly organised by the European Law Institute (ELI) and the European Banking Institute (EBI). They have been updated since to reflect new developments.

The book is divided into three parts. Part I addresses fundamental issues that cut across enforcement and insolvency. It starts with the core question of whether digital assets can be property, or rather 'the object of proprietary rights', which is essential for both fields. It will be discussed by one of the most eminent authorities

[1] See, eg, English Law Commission, *Digital assets: Final report* (Law Com No 412, 2023) para 1.3.

[2] See, eg, S Johnstone, *Rethinking the Regulation of Cryptoassets* (Cheltenham, Edward Elgar, 2021); I Sheridan, *Financial Regulation and Technology: A Legal and Compliance Guide* (Cheltenham, Edward Elgar, 2022); DA Zetzsche et al, 'The ICO Gold Rush: It's a Scam, It's a Bubble, It's a Super Challenge for Regulators' (2019) 60 *Harvard International Law Journal* 267.

on property law.[3] The first soft-law instrument to address property and insolvency law issues raised by the blockchain is the UNIDROIT Principles on Digital Assets and Private Law. It will be presented by two of the experts involved in its adoption.[4] Whether a particular digital asset can be the object of enforcement and the status of investors in insolvency proceedings depends on the applicable national law. For tangible assets, the location or *situs* plays a dominant role since it determines the competent forum to enforce a judgment debt as well as the question whether certain assets form part of the insolvency estate. However, where is the '*situs*' of a digital asset? This problem will be addressed in the next chapter.[5]

Part II is dedicated to enforcement issues. It analyses whether existing enforcement regimes are flexible enough to overcome the challenges raised by digital assets. The Global Code of Digital Enforcement, adopted by the International Union of Judicial Officers, provides innovative approaches in this respect and aims at inspiring national legislators when adopting specific provisions for enforcement in digital assets. Its content will be presented by one of the Union's leading members.[6] In many jurisdictions, the existing framework ensures efficient enforcement results. However, specific rules could enhance legal certainty, as discussed in the following chapter.[7] At the outset of enforcement proceedings, creditors face the issue of how to effectively trace and recover the debtor's (digital) assets. A practitioner will lay out strategies for coping with this problem.[8] Additionally, judgment creditors may wish to reduce the risk that the defendant transfers crypto assets prior to any enforcement attempt. How enforcement in such cases can be secured by interim remedies, eg, freezing injunctions or freezing orders, will be discussed by a leading UK practitioner.[9]

Part III tackles digital assets in insolvency law. Whether they form part of the insolvency estate and how they can be identified and recovered is a complex problem, which will be discussed from the perspective of various legal systems.[10] Since its inception, the crypto market has been plagued by insolvencies of crypto exchanges and custodians, such as Mt. Gox, Voyager Digital, FTX, and Celsius Network.[11] Such an insolvency can substantially impact the rights of crypto investors and holders. Several chapters cover these issues, again from the perspective of a variety of jurisdictions.[12] The insolvency of a party potentially disrupts the contractual framework on multiple levels. Insolvency law may, for instance, grant the insolvency administrator the right to terminate current contracts that have

[3] See Louise Gullifer, ch 2.
[4] See Anna Veneziano and Teresa Rodríguez de las Heras Ballell, ch 3.
[5] See Michael Ng, ch 4.
[6] See Jos Uitdehaag, ch 5.
[7] See Dominik Skauradszun, ch 6.
[8] See Anna K Wilke, ch 7.
[9] See Nik Yeo, ch 8.
[10] See Matthias Lehmann, ch 9, Thomas Nägele and Markus Stelzl, ch 10, and Benjamin Geva, ch 17.
[11] See Dirk Zetzsche and Areti Nikolakopoulou, ch 11.
[12] See Matthias Lehmann, ch 9, Thomas Nägele and Markus Stelzl, ch 10, Dirk Zetzsche and Areti Nikolakopoulou, ch 11, Oliver Völkel, ch 12, Hubert de Vauplane, ch 13, and Tetsuo Morishita, ch 14.

not yet been (entirely) fulfilled by the debtor or the respective counterparty. Furthermore, transactions or acts carried out before the commencement of insolvency proceedings that harm the community of creditors may be invalidated under transaction avoidance law. In this respect, 'transaction finality' is crucial, ie, the precise point in time when proprietary rights vest in the recipient, and when the parties' obligations are irrevocably fulfilled. As will be shown, transposing this concept to the blockchain is anything but easy.[13] In a similar vein, the application of transaction avoidance law raises complex questions as to whether transactions on the blockchain can be set aside in insolvency proceedings, which will be analysed.[14]

It is to be expected that different jurisdictions will solve the questions discussed here differently. Enforcement and insolvency law are the product of national traditions, interests and policy choices; therefore, they differ from country to country. However, distributed ledger technology is a worldwide phenomenon. Its problems occur in the same or in a similar manner in countries around the world. This suggests a uniform solution. Such an approach is all the more necessary as many of these problems can only be solved through cross-border coordination and cooperation between national authorities and courts. A transnational approach would benefit not only states, creditors and investors, but also the crypto industry, which requires a safe, harmonious and stable legal framework for its seamless functioning. We hope that this book will be a step on the way achieving this goal. In the editing process, we were assisted by Susanne Brück, Antonia Tieber, Julia Wachowicz and Anna Weber, to whom we owe a debt of gratitude.

[13] See Hossein Nabilou, ch 15, and Amy Held, ch 16.
[14] See Amy Held, ch 16.

2

Proprietary Rights in Digital Assets

LOUISE GULLIFER

I. Introduction

The subject matter of this book is digital assets in enforcement and insolvency. Leaving aside, for the moment, what is meant by 'digital assets'[1] a fundamental question is whether digital assets can be property, or, more accurately, whether they can be the object (or subject)[2] of proprietary rights.[3] It would be possible, though perhaps rather frustrating, to discuss issues of enforcement and insolvency on the basis that digital assets could not be the subject of proprietary rights. At each stage, we would be asking what personal rights each of the relevant players in a dispute had against each other, how those personal rights could be enforced, whether they survived insolvency, and so on. We might be having this conversation, for example, if we were discussing data or information in general. While jurisdictions vary, many consider that 'pure' information cannot be the subject of proprietary rights. That does not mean that, for example, breach of a duty of confidentiality cannot be enforced, but that the enforcement is of a personal right and not a proprietary right.

However, when the term 'assets' is used for the subject matter of our discussion, we instinctively feel that the organising structure of our discussion should be the law of property. We can see property law as an organisational structure to protect the control and circulation of wealth.[4] The law of property has grown up to protect the ability of people to exploit the value in 'assets' by using them,

[1] See s III.E.

[2] Whether the word 'object' or 'subject' should be used here is a matter for debate. The word 'object' appears to be in more common usage in civil law jurisdictions, while both words are used in common law jurisdictions (and 'subject' is used in the UNIDROIT Principles on the Private Law of digital assets). The word 'object' is used here, but is not intended to have a different meaning from 'subject' when that word is used in the same context.

[3] English lawyers sometimes use the word 'property' quite loosely, to mean both property rights and the subject of property rights: we talk about 'real property' and 'personal property'. Civilian lawyers are much more precise, and distinguish between the right and the object (or subject) of the right, as do many more rigorous English lawyers.

[4] See, eg, K Pistor, *The Code of Capital* (Princeton, Princeton University Press, 2019).

by transferring them in exchange for other assets, and by preventing others from using and transferring the assets they see as theirs. The use of property law as an organisational structure means that, in any one jurisdiction, consistent answers can be given to a number of questions. While there is scope for some variation of conclusion depending on the type and nature of assets,[5] there is a strong family resemblance between the consequences of any type of asset being the subject of proprietary rights.

A non-exhaustive list of such consequences gives an indication as to why one would want to know whether an asset is capable of being the object of proprietary rights. First, for example, proprietary rights are enforceable against third parties, although this rather sweeping statement hides a considerable degree of nuance between jurisdictions and in relation to different types of assets.[6] As a corollary, proprietary rights can be protected by specific remedies, such as an order for delivery up, or certain tracing remedies. These remedies typically include interlocutory remedies: applications for these remedies are the source, so far, of most of the English law decisions on whether digital assets can be the subject of proprietary rights.[7] Second, whether an insolvent person has a proprietary right in an asset usually determines whether that asset is available for distribution to its creditors or not. Third, a person can only dispose by will of assets in which they have a proprietary right. Fourth, proprietary rights include rights less than full ownership, such as security rights, and, in the common law, equitable rights against trustees, so that if an asset is capable of being the object of proprietary rights, a security right can be taken over it, and it can, in a common law jurisdiction, be held on trust.[8]

This chapter contains some reflections on the approach to be taken, in a legal system, to determine whether a particular type of 'asset'[9] is, or should be, capable

[5] See B McFarlane and S Douglas, 'Property, Analogy and Variety' (2022) 42 *OJLS* 161.

[6] In relation to tangibles, most systems accept that proprietary rights are enforceable against the world, although in some situations some jurisdictions, particularly common law ones, permit relative title. The position in relation to intangibles is more nuanced in both civil and common law jurisdictions: in relation to English law, see McFarlane and Douglas (n 5).

[7] *Vorotyntseva v Money-4 Ltd* [2018] EWHC 2596 (Ch); *Robertson v Persons Unknown* (15 July 2019, unreported); *AA v Persons Unknown* [2019] EWHC 3556 (Comr); *Toma v Murray* [2020] EWHC 2295 (Ch); *Ion Science Ltd v Persons Unknown* (21 December 2020, unreporte); *Fetch.AI Ltd v Persons Unknown* [2021] EWHC 2254 (Comr); *Wang v Darby* [2021] EWHC 3054 (Comr); *Mr Dollar Bill Ltd v Persons Unknown* [2021] EWHC 2718 (Ch); *Danisz v Persons Unknown* [2022] EWHC 280 (QB); *Jones v Persons Unknown* [2022] EWHC 2543 (Comr); *Osbourne v Persons Unknown* [2022] EWHC 1021 (Comr); *Piroozzadeh v Persons Unknown* [2023] EWHC 1024 (Ch).

[8] For discussion of whether a digital asset can be held on trust, see K Low, 'Trusts of Cryptoassets' (2021) 34 *Trust Law International* 191; G Cooper, Virtual Property as Trust assets and Investments' [2021] *Journal of International Banking and Financial Law* 751. Digital assets have been held to be capable of being held on trust in *Ruscoe v Cryptopia Ltd* [2020] NZHC 728 (New Zealand) and in *ByBit Fintech Ltd v Xin* [2023] SGHC 199 (Singapore).

[9] The word 'asset' is used as a neutral word in this chapter to refer to something about which the 'fundamental question' is asked. It does not necessarily connote that the asset has value (in any given case), although usually the fundamental question will only arise if at least some assets of that type have value. The word 'asset' is used rather than 'thing', since the word 'thing' is used in a different context (see s 3).

of being the object of proprietary rights. This question is called the 'fundamental question'. The chapter argues that there are two approaches to this question, which are not alternatives, but which can be combined in various ways. The next (second) section sets out these approaches (the deductive approach and the normative approach). The following section focuses on the deductive approach: considering the numerus clausus restricting the objects of a proprietary right and the characteristics which an object of proprietary rights might have, which would enable an argument from analogy to be made in relation to digital assets, as well as then suggesting a definition of 'digital asset' which would enable such an argument to be made, and finishes with a short discussion of why and how linked assets can be seen as the objects of proprietary rights. The fourth section reflects on the normative approach and the fifth section concludes, arguing that there are a preponderance of good arguments that digital assets (as defined) should be the object of proprietary rights, and that the application of the deductive approach provides a method and justification for an overall positive answer to the fundamental question.

II. Approaches to the Fundamental Question

The two approaches to the fundamental question are a deductive approach (is it?) and a normative approach (should it be?). The two approaches are not exclusive of each other but can operate in combination. Thus, if the answer to the first is a resounding 'yes' then the second may be more of a question of whether policy dictates that there should be any kind of restriction (such as is the case with body parts, for example[10]). If the answer to the first is 'maybe' or even 'as things stand, no' then a positive answer to the second will tip the balance in favour of adaptation of the existing legal position to accommodate the new type of asset within the general framework of property law.

The deductive approach involves deducing the answer to the question from existing legal principles. Within this process there are likely to be two questions, which I will address in turn in subsequent sections. The first is whether the asset is within a numerus clausus, that is, the list of assets that the law already permits to be the subject of proprietary rights.[11] Second, does it have the characteristics that other things which are capable of being the subject of proprietary rights have?[12] This second question involves reasoning by analogy, and has been used in the past to extend the types of assets that can be the object of proprietary rights and thus extend the numerus clausus. Ideally, both questions would be answered affirmatively in relation to an asset, but the questions could also be asked sequentially, in

[10] See, eg, *Yearworth v North Bristol NHS Trust* [2009] EWCA Civ 37, [2010] QB 1.
[11] See s III.A.
[12] See s III.D.

that if an asset did not readily fit into the numerus clausus, the 'characteristic test' could be used to show that they should, and that the taxonomy should be changed if necessary.[13] As mentioned above, at this stage the normative approach should also be used.

The normative approach involves a policy decision, taken by asking whether there are good reasons for the organisational structure of property law to apply to the asset. If such reasons exist, this approach would then involve consideration of whether the existing structure of a numerus clausus could be adapted to include it, and whether the definition of the asset should be limited to those assets with similar characteristics to other assets that are capable of being the object of proprietary rights. These points are considered in the following sub-sections.

III. The Deductive Approach

A. Numerus Clausus

In answering the fundamental question in relation to the law of a particular jurisdiction, the immediate reaction of most lawyers is to look at the law of that jurisdiction and ask, 'are digital assets within a category of asset that can already be the object of proprietary rights?'. In other words, they look at the existing law of property in their jurisdiction, and ask where digital assets fit in. This is because most, if not all, legal systems have a taxonomy of assets[14] that can be the object of proprietary rights. This taxonomy is likely to have grown up over a very long period of time, and is either enshrined in legislation[15] or entirely in caselaw.[16] Taxonomies in most (if not all) jurisdictions make a distinction between land (real or immovable property) and non-land (personal or movable property), although the lines may be drawn in slightly different places. Most also make some sort of a distinction between tangibles and intangibles, on the basis that this is reasonably easy to do as a matter of fact, but the consequences of such a distinction are more varied, and a matter of more contention.[17] Many jurisdictions, at least for certain purposes, also sub-divide these categories, so that the question asked in relation

[13] This is, broadly speaking, the approach that is being taken under English law.

[14] This is using this term in the sense set out in n 9 above.

[15] Legislation can either be general, (eg, arts 3.1, 3.2 and 3.6 of the Dutch Civil Code, which provide that property comprises of things and property rights, and then defines (briefly) things and property rights, the latter of which are broadly what are called 'claims' in s III.B: or can apply specifically for the purposes of the relevant piece of legislation, (eg, the definitions in US Uniform Commercial Code (as amended), §1:102(42) and (44) which give very detailed definitions of 'general intangibles' and 'goods').

[16] eg, English law. However, even in English law there are some examples of statutes which state that a particular type of asset is property eg, shares (Companies Act 2006, s 541: 'The shares or other interest of a member in a company are personal property (or, in Scotland, moveable property) and are not in the nature of real estate (or heritage)', Patents Act 1977, s 30(1): 'Any patent or application for a patent is personal property (without being a thing in action) …'.

[17] See, eg, n 6 above.

to digital assets is: 'What sub-category does it fall into?' Thus, in the United States, under Article 9 of the Uniform Commercial Code, one might ask whether an intangible is an account, a commercial tort claim, a deposit account, investment property, a letter-of credit right, money or a general intangible?[18]

Once we get down to this level of generality, we need to be very careful not to mix up private law categories with those established for the purposes of regulation, that is, categories established in order for the state to regulate certain activities or assets because of the systemic or other risk they pose. While there can be some overlap, this kind of functional taxonomy may well not map onto the private law taxonomy, which, to the extent that it does sub-categorise, may depend on characteristics of the assets categorised other than the risk they pose or their function. The debate in the United States over whether digital assets are money, securities or commodities[19] is a good example of this type of reasoning.

If we leave detailed sub-categories aside, in relation to movables we are left with the tangible/intangible distinction. This is where the question becomes more difficult, and where the different approaches of the civil law and common law jurisdictions begin to show. The civil law has a strict idea of numerus clausus, both in terms of proprietary rights[20] (rights effective erga omnes, that is, against all third parties) and in terms of the objects of such rights.[21] It is the latter (and less frequently articulated[22]) application of the numerus clausus principle that affects us here. Under the German system, for example, only tangibles can be the subject of ownership rights,[23] although the rule is less strict in relation to security rights over intangibles,[24] while the French system is less rigid, permitting incorporeal assets to be the subject of ownership rights in some specific situations,[25] as well as using the overall concept of 'biens' in its property law, which includes both tangibles and intangibles.[26]

[18] UCC art 9-102(2), (13), (29), (42), (49), (51). 'Money' is defined in UCC 1-102(24).

[19] For accounts of this debate in the courts and elsewhere, see C Goforth, 'U.S. Law: Crypto Is Money, Property, a Commodity, and a Security, all at the same Time' (2019) 49 *Journal of Financial Transformation* 102–10; J Allen, H Wells and M Mauer, 'Cryptoassets in Private Law: Emerging Trends and Open Questions from the First 10 Years' (2022) *SMU Centre for AI and Data Governance Research Paper*, papers.ssrn.com/sol3/papers.cfm?abstract_id=4206250.

[20] S van Erp, 'Comparative Property Law', in M Reiman and R Zimmermann (eds), *Oxford Handbook of Comparative Law*, 2nd edn (Oxford, Oxford University Press, 2019) 1042.

[21] S van Erp, 'Ownership of Data and the Numerus Clausus of Legal Objects' (2017) 6 *Brigham-Kanner Property Rights Conference Journal* 235; S Murphy and P Kenna (eds), 'eConveyancing and Title Registration in Ireland' Dublin, Clarus Press, 2019) 125; van Erp (n 20) 1050.

[22] See D Carr, 'Cryptocurrencies as Property in Civilian and Mixed Legal Systems', in D Fox and S Green (eds), *Cryptocurrencies in Public and Private Law* (Oxford, Oxford University Press, 2019) 7.09.

[23] See paras 90 and 903 BGB. Similarly, in Dutch law only 'things' can be the subject of ownership (Dutch Civil Code, arts 3.2 and 5.1), although 'rights' can be transferred (Dutch Civil Code, art 3.6). *cf* the position in Austria, where incorporeal things can be the object of ownership (ABGB, § 353).

[24] There can be a pledge of intangibles (see BGB, §1068 BGB) or a security assignment (a Sicherheitsabtretung, see S Van Erp and B Akkemanns (eds), *Cases, Materials and Texts on Property Law* (Oxford, Hart Publishing, 2012) 512.

[25] eg, there is specific legislation on intellectual property (the Code de propriété intellectuelle).

[26] J Bell, A Bell and S Boyron, 'Property Law' in J Bell, S Boyron and S Whittaker (eds), *Principles of French Law*, 2nd edn, (Oxford, Oxford University Press, 2008) 270.

The more rigid view has led to courts in some civil law jurisdictions to state that digital assets cannot be the subject of ownership rights. The *MtGox* case in Japan is an early example of this,[27] as is a Russian case in which, at first instance, the insolvency representative of a bankrupt was not permitted to access the bitcoin he controlled as it was not held to be 'property' under the Russian Civil Code.[28] The decision was overturned on appeal on the grounds that the Civil Code was about to be amended to include digital assets.[29] Article 128 of the Russian Civil Code was subsequently amended in 2019 to include digital rights, although it is not clear that this term includes digital assets.[30]

The common law also, arguably, has a taxonomy of objects of proprietary rights amounting to a numerus clausus, although the categories are broad, and the conceptual structure more flexible. Leaving aside land (immovable property) there are, at present, two categories of personal property in the common law: choses in possession and choses in action. Choses in possession are things that can be possessed, that is, tangibles. The common law so far has set its face against the possession of intangibles. Choses in action, however, while variously defined over the years, are usually said to be rights[31] enforced by action. There have been judicial statements that these two categories form the only two categories of objects of proprietary rights in the common law.[32] The question of whether digital assets, if capable of being the object of proprietary rights, are choses in action, choses in possession, or a third type of property is much debated in common law jurisdictions.[33] Before discussing this point, the more general division of movable assets into tangibles and intangibles (things and claims) will be discussed further.

[27] See the paraphrase of the 2015 Mt Gox judgment prepared by L Gullifer, M Hara, and C Mooney Jr, and available at www.law.ox.ac.uk/sites/default/files/migrated/mtgox_judgment_final.pdf. The context was the insolvency of the Mt Gox crypto-exchange, which controlled a number of bitcoin for its clients, although fewer than the number recorded in its books as controlled for its clients. The Mt Gox case was, at least in theory, resolved by a rehabilitation plan in 2021, and the plight of future crypto-exchange customers has been ameliorated by regulatory intervention in the insolvency of regulated crypto-exchanges by a statutory provision that customers have a preferential claim in relation to crypto assets held in compliance with the exchange's regulatory obligation to hold enough assets to satisfy its customer's contractual entitlement (Payment Services Act 2009, s 63-11-2 and 63-19-2(1), as amended in 2019 effective in 2020). For discussion of the Japanese position, see K Low and M Hara, 'Cryptoassets and Property', in S van Erp and K Zimmermann (eds), *Edward Elgar Research Handbook on European Property Law* (Edward Elgar, 2024).

[28] Arbitrazh Court No A40-124668/17-71-160 F, 5 March 2018.

[29] Ninth Arbitrazh Court of Appeals No 9AP-16416/18 in case No A40-124668/17, 15 May 2018.

[30] The matter was the subject of 'heated debate' during the enactment process, see EY Messenger, 'New amendments to the Russian Civil Code to introduce regulation for digital assets' (2019) assets.ey.com/content/dam/ey-sites/ey-com/en_ru/topics/tax/legal/march/ey-law-regulation-for-digital-assets-25-march-2019-eng.pdf.

[31] Usually the rights need to be transferable to fall within this category, although as long as the right is of a type that is transferable, even if a particular right is not transferable it is treated as property for some purposes, eg, on the insolvency of the person who has the right, see M Bridge and others, *The Law of Personal Property*, 3rd edn, London, Sweet & Maxwell, 2021) 4-012.

[32] *Colonial Bank v Whinney* [1885] 30 Ch D 261 (CA) 285; *Your Response Ltd v Datateam Business Media Ltd* [2014] EWCA Civ 281, [2015] QB 41.

[33] See s III.C.

B. Things and Claims

As indicated above, broadly speaking, in civil and common law systems, movable assets can be divided into two classes. The first class comprises 'things'[34] that can be the subject of proprietary rights: these are things that exist in the world irrespective of the application of law or a legal regime.[35] The proprietary rights of which 'things' are objects do require law to exist and to be enforced, but the things themselves do not.[36] These things are 'tangibles' or 'corporeals' in civil law systems and 'choses in possession' in common law systems. The law can impose some policy restrictions on whether certain 'things' are capable of being the object of proprietary rights,[37] but in the absence of such restrictions, all 'things' have this capacity.

The second class comprises 'claims'[38] that can be the subject of proprietary rights. These have no bodily or factual existence and therefore owe their existence to the law: without the operation of law for their creation and enforcement, they would not exist.[39] These 'claims' are 'intangibles' or 'incorporeals' in civil law, and 'choses in action' in the common law. These assets are themselves rights, so if they are the subject of proprietary rights, the proprietary rights are 'rights to rights'.[40] In many cases, these claims are rights against a specific person or persons, for example, a debt, a right to bring an action for damages, maybe shares in a company.[41] Sometimes, however, there can be assets that themselves appear to be rights against the whole world, for example, intellectual property.[42] The extent to which intellectual property should be in the same category as rights against specific persons is debatable.[43]

There are also hybrid assets, that is, assets with some characteristics of things and characteristics of claims. Documentary intangibles are an example of this phenomenon. A documentary intangible, such as a negotiable instrument or a bill of lading, is a right 'locked up' in a document, so that the transfer of the document transfers the right. The document is tangible, and the right is intangible, but the

[34] This is a word that is actually used in some systems, but all systems, whatever terminology is used, seem to have the concept.

[35] See, eg, the analysis in the Law Commission for England and Wales, Digital Assets: Final report (Law Com No 412, 2023) ('LC final report') para 3-19.

[36] See LC final report ch 3 fn 27.

[37] See, eg, *Yearworth* (n 10) in relation to human bodies and body parts.

[38] The term 'claims' is used in some states, and the term 'rights' in other states.

[39] LC final report para 3-19 and Law Commission for England and Wales, Digital Assets: Consultation Paper (Law Com No 256, 2022) ('LC consultation paper') paras 4-29–4-38. See also A Sanitt, 'What sort of property is a cryptoasset?' [2021] *Journal of International Banking and Financial Law* 83.

[40] See B McFarlane, *The Structure of Property Law* (Oxford, Hart Publishing, 2008).

[41] These are claim rights in the Hohfeldian sense.

[42] See, eg, McFarlane and Douglas (n 5) 177.

[43] See K Low, 'Bitcoin as Property' (2020) 136 *LQR* 345, K Low, 'Cryptoassets and the Renaissance of the *Tertium Quid*?' in C Bevan (ed), *Edward Elgar Research Handbook on Property Law and Theory* (Edward Elgar, 2024).

law fuses the two together to make what is often treated as a single asset. Their legal treatment involves some features of the treatment of things[44] and some features of the treatment of claims.

C. Digital Assets: Things or Claims?

Digital assets could also be said to be hybrid assets in the sense that they are intangible (in that they are not tangible)[45] but they are not claims, that is rights against an identified person or even rights against the whole world.[46] Moreover, unlike a claim as described above, a digital asset exists because of a state of the world (the system that enables factual control) rather than owing its existence to law, so it has features of a 'thing' while, of course, being intangible.[47] Thus, rather than being 'hybrid' in the sense of being a tangible and an intangible fused together, it is hybrid in the sense of having some features of a tangible and some of an intangible.

If this is correct, is a digital asset a thing or a claim? And if it is neither, does it matter? It would obviously matter if a jurisdiction had a strict numerus clausus governing what could be the object of proprietary rights, and if that numerus clausus consisted of (only) things, or consisted of (only) things and claims. However, if the application of the normative approach to the fundamental question, mentioned above, indicated that digital assets should be the subject of proprietary rights, perhaps the numerus clausus should be adapted.

In English law (and more generally in the common law)[48] there is a debate as to whether digital assets are choses in action or a third category of personal property.[49] One view equates 'choses in action' with 'intangible property', given that, already, the category of 'choses in action' has been extended to include rights against the world such as intellectual property rather than rights against specific people ('claims' or 'claim-rights').[50] The contrary argument is that there should be a third category of intangible assets, to encompass (at least) assets that do not owe

[44] eg, in English law it is possible to sue in conversion for interference with possession of a documentary intangible.

[45] It can be argued that since the record comprising the digital asset is held on tangible computers that digital assets have a tangible base, but since the digital asset cannot be separated from the rest of the tangible(s) it is hard to see how this argument assets in classifying them as tangibles.

[46] See, eg, LC final report para 3-32 stating that almost all consultees agreed that 'crypto-tokens' were not rights in themselves.

[47] See (n 39) above and also T Chan, 'The Nature of Property in Crypto-Assets' [2023] *Legal Studies* 1, who, in analysing the 'res' that is the object of proprietary rights, focuses on the factual features of a digital asset and, in particular, the factual abilities of the person in control of the private key to exclude and transfer (esp at 7–9).

[48] eg, the question has also been discussed in the Singapore courts, see *Janesh s/o Rajkumar v Unknown Person* [2022] SGHC 264, 60–68 and *ByBit* (n 8) 31–36.

[49] This, for present purposes, leaves aside the argument that digital assets cannot be the object of proprietary rights at all under the common law, since they are neither things nor claims, see R Stevens, 'Crypto is Not Property' [2023] 139 *LQR* 695.

[50] See the writings of Professor K Low, especially the two articles referred to in n 43. This argument has been accepted at first instance in the Singapore courts, see *ByBit* (n 8) 36.

their existence to law, and do not consist of a right enforced by legal action, but rather owe their existence to a combination of facts. Such assets (which include digital assets) are different enough from 'claims' (or 'choses in action') for exactly the same rules not to apply to both types of assets.[51] Thus, the legal consequences of such assets being the object of proprietary rights may differ in some respects from the legal consequences of things (on the one hand) or claims (on the other) being the object of proprietary rights. This is not surprising, given that such legal consequences in relation to things and claims already vary.[52]

A slightly different argument applies to the inclusion of intellectual property in the third category, since intellectual property depends on law for its existence rather than, as with digital assets, facts. The same is true of transferable licences or permissions, such as milk quotas and statutory carbon credits. These are not rights against the whole world, but exemptions from legal sanctions that a state or a person could otherwise impose on the person performing the relevant activity. However, unlike digital assets, they do depend on law for their existence. The common law courts have held such assets to be 'property' within the meaning of particular statutes in a number of cases.[53] These cases were decided as a matter of statutory interpretation rather than general principle, and may turn on the phrasing and intention of the statute. For example, the Theft Ordinance of Hong Kong, which is identical to the English Theft Act in this respect, refers to 'choses in action or other intangible property', thus suggesting that there is such a third category of movable property.[54] However, two cases have involved more general decisions on these types of assets. In one case, a milk quota was held to be 'property' capable of being the subject of a trust,[55] and, in another, a carbon trading unit was held to be 'property' so that it could be the subject of a trust and could form the basis of a proprietary restitutionary claim.[56]

For the purposes of the current discussion, however, what the common law debate does illustrate is that it is possible to bring digital assets within a numerus clauses of assets, which can be the object of proprietary rights either by keeping the existing categories and enlarging them or by creating a new category. Arguably, it is therefore possible for civil law jurisdictions to extend their numerus clausus in

[51] See, eg, LC final report paras 3.49–3.58.

[52] See McFarlane and Douglas (n 5).

[53] *Attorney General of Hong Kong v Nai-Keung* [1987] 1 WLR 1339 (Theft Ordinance of Hong Kong); *Re Rae* [1995] BCC 102 (Insolvency Act 1986, s 436); *Commonwealth of Australia v WMC Resources Ltd* (1998) 194 CLR 1 (Petroleum (Australia-Indonesia Zone of Cooperation) (Consequential Provisions) Act 1990); *Re Mineral Resources* Ltd [1999] 1 All ER 746 (Insolvency Act 1986, s 436), *Re Celtic Extraction* [2001] Ch 487 (Insolvency Act 1986, s 436).

[54] See *Attorney General of Hong Kong v Nai-Keung* (n 53) 1341–1342.

[55] *Swift v Dairywise Farms Ltd* [2000] 1 WLR 1177.

[56] *Armstrong DLW GmbH v Winnington Networks Ltd* [2012] EWHC 10 (Ch). In this case, the phrase 'other intangible property' was used to denote a third category at common law, although it was made clear by the judge that the decision did not turn on whether the asserts were choses in action or 'other intangible property'. The Property (Digital Assets etc) Bill has been put before the UK Parliament. It provides that something may be capable of attracting property rights even if it does not fit into either of the two categories of personal property discussed in s II C.

the same way, so that assets that are neither things nor claims can be accommodated within the list of possible objects of proprietary rights. As with the common law, the details of how proprietary rights operate in relation to this new type of asset would then need to be considered and developed.

D. Characteristics of an Object of a Proprietary Right

Under the deductive approach to the fundamental question, identified above, the second question is whether the asset has characteristics that other things that are capable of being the subject of proprietary rights have. If the answer is yes, or predominantly yes, then, reasoning by analogy, it is possible to argue that the asset is itself capable of being the object of proprietary rights. However, as mentioned above, the deductive approach and the normative approach need to go hand in hand. If, applying the normative approach, digital assets should be the object of proprietary rights, then the ability to reason by analogy based on characteristics gives the law the means by which to effect that normative conclusion.

This section considered what these characteristics appear to be in civil and common law. Although the terminology can sometimes be different, there seems to be relatively little substantive difference at a general level, although, at a detailed level, there is a difference in emphasis, and also some substantive differences, largely flowing from the flexibility available in the common law by the operation of equity. The various characteristics will be discussed, with differences between the two systems pointed out where appropriate.

A much-quoted case in English law on the 'characteristics of property' is *National Provincial Bank Ltd v Ainsworth*,[57] where Lord Wilberforce said 'it must be definable, identifiable by third parties, capable in its nature of assumption by third parties, and have some degree of permanence or stability'.[58] From this statement, it could be said that an important characteristic is transferability ('capable in its nature of assumption by third parties'). However, this is confusing. When an asset is, for example, sold, what is transferred is the proprietary right in the asset rather than the asset itself.[59] Therefore, to ask whether a proprietary right in the asset is transferable does not tell us whether the asset is capable of being the object of proprietary rights in the first place: one would have to say 'if the asset were the object of a proprietary right, would that right be capable of being transferred?'[60] However, what Lord Wilberforce was talking about in this sentence

[57] *National Provincial Bank Ltd v Ainsworth* [1965] AC 1175 (HL).

[58] ibid at 1247–1248.

[59] In relation to civil law, see, eg, G Gretton, 'Ownership and its Objects' (2007) 71 *The Rabel Journal of Comparative and International Private Law* 4, 802.

[60] This could be an important question if, in a given situation, it was possible to prevent, in fact or in law, the transfer of a proprietary right in the asset: there is then a real question whether that asset can be the object of a proprietary right at all (an example could be certain types of body parts). See also n 31 above.

(that is, he meant by 'it') was a right 'affecting property'. The issue in this case was whether a wife's right to occupy the matrimonial home was a property right in the land or a personal right. Thus, when Lord Wilberforce says that 'it' must be 'capable in its nature of assumption by third parties' that is, transferable, he is referring to the right and not to its object, which was, uncontentiously, the land.

Another of Lord Wilberforce's criteria is also more suitable to apply to the proprietary right than to the asset, namely identifiability by third parties. This has resonances with the requirement of publicity in civil law jurisdictions,[61] that is based on the idea that third parties should be able to discover proprietary rights, an idea which also applies in the common law, although perhaps less rigorously. In relation to tangibles, the principle of publicity can be fulfilled with the transfer of possession to the transferee of the proprietary right: it could also be fulfilled (in relation to both tangibles and intangibles) by registration or, in the case of intangibles, by notice to the person who owes the obligation that correlates with the claim. While, in relation to digital assets, it could be argued that the system on which an asset is recorded functions as a kind of register, thus fulfilling the requirement of publicity for proprietary rights in digital assets, this is far from a perfect analogy, given the pseudonymous nature of most systems.[62] While also not perfect,[63] a closer analogy is the transfer of control to the transferee, which is broadly functionally equivalent to the factual aspect of possession in relation to tangibles.[64]

The idea of permanence or stability also seems more appropriate in relation to a proprietary right (rather than the object of that right), and was particularly relevant in the *Ainsworth* case itself, where the right claimed by the wife was a right that her husband provide her with cohabitation and support. The content of this right was dependent on the exercise of the court's discretion.[65] As counsel for the bank said in argument, it was a 'right to reside until the court in its discretion ordered her to leave'.[66] This lack of permanence of the right was an important factor in the House of Lords' decision that the right was a personal and not a proprietary right. However, the question of permanence of the object of the right (the land) was not considered: land is, in any event, the most permanent of objects. While there are many objects of proprietary rights that have a degree of permanence, there are many that do not.[67] Permanence is, then, unlikely to be a

[61] Carr (n 22) 7.18–7.20.

[62] ibid 7.19.

[63] The transfer of control does not give complete publicity, since it is only visible on investigation (the same is true of possession) and there are other possible reasons for a change of control other than a transfer of proprietary rights (such as misappropriation or custody). However, this latter problem applies even more to tangibles, where possession can be given to a lessee, a borrower, a custodian and so on.

[64] See s III.E. below.

[65] *National Provincial Bank Ltd v Ainsworth* [1965] AC 1175 (HL), 1243–1247.

[66] ibid 1182.

[67] See the example given in *Ruscoe v Cryptopia Ltd* [2020] NZHC 728, 117 of a ticket to a football match as something that is likely to be of a short-lived nature, although note the point made in LC Consultation Paper ch 2 fn 123 that a physical ticket is not necessarily destroyed as soon as it is used.

determinative characteristic as to whether an asset can be the object of proprietary rights. Moreover, as the UK Jurisdiction Taskforce points out, digital assets 'appear to be as permanent as other conventional financial assets, which may exist only until they are, for example, cancelled, redeemed, repaid or exercised'.[68]

The characteristic identified by Lord Wilberforce that does apply more readily to the asset itself is 'definability', which seems to be similar to the civil law concept of specificity. Specificity of object is required so that all parties know to what the proprietary right relates. This is a strict requirement in civil law[69] (although it varies among jurisdictions, and is now often relaxed in relation to rights less than ownership, such as security rights), while it is somewhat more relaxed in common law jurisdictions, where, for example, there could be a valid transfer of a proprietary right in 'all my wine' or of an undivided share in a bulk storage of bottles of wine. However, this variation between civil and common law systems is not seen as a reason for a bottle of wine not to be capable of being the object of proprietary rights (even if, in a particular situation, it might not be the object of a particular proprietary right). The same is true of digital assets, provided that they are capable of individuation, even if they may, under certain circumstances, be mixed and treated as fungible in a way that might preclude the requirement of specificity being fulfilled in a particular jurisdiction (at least, without some form of relaxation).

One characteristic of (some) assets which are capable of being the object of proprietary rights in both civil law and common law is that they are capable of being possessed.[70] Possession plays a number of important functions, such as enabling the possessor to exclude others from using, possessing, or benefitting, from the asset (excludability can be seen as a necessary characteristic of an asset which can be the object of proprietary rights),[71] providing a degree of publicity for, and often evidence for, the proprietary right and, thus, enabling a proprietary right in the asset to be transferred by transfer of possession. While it is highly controversial to suggest (in many jurisdictions) that intangibles can be possessed, the factual element of possession, factual control, is possible in relation to digital assets, so long as the capability of being controlled is part of the definition of digital assets.[72]

There are some other possible relevant characteristics of assets that are capable of being the object of proprietary rights, which have been much discussed in relation to digital assets. The first, which builds on the idea of excludability, but is different from it, is that the asset is rivalrous.[73] Something is rivalrous if the

[68] UK Jurisdiction Task Force, 'Legal Statement on Cryptoassets and Smart Contracts' (2019) para 52.

[69] D Carr, 'Cryptocurrencies as Property in Civilian and Mixed Legal Systems', in D Fox and S Green (eds), *Cryptocurrencies in Public and Private Law* (Oxford, Oxford University Press, 2019) 7.16.

[70] ibid 7.15.

[71] Bridge, Gullifer, Low, and McMeel (n 32) 1-006; *Fairstar Heavy Transport N.V. v Adkins* [2013] EWCA Civ 886, 47; LC Consultation Paper paras 2.70–2.73.

[72] See s III.E. below.

[73] See LC final report paras 4.43–4.47.

consumption or use of it by one person precludes anyone else from consuming or using it, while something is not rivalrous if more than one person can use or consume it at the same time (information, therefore, is not rivalrous since it can be copied and used by many people at once). In relation to digital assets, it is the ability to transfer control of the digital asset that is rivalrous: once it has been exercised, it cannot be exercised again by the same person as they will no longer have the private key.[74] The data of which the electronic record that is the digital asset is comprised can, however, be copied easily: again, this shows that the definition of 'digital asset' is critical to whether the thing defined is rivalrous or not.

Another possible characteristic is that an asset that is capable of being the object of proprietary rights has value.[75] This is certainly true of many such assets, since it is the value (economic or otherwise) that provides the incentive for the enforcement of a proprietary right. The question of value can be viewed in two ways. First, is it necessary for an asset to have value to be capable of being the object of proprietary rights? Put like this, the answer must be negative. Many tangibles that can be the subject of proprietary rights have no value. Moreover, many valuable assets that are regarded as being capable of being the object of proprietary rights can lose their value in a market crash (such as bonds or digital assets). It would make no sense if they also lost their ability to be the object of proprietary rights. However, the second way of viewing value is to ask whether any asset that has value should be the object of proprietary rights. This question moves from the deductive approach to the fundamental question to the normative approach. The fact that something has value could be a good reason for it to be capable of being the object of proprietary rights.

As discussed in this section, the chief characteristics that the objects of proprietary rights usually have are that they are definable (or identifiable), they are capable of being possessed and therefore excludable, and they are rivalrous. The normative argument, therefore, that digital assets should be able to be the subject of proprietary rights, and that therefore the numerus clausus should include them, must relate only to those digital assets that have, or are capable of having, these characteristics, and this should be reflected in a definition of 'digital asset'.

E. The Definition of a Digital Asset

For it to be possible to reason by analogy that digital assets can be the objects of proprietary rights, either deductively or because of a normative decision that digital assets ought to be capable of being the subject of proprietary rights, there needs to be a definition of digital assets that has the result that digital assets, so defined, share most or all of the characteristics mentioned in the last section, so

[74] ibid 4.45. See also Chan (n 47).

[75] See R Goode, 'What is Property?' (2023) 139 *LQR* 1.

that they can fit within property law. This is what has been done in the UNIDROIT Principles of Digital Assets and Private Law.[76]

In these Principles, a digital asset is defined as an electronic record which is capable of being subject to control.[77] An electronic record is defined as information which is stored in an electronic medium and is capable of being retrieved.[78] This latter definition was chosen as it is consistent with various national definitions, but it is pointed out that it is really the record of the information that is the digital asset and not the information itself. Information (in general) is not specific or identifiable, as it can be duplicated so that many people have the same information, and it is not possible to identify which is *the* information that is the subject of the proprietary right.[79] This is why, in most jurisdictions, information cannot be the subject of a proprietary right. But, in relation to a digital asset, the combination of the record of information and the ability of that record to be controlled (which depends on the operation of the system on which the record exists) means that the digital asset is identifiable and specified. Thus, the digital asset is comprised of the data held on the system *plus* the operation of that system.

The other work in the definition comes from the definition of 'control'. This is defined as a factual concept and is therefore more similar to the factual aspect of possession in relation to tangibles than the concept of 'control' when applied to a claim or right. Since the right requires the law to be enforceable, control of the right is usually also a matter of law.[80] The use of a factual concept of control is deliberate. Although the Principles are designed to be technologically neutral, the definition is designed to cover electronic records held on systems that enable a person who holds a particular type of data to, as a matter of fact, do certain things in relation to that electronic record. Thus, while the definition is not limited to crypto assets and/or assets held on DLT systems,[81] such assets are a good example of what is covered because of the factual abilities of the person who has the private key.

Having control is defined in the Principles as having three abilities, which are the things that the protocol or system enables the person in control to do, as

[76] See www.unidroit.org/wp-content/uploads/2023/04/C.D.-102-6-Principles-on-Digital-Assets-and-Private-Law.pdf. A similar attempt is made by the Law Commission of England and Wales, see LC final report para 4.5 which sets out three criteria for something to fall within the proposed third category of personal property.

[77] Principle 2(2).

[78] Principle 2(1).

[79] In terms of characteristics, it is neither definable nor rivalrous, and is not excludable as a matter of fact, though it may be protected by a jurisdiction's rules on confidentiality and intellectual property.

[80] Control of a right is manifested in various regimes, such as the Financial Collateral Directive regime in the EU (and the Financial Collateral Arrangements (No 2) Regulations 2003 in the UK), the requirement of control as a perfection mechanism in relation to securities, bank accounts and other rights in the Uniform Commercial Code and the Canadian and Australian Personal Property Security Acts, and the requirement of control by the chargee which renders a charge over, eg, receivables a fixed and not a floating charge under English law (see *National Westminster Bank plc v Spectrum Plus Limited* [2005] UKHL 41, 2 AC 680).

[81] Systems based on distributive ledger technology.

a matter of fact. These are the ability to prevent others from obtaining substantially all of the benefit from the digital asset,[82] the ability to obtain substantially all the benefit from the digital asset[83] and the ability to transfer all three abilities to another person.[84] For there to be control (as defined) the first and third principles have to be exclusive: this means that the person in control must usually be the only person who has these abilities, but the exclusivity is relaxed in two ways.[85] First, the abilities can be shared with another by consent (for example, in a multi-sig arrangement) and second, the system can limit the control person's abilities, or can itself be programmed to make changes resulting in a change of control of the digital asset.

Thus, providing in the definition of a digital asset that it must be capable of being subject to control means that a digital asset has the characteristic identified above as 'being capable of being possessed' given that control is the equivalent of the factual aspect of possession, and achieves the excludability that possession achieves. It also facilitates the publicity that is a characteristic of proprietary rights in some civil law jurisdictions, at least to the same (or maybe greater) extent than possession does in relation to tangibles.[86] Moreover, if an asset is capable of being subject to control as defined, it is inherent in that definition that the control must be transferable to another person. While this does not necessarily mean that any proprietary right in the digital asset is transferable,[87] it facilitates evidence and publicity of that transfer if such a transfer is possible under the law of the relevant jurisdiction.

A combination of the idea of *an* electronic record and that fact that such a record must be capable of being subject to control also ensures that a digital asset is definable, even if, as a matter of fact, it is mixed with other digital assets and is treated as fungible. Moreover, even though there is no separate requirement of rivalrousness in the definition, this is also built into the concept of control. A change of control is defined as a transfer of the abilities to another person:[88] once they have been 'transferred' the person formally in control will no longer have those abilities, and the person to whom control has been changed will have those abilities. Control of the digital asset thus cannot be transferred twice by the same person.[89]

[82] Principle 6(1)(a)(i).
[83] Principle 6(1)(a)(ii).
[84] Principle 6(1)(a)(iii).
[85] Principle 6(3).
[86] See (n 63) above.
[87] See (n 60) above.
[88] Principle 6(2).
[89] This analysis deals with factual rivalrousness. As with virtually all assets it is possible for a person to purport to transfer proprietary rights in that asset to two different persons. The legal rules on priority of the relevant jurisdiction then apply to determine which transferee has the proprietary right (or the best proprietary right) to the asset.

F. Linked Assets

The discussion above has proceeded on the basis that a digital asset is an electronic record capable of being subject to control. Such an asset does not constitute a thing or a claim as discussed above in section III.B. However, in the real world, often such an electronic record purports to be linked in some way to a thing or a claim. While there are a number of possible 'links', the most usual one will be that the person who controls the digital asset (or, if different, has a proprietary right in it) also has a proprietary right in the other asset, and when the proprietary right in one asset is transferred the proprietary right in the other asset is also transferred to the same transferee.[90] The mere fact that there is a purported link does not, of course, necessarily mean that the link is effective as a matter of applicable law.

Does this possibility change the analysis in this chapter so far? The issue can be approached from either end of the 'telescope'. First, it could be said that a 'digital asset' linked successfully as a matter of law to a claim can be the subject of proprietary rights because it itself consists of a claim. It could, in addition, be said that a 'digital asset' linked successfully to a thing (or a claim) is not an asset at all, but merely a record of ownership of the thing or claim. The alternative approach is to say that a digital asset can be the subject of proprietary rights, therefore, it can be successfully linked to a claim or thing that can also be the subject of proprietary rights.

It is argued here that the second analysis is to be preferred because it is a cleaner analysis. It recognises that a digital asset that is linked to another asset is inherently the same as an unlinked one, and means that if the purported link is not successful (for example, in the case of a non-fungible token that does not give the holder any rights at all) there is still a digital asset that is capable of being the object of proprietary rights. This approach has the result that attention is focused on the existence, nature, and legal effect of the link, which will vary according to which jurisdiction's law is applicable. This approach is that followed by the UNIDROIT Principles on Digital Assets and Private Law.[91] The question of how to determine the law applicable to issues relating to the link is currently being considered in a HCCH project on Digital Tokens.[92]

If the link between the digital asset and the other asset is fully established under the applicable law,[93] so that the two 'fuse' together and become a 'hybrid' asset,[94] then the effect of the digital asset as a separate asset becomes much less marked. The closest analogy is a documentary intangible: the document is still a

[90] The UK Jurisdiction Taskforce call this type of link 'stapling' in their Statement on the Issuance and Transfer of Digital Securities under English Private Law (2023).

[91] Principle 4.

[92] See www.hcch.net/en/projects/legislative-projects/digital-tokens1.

[93] eg, by legislation.

[94] See s III.B. above.

piece of paper and, to that extent, a tangible asset, but the documentary intangible is often treated as a single, hybrid, asset. Here, the law on the hybrid asset becomes much more important than the law on pieces of paper, or the law on 'unlinked' claims. A similar situation occurs when a digital asset is successfully linked to another asset. It could also be that the effect of the link and the way the system is structured leads to the result that the electronic record is not subject to control under the definition above (for example, if the record is controlled by a third party registrar who does not obtain substantially all the benefit from the 'digital asset', but who has the power to rectify the electronic record that otherwise operates as the root of title or the best evidence of ownership of the other asset). In that case, the analysis is not of a fused or hybrid asset, but just of a record, albeit one held in a way which, if slightly differently structured, could have been a linked digital asset.

IV. The Normative Approach

As mentioned above, it is suggested here that whether a 'new' type of asset is capable of being the object of proprietary rights can be approached in two ways: the deductive approach and the normative approach. Sometimes the answer to the deductive approach is obvious. For example, 50 years ago there were no mobile phones. When mobile phones became a commercial reality in the early 1980s,[95] there was no question that they were capable of being the object of proprietary rights, since they were tangibles. The normative question was also easy to answer: there was no good reason why they should not be capable of being the object of proprietary rights, and so there was no discussion as to this issue.

If the answer to the deductive question in relation to digital assets in any jurisdiction is thought to be a clear 'yes', then the normative question becomes: is there a good reason for digital assets not to be the object of proprietary rights? However, as discussed earlier, the answer to the deductive question in most, if not all, jurisdictions is likely to be more equivocal. In order for digital assets to be the object of proprietary rights, it is likely to be necessary to extend the numerus clausus of such objects, either by expanding existing categories or by creating a new category altogether,[96] although the analysis in section III.D., combined with the limited definition of 'digital asset' suggested in section III.E. means that such extension can be justified by reasoning by analogy. Thus, the normative question acquires more importance: if there is a preponderance of good reasons why digital assets *should* be the object of proprietary rights,[97] the deductive approach provides the tools to enable a jurisdiction to justify.

[95] See www.sciencemuseum.org.uk/objects-and-stories/invention-mobile-phones.
[96] See s III.A. above.
[97] That is, if the reasons in favour outweigh the reasons against.

Various good reasons why digital assets *should* be the object of proprietary rights have already been identified. Watts and Low[98] argue that, because digital assets have been invented, and are 'held' and transacted with on a relatively large scale, and because those carrying out the transactions reasonably expect certain legal conclusions (for example, to receive some protection against unauthorised transactions, to be able to bequeath digital assets in a will, to be able to grant security over digital assets and for digital assets to form part of an insolvent person's estate)[99] the most 'expedient'[100] way to meet these expectations is for digital assets to be capable of being the object of proprietary rights. In support of this argument, they cite the 'relatively straightforward' resolution of the *Cryptopia* case,[101] compared to the difficulties encountered under Japanese law in relation to the MtGox case.[102] This argument is compelling, especially when it is bolstered by judicial decisions which proceed on the basis that digital assets can be the object of proprietary rights, as has been the case in many common law jurisdictions,[103] although it should be noted that many of these decisions are in preliminary rather than final determinations and none have been by apex courts. Many civil law jurisdictions have legislated in order to enable digital assets (or at least a sub-set of them) to be the object of proprietary rights.[104] Of course, one could argue that these decisions are wrong, and that the legislation is misguided, or, at least, that deductive analysis (as contained in section III. above) is necessary in order to justify the expedient conclusion. The argument from expediency is attractive, since in all jurisdictions there is a well-developed law of property enabling issues such as the ones listed above to be resolved readily and with reasonable consistency with the resolution of such assets in relation to other objects of proprietary rights, although the conclusion of McFarlane and Douglas,[105] namely, that the legal consequences of different types of assets being the object of proprietary rights vary according to the nature of those assets, must always be borne in mind.[106]

The argument in favour of a positive answer to the normative question can also be put on an economic basis. Thus, it can be argued that the legal certainty that flows from the conclusion that digital assets can be the object of proprietary rights will reduce transaction costs in relation to such assets, and will enable markets to function more efficiently, thus increasing economic benefits. Given the predominance of cross-border transactions in digital assets, these benefits are best

[98] P Watts and K Low, 'The Case for Cryptoassets as Property', in S Agnew and M Smith (eds), *Law At The Cutting Edge, Essays In Honour Of Sarah Worthington* (Oxford, Hart Publishing, 2024) ssrn.com/abstract=4354364 or http://dx.doi.org/10.2139/ssrn.4354364.

[99] See s I. above.

[100] Watts and Low (n 98) 14.

[101] See n 65.

[102] Watts and Low (n 98) 10–12.

[103] See the cases cited in nn 7 and 8, and also *Re Gatecoin Ltd* [2023] HKCFI 914. See also Allen, Wells and Mauro (n 19).

[104] eg, see the Russian legislation (n 30), the Liechtenstein Blockchain Act 2019.

[105] McFarlane and Douglas (n 5).

[106] Watts and Low (n 98) 6.

realised if a harmonised approach to the fundamental question is adopted.[107] A similar argument can be made that digital assets have value, and therefore should be treated as 'property'[108] (that is, they should be capable of being the object of proprietary rights).

Arguments[109] against a positive answer to the normative question tend to be either based on a lack of consistency with existing property law,[110] or on policy considerations. In relation to the first of these, while some differentiation in legal conclusions from those applying to other types of assets is likely to flow from recognition that digital assets are capable of being the object of proprietary rights, this is not inconsistent with the way property law operates in other contexts.[111] In terms of policy, recent events have certainly shown the dangers of an unregulated market in digital assets, especially for consumers,[112] and other objections, such as the impact on climate change of proof of work,[113] can also be raised. However, even if a state did wish to reduce the market in digital assets, to protect consumers and the environment, for example, it is hard to see that refusing to recognise digital assets as a potential object of proprietary rights would have sufficient effect on people's behaviour (particularly that of consumers) to achieve any particular policy goal. Both criminal law and regulatory law are more effective ways of managing widespread risk, and there is no reason why these techniques cannot be used in conjunction with a positive answer to the fundamental question.

V. Conclusion

This chapter argues that, when considering whether digital assets are, as a matter of a jurisdiction's law, capable of being the object of proprietary rights, there are two inter-connected approaches. The deductive approach, which involves deducing the answer from existing legal principles, renders an ambiguous reply: there are sufficient similar characteristics for analogical reasoning to operate, but an extension in some way to the numerus clausus is required in most jurisdictions. The balance in favour of a positive answer to the fundamental question can be swung by a positive answer when applying the normative approach. It is suggested,

[107] See UNIDROIT Principles of Digital Assets and Private Law paras 0.1–0.4.

[108] See Goode (n 75). Note that the argument made in the text is a normative argument and not a deductive argument, that is, it is not based on the premise that everything that has value is capable of being the object of proprietary rights, nor that something without value is not so capable. See s III.D. above.

[109] See Watts and Low (n 98) 12–13.

[110] See Stevens (n 49).

[111] See s III.C. above and McFarlane and Douglas (n 5).

[112] eg, the 'crypto-bankruptcies' of intermediates such as Celsius and FTX have led to high-profile cases and potential losses to consumers.

[113] See, eg, the Cambridge Bitcoin Electricity Consumption Index at ccaf.io/cbnsi/cbeci although steps are being taken to reduce the environmental impact of other digital assets, see www.jbs.cam.ac.uk/2023/blockchain-sustainability-ethereum/.

for the reasons set out in section IV that, the arguments in favour of a conclusion that digital assets *should* be capable of being the object of proprietary rights outweigh the arguments against. With this overall positive answer, the application of the deductive approach provides a method and justification for an overall positive answer to the fundamental question.

This positive answer comes with some caveats. First, it is predicated on a narrow definition of digital assets. It is suggested that the definition in the UNIDROIT Principles is suitable. It is important that the definition is narrow enough to exclude potential assets that do not bear the characteristics of definability, excludability and rivalrousness.[114] Many electronic records will, therefore, fall outside the definition of digital assets.[115] Second, the ways in which the legal conclusion that digital assets are capable of being the object of proprietary rights will vary depending on the legal culture of the jurisdiction, and maybe also on other factors. One possibility is for this conclusion to form part of bespoke legislation on digital assets.[116] This has the advantage that many other issues in relation to digital assets can be included in the same piece of legislation. Another is for existing legislation on property law to be amended, either minimally[117] or with detailed rules.[118] Yet another, which reflects the common law approach at least, is for the conclusion to be recognised by the courts and its contours to be developed by the judiciary.[119] Whatever the method, it is suggested that consistency with the UNIDROIT Principles will enable cross-border harmonisation, which will bring economic benefits, in addition to those brought by domestic law reform, to this global market.

[114] As discussed in s III.D. above.

[115] See UNIDROIT Principles of Digital Assets and Private Law commentary, 2023, paras 2.14–2.17, available at www.unidroit.org/wp-content/uploads/2024/01/Principles-on-Digital-Assets-and-Private-Law-linked-1.pdf.

[116] eg, see the Liechtenstein Blockchain Act 2019.

[117] See the Russian legislation (n 30).

[118] See the 2022 amendments to the Uniform Commercial Code especially the new art 12.

[119] See, however, the minimal legislative intervention recommended by the Law Commission of England and Wales, which was, apparently, included after feedback from the judiciary, LC Final report paras 3.66 to 3.76. This legislative intervention is said to confirm the existing law rather than to change the law (para 3.71). The proposed legislative intervention is also in a negative form, namely that 'a thing will not be deprived of legal status as an object of personal property rights merely by reason of the fact that it is neither a thing in action nor a thing in possession'.

3

Digital Assets in Insolvency and Enforcement Proceedings: Some Insights from UNIDROIT's Work

ANNA VENEZIANO AND TERESA RODRÍGUEZ DE LAS HERAS BALLELL*

I. Introduction

Cryptocurrencies and non-fungible tokens (perhaps the most well-known digital asset sub-classes) have increasingly – and dramatically – gained public visibility and economic importance in recent years, entering the investment portfolios of a growing number of companies and individuals worldwide. Such an increased popularity of a hitherto non-existent class of assets has triggered the attention, and oftentimes the concern, of several public bodies, including legislators and central banks, as well as of private trade organisations. Thought has particularly been given to the challenges of reconstructing a new taxonomy and reassigning institutional responsibilities and roles in the field of international payments and finance from a regulatory and public law perspective,[1] and on regulatory frameworks for digital asset custodians.[2] However, there is the no less relevant need to consider the repercussions and the strain on traditional legal approaches to private law issues arising in the context of the use and exchange of digital assets, which oftentimes involve a cross-border dimension. When faced with legal uncertainty,

* While this chapter is the result of a joint effort and both authors take responsibility for any error or omission, sections I, II, and IV are attributable to Anna Veneziano and section III to Teresa Rodríguez de las Heras Ballell.

[1] In relation to CBDCs, see among others the IMF publication by G Soderberg, J Kiff, M Bechara et al, *How Should Central Banks Explore Central Bank Digital Currency?: A Dynamic Decision-Making Framework*. IMF Fintech Note 2023/008. For a recent survey and discussion see also F Zatti and RG Barresi (eds), *Digital Assets and the Law – Fiat Money in the Era of Digital Currency* (Abington, Routledge-Giappichelli, 2024).

[2] eg, 'ISDA, Navigating Bankruptcy in Digital Assets Markets: Digital Assets Intermediaries and Customer Asset Protection' (May 2013) 10 www.isda.org/a/CrLgE/Navigating-Bankruptcy-in-Digita l-Asset-Markets-Digital-Asset-Intermediaries-and-Customer-Asset-Protection.pdf.

market participants, legal counsels, as well as adjudicators and legislators look for greater predictability and clearer rules, which are especially crucial regarding the enforceability of proprietary rights and their treatment in insolvency.[3]

In the following pages, we will focus on a recent effort to provide harmonised, soft-law guidance to legislators and other interested stakeholders on the treatment of digital assets in private law undertaken by the International Institute for the Unification of Private Law (UNIDROIT), which culminated in the adoption of the UNIDROIT Principles on Digital Assets and Private Law in 2023 (UNIDROIT DAPL Principles).[4] Their approach to digital assets in enforcement and insolvency will be highlighted (see below, section II) as well as some selected issues that were discussed within the ongoing project at UNIDROIT regarding *Best Practices for Effective Enforcement* (BPEE project),[5] with particular regard to judicial enforcement on digital assets. The latter project originally stemmed from a proposal of the World Bank Group, and the instrument will contain dedicated recommendations on this topic (see below, section III).

II. Enforcing Rights Over Digital Assets under the UNIDROIT Principles on Digital Assets and Private Law (DAPL Principles)

A. The UNIDROIT DAPL Principles: A Brief Overview

The UNIDROIT Principles on Digital Assets and Private Law, one of the most recent instruments adopted by UNIDROIT[6] and the first global uniform law instrument entirely dedicated to the private law legal issues arising from the use of digital assets in market practice, aims to provide legal guidance in the form of principles, accompanied by extensive commentary, focusing on specific private law issues relating to the holding, transfer, and use as collateral of digital assets,

[3] See ISDA, 'Navigating Bankruptcy in Digital Assets Markets: Netting and Collateral Enforceability' (January 2023) www.isda.org/a/mIxgE/Navigating-Bankruptcy-in-Digital-Asset-Markets-Netting-and-Collateral-Enforceability.pdf, and ISDA (n 2).

[4] See www.unidroit.org/instruments/digital-assets-and-private-law/ for the text of the Principles, their preparatory works, and information on the members and observers of the Working Group (chaired by Prof. Hideki Kanda) and the Drafting Committee of the project (chaired by Prof. Louise Gullifer). The project benefited from the additional input of a Steering Committee composed of experts nominated by Unidroit Member States and chaired by Prof. Monika Pauknerová, on which see UNIDROIT DAPL Principles, at VIII. For a detailed academic account of the DAPL Principles see the contribution by Louise Gullifer and Ignacio Tirado, *Proprietary Rights and Digital Assets: A "Modest Proposal" from a Transnational Law Perspective*, Law and Contemporary Problems 2024 (forthcoming).

[5] For information on this project, chaired by Ms Kathryn Sabo, and on the members and observers of the Working Group see www.unidroit.org/work-in-progress/enforcement-best-practices/.

[6] The UNIDROIT Governing Council adopted the instrument in May 2023.

particularly when rights are to be asserted against third parties.[7] Thus, as a matter of principle, they do not cover areas of the law that traditionally fall outside private law, such as rules of a regulatory nature[8] (eg, among others, the regulation of the markets in which digital assets are traded; the regime applied to the activity of intermediaries; the information duties connected with the use of certain digital assets, etc). As we will see below, however, in specific cases the Commentary does offer soft guidance to legislators as to potential areas outside private law where action might be usefully taken.

Moreover, the drafters chose a neutral approach both to legal concepts and to different types of assets and technologies, seeking to offer internationally harmonised standards to enable jurisdictions to follow a set of common principles, whilst avoiding imposing a specific legal characterisation on the interests and rights created on digital assets. Legislators are therefore free to implement the Principles in their own jurisdiction, for instance by adopting a specific statute, amending general rules, or influencing the application of existing rules. Moreover, legislators are free to adopt the legal characterisations that are suitable for their own legal culture, as long as the general aim to facilitate the legal treatment and effective transactions regarding digital assets is preserved. Further, in line with their principled nature, the DAPL Principles do not purport to exhaustively cover all the issues that are generally included in their scope of application but leave many of them to 'other law', ie, state law that does not fall under the definition of Principles law.

According to Principle 2 (2), the DAPL Principles apply to a subset of assets that are known as 'digital assets', namely those most commonly used in commercial transactions.[9] They are defined as electronic records 'capable of being subject to control', where 'control' is functionally defined in Principle 6 with reference to factual abilities[10] and as a requisite for the application of the subsequent Principles on transfer,[11] innocent acquisition,[12] effectiveness of a security right created on the

[7] *cf* DAPL Principle 1, paras 1.1. and 1.2.

[8] This point is clearly stated in the Principles themselves and in the Commentary (eg, Introduction, para. 0.9; Commentary to Principle 1, para.1.1., and Principle 3).

[9] *cf* Principle 2 (1) and (2). The Commentary to this provision contains numerous examples and illustrations that are helpful in better understanding the type of asset, and arrangement, to which the Principles apply.

[10] Principle 6 lists three factual abilities of a person having 'control' of the digital asset (the exclusive ability to prevent others from obtaining substantially all of the benefits from the digital asset; the ability to obtain all such benefits; and the exclusive ability to transfer these abilities to another person); one additional element (the person is allowed to identify itself as having the afore-mentioned abilities); and a qualification regarding the element of 'exclusivity' (reserved to the situations where the digital asset, or the relevant protocol or system, limits the use of, or is programmed to make changes to, the digital asset, including change or loss of control, or the person in control has agreed, consented to, or acquiesced in sharing that ability with one or more other persons). Once again, the Commentary provides useful illustrations of different scenarios.

[11] *cf* Principle 6 (1) (iii), (2), and Principle 9.

[12] *cf* Principles 8 and 12.

digital asset,[13] and for the definition of a custody agreement.[14] Another cornerstone in the DAPL Principles is the proposition that 'a digital asset can be the subject of proprietary rights' (Principle 3 [1]). While this is a basic rule on which many subsequent Principles are based, as mentioned above, it does not require a characterisation of the digital assets as 'property', 'goods', or other concepts, as long as the legal consequence of third-party effectiveness is achieved. Finally, the legal guidance contained in the DAPL Principles is completed by a provision on the applicable law (Principle 5), by a reference to 'linked assets' (Principle 4), and by two Principles relating to digital assets in insolvency (Principle 19), enforcement of security rights (Principle 17), and general enforcement (Principle 18). The three latter topics will be the focus of the following paragraphs.

B. Digital Assets in Insolvency (UNIDROIT DAPL Principles, Section VII, Principle 19)

Unsurprisingly, the treatment of digital assets in insolvency has catalysed the attention of domestic legislators and international market players. From the onset of the project, the UNIDROIT Working Group on the DAPL Principles included this topic in the list of legal issues for which predictable and clear rules would be necessary in order to reach the goal of facilitating transactions on the digital assets that are most commonly used in commerce.[15] Thus, the DAPL Principles expressly contain a Section dedicated to the effect of insolvency on rights over the subset of digital assets they cover.

i. Pre-insolvency Proprietary Rights Generally Effective in Insolvency-related Proceedings

Principle 19 provides that proprietary rights that have been made effective against third parties under the DAPL Principles themselves or under 'other law' are generally effective in insolvency-related proceedings. This statement, contained in Principle 19 (1), is a confirmation of the general Principle according to which

[13] *cf* in particular Principle 15, according to which a security right can be made effective against third parties by control if the secured creditor has control as defined in Principle 6, or if a custodian maintains the digital asset for the secured creditor and has control of the digital asset, or enters into a custody agreement with a sub-custodian, provided that the custodian was authorised by the secured creditor or by other law and the sub-custodian is bound by the duties set out for a custodian the Principles.

[14] On which see below, section II.3.

[15] *cf* the first issues paper available at UNIDROIT 'Digital Assets and Private Law Working Group Issues Paper, Study LXXXII' (November 2020) at 18 ('Private-law property rules provide an incomplete picture of the legal treatment of digital assets unless the treatment of those rights in insolvency proceedings also are considered') www.unidroit.org/english/documents/2020/study82/wg01/s-82-wg01-02-e.pdf.

'digital assets can be the subject of proprietary rights' (Principle 3 [1]), which implies the opposability of the right of a person who has a proprietary right in a digital asset if this right has been made effective as against relevant parties. In other words, pre-insolvency proprietary rights on the assets that are rendered effective against third parties under applicable law generally continue to be effective against the insolvency representative, creditors, and any other third party in an insolvency-related proceeding, though this may be further nuanced depending on the circumstances and the specific rules of the applicable law. In this regard, the Commentary refers to the guidance contained in the UNCITRAL *Legislative Guide on Insolvency*,[16] whereby the insolvency estate should comprise 'assets of the debtor', ie, using the terminology of the DAPL Principles, those assets in which the debtor has a proprietary right and to the extent of that proprietary right (which could be a limited right in-rem or other interest short of full ownership).[17]

In most circumstances, the law under which the proprietary right is made effective will be 'other law', that is, any part of the law of a state that is not Principles law (as defined in Principle 2 [4]). There are, however, two situations where the DAPL Principles themselves would determine the effectiveness of a right on digital assets. First of all, as noted above (section II.A.), the DAPL Principles regulate innocent acquisition of a proprietary right in a digital asset, defining the conditions under which a transferee can qualify as an innocent acquirer[18] and the consequences thereof.[19] Second, there is a special provision regarding the effectiveness of a security right on digital assets in Principle 15 (on this provision, see below, section II.C.).

In order to facilitate a better understanding of Principle 19, the Commentary provides concrete examples of typical situations to which it would apply, particularly focusing on insolvency-related proceedings resulting in a distribution to creditors.[20] A first scenario concerns the insolvency of a person who has a proprietary right over the digital asset (eg, a person who 'owns' the digital asset or a creditor who has acquired a security right on the digital asset). The person who owns and controls a digital asset might hold them in a self-custody arrangement, whereby the private key that guarantees control is held on a personal computer or other personal device, or in cloud-based software that provides a wallet service without offering custodial services.[21] The digital assets may also be held through a custodian. In both cases, the insolvent person's proprietary right continues to be effective if made effective under the applicable law or Principles' law (and subject

[16] UNCITRAL 'Legislative Guide on Insolvency' (2004), available at uncitral.un.org/sites/uncitral.un.org/files/media-documents/uncitral/en/05-80722_ebook.pdf.

[17] ibid, Recommendation 35, at 82.

[18] *cf* Principle 8, (1) and (5).

[19] *cf* Principle 8, (2), (3), (4).

[20] *cf* Commentary to Principle 19, paras 19.3–19.8. For the meaning of 'insolvency-related proceedings' in the context of the UNIDROIT DAPL Principles see below, paragraph accompanying n 27.

[21] Useful illustrations of self-custody scenarios are found in the Commentary to Principle 10 (particularly paras 10.16 and 10.17).

to the limitations contained in Principle 19 [2], which will be addressed below). Under insolvency law, the insolvency representative will usually 'step into the shoes' of the insolvent 'owner' and exercise its rights, which, as clarified in the Commentary, might be easier in the situation of a custodian that may be instructed by the insolvency representative to transfer the control of the digital assets to the representative itself or a third party.[22] When the assets are held in a private wallet, however, transfer of control might entail the need to ensure the cooperation of the insolvent person in relinquishing the private key;[23] the extent to which such cooperation may be coerced will depend on the applicable (insolvency) law.[24] Similar considerations would apply to the insolvent creditor who has obtained control of the asset in order to render its security right effective as against third parties, has achieved third-party effectiveness of its right through other methods available under applicable law, or has availed itself of the services of a custodian.[25] In all these situations, Principle 19 (1) ensures that the rights in the digital asset remain part of the insolvent creditor's estate and remain effective in insolvency.

Another constellation of cases to which Principle 19 would apply regards the insolvency of a debtor who has granted a security right over the digital asset. A security right made effective under the applicable law will, in principle, have the same effects (and the same limitations) as security rights over any other assets, but this will depend on the applicable insolvency law. Creditor's rights will also be subject to Principles 15–17 dealing with security rights in digital assets (see below, B.iii.).

The realm of application in terms of types of proceedings of Principle 19 should also be clarified. The DAPL Principles contain a definition of 'insolvency-related proceedings' in Principle 2 (6), whereby this expression means

> a collective judicial or administrative proceeding, including an interim proceeding, in which, for the purpose of reorganisation or liquidation, at least one of the following applies to the assets and affairs of the debtor: (a) they are subject to control or supervision by a court or other competent authority; (b) the debtor's ability to administer or dispose of them is limited by law; (c) the debtor's creditors' ability to enforce on them is limited by law.

As clarified in the Commentary, this definition is not meant to replace the general definition found in UNCITRAL's texts (particularly the *UNCITRAL Legislative Guide on Insolvency*[26]). It is rather aimed at expressly including those situations where the debtor is not necessarily subject to control or supervision by a public

[22] See Commentary to Principle 19, para 19.5.

[23] It should be noted that 'control' is used in Principle 19 (1) in a broad sense, defined by the applicable law, and not in the specific meaning of 'control' under Principle 6 (Commentary to Principle 19, para 19.4).

[24] For the *Best Practices for Effective Enforcement (BPEE)* project's recommendations so far in this regard, see below, B.iii.

[25] See Commentary to Principle 19, paras 19.6 and 19.7.

[26] See above, n 16.

body, but its ability to administer or dispose of assets and affairs outside of the ordinary course of business is limited by law, or even those situations where only the debtor's creditors' ability to enforce on them is limited, such as through a temporary stay of enforcement against the debtor's assets necessary for the continuation of the business activity.[27]

ii. Limitations to the Application of Principle 19 (1)

Principle 19 (2) makes it clear that the protection enjoyed by the general rule under Principle 19 (1) is not absolute. In order to do so, it lists three typical examples of limitations that the applicable law ('other law') may provide, which can be contained in insolvency law or in other laws (such as general procedural law, tax law, etc).[28] In line with the 'principled' nature of the instrument, this is a list provided by way of example that is meant to cover the most common situations where limitations may be found. The important message to legislators is that there should be sufficient clarity in relation to the applicable limitations, be they qualified as procedural or substantive in nature, and that such limitations should be triggered by an insolvency-related proceeding.

iii. Insolvency of the Custodian of a Digital Asset

As mentioned above (section B.i.), the UNIDROIT DAPL Principles address matters relating to custody of digital assets in a specific section (section V) and complete that section with an express coverage of the insolvency of a custodian (Principle 13 [2]–[7]) and a sub-custodian (Principle 13 [8]).

Following the functional approach generally adopted in the drafting of the Principles, Principle 13 sets out the practical consequences of the opening of an insolvency-related proceeding against a custodian by providing that the digital asset maintained by a custodian for its client pursuant to a custody agreement as defined in the Principles 'does not form part of the custodian's assets available for distribution to its creditors' (Principle 13 [2]).[29] Once again, the underlying idea is that legislators would be free to use their own categories and legal concepts to

[27] Principle 2, Commentary 2.28.

[28] The three examples include the rules on the ranking of categories of claims (eg, preferences or liens with priority which are commonly granted to certain categories of persons or claims, and which depend on the policy decisions of a given jurisdiction); the rules on fraudulent transfers; and the limitations applicable when an insolvency representative has taken control of the digital asset and special rules apply, such as a stay on enforcement by a secured creditor. The Commentary clarifies that this latter case may need the cooperation of third parties (eg, the system that operates the digital asset or contains the record of the digital asset): Commentary to Principle 19, para 19.12.

[29] The same rule applies when a custodian maintains a digital asset for a client with a sub-custodian, and the custodian enters into an insolvency-related proceeding (Principle 13 [3]). In this latter case, the custodian's rights against the sub-custodian are not part of the custodian's assets available to its creditors.

reach this outcome, be it through adaptation/interpretation of existing rules or through a specific legal framework for digital assets. The Commentary, however, makes it clear that should a state apply a special insolvency regime to certain types of financial institutions (among which there could well be 'custodians' as defined by the DAPL Principles), it should ensure that the definition of insolvency-related proceeding encompasses the insolvency of those custodians, and that the consequences set out in Principle 13 are possible under that special regime.[30]

It is important to note that the DAPL Principles contain a presumption, included in the definition of a custody agreement, according to which these consequences apply unless the agreement between the service provider and the client makes it clear that the service provider's assets would be available for distribution to its creditors in an insolvency-related proceeding.[31] The function of this presumption is to address the line between a veritable custody agreement and other types of agreements under which, though the service provider acts in a similar way than a custodian by 'maintaining an account in which the client's entitlement on the digital asset is recorded' and by ensuring that the client does not retain control of the assets, the client is 'exposed to the insolvency risk of the account provider'.[32] Thus, this provision has a protective function vis-à-vis the client, who may be a consumer or an otherwise vulnerable party, and serves the purpose of flagging a potential risk to the client while offering a strong incentive to service providers to expressly clarify the nature of their agreement.

In this regard, we would like to particularly emphasise three points. First, the DAPL Principles do not call for a specific wording to be used, and we start from the assumption that the rules of contract interpretation of the applicable law will determine whether there is sufficient clarity as regards the nature of the agreement. The DAPL Principles, however, use the expression 'if it is clear from the agreement', thereby implying a potentially higher threshold (depending on the applicable law) of which interpreters, or legislators, should be aware. Second, the Commentary to Principle 10 helpfully contains several practical illustrations of custody and non-custody agreements,[33] which may guide parties in drafting suitable language in their contract, and interpreters in reaching a common understanding of the dividing line between the two situations. Third, while the DAPL Principles do not purport to address regulatory issues and only apply to a selected number of private law issues, the Commentary to this provision contains additional 'soft' advice to legislators regarding mitigation of the risk for clients in some situations. In particular, the Commentary refers to those arrangements where the service provider is obliged to deliver a certain quantity of a digital asset to a client, which it keeps in an account (similar to a bank account, with no additional obligations towards the client than the obligation to deliver) and the client's claim would likely be treated

[30] Principle 13, Commentary para 13.2.
[31] *cf* Principle 10 (4).
[32] The quotations are taken from the text of Commentary para 10.7 to Principle 13.
[33] *cf* Commentary to Principle 10, paras 10.10 to 10.22.

as an unsecured claim in the insolvency of the provider.[34] Legislators are invited to consider regulatory mitigation tools that would provide additional protection to (vulnerable) clients, including requirements for specific disclosure of the risks, limitations of the provision of such services to regulated entities, or limitations as to the type of persons that could become clients.[35]

Principle 13 provides some further (non-exhaustive) guidance, relevant for the effective enforcement of the client's rights, on the duties of the insolvency representative, who must take reasonable steps to ensure that control of the digital asset is changed to the control of the client or another custodian nominated by the client, and that the rights the custodian has against any sub-custodians to be transferred or otherwise made accessible to the client (or to the custodian the client has nominated).[36] Finally, Principle 13 is completed by a provision applying to the insolvency of a sub-custodian,[37] and by more specific guidance on the situations where the custodian maintains digital assets of the same description for two or more clients in an undivided pool and there is a so-called 'shortfall' of digital assets when the custodian enters in an insolvency-related proceeding.[38]

C. Enforcing Security Rights on Digital Assets (UNIDROIT DAPL Principles, Section V, Principle 17)

As mentioned above (section B.i.), the drafters of the UNIDROIT DAPL Principles devoted special attention to security rights over digital assets, which are among the most important types of transactions currently used in commerce and for which it was thought that some guidance regarding creation, third-party effectiveness, priority, and indeed enforcement would be useful.[39] In relation to enforcement, it should be noted that the 'black-letter' text of Principle 17 primarily refers to 'other law', especially regarding judicial enforcement, and avoids prescribing particular enforcement methods. Nevertheless, Principle 17 and its Commentary do provide some additional guidance for legislators and adjudicators, starting with the general principle that all enforcement actions available to creditors for other types of collateral should be generally available (unless the nature of the digital asset or the way it is held prevents the use of certain remedies in practice), and that existing international standards on secured transactions (such as the UNCITRAL Model Law on Secured Transactions[40]) appear to be sufficiently

[34] *cf* for more details and nuances, Illustration in Commentary to Principle 10, para 10.20.
[35] *cf* Commentary to Principle 10, para 10.21.
[36] *cf* Principle 13 (4) and for more details and practical constellations Commentary at paras 13.5–13.6.
[37] *cf* Principle 13(8).
[38] *cf* for more details Principle 13 (5) to (7) and Commentary paras 13.7 to 13.9.
[39] *cf* Principles 14 through 17 and related (extensive) Commentary.
[40] UNCITRAL Model Law on Secured Transactions, available at uncitral.un.org/sites/uncitral.un.org/files/media-documents/uncitral/en/19-08779_e_ebook.pdf.

flexible to accommodate enforcement on digital assets.[41] Usefully, the Principle and its Commentary highlight potential practical difficulties or situations that would require special attention by legislators.[42] One such situation that found its way into the black-letter text of Principle 17 concerns a custodian maintaining the digital asset for a client who then grants a security right over it. Should the creditor wish to enforce its rights extra judicially, the custodian may be reluctant to follow its instructions unless it has agreed to do so (which will typically be the case when the intermediary continues to maintain the digital asset for the secured creditor after a security right is made effective by control). When the security right is made effective by registration, the creditor will need to obtain an order from a court or other public authority if the custodian does not agree to act on the secured creditor's instructions.[43]

D. Procedural Law Including Enforcement in the UNIDROIT DAPL Principles (Section VI, Principle 18)

In relation to procedural law matters, including enforcement of rights relating to digital assets, the DAPL Principles generally provide for the application of 'other law'. Principle 18 clarifies that ordinary procedural law of a state will apply to court proceedings concerning rights relating to digital assets and to proceedings for the enforcement of court orders or execution by way of authority with respect to digital assets. The Commentary, however, highlights that adaptations of the ordinary enforcement rules may be necessary to ensure a more effective exercise of enforcement rights by the creditor, particularly considering the need for the debtor's or third party's cooperation in transferring control over the asset, the need to specify the duties of custodians in the case of enforcement procedures, or the potential difficulties in identifying the person who is in control of the digital asset.[44] Thus, the DAPL Principles expressly refer to the current work carried out by the *Best Practices for Effective Enforcement* project.[45]

[41] Principle 17 (1) expressly refers to the requirement to enforce according to the general principle of good faith, or in a commercially reasonable manner, or both, that may be provided for in the applicable 'other law', and that is contained in Art 4 of the UNCITRAL Model Law on Secured Transactions (n 40). The Commentary refers to other rules that characterise modern secured transactions laws and are embodied in the Model Law, such as notification duties on the secured creditor, respect of priority rules in the distribution of the proceeds, or differentiated (and more limited) enforcement requirements for creditors that have acquired an intangible asset outright as opposed to obtaining rights on it by way of security, etc (Commentary, paras 17.2 and 17.3).

[42] eg, the Commentary (paras 17.5 to 17.7) refers to the exceptions to the general secured transactions rules that impose notification duties on secured creditors enforcing their rights extra judicially, exceptions which would apply when the asset may speedily decline in value or is sold on a recognised market (eg, Art 78 [8] of the UNCITRAL Model Law), and which would concern some types of digital assets only (eg, bitcoins as opposed to stable coins). An analogous exception is suggested in Part II of the UNIDROIT draft Best Practices on Enforcement that cover enforcement of security rights.

[43] Principle 17 (2).

[44] Commentary to Principle 18, paras 18.3 to 18.7.

[45] *cf* Commentary to Principle 18, para 18.8.

III. Enforcing Creditor's Rights on Digital Assets: Open Issues, and Some Insights from the Draft UNIDROIT Best Practices on Enforcement (BPEE Project)

As mentioned in the introduction, the use of digital assets in the market and litigation involving digital assets are on the rise. Creditors want to be reassured that they can effectively enforce their rights, even if these are related to such assets. In addition to the general circumstances that can traditionally render the enforcement of creditors' rights costly, ineffective, or unsuccessful, specific complexities linked to the functional, structural and operational characteristics of digital assets can add costs, uncertainties or inefficiencies to the enforcement proceedings. Therefore, special attention is being paid to ensure the effectiveness of the enforcement of rights on digital assets within the framework of the UNIDROIT *Project on Best Practices for Effective Enforcement* (BPEE).

While the key policy premise is that digital assets are susceptible to enforcement and, therefore, that general enforcement rules should apply, the BPEE Working Group has acknowledged that some of the methods and procedures for enforcement show inadequacies, limitations, or have simply proven to be unsuited to the specificities of digital assets. Hence, it may be advisable to adapt the general rules, measures, or procedures. In principle, ad hoc legal solutions for digital assets may be necessary only in rare cases, and therefore, most of the recommendations that are being developed for the future instrument are mainly of a practical nature, aimed to help authorities, practitioners, courts, and enforcement agents in the application of existing rules and enforcement methods to digital assets. Five general issues that have been discussed by the BPEE Working Group will be highlighted in the following paragraphs, which will mention the solution retained in the draft instrument where relevant, with the caveat that the instrument is still work in progress and that more detailed recommendations are in the process of being developed.

A. Distinctive Features of Digital Assets with Relevance for Enforcement

Although the amply accepted finding is that solutions for digital asset enforcement can be found in general enforcement law, the novelty, the popularity, and the technological complexity underlying the operation of digital assets, as well as the limited familiarity with these classes of assets in certain circles, moved the Working Group to consider drafting or at least collating specific recommendations for digital assets with special consideration of their distinctive features. A separate set of recommendations was considered to provide more effective advice when considering the practical difficulties encountered in enforcement proceedings involving digital assets.

Should the premise be that general rules apply to digital assets, but their distinctive features require adaptation, a proper understanding of such singular characteristics and their implications for enforcement is a prerequisite. The different methods of holding digital assets, their natural cross-border nature, the elusive notion of location, the risk of dissipation of value, and the problem of identification, not only of the assets but also of the debtor itself, are the most revealing features that underscore the need for adaptation in the enforcement stage.

B. The Uncertainties Regarding the Status of Property Rights on Digital Assets and the Significance for Enforcement

The concept of a digital asset is neither uniformly defined nor clearly delimited. It is indeed a broad category of undefined contours that comprises different subclasses, ranging from cryptocurrencies, to stablecoins, and non-fungible tokens (NFTs). Each type has different variables that may intensify or diminish certain legal challenges and alter the legal analysis. The heterogeneity of these asset classes complicates the legal debate on the legal characterisation of digital assets even more. The legal nature and the status of property rights on digital assets remain debated at the domestic law level and are still unresolved on a harmonised basis. Nevertheless, the express recognition of the fact that a digital asset can be the subject of proprietary rights in the *UNIDROIT DAPL Principles*,[46] however differently they may be characterised in domestic laws, is certainly a step in the right direction in terms of admitting third-party opposability of such rights over a digital asset.

The property status may have an impact on enforcement, as selected case law demonstrates. In *Kleiman v Wright*,[47] a Florida court discussed whether bitcoins were 'money'[48] and thus capable or incapable of being the subject of an action of conversion under Florida law. Contrary to this ruling that admitted the action, an English court refused the applicability of conversion in *OBG v Allan*,[49] on the grounds that in English law conversion has traditionally required physical possession of the object at stake. Likewise, the granting by a court of a proprietary

[46] *cf* Principle 3 (1).

[47] [2018] WL 6812914.

[48] The legal categorisation of digital assets is also relevant for the purposes of financial regulation. Disparate solutions have led to inharmonious regulatory approaches: taking the US as an example, some court decisions held that bitcoin is 'money', eg, *United States v Harmon* (US District Court, District of Columbia, 474 F.Supp.3d 76 [2020]), *United States v Faiella* (US District Court, Southern District of New York, 39 F.Supp.3d 544 [2014]), *SEC v Shavers* (US District Court, Eastern District of Texas, [2013] WL 4028182), while other decisions refused this categorisation – *United States v Petix* (US District Court, Western District of New York, 15-CR-227A [W.D.N.Y. Dec. 1, 2016]), *State v Espinoza* (US District Court, 11th Circuit Florida, F14-2923 [22 July 2016]).

[49] [2007] UKHL 21.

injunction,[50] an asset preservation order,[51] or a proprietary freezing order[52] in respect of digital assets depends upon the response to the question of the legal characterisation.

As the examples selected above illustrate, the uncertain and unresolved legal characterisation of digital assets has a decisive impact on enforcement.

The draft BPEE do not directly solve this matter by determining a specific legal characterisation, but by conclusively affirming that digital assets are capable of enforcement and providing recommendations aimed to facilitate the adaptation of methods and procedures to the distinctive features of digital assets. The approach to this matter is therefore a pragmatic one.

C. The Identification Problem

The identification of the parties holding the digital asset relevant for the enforcement proceeding may be difficult, due to the anonymity or the use of pseudonyms as a distinctive feature of digital assets operating on DLT (*Distributed Legal Technologies*) models, or may require the cooperation of third parties. As the court acknowledged in the *Tulip Trading Ltd v Bitcoin Association for Bitcoin SV (BSV) and others* judgment,[53] '(t)he amounts held at every address are public, but the identity of the parties is not. The blockchain does not reveal the relationship between the digital addresses and any persons'. The draft BPEE considers this issue by alerting legislators of the need to consider this factor, particularly in determining the rules on disclosure in judicial enforcement of digital assets.

D. The International Nature and the Notion of Location

The operation of digital assets primarily on DLT models and the habitual multi-jurisdictional nature of transactions and conflicts involving digital assets considering the parties involved – debtor, creditor, custodians, other intermediaries – add complexities to enforcement proceedings. While location is a usual connecting factor to determine the applicable law or *forum*, it can also be relevant at the enforcement stage in ensuring the effectiveness of an enforcement order or in determining the territorial jurisdiction of enforcement agents.[54]

[50] In the Japanese case *Mt. Gox*, for example, the court ruled that the lack of corporeality of bitcoins and the fact that they cannot be controlled in an exclusive manner by a person entailed that no proprietary remedy could be granted to the claimant: *Tokyo District Court, MtGox Co. Ltd. Case*, ref. number: 25541521. Final judgment: 5 August 2015.

[51] Granting the order, *Shair.Com Global Digital Services Ltd v Arnold* (Unreported, 15 July 2019).

[52] In the affirmative, *Vorotyntseva v Money-4 Ltd* [2018] EWHC 2596 (Ch).

[53] [2022] EWHC 667 (Ch).

[54] International Union of Judicial Officers (UIHJ), *Global Code of Digital Enforcement* (September 2021) Article 12 – Territorial jurisdiction of judicial officers or enforcement agents. The competence of

Efforts to link the 'location' of digital assets with the residence, domicile or place of business of the holder or the intermediary come up against the diversity of holding models and their implications. Digital assets can either be directly held by a wallet native to the protocol, held in an internet-based wallet offered by a third-party provider, or held by relying on a custodial wallet provider.

The significance of the variety of holding models for enforcement is two-fold. On the one hand, it shows how a typical connection factor, ie, location, becomes elusive, uncertain, or even totally irrelevant as regards digital assets. Users can hold crypto assets in their own wallets (on a specific device), in internet-based wallets ('hot wallets'), or in wallets offered by third parties (established in a certain country). It is then uncertain whether the user's domicile, the custodian's establishment, the technological devices' location, or other factors might be relevant for enforcement purposes. On the other hand, the diversity of holding models leads to different scenarios in enforcement, where it is necessary to identify the person who has to cooperate for the purposes of enabling the enforcement actions. The draft BPEE emphasises the essential role of cooperation of the debtor and/or third parties during the successive stages of enforcement and for the purposes of disclosure of information, seizure, or transfer.

E. The Relevance of the Cooperation of the Debtor and/or Third Parties for Enforcement

The diversity of holding models reveals that cooperation may be required from the debtor, in some cases, or from third parties that provide various services of custody, trading or intermediation, in other cases. Should the debtor or the third parties not cooperate on a voluntary basis, adequate measures need to be granted. Although *in personam* measures are, in principle, deemed a last resort, they prove to be particularly adequate in the enforcement of digital assets.[55] These measures should be proportionate and adequate, and priority should be given to less invasive and less costly measures, taking into account the circumstances and the interests and rights at stake. Special consideration needs to be paid to the protection of third-party rights, the risk of exposure of trade secrets and confidential information, cybersecurity risks, and privacy issues.

The cooperation of the debtor in asset disclosure renders enforcement much easier and more practical. In some cases, however, the technological complexity of

judicial officers or enforcement agents to identify digital assets and the place where they are accessible should be governed by the debtor's domicile. The competence of judicial officers or enforcement agents to seize and sell a digital asset should be governed by the place where it is identified and accessible.

[55] In the *Tsarkov* case, for example, the Court ordered the defendant to provide the password to his crypto-wallet to the insolvency administrator – First instance – *Moscow Arbitrazh Court; Appellate court – Ninth Arbitrazh Appellate Court, civil matters – Mr Tsarkov case*, case No. A40-124668/17. Resolution of the Appellate court: 15 May 2018.

digital assets may require the assistance of technical experts to ensure full compliance with disclosure obligations. Besides, enforcement organs can search for information in publicly-accessible registers – such as movables/security rights registries, or company registers, provided that applicable law requires such registration – insofar as this is necessary. The increase of disclosure obligations provided for by financial regulation, tax legislation, or other regulatory instruments facilitates access to relevant information provided by third parties and reinforces the need for cooperation of private entities and public authorities with competent enforcement organs in respect of digital assets. The duty of disclosure by third parties is related but is not limited to the identification of users and digital assets. Disclosure can refer to any information relevant for the enforcement proceedings.

Cooperation becomes particularly critical to effectively and efficiently seize and transfer the digital assets. Based on the concept of 'control' of the *UNIDROIT DAPL Principles* (Principle 6), the BPEE articulates the seizure and the transfer of digital assets for enforcement purposes. To that end, depending on the holding model, the debtor's cooperation can be crucial and irreplaceable – ie, in the case of 'cold wallets' – to provide access and taking of control, or third parties' cooperation can be necessary (eg, when the debtor is unwilling or unable to cooperate, for instance, because it cannot provide the required information or perform the required actions to transfer control; or on the basis of the service provision agreement, or of any technological consideration, the cooperation of the debtor is insufficient or ineffective, because the third party retains control over the private key or a multi-signature arrangement is in force). It should be noted that resistance to cooperate or unsuccessful cooperation, despite the provision by the applicable law of dissuasive (effective, proportionate, and adequate) sanctions, may still lead to ineffective or even totally unsuccessful enforcement.[56]

F. The Realisation of Value

The special characteristics of digital assets may add two different elements of complexity in the realisation of value: lack of liquid markets, or high volatility. Certain digital assets may lack a liquid market, rendering the valuation of the assets and the conversion into money challenging. Other digital assets, such as cryptocurrencies, do have a liquid market but are highly volatile. Therefore, the value may vary drastically from the moment of taking control of the digital assets

[56] eg, the Australian case Blockchain Global – *Chen v Blockchain Global Ltd; Abel v Blockchain Global Ltd* – where a Security '2 of 2' wallet has been employed, which means that 2 out of 2 signatories need to authorise a transaction to make a transfer out of it, if any of seed phrase is lost, forgotten or corrupted, the Bitcoins will become inaccessible, which would amount to the destruction of bitcoins. In fact, in *Tulip Trading Ltd v Bitcoin Association for BSV* [2022] EWHC 2 (Ch), the private keys have been lost in a hack, likely stolen, and consequently, without its private keys Tulip could not access its assets or move them to safety.

by the enforcement agent and the actual realisation of the value for the creditors. Volatility and uncertainties on the reference value for realisation will affect the effectiveness of enforcement actions. Therefore, the draft BPEE recommends that clear, predictable, and adequate criteria and procedures for valuing digital assets in due consideration of these particular characteristics should be considered. Existing criteria, procedures, and enforcement rules available for assessing the value of assets other than digital assets but with similar characteristics may be used as useful benchmarks to the extent possible.

Insolvency proceedings, in particular, provide revealing insights on this matter. As the Japanese case *Mt. Gox*[57] proves, valuation methods for digital assets can be diverse and lead to significantly disparate consequences in terms of value. Two methods of bitcoin valuation were applied depending upon the type of proceedings.[58] In insolvency proceedings, non-monetary claims, including bitcoin claims, were converted into monetary claims based on the valuation as at the time of the commencement of insolvency proceedings; while in civil rehabilitation proceedings, non-monetary claims, including bitcoin claims, are not required to be converted. Given the volatility of bitcoins, the relevant date for conversion becomes critical. The Court held in *Mt. Gox* that the relevant date was that of the start of the civil rehabilitation proceedings, while an Italian court decided in the two proceedings of the *BitGrail case*[59] that the date of the declaration of bankruptcy should be referenced.

IV. Conclusions

The UNIDROIT DAPL Principles and the BPEE project address the need for more clarity and predictability of the legal regime applicable to the enforcement of rights in digital assets outside insolvency and, as regards the DAPL Principles, also within insolvency. They do so by offering soft law guidance to legislators and other stakeholders, which can then be adapted to the specificities of each legal system while preserving the objectives and the harmonised legal framework introduced with the uniform law instrument. As one may expect, once formally adopted, such global instruments face the challenge of being (correctly) implemented and accepted by their intended addressees. In this respect, one should recall that the methodology used in the development of uniform law, particularly at UNIDROIT, includes active participation of stakeholders and international organisations involved in

[57] Tokyo District Court of 2015, MtGox Co. Ltd. Case, ref. number: 25541521. Final judgment: 5 August 2015.

[58] Answers to Frequently Asked Questions, Announcement of Commencement of Civil Rehabilitation Proceedings, 22 June 2018, available at www.mtgox.com/img/pdf/20180622_announcement_en.pdf.

[59] Court of Florence – Mr Francesco Firano's case No. 17/2019, bankruptcy docket No. 178/2018 and 205/2018; BitGrail case No. 18/2019, bankruptcy docket No. 179/2018 and 505/2018. Mr Francesco Firano's Decision No 17/2019, 21 January 2019; BitGrail Decision No. 18/2019, 21 January 2019.

work on the ground[60] as well as of the experts that are appointed as members of the Working Group responsible for the drafting of the instrument. The process also involves consultations with governmental experts and other interested parties prior to the instrument's submission to the competent organs for adoption.[61] This is purposely done to ensure that the instrument adequately responds to the needs of the specific sector or market, and balances the interests at stake, while raising awareness among the principal addressees of the instrument, thus preparing them to support its practical implementation. While the DAPL Principles have just been adopted and the BPEE project is still awaiting completion, they appear to be well suited to serve their respective aims, and, in relation to the specific topic of enforcement of rights in digital assets, to contribute to increasing certainty and effectiveness of the legal framework within domestic laws and across borders.

[60] Among the institutional observers in the DAPL Principles Working Group were, for example, representatives of the private sector such as ISDA, the Association of Global Custodians, or the Banking Law Committee of the IBA, as well as international organisations active in advising on financing matters such as the World Bank Group, the IMF, or think tanks such as the European Banking Institute. A complete list of observers is found at pages III–VI of the DAPL Principles (n 4 above). The BPEE project counts as observers, among others, the International Union of Judicial Officers (UIHJ) as well as the WBG and the EBRD. For more information see above, n 5.

[61] As already mentioned (n 4 above), the DAPL Principles were subject to multiple consultations, including the setting up of a Steering Committee of experts nominated by States in a consultative capacity, which was consulted twice before adopting the instrument, and a wider consultation exercise on the latest draft before completion. As evidence of the keen interest of legislators and domestic regulators in the DAPL Principles, the Working Group was also directly joined by observers of several domestic law-making bodies and regulatory or banking authorities (for a complete list see DAPL Principles, at III–IV, n 4 above). The BPEE has already benefited from targeted consultations facilitated by the UIHJ, the EBRD, and the World Bank Group.

4

The Role of the Situs of Digital Assets for Enforcement and Insolvency Proceedings

MICHAEL NG

I. Introduction

The location or situs of property is a core concept in private international law. For example, in disputes where there are competing claims to priority over ownership of all kinds of property, the law applicable to determine the dispute has been the lex situs.[1] Whether the forum will recognise the validity of a government expropriation of property similarly generally depends on whether the property in question was within the territorial jurisdiction of the expropriating state.[2] Similarly, whether the forum will enforce a judgment debt against property or recognise such an enforcement by a foreign court depends on whether the property was within the territorial jurisdiction of the enforcing court.

This chapter seeks to re-evaluate the monopoly status of the concept of situs in light of the emerging crypto economy. This emerging market is built upon a novel type of property – crypto-tokens, which are a type of digital asset. Indeed, the UK Law Commission has adopted the view that this new type of asset is so novel that a new class of property under English law, has been proposed for it.[3] The suitability of the concept of a situs for crypto-tokens would depend on whether the concept of a situs for property continues to serve its intended purposes for crypto-tokens.

This introduction forms section I of this chapter. Section II starts off with a description of digital assets in light of the subject matter scope of the book as a whole. It then zeroes in on the subject matter of this chapter – crypto-tokens.

[1] A Held, 'Crypto Assets and Decentralised Ledgers: Does Situs Actually Matter' in A Bonomi, M Lehmann and S Lalani (eds), *Blockchain and Private International Law* (Leiden, Brill, 2023) 210.

[2] *Luther v James Sagor & Co* [1921] 3 KB 532.

[3] Law Commission, *Digital Assets* (Law Com No 256, 2022).

Instead of surveying the panoply of crypto-tokens available on the market today to produce a full taxonomy, a selection of crypto-token projects are contrasted with the well-known Bitcoin system to illustrate certain key design choices for different crypto-tokens that may be relevant for private international law purposes. Section III then sets out when the concept of a situs of crypto-tokens is and is not relevant in the insolvency and enforcement scenarios. Section IV then considers the rationales for adopting the concept of a situs of property to resolve: (i) choice of law questions for proprietary issues; and (ii) limiting the court's enforcement jurisdiction against property. Following that, it is argued that the rationales identified in section III continue to be relevant in deciding what connecting factor is appropriate for selecting an applicable law for property issues involving crypto-tokens.[4] Section V then evaluates the existing panoply of candidates for determining the situs of crypto-tokens according to how they fulfil the rationales identified in section III, before proposing a structured way for identifying the situs of crypto-tokens. It is also observed in section V that the rationale underlying the situs limitation in enforcement action involves different considerations than those for choice of law, with the result that a divergent approach may be appropriate. Section VI concludes.

II. Digital Assets and Crypto-tokens

There does not yet appear to be a consensus on the meaning of the term 'digital assets'. On the one hand, the UK Law Commission uses the term broadly. On this view, everything from digital files and records of themselves to crypto-tokens are digital assets.[5] From that starting point, only some digital assets replicate the primary characteristics of objects of property rights[6] and are therefore objects of property rights.[7] Others are purely information.[8] UNIDROIT, on the other hand, defines digital assets as 'an electronic record which is capable of being subject to control',[9] where an 'electronic record' means 'information which is (i) stored in an electronic medium and (ii) capable of being retrieved'.[10]

[4] M Lehmann, 'Extraterritoriality in Financial Law' in A Parrish and C Ryngaert (eds), *The Cambridge Handbook on Extraterritoriality* (Cambridge, Cambridge University Press, 2022).

[5] The category would cover digital files and digital records, email accounts, certain in-game digital items, domain names, various credits and allowances under carbon emissions trading schemes and crypto-tokens: see Law Commission (n 3) chs 6 to 10 generally.

[6] Law Commission (n 3) para 1.8.

[7] ibid para 1.10.

[8] ibid para 1.6.

[9] UNIDROIT 'Digital Assets and Private Law Working Group Issues Paper, Study LXXXII' (June 2021) Principle 2(2) www.unidroit.org/wp-content/uploads/2023/03/W.G.8-Doc.-2-Draft-Principles-and-Commentary-Clean.pdf.

[10] UNIDROIT (n 9) Principle 2(1).

Thus, the final draft of this chapter written on Microsoft Word would fall within the UK Law Commission's definition of 'digital assets' but not UNDROIT's definition, where it would merely be an 'electronic record'. However, despite the difference in the use of labels, the UK Law Commission and the UNDROIT Working Group are in fact in agreement that what turns information into a proper object of property rights is when it is capable of being controlled by a particular person.[11] In other words, where the digital architecture renders the use of the information rivalrous by assigning exclusive control of that information to a particular person, it becomes a proper object of property rights.

Thankfully, resolving these differences in terminology falls outside the scope of this chapter. The subject matter scope of this chapter is rather more modest, being confined to crypto-tokens as a sub-set of all digital assets. This is because the often decentralised and thus delocalised nature of crypto-tokens poses unique challenges to private international law reasoning. For this purpose, I gratefully adopt the UK Law Commission's definition of crypto-tokens:[12]

> **Crypto-token** means a particular, individuated data structure which:
>
> 1. is constituted by the Protocol Rules of the Crypto-token System in which it is instantiated using one or more distributed ledgers or structured records; and
> 2. is recognised by the Protocol Rules of the Crypto-token System in which it is instantiated as, at any one time (including by reference to the state of the distributed ledger(s) or structured record(s) and the Protocol Rules relating to state transitions, if applicable):
>   a. capable of being uniquely attached to or associated with a particular Data Address, and
>   b. capable of Authentication of an operation in respect of the particular instantiation of the data structure (including, if applicable, an operation to effect a change of state of the distributed ledger or structured record).
>
> In this description the following terms have the following meanings:
>
> **Authentication** means cryptographic authentication via computational or computing means.
>
> **Crypto-token System** means the system manifested or realised by the operation of a particular set of Protocol Rules.
>
> **Data Address** means a unique individuated data structure or a particular set of associated data structures or identifiers (including, but not limited to, an asymmetric cryptographic value) which is/are recognised by the Protocol Rules of the relevant Crypto-token System.

[11] Law Commission, *Digital Assets* (Law Com No 256, 2022) chapter 11 generally; UNIDROIT issues paper (n 9) Principle 6.

[12] Law Commission (n 3) Appx 4.

Protocol Rules means software code that specifies or embodies rules or algorithms for:

1. the generation, Authentication, sending and validation of data within the particular Crypto-token System;
2. determining and effecting changes to the distributed ledger or the structured record of the particular Crypto-token System by a process of Authentication such that the state of the relevant distributed ledger or structured record is capable of verification by other participants in the Crypto-token System; and
3. determining and effecting changes to the particular Crypto-token System and/or the Protocol Rules themselves.

The above definition is useful because it is capable of capturing the variety of crypto-tokens that are available in the market. However, it leaves us with a wide variety of crypto-tokens to address. It would not be possible to analyse each existing crypt-token individually in this chapter. It is, however, important to have a sense of how crypto-tokens vary in order to determine whether the differences are material to the issue at hand. The various ways in which crypto-tokens can be categorised have been explored in detail by others.[13] This section, in the interests of brevity, will instead set out the main differentiating factors using Bitcoin and a relevant comparator for illustration:

Permission-less vs permissioned networks: In permission-less blockchains, any person can become a participant and be authorised to add entries to the distributed ledger without prior approval by any authority.[14] Permission-less systems instead rely on a particular protocol to validate such additions to the ledger. The Bitcoin network is a permission-less system where anyone who downloads the Bitcoin core client can become a participant and add entries to the distributed ledger. Such entries are validated by a proof-of-work.[15] By contrast, the Ripple network is a permissioned network where only participants approved by the centralised authority are able to add entries to that distributed ledger.[16]

Fungibility: This is whether one crypto-token native to a network is distinguishable from another. Bitcoin is the prime example of a fungible crypto-token. What we think of as 1 BTC is actually unspent transaction output associated with an address on the Bitcoin network. Where bitcoins from two sources are mixed in a single address, there is no precise way to separate them again. Other crypto-tokens are by design unique and therefore non-fungible. The best known example would probably be OpenSea's Bored Ape Yacht Club non-fungible tokens.[17] Even

[13] See for instance F Krysa, 'Taxonomy and Characterisation of Crypto Assets in Private International Law' in Bonomi, Lehmann and Lalani (n 1).

[14] A Lewis, 'A gentle introduction to blockchain technology' (*Bits on blocks*, 9 September 2015) https://bitsonblocks.net/2015/09/09/a-gentle-introduction-to-blockchain-technology/.

[15] ibid.

[16] SK Krause, H Natarajan and HL Gradstein, *Distributed Ledger Technology (DLT) and blockchain: Fintech Note No. 1* (Washington DC, World Bank, 2017).

[17] opensea.io/collection/boredapeyachtclub.

the venerable Sotheby's holds auctions for digital art non-fungible tokens hosted on their own metaverse.[18]

Real-world asset link: Some crypto-tokens purport to represent rights in or ownership of certain real-world assets, much like how bills of lading represent title to goods in transit by sea. Bitcoin is not this type of crypto-token. Owning a bitcoin does not even purport to represent ownership of any real-world asset, including any contractual or other rights against a counterparty. By contrast, the Hong Kong government has issued green bonds on Goldman Sachs' new tokenisation platform, GS DAPTM.[19] The crypto-token issued would represent ownership of an investor's rights as a lender under the terms of the bond.

Stablecoins: Some crypto-tokens purport to have their values linked to a fiat currency, and are thus seen as less volatile than other independent crypto-tokens like Bitcoin. The most well-known example of this is Tether, whose value is linked to the US dollar. These crypto-tokens are often called stablecoins. There are, however, two versions of stablecoins. One version, like Tether, is backed by ownership of the asset linked to the crypt-token. The other version, such as the failed Luna, relies on a computer algorithms and smart contracts to maintain its peg.

Payment/utility/security: Finally, securities regulators[20] generally use some version of this trichotomy to determine whether the issuance of a particular crypto-token attracts securities regulation.[21] On this axis, Bitcoin is a payment token, largely because it was intended as a medium of exchange. A utility token represents rights against the provider of a product or service, much like airline miles programs. An example would be Filecoin, where Filecoin's native token is required to access its decentralised data storage services. The aforementioned Hong Kong government green bonds would be a security token, representing rights based on the performance of a stated venture.

III. Insolvency, Enforcement and Situs

Before delving into whether the concept of a situs for crypto-tokens is appropriate in the enforcement and insolvency scenarios, we begin by defining the two scenarios and identifying when the concept of situs would (and would not) be relevant in each.

[18] metaverse.sothebys.com/.

[19] www.hkma.gov.hk/eng/news-and-media/press-releases/2023/02/20230216-3/.

[20] Outside of the US.

[21] Swiss Financial Markets Supervisory Authority, *Guidelines for enquiries regarding the regulatory framework for initial coin offerings (ICOs)*, s 3.1; P Hacker and C Thomale, 'Crypto-Securities Regulation: ICOs, Token Sales and Cryptocurrencies under EU Financial Law' [2018] *European Company and Financial Law Review* 645.

A. The Enforcement Scenario

The enforcement scenario involves a successful claimant seeking to enforce the fruits of his successful litigation or arbitration against crypto-tokens owned by the defendant[22] with the assistance of a national court. Traditionally, unlike in the insolvency scenario discussed below, the issue is not thought of as one of choice of law. Instead, the issue has been framed in terms of whether the national court petitioned has jurisdiction over the subject matter to effectively expropriate them from the defendant for the satisfaction of the claimant's judgment or award debt. One justification for this limitation is that since the enforcement process is akin to a seizure or confiscation of property,[23] it should be confined to property within the territorial jurisdiction of the forum because 'it is a general principle of international law that one sovereign state should not trespass upon the sovereignty of another, by attempting to seize assets situated within the jurisdiction of the foreign state'.[24] Thus, at least when it comes to traditional asset classes, a national court will generally only enforce a judgment or award against an asset if it is located within its territorial jurisdiction.

Thus, in *Societe Eram*,[25] the House of Lords held that it could not enforce a judgment debt against a debt owed to the judgment debtor by a bank in Hong Kong because the debt was situated in Hong Kong. The nature of the enforcement order was proprietary in nature, and therefore, for reasons of comity owed to the Hong Kong court, the debt was beyond the subject matter jurisdiction of the English court.[26] By contrast, in *Taurus Petroleum*, Taurus successfully enforced an arbitral award against debts owed under letters of credit issued by the London branch of Credit Agricole in favour of SOMO on the basis that the situs of the letters of credit was in England.[27]

The question of whether a claimant can enforce its judgment or award debt against certain crypto-assets therefore traditionally turns on whether those crypto-tokens are located within the territorial jurisdiction of the enforcing court.

[22] There may also be situations where a third party contends that he, and not the defendant, is the true owner of the crypto-tokens in the course of enforcement proceedings. That issue falls outside of the enforcement problem per se. It is a pure ownership dispute, and falls to be determined along the same lines as disputes over whether certain crypto-tokens fall within the insolvency estate discussed in III.B. below.

[23] Lord Collins of Mapesbury and J Harris (eds), *Dicey, Morris and Collins on The Conflict of Laws*, 16th edn (London, Sweet & Maxwell, 2022) 25-090.

[24] *Societe Eram Shipping Co Ltd v Cie Internationale de Navigation and others* [2003] UKHL 30, [2004] 1 AC 260 para 54 per Lord Hoffmann.

[25] *Societe Eram Shipping Co Ltd v Cie Internationale de Navigation and others* [2003] UKHL 30, [2004] 1 AC 260.

[26] *Societe Eram Shipping Co Ltd v Cie Internationale de Navigation and others* [2003] UKHL 30, [2004] 1 AC 260 paras 24–26 per Lord Bingham.

[27] [2017] UKSC 64 para 41; also overruling *Power Curber International Ltd v National Bank of Kuwait SAK* [1981] 1 WLR 1233 on the lex situs of letters of credit.

B. The Insolvency Scenario

The relevance of the concept of situs in the insolvency scenario is more complex. The basic contours of the scenario are that an entity has entered into insolvency proceedings in the forum concursus, usually the courts of the centre of main interest of the entity where the UNCITRAL Model Law on Cross-Border Insolvency applies.[28] In the short and volatile history of the crypto-economy, the insolvent has more often than not been a crypto-token exchange. Many of the issues that arise in insolvency are arguably proprietary in nature. The applicable law for determining them has therefore traditionally been the lex situs. Yet, this is not the case for all issues. The differences are examined below.

i. Where Situs is Relevant in Insolvency

Within an insolvency proceeding, several choice of law issues[29] which could involve crypto-tokens arise where the connecting factor has traditionally been the lex situs. These issues tend to revolve around either: (a) whether certain assets, in the case of this contribution crypto-tokens specifically, fall within the scope of the insolvency estate for distribution to creditors; or (b) whether certain creditors have valid security interests over crypto-tokens and therefore have priority over the general body of creditors.

a. Determining the Scope of the Insolvency Estate

The scope of the insolvency estate has to be determined as part of any insolvency process, regardless of whether the process is viewed from a substantive law or private international law perspective. As Savigny observed:[30]

> The functions of the judge in bankruptcy (Concurs) consists of two distinct portions – preparatory acts, and the division of the estate (competition, Concurs). Among the preparatory acts are the determination of claims themselves (liquidation), then *the formation and determination of the estate in bankruptcy (common fund, Concursmasse) by elimination of all portions not belonging to the estate of the debtor (Vindicanten, Separatisten)*, by collection of all portions really belonging to the estate, and by converting them into cash by sale. (emphasis added)

Within this process, several issues arise that would traditionally be governed by the lex situs.

[28] It is beyond the scope of this chapter to discuss the intricacies of determining where the main insolvency proceedings should be opened.

[29] Since the focus of this contribution is on crypto-tokens, we can safely leave to one side the jurisdictional limitations in the so-called *Mocambique* rule in relation to suits over foreign immovables.

[30] FC von Savigny, *Private International Law: A Treatise on the Conflict of Laws, and the Limits of their Operation in Respect of Place and Time* (William Guthrie trans, Edinburgh, T&T Clark, 1869) 209–210.

First, there is the question of whether crypto tokens are properly the object of substantive property rights at all. There appears to be a divergence in national laws on this issue. Here, most common law jurisdictions applying the *Ainsworth*[31] criteria have had little trouble accepting that crypto-tokens can be the object of property rights.[32] The position is less clear in civilian legal systems. German law, for example, does not appear to embrace crypto-tokens as an object of property rights.[33] During the administration of the insolvency of Mt Gox, Japanese law had taken the same position[34] although Japanese law has since been amended.[35] Nevertheless, when the insolvency forum is confronted with the question of whether crypto-tokens are properly objects of property rights, it would be parochial to determine this question based on the lex fori. The characterisation of property in the conflict of laws should be untarnished by domestic preconceptions,[36] leaving the question of whether property rights can attach to the applicable law:

> The capacity of a thing to become subject to private property, and therefore not to belong to the res quarum commercium non est, is to be judged by the law of the place at which the thing is situated.[37]

Second, issues could arise over whether the insolvent entity had validly acquired title to crypto-tokens from a seller prior to the onset of insolvency vis-à-vis another buyer or an upstream transferor. The textbook scenario is where the insolvent entity has either been the victim of theft or purportedly acquired stolen crypto-tokens.

To illustrate, in *Winkworth*,[38] some works of art were stolen from Winkworth in London, and then sold by the thief to one D'Annone in Italy. The works were then sent back to Christie's in London to be sold by auction. Winkworth then claimed them in England, and a dispute arose as to who had superior title. Even today, under English law, stolen goods remain the property of the owner even if resold, subject to limited exceptions at common law (now codified in the Sale of Goods Act) and in statute.[39] Under Italian law, the subsequent buyer would have

[31] *National Provincial Bank v Ainsworth* [1965] AC 1175.

[32] *AA v Persons Unknown* [2019] EWHC 3556 (Comm), [2020] 4 WLR 35; *Ruscoe v Cryptopia Ltd (in liq)* [2020] NZHC 728; *Quoine Pte Ltd v B2C2 Ltd* [2020] 2 SLR 20 (CA); *ByBit Fintech Ltd v Ho Kai Xin and others* [2023] 5 SLR 1748 (HC).

[33] S 90 of the German Civil Code (BGB) defines 'things' that are objects of German property law as 'corporeal things': see M Lehmann and H Meyle, 'The Law Applicable to Stablecoins' in Bonomi, Lehmann and Lalani (n 1) 382.

[34] Kyodo, 'Bitcoins lost in Mt. Gox debacle 'not subject to ownership' claims: Tokyo Court' (*The Japan Times*, 6 August 2015) www.japantimes.co.jp/news/2015/08/06/national/crime-legal/bitcoins-lost-in-mt-gox-debacle-not-subject-to-ownership-claims-tokyo-court-rules/#.WqWJlSi5vD4.

[35] GM Nori and M Girolametti, 'International Insolvency Law and Cryptocurrencies' in Bonomi, Lehmann and Lalani (n 1) 441.

[36] JM Carruthers, *The Transfer of Property in the Conflict of Laws* (Oxford, Oxford University Press, 2005), para 1.09.

[37] von Savigny (n 30) 138.

[38] *Winkworth Christie Manson and Woods Ltd* [1980] 2 WLR 937.

[39] M Bridge, L Gullifer, G McMeel and S Worthington QC (eds), *The Law of Personal Property* (London, Sweet & Maxwell, 2013) ch 13, but doubt has been cast of whether the same applies to intangibles (para 15-093).

acquired title if he was a bona fide purchaser. The outcome was therefore dependent on the lex situs. The same reasoning would apply to crypto-tokens.

A related but important issue here is whether certain crypto-tokens is considered money under the applicable law. Under English law, a *currency* rule applies to money such that a bona fide purchaser for value receives indefeasible title to the money.[40] Thus, conversion does not lie for money taken and received as currency.[41] Further, title to money passes regardless of the validity of the underlying transaction[42] and is untraceable.[43] The combined effect of these legal rules promotes the circulation of money and equivalence between the value of money as a medium of exchange and as a unit of account.[44] In this respect, El Salvador is the first country to recognise Bitcoin as legal tender. Once so recognised, a country is likely to apply the currency rule to that crypto-token.

This raises a question of whether a transfer of crypto-tokens should be understood as similar to a transfer of tangible movables or as an assignment of a chose in action. If transfers of crypto-tokens are understood as analogous to the former, whether the insolvent obtains title would depend on the lex situs. If, on the other hand, such transfers are considered analogous to assignments, then following the approach set out in *Raffeisen*,[45] the competing title claims would be governed by the legal system that is analogous to the proper law of the contract creating the contractual right being assigned.

It is submitted that crypto-tokens in general are closer to the case of tangible movables than to choses in action, even where the crypto-token represents entitlements to contractual rights. This is because a crypto-token in and of itself is not a legal right against any counterparty. The necessary element in the assignment analysis of a proper law of the underlying contractual right is therefore non-existent. Thus, the UK Law Commission rightly classifies crypto-tokens as a third thing rather than choses in action because the economic value in them is realised by control and not enforcement of any rights under any law before any court. The concept of a situs for crypto-tokens is therefore relevant to the proprietary effect of transfers.

In this respect, a distinction should be drawn conceptually for asset-linked crypto-tokens between the crypto-token itself and the exogenous legal rights linked to the token in a similar manner to how there is a conceptual separation between the physical paper and the rights represented by that paper in relation to negotiable instruments such as bearer share certificates. For the latter, it is lex incorporationis of the shares that first provides that the holder of the certificate is a shareholder of the company. That then raises the incidental question of who holds the certificate, which is determined by the lex situs of the certificate. Thus, where

[40] D Fox, *Property Rights in Money* (Oxford, Oxford University Press, 2008) para 1.61; Bridge (n 39), paras 36-002 and 36-009.

[41] *Lipkin Gorman v Kaprnale Ltd* [1988] UKHL 12, [1991] 2 AC 548, 572–573.

[42] D Fox (n 40) para 1.61.

[43] ibid.

[44] ibid para 1.62.

[45] *Raffeisen Zentralbank Osterreich Ag v Five Star Trading LLC (The Mount I)* [2001] QB 825. The approach is the same under Article 14 of the Rome I Regulation.

the shares are for instance expropriated by the state of incorporation in a manner recognised by the lex incorporationis, that expropriation will be considered effective even when the certificate is held by a person in another jurisdiction.[46] This remains the case even though, as discussed below,[47] it could be desirable for the lex situs of asset-linked tokens and the law governing the underlying rights to coincide for simplicity and certainty. Conceptually, there remain two distinct things. All that has happened is that the law governing the legal right is deemed the situs of the crypto-token.

Nevertheless, it is further suggested that the difference between the approaches to the transfer of tangible movables and to the assignment of choses in action may boil down to a peculiar turn taken in common law systems. The common law regards the situs of a debt as the place where the debtor resides.[48] The proper law of the debt is regarded as a matter of contract only. As a result, it is thought that whether the law of the place of the debtor or the proper law of the debt should apply depends on whether the issue is characterised as contractual or proprietary.[49] Thus, it is said that in relation to competing claims to entitlement to be paid by the debtor, the approach in *Raffeisen* and Article 14 of Rome I 'treats the question of as fundamentally contractual'.[50] Yet, given the absence of a contractual relationship between the competing creditors, that characterisation is rather surprising. Certainly, it is not the only possible way to ascribe a notional situs to debts, despite it being 'the oldest and most universal of the fictional situs rules'.[51] The proper law of the debt could be a competing candidate for the lex situs of a debt as a type of lex creationis.[52] This would have the added benefit of resolving a concern about whether a debt situated in the forum but governed by foreign law is truly discharged by an enforcement order made by the forum.[53] Thus, if the lex situs of the debt were instead the proper law of the debt, the difference in approaches disappears.[54] Ultimately, the vintage of a rule by itself is not indicative

[46] M Ooi, *Shares and Other Securities in the Conflict of Laws* (Oxford, Oxford University Press, 2003) 2.25, citing *Brown v Beleggings-Societeit* (1961) 29 DLR (2d) 673, and 5.38. Although *Brown* was criticised by Staughton LJ in *Macmillan*, Ooi has argued at 2.27 that the position is in fact supported by the English case of *Williams & Humbert Ltd v W 7 H Trade Marks (Jersey) Ltd; Rumasa SA v Multinvest* (UK) Ltd [1986] AC 368. Indeed, 'all assertions to title to shares and membership rights against the company can only be determined by the law of the place of incorporation' (2.27). A similar argument has been made for documents of title vis-à-vis the goods themselves. Thus, it has been suggested that the lex situs of the chattel at the time the document is issued determines whether property may pass by transfer of the document while the lex situs cartae determines whether property has been transferred by the relevant document transfer: YTM 14.032, citing *Hardwick Game Farm v Suffolk Agricultural Poultry Producers Association* [1969] 2 AC 31, 101.

[47] See s V below.

[48] Lord Collins of Mapesbury and Harris (n 23) 23-026.

[49] ibid 25-059.

[50] ibid 25-060.

[51] Carruthers (n 36) para 1.35.

[52] TM Yeo, *Commercial Conflict of Laws* (London, Academy Publishing, 2023) para 14.038; by analogy with the lex situs of shares.

[53] Lord Collins of Mapesbury and Harris (n 23) 25-090.

[54] It should finally be noted that neither the place of the debtor nor the proper law of the debt as connecting factors are capable of addressing the risk taken by assignees in bulk assignment cases since

of merit. The original reasons for locating debts at the place of the debtor had nothing to do with choice of law. Instead, they concerned the power of the Ordinary[55] to give a debtor a good discharge on payment as against a deceased creditor, thus protecting the debtor from double liability.[56] The alternative explanation advanced in *Commissioner of Stamps v Hope*[57] that the assets to satisfy debt are presumably where the debtor is, and hence that a debt can most likely be enforced carries little weight in an era where debtors can hold assets in multiple jurisdictions and readily move from place to place.

Third, in the case of the insolvency of intermediaries such as crypto-token exchanges, an issue commonly arises as to whether assets held in the name of the intermediary, but which are reflected on the exchange's books as held for the account of the customers, are the property of the customers of the exchange or part of the insolvency estate, ie, owned by the exchange and available for liquidation and distribution to the general creditors of the exchange. The outcome of this third question could turn on differences in the applicable law on the conditions that must be fulfilled before the customers have a proprietary interest in the underlying asset.

The basic problem is as old as gold. In *Re Goldcorp*,[58] an issue arose under New Zealand law in the event of a company in the business of holding gold coins and ingots for customers wishing to invest in gold. While the company represented to customers that it would maintain a separate stock of each type of bullion to meet customer demand, it in fact did not do so. The Bank of New Zealand was owed money by the company and petitioned for the company to be wound up. The dispute was ultimately between the customers and the bank over whether the gold in stock belonged to the customers or to the company (and was therefore subject to a charge in favour of the bank). The bank prevailed in *Re Goldcorp* because under New Zealand (and English) trust law, the gold had to be segregated in favour of the customers in order for the certainty of subject matter to be satisfied.

A possible example of differing results could arise in relation to shares being held by an intermediary, such as on the facts of *Re Harvard Securities*,[59] where outcomes could differ depending on how the certainty of subject matter in

the mass of debts assigned would have varying proper laws and debtors resident in different jurisdictions. It is submitted that the case of bulk assignments is a red herring for choice of law purposes. The short answer must be that the assignee in a bulk assignment who takes an assignment of debts governed by different laws or owed by debtors in different jurisdictions takes the risk that comes with acquiring the assets at a discount. This can be tested by an assignee taking a bulk assignment of mortgage securities over immovables in several jurisdictions. That assignee can hardly be heard to demand that the effectiveness of its acquisition of security over land be governed by a single legal system.

[55] This was the ecclesiastic officer with power to grant probate and administer intestacies in England: *AG v Bouwens* (1838) 4 M & W 171, 191–192.

[56] PJ Rogerson, 'The Situs of Debts in the Conflict of Laws – Illogical, Unnecessary and Misleading' [1990] *CLJ* 441, 442.

[57] [1891] AC 476, 481.

[58] *Re Goldcorp Exchange Ltd* [1995] 1 AC 74.

[59] *Re Harvard Securities Ltd* [1997] 2 BCLC 69.

trust law referred to above applies to intangibles. In the case of shares held by an intermediary, Staughton LJ held that the lex situs of the shares themselves governed the issue in *Macmillan*.[60] The English substantive law position following *Hunter v Moss*[61] does away with the segregation requirement that applies to tangible movables like bullion. By contrast, some commentators have noted that the stricter position in *Re Goldcorp* may continue to apply to intangibles under Singapore law,[62] which would lead to divergent results.

Staughton LJ's approach could, however, be subject to one further refinement. Certain authorities concerning indirect holdings of crypto-tokens appear to apply the law governing the relationship between the customer and the intermediary as determinative of competing proprietary claims between customer and creditor.

In *Ruscoe v Cryptopia Ltd (in liq)*,[63] the New Zealand High Court held, applying New Zealand law, that the three certainties for creating a trust were satisfied based on the terms and conditions between Cryptopia and its customers, who therefore took priority over Cryptopia's general creditors. On the other hand, in a non-insolvency context, the breach of trust claim in *Quoine Pte Ltd v B2C2 Ltd*[64] failed because the Court of Appeal found that under Singapore law the terms of the agreement between Quoine and its customers were inconsistent with a trust relationship.[65] Neither decision, however, addressed the situs of the relevant crypto-tokens.

The decisions can be rationalised within an orthodox choice of law analysis – the question of whether a trust arises on the terms between an exchange and its customers arises as an incidental question. This maintains the separation between the law governing the relationship between exchange and customer, and the law applicable in disputes between those customers and third parties. The main question is whether the customers have property rights in the crypto-tokens held by the exchange. That main question ought to be governed by the law applicable to property issues for crypto-tokens rather than the law governing the relationship between exchange and customer. This is because the interests of the general creditors of the exchange are affected by the answer. Yet, it is expected that the law applicable to the main question will provide a conditional answer, ie, that the customer will have property rights in the crypto-tokens if the exchange is under an obligation to hold the crypto-tokens on trust or as belonging to the customer under the law that governs their relationship inter se, including any regulations.[66] Whether such an obligation arises is therefore an incidental question.

[60] [1996] 1 WLR 387, 396.

[61] *Hunter v Moss* [1994] 1 WLR 452.

[62] C Hare and V Ooi, *Singapore Trusts Law* (London, LexisNexis, 2021) [2-80].

[63] [2020] NZHC 728.

[64] *Quoine Pte Ltd v B2C2 Ltd* [2020] 2 SLR 20 (CA).

[65] It should be noted that although the Singapore Court of Appeal reversed the Singapore International Commercial Court in finding that there was no trust, the breach of trust claim was a personal claim by the customer against the intermediary. There were no third party interests involved in *B2C2*.

[66] Such as Regulation (EU) 2023/1114 of the European Parliament and of the Council of 31 May 2023 on markets in crypto-assets, and amending Regulations (EU) No 1093/2010 and (EU) No 1095/2010 and Directives 2013/36/EU and (EU) 2019/1937 [2023] OJ L150/40.

In the discussion so far, the insolvent exchange is the sole intermediary between the customer and the crypto-token. The situation can be illustrated as follows:

Figure 4.1 Single Intermediary Situation

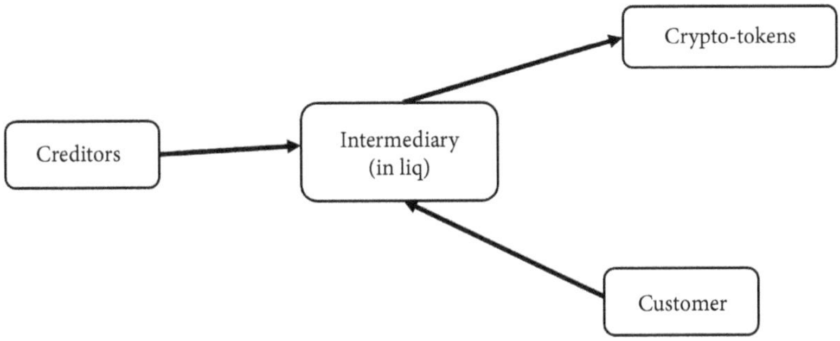

A possible further issue concerning intermediation arises if there are multiple layers of intermediaries, such as where one crypto-exchange is itself the customer of another crypto-exchange.[67] In such situations as applied to shares, more than one commentator has argued that Staughton LJ's the lex situs approach in *Macmillan* is inappropriate.[68] There is, however, considerable debate about what the correct approach should be.[69] While there is agreement that an approach that 'looks through' the intermediaries all the way to the underlying asset does not adequately serve the needs of participants in intermediated holding systems, the appropriate approach remains the a matter of continued debate over the characterisation of the res that forms the subject matter of choice of law analysis. The issue is, however, unlikely to be relevant to disputes involving insolvencies of crypto-token exchanges, who are usually the sole intermediary in the equation. In any event, to the extent that the debate turns on the proper characterisation of the res, it falls outside the scope of this chapter.

b. Security Interests

The issues concerning security interests discussed below may not be entirely distinct from the issues concerning the scope of the insolvency estate. These issues have nevertheless been singled out for discussion because of the significance of the validity of security interests in insolvency proceedings.

[67] Such scenarios invite comparisons with the indirect holding system for shares where there is no consensus on the appropriate approach to be taken. There, multiple layers of intermediaries are common because to either immobilise registered shares or dematerialise certified securities, there will be a first-level operator intermediary who either serves as the sole registered shareholder or sole holder of all the certificates. There is then usually one intermediary, an exchange or a brokerage, between the operator and the actual investor: Ooi (n 46) para 6.20.

[68] Lord Collins of Mapesbury and Harris (n 23) 25-077; Ooi (n 46) para 5.42.

[69] Contrast Ooi (n 46) paras 6.30 and 6.31 with Lord Collins of Mapesbury and Harris (n 23) 25-079.

Within the category of security interests, there are arguably two different sets of issues. The first relates to security interests granted by the insolvent entity. The second relates to whether security interests taken by the insolvent entity continue to be valid. The second bears a close relation to the above issue on the transfer of crypto-tokens.

bb. Security Interests Granted by the Insolvent Entity

First, charges granted by the insolvent entity in favour of a lender, such as the one granted by the company in *Re Goldcorp* highlight the dual contractual and proprietary analyses that can be run in parallel. While the creation, validity and scope of a charge is governed by the law of the instrument creating the charge[70] (implying a contractual characterisation), the proprietary effect of the security interest, usually in competition with the rights of third parties, depends on the lex situs of tangible property or the lex causae of intangible property as the case may be.[71]

bbb. Security Interests Granted by the Insolvent Entity

Second, it is common in the trade of tangible movables that one party takes a non-possessory security interest over that tangible movable. The same transactions, namely conditional sales and chattel mortgages, readily apply to crypto-tokens.

In a conditional sale,[72] B (who lives in country Y) buys crypto-tokens from A (who resides in country X) under a contract that provides that title will not pass to B until the price is fully paid. Before she has paid for them, B sells them to C, representing that she has full title to them. C takes the crypto-tokens in good faith.

In a crypto-token mortgage,[73] B (who then resided in country X) mortgages a crypto-token to A. With A's consent, B remains in possession. Before the mortgage is redeemed, B changes her residence to country Y and sells it to C, representing that she has an unencumbered title. C takes it in good faith.

In both situations, the insolvent entity could actually be one of A, B or C. The most difficult questions arise where it is B, the purported security-giver, who has become insolvent. It leads to a contest for priority between C and A, who are strangers to each other. In general, the contest is resolved by applying the *lex situs* of the crypto-token at the time of the transfer to C. In this sense, the approach to resolving the dispute is no different from the case of *Winkworth* discussed above. The underlying policy debate is the familiar one between security of transactions and security of title.[74]

[70] L Collins, *Essays in International Litigation and the Conflict of Laws* (Oxford, Oxford University Press, 1996) ch 12.

[71] TM Yeo (n 52) para 14.056; M Haentjens and M Lehmann, 'The Law Governing Secured Transactions in Digital Assets' in Bonomi, Lehmann and Lalani (n 1) 460.

[72] Adapted from Lord Collins of Mapesbury and Harris (n 23) para 25-029.

[73] ibid para 25-031.

[74] ibid para 25-029.

The difference in analysis between tangible movables and crypto-tokens turns on whether the changes in residence of B matter to determining the lex situs. This depends on how a notional situs ought to be ascribed to crypto-tokens, which is discussed in section V below. For now, it need only be noted that these transactions are less complex in the case of crypto-tokens than for tangible movables when the situs of crypto-tokens is not tied to the residence of the holder at the time of the relevant transaction. If the situs of crypto-tokens follows the current holder, then it would be the law of Y that determines whether C takes good title over A's security interest. If the situs of crypto-tokens uses a different connecting factor, such as the proper law of the network, then that law would determine the competing proprietary claims.

For tangible movables with a physical situs, a further complication in relation to condition sales and chattel mortgages arises from mandatory requirements of the situs at the first (A to B) and second (B to C) transactions. Some jurisdictions have legislation providing that securities granted over movables must be registered in order to be valid against third party purchasers in good faith.[75] Whether such legislation, or other substantive rules favouring the third party buyer, are applicable would also depend on the situs of the crypto-token at the time of transfer.[76] The editors of Dicey explore seven scenarios involving non-possessory security interests in tangible movables that need not be explored in full here. It suffices to say that knowing the situs of the property is crucial to resolving the question of the validity of the security against the third party buyer C.

ii. *Where Situs is Not Relevant in Insolvency*

The breadth of the concept of a situs for crypto-tokens in an insolvency should not however be over-stated. There are issues for which the governing law is not determined by reference to the situs. As aforementioned, the validity of the contracts that create the security interests are governed by their proper laws.

A particular issue that stands out for clarification is what law governs whether certain transactions entered into by the insolvent entity (whether they involve crypto-tokens or not) can be avoided by the liquidator or trustee in bankruptcy under the relevant insolvency avoidance provisions. The prevailing view is that the forum concursus applies its own insolvency avoidance provisions.[77] These are applied as the forum's mandatory rules. As a result, their application to transactions with foreign elements is not at first blush controlled by the forum's choice of law rules, but by whether the relevant avoidance provisions would be interpreted to have extraterritorial effect[78] against the general presumption against the

[75] ibid para 25-035. The editors of Dicey have also noted that it is possible that such legislative provisions could be interpreted as not applying to foreign security arrangements.

[76] Lord Collins of Mapesbury and Harris (n 23) paras 25-035 to 25-042.

[77] ibid para 30-127.

[78] LC Ho, 'Conflict of Laws in Insolvency Transaction Avoidance' [2008] *Singapore Academy of Law Journal* 343.

extraterritorial application of statutes.[79] Here, the English position is that English avoidance provisions would only apply to a foreign transaction where there is a sufficient connection between the forum and the transaction.[80] A further control exists in taking jurisdiction in avoidance claims over foreign defendants.[81]

One commentator has however argued that the forum should not shy away from the extraterritorial application of its avoidance provisions where it is either the sole forum or the centre of main interest of the insolvent entity,[82] rejecting the sufficient connection test. The forum would only apply foreign avoidance provisions when that forum is the centre of main interest seeking assistance from the forum, although this appears to be on the basis that such application of foreign mandatory rules is expressly provided for in local legislation.[83]

Neither the existing nor the proposed approaches connect the question of whose avoidance provisions should apply to the situs of any property. It can therefore safely be said that the lex situs of the subject matter of the impugned transaction would not amount to a connecting factor in this situation.[84]

iii. Synthesis

To round off this section, essentially the concept of situs is traditionally in private international law to resolve disputes between two parties who have no contractual relationship with each other where they make competing claims for priority over property, in our case crypto-tokens. Such disputes often become particularly acute in insolvency proceedings where the insolvent entity has insufficient assets to satisfy all claims.

IV. Rationale for the Lex Situs Rule for Tangible and Intangible Property before Crypto-tokens

Section III explored the many scenarios where proprietary issues involving crypto-tokens could arise in the enforcement and insolvency scenarios. There is a

[79] *Clarke v Oceanic Contractors* [1983] 2 AC 130, 144–145; 152.

[80] *Re Paramount Airways Limited* [1993] Ch 223.

[81] *Orexim Trading Limited v Mahavir Port and Terminal Private Limited* [2018] EWCA Civ 1660.

[82] Ho (n 78) 343.

[83] S 426(5) UK Insolvency Act.

[84] In any event, both approaches adopt a unilateralist view of the conflict of laws in rebuttal to the multilaterlist approach embedded in conventional choice of law methodology: WS Dodge, 'Extraterritoriality and Conflict-of-Laws Theory: An Argument for Judicial Unilateralism' (1998) 39 *Harvard International Law Journal* 106–121. The multilaterlist approach is the one we have inherited from Savigny, which focuses on finding the legal system most closely connected to the seat of a relationship: Ho (n 78) 343 para 33. The unilateralist view, championed by Brainerd Currie, determines whether there is a 'true conflict' in the sense that more than one state have an interest in applying their laws to a dispute based on the spatial reach of each state's laws (Ho [n 78] 343 para 31). In one sense, the unilateralist approach succeeds the approach to conflict of laws taken by the statutists.

remarkable degree of consensus across jurisdictions that the law applicable to such issues is the lex situs.[85] In this section, we look at the rationales that gave rise to this consensus by tracing its development from immovable property and tangible movables,[86] where it was originally developed, to intangibles.

A. Lex Situs of Land

There is a clear consensus for the application of the lex situs to issues of competing ownership claims over immovable property.[87] As a matter of physical location, '[l]and could not without absurdity be treated as situate in any country other than that where it is situated.'[88] More importantly, any legal interest in land is situate where the land is physically situated.[89] The rationales that have been advanced for this rule are:

1. the ultimate control of the situs over the immovable property.[90] Thus, it is said that '[a]ny other rule would be ineffective, because in the last resort land can only be dealt with in a manner which the lex situs allows.'[91] Indeed, it is difficult to see how any other court applying another law could enforce its rulings over land in another jurisdiction without infringing the situs' territorial sovereignty;
2. the need to respect the social and economic policies of the situs in the protection and transmission of rights in immovable property.[92] This can be understood as a facet of the multilateralist approach to choice of law as reflective of international comity; and
3. it is an obvious, convenient and visible connecting factor for transacting parties.[93] In other words, it would accord with the reasonable expectations of honest people dealing with land that the lex situs determines competing ownership claims. One might say that the lex situs is clearly the legal system with the closest and most real connection to the issue.

B. Lex Situs of Tangible Movables

A review of the reasons for the adoption of the lex situs rule for immovables alone cannot explain the ascendancy and hegemony of the lex situs rule for all property

[85] Held (n 1) 210.
[86] Held (n 1) 250.
[87] Lord Collins of Mapesbury and Harris (n 23) para 24-069.
[88] ibid para 23-051.
[89] ibid para 23-051.
[90] Yeo (n 52) 14.020.
[91] Lord Collins of Mapesbury and Harris (n 23) para 24-069.
[92] Yeo (n 52) 14.020.
[93] ibid 14.021; and therefore convenient and expedient: Dicey (n 23) 24-069.

types, perhaps because the application of the lex situs to immovables is too obvious. The reasons become even clearer when the case of tangible movables is examined.

The lex situs rule for tangible movables has been judicially described as being 'long established beyond challenge', which for all practical purposes it certainly now is.[94] In detail, the rule states that the proprietary effects of a transfer of tangible movables are generally governed by the law of the country where the movable is at the time of the transfer.[95] While there are three recognised exceptions to the rule (for ships,[96] aircraft[97] and goods in transit[98]), all of which involve tangible movables that are expected to be in transit most of the time, such that their physical location at any point in time is considered fortuitous.

Yet, why has the common law steadfastly adhered to this position despite the diversity of subject matter within the category of tangible movables?[99] There is more to the longevity of the lex situs rule than mere 'history aided by frequent repetition of often superficial argument by textwriters and judges'.[100]

The main arguments advanced for the application of the lex situs rule to tangible movables are:[101]

1. Practical control over the property;[102]
2. Certainty deriving from an i. objective, ii. easily ascertainable and ii. therefore readily applicable connecting factor for transacting parties;[103]
3. Neutrality as between the disputing parties;[104] and
4. Consistency of principle.[105]

To a large extent, they explain why other connecting factors used were successively discarded in favour of the lex situs.

One of the oldest connecting factors found in the case law is the law of the owner's domicile.[106] While it remains to have some attraction for bulk assignments and continues to apply to matters of succession, modern writers and judges have

[94] Dicey (n 23) 25-002; *Air Foyle Ltd v Center Capital Ltd* [2002] EWHC 2535 (Comm).
[95] Lord Collins of Mapesbury and Harris (n 23) para 25R-001.
[96] ibid Rule 136(3), Exception 1.
[97] ibid para 136(3), Exception 2.
[98] ibid para 25E-016; Yeo (n 52) 14.031.
[99] ibid para 25-002.
[100] *Cf* IF Baxter, 'Conflicts of Law and Property' [1964] *McGill Law Journal* 1, 34.
[101] Generally Lord Collins of Mapesbury and Harris (n 23) para 25-005.
[102] *Glencore International AG v Metro Trading International Inc (No.2)* [2001] 1 All ER (Comm) 103; [2001] 1 Lloyd's Rep 344, paras 31–32.
[103] *Re Anziani, Herbert v Christopherson* [1930] 1 Ch 407, 420; *Macmillan Inc v Bishopgate Investment Trust plc (No 3)* [1996] 1 WLR 387, 399; GC Cheshire, *Private International Law*, 3rd edn (Oxford, Clarendon Press, 1947) 563; Yeo (n 52) 14.028.
[104] Carruthers (n 36) para. 8.10, citing GC Cheshire (n 103) 563.
[105] *Glencore International AG v Metro Trading International Inc (No.2)* [2001] 1 All ER (Comm) 103; [2001] 1 Lloyd's Rep 344.
[106] Lord Collins of Mapesbury and Harris (n 23) para 25-003; *Sill v Worswick* (1791) 1 H.Bl. 665, 690; *Re Ewin* (1830) 1 Cr. & J. 151, 156. This connecting factor bears more than a passing resemblance to the proposition that crypto-tokens are situate where the holder is resident.

largely discarded the connecting factor.[107] Primarily, the choice of the owner's domicile may have been acceptable in earlier times where a person's possessions were few and usually situated in the owner's domicile, but this is far from the case in modern commerce.[108] As a result, this connecting factor fell into disuse.

Next are the laws of the place where the transfer takes place (the lex loci actus) and the proper law of the contract or other transaction (the lex loci contractus). Neither is an attractive option compared to the lex situs. The main reason for preferring the lex situs appears to be commercial certainty that arises from having an objective and easily ascertainable connecting factor bearing in mind the likely shape of a property dispute – that it is a dispute between strangers who have no other relevant legal relationship with each other. They are likely to be parties to separate transactions with at least one other party, such as in the case of *Winkworth* above. Thus, Moore-Bick LJ grounds the rationale of the lex situs rule not so much on the fact of one state's practical control over the property but in the 'expectation that a transaction which would be effective by the law of that state to pass a good title will in fact do so'.[109] That is the best way to understand Maughum J's dictum that '[b]usiness could not be otherwise'.[110]

Nevertheless, when it comes to tangible movables, Yeo has astutely pointed out that the notion of practical control is not the primary consideration.[111] This is inherent in how the lex situs rule operates in relation to successive transfers – that the latest recipient can obtain good title if the lex situs at the time of the last transaction confers good title even if a different result follows under the lex situs of an earlier transaction.[112] The focus of the analysis on the situs at the time of transfer shows that the law is making a choice in favour of upholding certainty of transactions by providing a visible point of reference for all parties involved.[113]

The emphasis on certainty of transactions and ease of effecting transfers makes sense when the nature of tangible movables is contrasted with immovables. In physical terms, the physical location of movables can be changed while that of immovables cannot.[114] However, that is not the material difference. Owing in part to the relative ease of transfer, there is a greater expectation that movable property will be more liquid than immovable property. To facilitate that liquidity, in selecting a choice of law rule for property issues involving tangible movables, one that tends to uphold the certainty of transactions and therefore promote such

[107] Lord Collins of Mapesbury and Harris (n 23) para 25-003; *Provincial Treasurer for Alberta v Kerr* [1933] AC 710, 721 (PC).

[108] Lord Collins of Mapesbury and Harris (n 23) para 25-003.

[109] *Glencore International AG v Metro Trading International Inc (No.2)* [2001] 1 All ER (Comm) 103; [2001] 1 Lloyd's Rep 344, paras 31–32.

[110] *Re Anziani, Herbert v Christopherson* [1930] 1 Ch 407, 420.

[111] Yeo (n 52) 14.028.

[112] Lord Collins of Mapesbury and Harris (n 23) para 25R-020.

[113] Yeo (n 52) 14.028.

[114] It is suggested that while the physical location of immovables cannot change, it is possible to change their legal locations. Thus, ownership of land located in the former Yugoslavia and now in the Czech Republic would today be governed by Czech law.

transactions is preferred. In economic terms, this would improve the efficiency of the allocation of resources.

C. Lex Situs of Intangibles

It is then perhaps striking that the inclination toward transferability is not as obvious when it comes to intangibles. Prior to the advent of crypto-tokens, all intangibles represented rights against a counterparty and were therefore choses in action. At the same time, however, the category comprised of a diverse category of rights[115] covering a very wide spectrum including the full array of financial instruments that underpin the capital markets of the developed world.[116] The range of rights falling within this category is so broad that it has been suggested that 'the category of 'intangible things' is no longer sufficiently coherent for it to be given a uniform rule for choice of law'.[117] Nevertheless, one of the benefits of applying the lex situs rule to intangibles is to accommodate the possibility of differing sub-rules for different intangibles within the rubric of ascribing a notional[118] situs to each intangible independently.

How this notional situs is ascribed sheds light on the rationales for selecting a particular notional situs and therefore a connecting factor. Some, but not all intangibles, have an obvious reference point despite having no physical location.[119]

Although the most common intangible is the debt, it will be discussed last because of its complexity and its status as somewhat an outlier among intangibles. In this author's view, for all intangibles apart from debts (before crypto-tokens), the reference point selected for property issues arising from then has essentially been their lex creationis – that is, the legal system that gives rise to the rights that can be enforced.

Thus, the lex situs for shares is ultimately the lex incorporationis.[120] The lex situs of non-contractual obligations such as rights accruing in tort, is the law applicable to the tort. Within the European Union (and the United Kingdom, where the Rome II Regulation is retained EU law), that is the lex obligationis as identified by that Regulation.[121] Where the double actionability rule still applies, this would generally be the lex loci delicti unless a flexible exception applies.[122] Intellectual property rights, being purely territorial monopolies conferred by statute, are located where they are conferred.[123] On one interpretation of the PRIMA rule, it

[115] Yeo (n 52) 14.037.
[116] Lord Collins of Mapesbury and Harris (n 23) para 25-058.
[117] ibid.
[118] Carruthers (n 36) paras 1.31–1.34.
[119] Yeo (n 52) 14.037.
[120] See s III.B.i above.
[121] Lord Collins of Mapesbury and Harris (n 23) para 25-074.
[122] See generally Yeo (n 52) 13.011–13.021.
[123] Yeo (n 52) 14.017.

follows that the situs of a right against the relevant intermediary is the location of that intermediary since that is usually also the governing law of the most significant mandatory rules rights against the relevant intermediary.

The case of debts (and other contractual rights) has been discussed briefly[124] and is an interesting case. In a case of multiple assignments by the same assignor, the competing assignees' priorities to the debt are governed by the proper law of the debt.[125] On the same characterisation of the problem as contractual in nature, the law of the place of a debtor's incorporation cannot directly discharge the debtor from a debt governed by another law.[126]

On the other hand, the common law has taken a consistent view that the situs of a debt is at where the debtor is. Thus, for debts, the problem is not the lack of an obvious reference point but the existence of more than one such reference point.

The rationale for preferring the place of the debtor as situs is that the residence of the debtor is the jurisdiction where the debt can most likely be enforced.[127] This reflects an emphasis on the control rationale for selecting a notional situs in the case of debts. Yet, in modern commerce, the justification is hardly adequate when a debtor can have multiple residences and assets that can be enforced against in even more jurisdictions.[128]

The strain caused to this version of the lex situs rule for debts when the debtor has multiple residences is illustrated by the notable case of *Jabbour v Custodian of Israeli Absentee Property*.[129] In that case, the claimants had taken out certain policies with an English insurer through the insurer's agency in Palestine, covering certain buildings in what was then Palestine. The buildings were subsequently blown up. The claimants took up residence in Egypt. A few months later, the British Mandate in Palestine was terminated and the state of Israel was proclaimed. The new Israeli government then enacted measures confiscating the property of a category of persons which included the claimants. At issue was whether the proceeds of the insurance policy had been validly confiscated by the Israeli government. That depended on whether the debt owed by the insurer was located in England or Israel. It was held that the debt was located in Israel and validly confiscated because the debt was primarily payable in Israel. The judge also held that the proper law of the insurance policy was the law of Palestine before the termination of the Mandate and the law of Israel afterward. However, as the editors of Dicey have argued, England had far greater control over the insurer since England was the insurer's primary place of business, the insurer acted through an agent in Israel

124 See s III.B.i above.

125 Lord Collins of Mapesbury and Harris (n 23) para 25-R57.

126 *Dubai Islamic Bank PJSC v PSI Energy Holding Co BSC* [2013] EWHC 3186 (Comm.), paras 40–41, considering *Adams v National Bank of Greece* [1961] AC 255. It appears, however, that if the government of the place of incorporation first expropriated the debt from the existing debtors as the lex situs, then proceeded to waive the debts under the proper law of the debt, such an exercise would be effective.

127 Lord Collins of Mapesbury and Harris (n 23) para 23-026.

128 ibid para 23-025.

129 [1954] 1 WLR 139.

with no office of its own, and had actually ceased to do business in Israel altogether by the time the case was decided.[130]

The same result in *Jabbour* would have been reached if we treated the debt as located in the legal system where it was created. The proper law of the debt was found to be the law of Israel at the time of the hearing. Aligning the lex situs of a debt to the broader lex creationis theme therefore avoids the problems arising from debtors having multiple residences and having to find a means of choosing between them based loosely on the rationale of control. It also avoids the problem of trying to explain how, at least in enforcement cases, a law other than the proper law of the debt could discharge the obligation of repayment. The proper law of the debt arguably provides a more visible and objective reference point for commercial parties. The argument in favour of the proper law of the debt is least forceful where there is no express choice of law. Yet, even then, there are developed choice of law rules for determining the governing law of a contract in contrast to the uncertainties in choosing between residences of the debtor. Finally, while using the proper law of the debt does not resolve the challenges faced in bulk assignments,[131] looking to the residence of the debtor (and not the creditor) creates the same problems.

D. Synthesis

Having surveyed the field for the rationales behind the lex situs rule, the commentaries largely circle around two broad rationales: 1. practical control over the property; and 2. providing an objective and visible reference legal system for resolving proprietary disputes.[132] For land, and for intangibles including shares, non-contractual rights of action and intellectual property rights, both rationales pull in the same direction to identify the situs of the property. In essence, the legal system with ultimate practical control over the property also provides an obvious and visible reference point which commercial parties would reasonably expect to govern competing ownership claims.

It is where the two rationales pull in different directions where we need to ask which force should have the greater sway. When we favour fulfilling the reasonable expectations of commercial parties, we run the risk of undermining the practical control that a legal system has over something 'within' its territory. That could potentially offend international comity or even be seen as an inroad into that jurisdiction's territorial sovereignty. While some modern writers scoff at the importance of territorial sovereignty and see it as an obstacle to global reforms, territorial sovereignty is one aspect of the principle of the sovereign equality of states which Article 2 paragraph 1 of the Charter of the United Nations makes clear is one of the fundamental principles of the international legal order.[133] All the more

[130] Lord Collins of Mapesbury and Harris (n 23) para 23-030.
[131] ibid para 25-060.
[132] ibid para 23-025.
[133] *Jurisdictional Immunities of the State (Germany v Italy)* [2012] ICJ Rep 99 para 57.

so in deciding private disputes, care needs to be taken when a choice of law rule may be seen as offending this fundamental principle.

On the other hand, when we choose the state with the perceived greatest practical control, we tend to upset the reasonable expectations of transacting parties. There is within this the risk of parochialism, where the forum perceives itself to have the greatest practical control.

It is suggested that how we strike a balance between these two rationales when they diverge is in considering the nature of the property in question. The connection between immovable property and territorial sovereignty is the strongest. At the same time, reasonable commercial parties could hardly expect the law of another sovereign to apply to their competing title claims. For tangible movables, as we have seen, the applicable legal system (outside of enforcement proceedings) is not the one where the property is located at the time of the dispute. Tangible movables, by their very nature, are also amenable to being moved from one jurisdiction to another. Outside of cultural property, no jurisdiction has any special claim to that tangible movable. For these reasons, it is sensible to favour the certainty of the expectations of commercial parties for tangible movables. Any potential inroad into territorial sovereignty is in any event likely to be limited.

When we come to intangibles, although they are movables, the general focus on the control of the lex creationis is also understandable. Companies are creatures of a particular legal system. Together with the relevant legislation, their constitutional documents under the law of incorporation define the rights and obligations attached to the shares. At common law, the company's constitution forms a statutory contract between the shareholders *inter se* and with the company. Very recently, the Singapore Court of Appeal ruled in a similar vein that the lex incorporationis decides when the corporate veil can be lifted.[134] Intellectual property rights are in some sense very similar, being creatures of statute. As conferred monopolies, they are confined within the territory of the granting state because of the principle of territorial sovereignty. When the lex creationis revokes those rights, they simply cease to exist. Again, however, there is no tension between the two rationales for most intangibles.

The tension really comes to the fore with debts. Here, the common law position exhibits an odd preference for the appearance of control over what I have argued to be the more obvious reference point for commercial parties taking over rights under an existing agreement.

Having brought two key rationales into focus and addressed how tensions between the two could be resolved when there are competing connecting factors that pull in different directions, the criticisms of using a notional situs for intangibles can then be addressed.

First, it bears emphasis that 'the conflict of laws does not depend (like a game or even an election) upon the application of rigid rules, but upon a search for appropriate principles to meet particular situations'.[135] The 'appropriate principles'

[134] *Nicholas Eng Teng Cheng v Government of the City of Buenos Aires* [2024] SGCA 15.
[135] *Raffeisen Zentralbank Osterreich Ag v Five Star Trading LLC (The Mount I)* [2001] QB 825 para 29.

that have led to the adoption of the lex situs rule thus far are the aforementioned twin rationales. As demonstrated earlier, how the general lex situs rule applies to each category of property differs depending on the interplay between those two rationales. It is therefore not the case that the lex situs was arbitrarily adopted as some 'absolute connecting factor' or for 'no compelling reason'.[136] Choice of law for any type of property must necessarily bear both the rationale of practical control grounded in territorial sovereignty and the rationale of the reasonable expectations for commercial parties in mind.

Second, the argument that the lex situs rule for intangibles depends on a legal fiction only holds water if we approach the issue superficially, ie, if we continue to pretend that the objective is to ascribe a physical location to something without a physical existence. Once we look deeper to perceive that we are ultimately seeking a connecting factor for proprietary issues, which means grappling with the two primary rationales, the objection falls away. The real endeavour is to reach a governing law that does conflicts justice between the disputing parties[137] while balancing that against territorial sovereignty concerns.

As a result, the only argument against the application of the lex situs rule for intangibles is one that says that intermediating the lex situs and then directing a court to a sub-rule that ascribes a notional situs is unnecessary. The formulation of the choice of law rule for intangible property admittedly appears clumsy. Yet, the invocation of the lex situs principle is how courts and lawyers are reminded that the search is for an applicable law to resolve proprietary issues that as far as possible fulfils the two primary rationales.

Ascribing a situs to crypto-tokens also serves as a means for determining which jurisdiction has enforcement jurisdiction over the crypto-token. However, as mentioned below, their omni-territoriality strains the application of Westphalian concepts to crypto-tokens.

It is therefore submitted that the lex situs concept remains relevant for intangible property in general. The next section considers how the rationales undergirding the lex situs concept could help to select the notional situs of different types of crypto-tokens.

V. Ascribing Crypto-tokens with a Situs for Choice of Law

The nature of crypto-tokens presents new challenges to how the rationales of practical control and reasonable expectations apply to them. In particular, the

[136] *cf* Held (n 1) 251–252.

[137] Conflicts justice refers to having choice of law rules in place that will select an applicable law without regard to the perceived quality of the outcome: see SC Symeonides, *The American Choice-of-Law Revolution: Past, Present and Future* (The Hague, Hague Academy of International Law Monographs, 2006) 405–406. It is contrasted with the concept of material justice, which refers to selecting the fairest

very nature of crypto-tokens tends to reduce the weight that could reasonably be attributed to the practical control rationale with its territorial sovereignty underpinnings. First, crypto-tokens in and of themselves are not legal rights. They have no lex creationis,[138] unlike shares or intellectual property. Second, many of them exist on decentralised blockchains where no person or entity exercises control over the distributed ledger. The result is that the crypto-token appears 'omni-territorial', ie, that instead of the absence of any valid 'genuine link' between such assets and a given state, there is an abundance of equally genuine links to several states.[139] The claim of any one state to have sovereignty over a crypto-token is therefore greatly diminished. Third, the very purpose of most tokens is that they and any rights they represent are transferable.[140] For example, in the case of real estate tokenisation, the point of the exercise is to make interests in real estate for liquid. Given this functional feature of crypto-tokens, greater weight should then be given to meeting the reasonable expectations of market participants, enhancing legal certainty, and thereby facilitating trade. Taken together, this means that in ascribing a notional situs to crypto-tokens, we should emphasise solutions that give effect to the second rationale.

Having clarified the relevant principles, we can now quickly evaluate the existing proposals for siting crypto-tokens based on how well they align with the rationale of proving certainty to commercial parties by aligning with their reasonable expectations for a visible and neutral applicable law. The various proposals are discussed within Wendehorst's framework taxonomy of proposals, which sorts them into connecting factors that are: a. party-focused, b. asset-focused, and c. coder-focused and is adopted for ease of reference.[141]

First, the party-focused connecting factors are: i. the law of the habitual place of the assignor,[142] and ii. The residence of the holder or the crypto-token at the relevant time.[143] Ultimately, all three proposals under this category anchor the choice of law issue with a location associated with the transferor. In the context of the assignment of debts, the assignor is the creditor. Choosing the assignor creditor's

possible result between the parties. Conflicts justice accords with the generally multilateral weal of choice of law methodology given that different legal systems will diverge on what they consider to be the fairest outcome. In property disputes, the perennial tension is between security of title and security of transaction.

[138] Held (n 1) 250.

[139] Held (n 1) 250; Lehmann (n 4).

[140] With the notable exception of soulbound tokens.

[141] C Wendehorst, 'Proprietary Rights in Digital Assets and the Conflict of Laws' in Bonomi, Lehmann and Lalani (n 1) 110 eq seq.

[142] By analogy with the draft EU Regulation on Third-Party Effects of Assignments of Claims (see Proposal for a Regulation of the European Parliament and of the Council on the law applicable to the third-party effects of assignments of claims, [2018] COM/2018/096 final) and the UNCITRAL Model Rules on Secured Transactions (see UNCITRAL, 'UNCITRAL Model Law on Secured Transactions [2016]' uncitral.un.org/en/texts/securityinterests/modellaw/secured_transactions.

[143] A Dickinson, 'Cryptocurrencies and the Conflict of Laws' in D Fox and S Green (eds), *Cryptocurrencies in Public and Private Law* (Oxford, Oxford University Press, 2019) para 5.107; Financial Markets Law Committee, 'Distributed Ledger Technology and Governing Law: Issues of Legal Uncertainty' (27 March 2018) para 6.23 fmlc.org/wp-content/uploads/2018/05/dlt_paper.pdf.

place of habitual residence as the law governing the validity of the assignment as between the debtor and the assignee would likely fall outside the expectations of the debtor. Prior to such proposals, the competing candidates were the residence of the *debtor* as lex situs or the proper law of the debt.

For crypto-tokens, the focus on the transferor has been criticised for assuming what it needs to prove.[144] However, as long as the rule is understood to refer to the residence of the holder at the time of the relevant transaction, then the criticism does not quite hold water.[145] Take a *Winkworth*-type scenario where X steals a crypto-token from C by breaking to C's home in Ruritania using C's private key stored on a thumb drive to transfer the crypto-token to X's address. X is residence in neighbouring Lusitania. After returning home to Lusitania, X sells the crypto-token to the unwitting D and transfers the crypto-token to D's address using X's own private key stored on his computer in Lusitania. D now has control over the crypto-token, and is resident in Sokovia. The issue of whether D has obtained good title despite C's interest is governed by the lex situs at the time of X's transfer to D, which would be Lusitania, the habitual residence of X.

The more significant problem with the proposal is that it is very difficult to apply to blockchains where participants are either pseudonymous, as with Bitcoin, or even completely anonymous. In the above scenario, the litigants are C and D, who in the course of proceedings will generally disclose to each other their habitual residences. Yet, the approach requires the determination of the habitual residence of the pseudonymous X. That may be a challenge to the point of making the connecting factor impracticable. Worse still, ex ante, the habitual residence of any transferor for on-chain transfers is opaque to all participants. Selecting this connecting factor would clearly undermine the rationale of providing certainty with an obvious and visible reference point upon which commercial parties can ground their reasonable expectations. It selects as a connecting factor something that is invisible to participants ex ante.

It also appears to be a re-introduction of the discarded connecting factor of the law of the owner's domicile for tangible movables.[146]

Second, there is a narrow category of coder-focused connecting factors. This has variously been labelled the lex codicilis or lex digitalis. Both essentially refer to the primary residence of the coder. The residence of the coder in and of itself is not an attractive connecting factor when the coder does not retain control of the blockchain, which is often the case.[147] Further, such as in the case of Bitcoin, the original coder could be pseudonymous and cannot be located.[148] Even for

[144] A Held, 'Does Situs Actually Matter when Ownership to Bitcoin is in Dispute?' [2021] *Journal of International Banking and Financial Law* 269.

[145] In two party scenarios such as the one in *Tulip Trading Limited v Wladimir Jasper van der Laan and others* [2023] EWCA Civ 83, the problem is concealed only because the situs at the time of the transfer would be the habitual residence of C.

[146] See IV.C. above.

[147] Financial Markets Law Committee (n 143) para 6.28.

[148] Held (n 1) 214.

crypto-tokens like Ethereum, where the original coder is visible, it is not obvious why his habitual residence ought to be a controlling connecting factor.

The third category is the broadest category itself, comprising a variety of connecting factors. Four of them, the place of the relevant operator approach ('PROPA'), the primary residence of the private encryption master key approach ('PREMA'), the place of the relevant intermediary approach ('PRIMA') and the location of the issuer master account approach ('LIMA') rely on the existence of a centralised point in the crypto-token economy. In situations where public law requires certain crypto-tokens to be entries in a public register, the place of that register could also fall within this group.

The PROPA and PREMA proposals rely on the existence of a legal person with control over the blockchain, ie, on the blockchain being centralised. The law that has the greatest control over that person is then seen as a visible reference point around which reasonable commercial parties can order their transactions.

The LIMA proposal is a variation on the theme. Instead of control over the blockchain, there is a legal person issuing the crypto-tokens with whom at least all initial participants will have a legal relationship. That forms another type of visible reference point. The PRIMA proposal draws from solutions adopted for dematerialised or immobilised securities trading. As seen above, there is some debate over whether it involves characterising a new *res* or a distinct sub-rule for the lex situs connecting factor for shares.[149]

A different proposal that stands out from the others within this category is the elective situs. This envisions that a blockchain can be designed at the outset with an express choice of law for either just property issues involving its native crypto-tokens or even for relations between participants inter se as a whole.[150] Where the choice is express, it is expected that it would be visible and obvious to any participants on the blockchain. Commercial parties taking interests in the crypto-tokens can then be expected to know about the chosen law, and in taking their interests, they have consented to their interests being governed by that law. This connecting factor therefore readily fulfils the rationale of meeting the reasonable expectations of transacting parties.

Where no express choice has been made, we are still required to find a connecting factor that fulfils the rationale of meeting parties' reasonable expectations. At this stage, we are in reality seeking the legal system with the closest and most real connection to the blockchain as the objective law governing all relations on the blockchain *inter se*.[151] This will depend on the particular features of the exact crypto-token.[152] Indeed, we can actually view several of the asset-related

[149] See III.B.i.bb above.

[150] M Ng, 'Choice of law for property issues regarding Bitcoin under English law' [2019] *Journal of Private International Law* 315, 332. However, there do not appear to be any prominent blockchains that have made an express choice.

[151] Ng (n 150) 336.

[152] Although it appears that fungibility does not make a difference to any analysis.

connecting factors as variations on the theme. Where there is an underlying asset to which the crypto-token is linked, the lex situs of the underlying should be the lex situs of the crypto-token for simplicity and visibility to commercial parties looking to acquire the crypto-token. Absent a link to a real-world asset, where the crypto-token is controlled by a centralised entity, the location of that entity becomes a visible reference point. The most difficult problems concern crypto-tokens like Bitcoin that are decentralised and pseudonymous. The pseudonymous aspect, as argued earlier, make reliance on the habitual residence of the holder at the relevant time impossible to rely on. It was in this vein that this author at one point suggested that for Bitcoin, the closest and most real connection in relative terms lay with the US State of Massachusetts where the developers of the Bitcoin core client are based.[153]

However, when it comes to issues of enforcement, it becomes more difficult to accord greater weight to the reasonable expectation rationale over the practical control rationale given how enforcement against things has been seen as an exercise of sovereign power. For the moment, it is provisionally suggested that situs is no more than shorthand for whether it is within the limits of a state's sovereignty to order execution against property. Where there is a multiplicity of genuine links to the property, the better view may be to defer to the jurisdiction with personal jurisdiction over the controller, ie view enforcement against crypto-tokens as a matter of *in personam* orders instead of *in rem* orders.

VI. Concluding Thoughts

This chapter has sought to identify the various situations within the insolvency scenario where the situs of various tangible movables and particularly intangibles have been relevant. It then argues that the same concept continues to be relevant for crypto-tokens in these same scenarios, provided that we correctly understand the concept to be based on the twin rationales of practical control over property and providing a visible reference point that forms the basis of the reasonable expectations of commercial men as to when and what rights they will acquire in that property, rather than a narrow focus on territorial control and viewing the exercise as physically anchoring the intangible. In other words, the concept of situs remains relevant as a connecting factor based on principle, rather than as a rigid application of rules developed for another class of property. By contrast, the greater difficulty appears to be with the concept of situs for the purposes of enforcement.

[153] Ng (n 150) 337–338.

PART II

Enforcement in Digital Assets

5

The Global Code of Digital Enforcement

JOS UITDEHAAG

I. The International Union of Judicial Officers

The International Union of Judicial Officers (UIHJ) was established in 1952. Currently, there are 102 organisations representing the profession of judicial officer or enforcement agent in 98 countries, covering five continents, who are members of the UIHJ. Its mission is to represent its members with respect to international organisations and to bring about cooperation with professional organisations at national the level. It contributes to the improvement of national legal procedures and international agreements and the promotion of the ideas, projects, and initiatives aimed at advancing and improving the independent status of the judicial officer or enforcement agent.

At a global level, the UIHJ is a member of the Economic and Social Council of the United Nations (UN) and is an observer member of the United Nations Commission on International Trade Law (UNCITRAL). It is in close contact with the World Bank, with UIHJ experts regularly participating in projects financed by the World Bank on various continents. The UIHJ is in contact with the IMF through missions carried out by its experts. The UIHJ collaborates in the work of the Hague Conference on Private International Law, particularly in the development of conventions relating to the service and notification of judicial documents and enforcement. The UIHJ participates in Unidroit discussions, particularly in the context of enforcement. It also regularly participates in projects and expert missions organised by USAID.

In Europe, the UIHJ is associated with the reflections of the Council of Europe for the implementation of treaties, conventions, charters, recommendations, guidelines, and other tools, intended for the constitution of the European area of justice. As an international non-governmental organisation, it closely cooperates with the Council of Europe. It is a permanent observer member of the Council of Europe's Commission for the Efficiency of Justice (CEPEJ) and, as such, participates in the meetings of the various working groups of the CEPEJ. The UIHJ actively collaborated in the development of the CEPEJ Guidelines on Enforcement[1] and was asked in 2015 to draft the Good Practice Guide on enforcement. The UIHJ is also contacted by the CEPEJ in the context of its reports on European judicial systems.

In Africa, the UIHJ promotes the establishment of a harmonised status of the judicial officer or enforcement agent. The UIHJ maintains close relations with the permanent secretariat of Ohada in Yaoundé, Cameroon. It has been a technical partner of Ohada since 2017. As such, it participates in meetings of the Council of Ministers of Ohada. A partnership was signed in 2018 with the Ohada Higher Regional School of Magistracy (Ersuma). The UIHJ participated in the work to revise the Ohada Uniform Act, organising simplified recovery procedures and enforcement proceedings.[2] The UIHJ also maintains ongoing relations with the West African Economic and Monetary Union (WAEMU) and collaborates with the Southern African Development Community (SADC).

In Asia, the UIHJ is in contact with the Association of Southeast Asian Countries (ASEAN). Also here, UIHJ is active in projects in the field of (legal) reform of enforcement in various countries. The UIHJ is active on the American continent, particularly in the US, South America, and the Caribbean area.

II. Introduction

In 1776 the economist Adam Smith in his famous book *Wealth of Nations*[3] wrote:

> Commerce and manufacturers can seldom flourish long in any state which does not enjoy a regular administration of justice, in which the people do not feel themselves secure in the possession of their property, in which the faith of contract is not supported by law …

Smith referred to economic growth. For such economic growth, several factors can be considered important, among them stable macro-economic conditions, competition, investments, the use of science, the development of a consumer-orientated society, and work ethic. Plus: the respect for the principles of the Rule of Law, or, more specifically, a system of well-specified and enforced property rights and contracts.

Indeed, development of markets is not just economic development. For markets to develop, a legal infrastructure is necessary. Markets exchange property rights and contracts. For this, a clear legal framework is necessary: transparency

[1] CEPEJ Guidelines for a better implementation of the existing Council of Europe's recommendation on enforcement, 17 December 2009 CEPEJ(2009)11REV2 (CEPEJ 2009 Guidelines).

[2] Ohada Uniform Act organising simplified recovery procedures and enforcement proceedings of 10 April 1998, adopted on 17 October 2023 in Kinshasa (Democratic Republic of Congo) by the Council of Ministers of Ohada during its 56th meeting.

[3] A Smith, 'An inquiry into the Nature and Causes of the Wealth of nations' (first published 1776, Oxford, Oxford University Press, 2008) V, iii.

of legislation, publicly declared, certainty and equality of law and legal procedures, and recognition of individual rights and freedom, ie, the Rule of Law principles. Those principles guarantee economic growth, guarantee economic development: ownership is assured, agreements will be observed, the government is controlled, there is a control on corruption, and private possessions are regulated. If not: there will be no trading or investments. International organisations such as the World Bank during the years have published a large number of reports indicating the need for these legal principles for economic growth.[4]

For a well-functioning society, these principles demand an independent, impartial, and efficient judiciary. Any judicial system that lacks an efficient, transparent, independent judiciary will face problems. A non-functioning, inefficient (or overregulated) legal system will result in long delays within the legal system. Litigation procedures will not be finished in a reasonable time. Unwilling parties, eg, through delay tactics, will benefit from the system. This will result in massive backlogs in courts, in civil proceedings, but also in enforcement proceedings. The legal system will become unattractive for market parties and foreign investors. It will result in a lack of trust of the general public in the legal system; after all, what is the use of contracting a party in case contractual obligations in case of non-compliance cannot be enforced? Non-enforcement of judgments will lead to liquidity problems. Corruption practices will flourish.

In 1997, this was also confirmed by the European Court of Human Rights. In the case of *Hornsby v Greece*,[5] the ECtHR ruled that the right to a fair trial (Article 6 of the ECHR) includes the right to the execution of an enforceable title once obtained. This requires an effective and efficient organisation of enforcement law. Without such a guarantee of legal certainty, citizens will lose respect for the Rule of Law and economic development will stagnate.

It is against this background that UIHJ has developed the Code Mondiale d'Execution (the World Code on Enforcement, hereafter: Comonex), a set of principles on enforcement based on international best practices. In 2015, at the UIHJ Congress in Madrid, the first set of principles was published, universal principles aiming at the general modernisation of attachment and enforcement law and its adaptation to the current economic and social climate. The second set of principles was introduced in 2021. This second set, the Global Code of Digital Enforcement, focusses on the digitisation of enforcement. Such digitisation, in Comonex, not only refers to the procedural aspects of enforcement, but also to substantive aspects, such as the enforcement against digital assets. Recently (May 2024), a third set of principles has been published, which focusses on the ethical and professional

[4] See, eg, Jamal Ibrahim Haidar (World Bank and the Paris School of Economics) who in 2012 concluded on the causal connection between a well-developed system of judiciary and countries' prosperity, that on average, each business regulatory reform is associated with a 0.15% increase in growth rate of GDP. (JI Haidar, 'The impact of business regulatory reforms on economic growth' [2012] *Journal of the Japanese and international economies* 285).

[5] *Hornsby v Greece* App no 18357/91 (ECtHR, 19 March 1997) para 40.

standards for enforcement agents. Enforcement agents are an essential element of the rule of law. They ensure the effectiveness of judicial decisions, without which the right to have recourse to a judge would be illusory. An efficient enforcement system is a major contribution to the protection of fundamental rights by ensuring fair enforcement and legal certainty. It also contributes to economic development. In order to gain public trust, Comonex and other international principles expect a high level of competence, reliability, and respectability from the enforcement agent. The third set of principles brings together the universally shared ethical principles and the standards of good practice within the enforcement profession.

III. The Global Code of Digital Enforcement

A. Introduction

Digitalisation is embedded in our economy and in our personal lives. The COVID-19 pandemic has shown that new technology is necessary to communicate when 'face-to-face' contact is no longer possible. In recent years, digitalisation has also taken off in the enforcement profession: as an effective tool for implementation, digital case management, electronic communication of documents, access to electronic databases, or the use of artificial intelligence. Digital assets such as cryptocurrencies are forcing us to think further about modernising or at least adapting attachment and enforcement law. The second set of UIHJ principles governs such future aspects of enforcement. This second set was presented in November 2021 in Dubai during the 24th UIHJ congress.[6] It consists of seven different chapters that govern the use of digital technology in enforcement: general principles of digital enforcement; applicable law to enforcement; the principles specific to the activity of judicial officers or enforcement agents; the digital enforcement procedures; enforcement against digital assets; the use of artificial intelligence in the enforcement and the seizure of crypto assets.

B. Fundamental Rights

To the extent possible, digital enforcement needs to be carried out on the same basis as traditional enforcement. This is a key principle of Comonex. The principles of traditional enforcement therefore also apply to digital enforcement, though, sometimes, with a focus on digital enforcement, these traditional principles have a broader meaning. For example, the principle of proportionality of the enforcement

[6] The work was carried out by the Scientific Council of the UIHJ (chaired by Marc Schmitz, President of the UIHJ).

measure and the amount of the claim refers also to the choice of either a traditional or a digital enforcement measure.[7]

Comonex pays a lot of attention to the 'human factor' in enforcement. Priority should be given to reaching an agreement between parties rather than enforcement, as is also confirmed by the UNCITRAL Model Law on International Commercial Conciliation.[8] Reaching such an agreement implies that parties have a duty to cooperate in the enforcement process. Article 59 Comonex underlines the importance of such a principle: digitalisation should not deprive the debtor of the right to establish physical contact with the enforcement agent as part of the enforcement process, nor should it deprive the parties of the right to appeal to a judge to sanction an irregularity, to check the proportionality of the enforcement measure, or to repair the possible damage when the lawfulness of the enforcement agent's actions or the proportionality of enforcement is at stake or the parties have suffered damage as a result of the enforcement agent's actions.[9] The enforcement agent is obliged to provide the parties with clear and understandable information about the use of digital debt collection.[10]

Access to justice and the right to compensation for damages within the framework of a fair trial constitute a necessary framework to ensure respect for fundamental rights.[11] The protection of fundamental rights needs to be ensured, no matter the legal nature of software, algorithms, artificial intelligence, or so that is used.[12] National law that provides for digital enforcement should secure compliance with the deontological and ethical principles recognised by international conventions and charters:

- *Respect for human dignity*[13] imposes, inter alia, the obligation to define and delimit the use of digital technology in view of the needs and the expectations of individuals, without hindering or endangering them.
- The Principle of *Non-Discrimination, Fairness and Solidarity*[14] prevents individuals and groups from being discriminated against, directly or indirectly, on the basis of illegal or unlawful criteria. All people should have equal access to the benefits of artificial intelligence.
- '*Transparency and predictability*'[15] mean that stakeholders should be properly informed, in a language they understand, about the purposes, modalities and possible implications of the use of digital systems.

[7] Comonex, Arts 27 and 38.
[8] ibid Art 10. See also CEPEJ 2009 Guidelines (n 1) Guideline 70.
[9] ibid, Art 40.
[10] ibid, Art 39.
[11] ibid, Art 40.
[12] ibid, Arts 35 and 36.
[13] ibid, Art 36.1.
[14] ibid, Art 36.2.
[15] ibid, Arts 36.3 and 39.

- *'Quality and Safety'*[16] guarantee the existence of a basis based on the law or jurisprudence and that only certified and correct legal data are used.
- *'Respect for personal data and privacy'*[17] provide for the protection of privacy. Intelligent systems must guarantee the confidentiality of data and the anonymisation of personal profiles.
- *'Developer social responsibility'*:[18] autonomous systems should only be developed and used in a way that serves the public interest and respect the different norms and values in society.
- *'Trust'*[19] : Artificial intelligence algorithms must be secure, reliable and robust enough to face and correct mistakes. Publicly empowered organisations, made up of representatives of all stakeholders, should implement a certification process to ensure the ethical compliance of artificial intelligence systems.
- *'Technological neutrality'*[20] : algorithms must adhere to a principle of neutrality and intellectual integrity and make data processing methodologies accessible.

C. Adaption of the Enforcement Measure

An important provision in Comonex is Article 52. Enforcement agents should always have the power to adapt the enforcement measure to the situation of the creditor and that of the debtor, to proceed with enforcement in accordance with non-digital procedures and to continue enforcement by 'traditional' enforcement (or vice versa). This means that there should not be a clear distinction between digital enforcement and non-digital enforcement: when a seizure or another enforcement measure begins in a dematerialised way and difficulties arise, it should be possible to continue in a non-digital way, *without losing the procedural benefit of what has already been accomplished.* Conversely, a non-digital enforcement procedure should be able to continue digitally. Enforcement agents should always be able to intervene, allowing them to end or modify digital enforcement.

This also applies to the use of artificial intelligence. Enforcement agents should have the power to override a decision made by artificial intelligence which does not appear to comply with the fundamental principles of enforcement.

D. The Digital Activities of the Judicial Officer

Technological neutrality, as mentioned in the previous paragraph, is an important deontological and ethical principle when it comes to the use of IT in enforcement.

[16] ibid, Art 36.4.
[17] ibid, Art 36.5.
[18] ibid, Art 36.6.
[19] ibid, Art 36.7.
[20] ibid, Art 36.8.

Comonex supports the use of information technology in the profession of enforcement agents. National law should allow enforcement agents to use digital tools, such as online enforcement proceedings and videoconferencing, in the performance of their function.[21] Such legislation should, for example, enable the enforcement agent to create a digital identity to perform their activities;[22] the use of secure electronic platforms for online mediation, including post-judicial or amicable debt recovery services[23] and the access of enforcement agents to dematerialised registers (such as bank accounts, motor vehicle registrations, and registers for asset declarations).

The IT systems at most enforcement agents' offices provide for automated processes in terms of case and financial management, litigation service, document processing, remote access to case data, and so on. Nevertheless, in a large number of countries, the enforcement process itself still materialises and processing takes place via physical documents. For example, the e-judgment is used sporadically; there is a limited use of IT in the seizure of movable property, and in many countries the e-attachment of the bank account or income has not yet been introduced. Even in cases where electronic means can be used, in a number of countries the electronic data related to an enforcement case are just an image reflection of the paper original. The paper original is considered solely authentic and relevant in case a dispute is raised, whether a certain claim, objection, ruling, or other relevant legal action has occurred.

A well-functioning enforcement case management system (CMS) not only relates to the automated functioning of all procedural implications (title and parties, document templates and process service, attachment and asset processing, debt calculation and accounting, cash flow processing, etc on a national scale), but also provides reliable statistical data and facilitate access and control over the civil enforcement operations.

Article 50 Comonex focusses on these challenges. National laws should provide for the organisation of the profession so that all enforcement agents are properly trained (initial training and continuing training) in the use of digital tools. In addition, enforcement agents should be sufficiently equipped to effectively participate in the digitalisation of justice. This means, for example, electronic communication with the courts, the ability to serve legal documents in a dematerialised way, and to carry out enforcement through electronic means.

E. The Automated Attachment Procedure

With regard to the enforcement through electronic means, it is important to define certain principles. A good example of such a need is a recent development in

[21] ibid, Art 47.
[22] ibid, Art 48.
[23] ibid, Art 49.

England. In the English enforcement system, physical presence is a legal requirement to seize or gain control over the debtor's movable property. To this end, the enforcement agent has the authority to enter buildings and make an inventory of the goods to be seized. An English company, Just Digital Marketplace Ltd, filed an application with the Supreme Court asking the Court for confirmation that English law does not prevent 'virtual' attachment of movable property.[24] Such virtual enforcement means a seizure or taking over of the debtor's movable property without the need for the physical presence of the enforcement agent. The purists among us would say – never. The question therefore arises: in the future, will the enforcement agent be able to seize the assets of the debtor through a 'virtual visit' (online via video link) to the debtor's premises? The Court concluded that Schedule 12 of the Tribunals Courts and Enforcement Act 2007 does not prohibit remote contact with the debtor. Nor does this Act prohibit the conclusion of a Controlled Goods Agreement without physical access to the home in order to take control of the goods.

With such an example in mind, it is obvious that legislation is needed to regulate dematerialised attachment procedures.[25] Article 57 Comonex states that national laws should provide for dematerialised procedures to carry out seizures of movable, immovable, or digital properties, and to allow the dematerialised circulation of the necessary documents. At the same time, we need to realise that e-enforcement will never be able to completely replace traditional enforcement. Hence, Article 58 Comonex invites legislators to also indicate clearly in law when the physical presence of the enforcement agent is mandatory. Consider, for example, the eviction. Besides, the digitalisation of the attachment procedure should not deprive the debtor of the right to contact the enforcement agent in person as part of any enforcement process, including a digital process.[26]

In order to combat corruption and improve the effectiveness of implementation, e-auction has been introduced in many countries. Comonex promotes these developments: national legislation should provide for the possibility of auctioning seized goods electronically. Payments could also be made electronically.[27]

As regards the enforcement costs of the digital enforcement procedure, Comonex provides that those costs are clear, predictable, and reasonable. Digital enforcement should not be more expensive than traditional enforcement.[28]

F. Electronic Service

For efficient and effective enforcement, communication, and access to information about the enforcement process are important. In that respect, a well-organised

[24] *Just Digital Marketplace Ltd v High Court Enforcement Officers Association* [2021] EWHC 15, QB.
[25] ibid, Arts 50 and 57.
[26] ibid, Art 59.
[27] ibid, Art 67.
[28] ibid, Art 60.

system for service of documents plays a crucial role. This is also underlined by the Council of Europe and CEPEJ.[29]

In accordance with legal international instruments, national law should allow enforcement agents to transmit all documents relating to enforcement measures by secure electronic means to the court and to the authorities concerned.[30]

In many countries, enforcement agents are charged with the service of procedural documents, not only in enforcement procedures, but also the documents initiating proceedings. This method of service provides unparalleled legal certainty.

Though e-service of documents is not common in a number of countries, we see a growing trend to introduce such system. The European Union has a strong belief in the use of e-service. Article 19 of the Service Regulation[31] allows electronic service of documents, provided certain requirements are met.[32] Such prior conditions refer to the existence of a 'guaranteed' electronic address or prior consent of the recipient or an agreement with the third party (ie, bank or employer) on the technical specifications and method of communication.

In order for the e-service of documents to be successful, Comonex advocates the introduction of an electronic judicial address or, failing that, an electronic address chosen for service. It is important that there is an authentic source for all records of notification and service: all reports are recorded there with all the necessary additional information. This can be achieved through the creation of an e-service platform and/or the use of DLT (blockchain).[33]

As a best practice, the e-service system as developed in Belgium can be mentioned. This system combines the possibility of e-service of (enforceable) documents with the traditional systems of document service. This country has the

[29] See, eg, Council of Europe Recommendation Rec(2003)17 of the Committee of Ministers to Member States on enforcement (Rec 17/2003) II.2.d; Council of Europe Recommendation Rec(2003)16 of the Committee of Ministers to member states on the execution of administrative and judicial decisions in the field of administrative law (Rec 16/2003) 2A iii; CEPEJ 2009 Guidelines (n 1) Guidelines 17–19.

[30] ibid, Art 76.

[31] Regulation (EU) 2020/1784 of the European Parliament and of the Council of 25 November 2020 on the service in the Member States of judicial and extrajudicial documents in civil or commercial matters (service of documents) (recast) [2020] OJ L405/40.

[32] Art 9 para 1: The service of judicial documents may be effected directly on a person who has a known address for service in another Member State by any electronic means of service available under the law of the forum Member State for the domestic service of documents, provided that:

(a) the documents are sent and received using qualified electronic registered delivery services within the meaning of Regulation (EU) No 910/2014 and the addressee gave prior express consent to the use of electronic means for serving documents in the course of legal proceedings; or
(b) the addressee gave prior express consent to the court or authority seised of the proceedings or to the party responsible for service of documents in such proceedings to the use of email sent to a specified email address for the purpose of serving documents in the course of those proceedings and the addressee confirms receipt of the document with an acknowledgement of receipt, including the date of receipt.

[33] Comonex, Art 77.

dematerialised notification procedure introduced in the Judicial Code. In order to notify a document electronically, certain prior conditions must be fulfilled:

- The circumstances of the case must allow for this.
- The recipient of the deed (private individual or legal entity) must hold an 'electronic judicial address'[34] or, failing this, an 'elected electronic address for service'.[35] In the latter case, express prior consent – which can be obtained by dematerialised means – is required.

For the e-service, Belgium introduced a special e-notification platform that functions as an authentic source for all records of notification and service: all notifications are recorded on this platform. The platform functions as a communication system through which the requests for service can be forwarded to the territorially competent and available enforcement agent. The platform also registers the receipt of service by the recipient. In case such a receipt is not received within a certain period, service still needs to be carried out 'traditionally'.

G. The Use of Artificial Intelligence

The Dutch childcare benefits scandal is a good example of the risks associated with the use of algorithms in the field of debt collection. In the case of the Dutch Data Protection Agency (DPA) against the Dutch Tax Administration, the unlawful processing by means of an algorithm in enforcement led to a violation of the right to equality and non-discrimination. The Tax Administration processed data on the (dual) nationality of childcare benefit applicants in an unlawful, discriminatory, and therefore improper manner and processed the nationality data of childcare benefit applicants for the purpose of combating organised fraud, even though this data was not necessary for this purpose. Lastly, it used applicants' nationality (Dutch/not Dutch) as an indicator in a system that automatically designated certain applications as risky.[36]

Algorithms make decisions based on digital data. In other words, there is little room for customisation or adaptation to a debtor's personal circumstances, while it is precisely this human factor, also in the vision of the UIHJ, that is important. Comonex has formulated a number of principles on the use of artificial intelligence and algorithms in the enforcement process.

[34] 'Electronic judicial address' means 'the unique e-mail address assigned by the competent authority to a private individual or a legal entity'.

[35] 'Elected electronic address for service' means 'any other electronic address to which notification can be made in accordance with the Judicial Code, following express prior consent of the recipient for every notification in question'.

[36] See www.autoriteitpersoonsgegevens.nl/en/current/tax-administration-fined-for-discriminatory-and-unlawful-data-processing and www.autoriteitpersoonsgegevens.nl/en/current/tax-administration-fined-for-fraud-blacklist.

Enforcement agents should be able to set up a 'smart enforcement' mechanism and use blockchain technology together with the debtor and the creditor to establish an automatic process of compulsory enforcement, particularly when payments are made with a cryptocurrency. National laws should give judicial officers or enforcement agents exclusive authority to intervene as an oracle of blockchain or distributed ledger technology.

The data entered into the algorithm must be exhaustive, transparent, unbiased, and representative to enable authentication of the data.[37] Artificial intelligence should focus on *assisting* the enforcement agent in the assessment of the appropriate enforcement measures.[38] Such a system requires rules, guidelines and an ethical framework that makes it possible to monitor and certify the risks of using the system.[39] States should be required to develop a regulatory framework to avoid risks posed by artificial intelligence and to guarantee the rights of parties in its implementation.[40] National law should also provide for a judicial procedure to remedy the damage suffered during automated enforcement.[41]

H. Electronic Access to Information

International standards recognise the importance of access to information on the domicile and assets of a debtor.[42] In fact, CEPEJ recommends to establish a unique multi-source restricted access database about debtors' attachable assets.[43] The development of such a database, in the view of CEPEJ, will demand co-operation between the various organs of state and private institutions subject to compliance with the data protection legislation.[44] In order to facilitate efficient enforcement, the CEPEJ 2009 Guidelines recommend to introduce the obligation for state authorities to provide the information to the enforcement agent.[45] The Guidelines further recommend that national legislation is scrutinised in case it needs to be adapted to allow for efficient enforcement procedures.[46]

When it comes to access to information, automated access to the databases, an exhaustive content of such databases, and the interconnectivity of such databases are crucial. Such access to information should also extend to the debtor's digital assets. National law should provide that public and private entities, as well as all

[37] Comonex, Art 37.
[38] ibid, Art 78.
[39] ibid, Arts 37 and 68.
[40] ibid, Art 37.
[41] ibid, Art 80.
[42] See, eg, Council of Europe Rec 17/2003 (n 29) III.6 and CEPEJ 2009 Guidelines (n 1) Guidelines 39 and 47.
[43] CEPEJ 2009 Guidelines (n 1) Guideline 41.
[44] ibid Guideline 42.
[45] ibid Guideline 43.
[46] ibid Guideline 44.

those who hold or manage digital assets, communicate, preferably by electronic means, to enforcement agents all the information at their disposal concerning the domicile, registered office, or place of business of the debtor, as well as the elements forming his patrimony, without being able to oppose professional secrecy.[47] Legislation must provide for a time limit within which enforcement agents are informed. Where national law provides for the existence of dematerialised registers (such as bank accounts, motor vehicle registrations, and declarations of assets), the enforcement agent must be able to connect electronically to these registers in order to carry out enforcement.[48]

With regard to information on the domicile of the debtor, in most countries the enforcement agent has (electronic) access to this information. However, the main problem here is the accuracy of such domicile registers or commercial registers. In a lot of countries, citizens are not very inclined to inform the register authorities when they change residence. Companies registered in the commercial register only exist on paper. A stricter legislative regime, combined with sanctions, might lead to a more reliable system. It also means that enforcement agents are dependent on various other sources (databases) to locate a debtor.

Due to the cross-border nature of digital assets, Comonex recommends that states cooperate and exchange information on debtors.[49] Such cooperation should also cover the electronic exchange of documents, evidence or other information.[50] States should provide for the interoperability of national digital systems and define international mutual assistance.[51]

The debtor's privacy must be safeguarded.[52] For the purposes of enforcement, the enforcement agent is entitled to create electronic files and collect personal data, in accordance with national law and international instruments.[53] Legislation should allow the enforcement agent to re-use information about a debtor's assets in subsequent enforcement proceedings to which the same debtor is a party. It is important that the re-use of such information is subject to a clear and precise legal framework (eg, with regard to the period for which this data may be retained).[54]

[47] Comonex, Arts 61 and 62.
[48] ibid, Art 51.
[49] ibid, Art 66.
[50] ibid, Art 69.
[51] ibid, Art 70.
[52] ibid, Arts 36 and 53.
[53] ibid, Art 53.
[54] ibid, Art 54. Here we see the global influence of Comonex. The provision is in accordance with international standards; for example, CEPEJ 2009 Guidelines (n 1) Guideline 46 states explicitly:

> Member states are invited to consider allowing enforcement agents to reuse information on the defendant's assets in subsequent procedures that involve the same defendant.

However, there are dissenting opinions if the provisions of GDPR allow such re-use of information on the debtor's assets.

Especially to search information on digital assets, the law should authorise the enforcement agent to obtain access to personal data on digital media with the assistance of a computer expert and with the authorisation of the court.[55]

I. Applicable Law

Which law governs the enforcement of a digital asset?

To answer this question, the drafters first sought a definition of a digital asset, a huge challenge as it appeared. Hence, the description of digital assets in Comonex (glossary) is rather general: a digital asset is a 'Product or service with patrimonial or extra-patrimonial value, digitally stored, displayed, transferred, and administered, natively or otherwise.' A more detailed definition of digital asset, in line with the description in Comonex, was developed by the Access to Digital Assets Working Group of the European Law Institute (ELI), in its report 'ELI Principles on the Use of Digital Assets as Security':[56]

> Digital asset means any record or representation of value that fulfils the following criteria:
>
> (i) it is exclusively stored, displayed and administered electronically, on or through a virtual platform or database, including where it is a record or representation of a real-world, tradeable asset, and whether or not the digital asset itself is held directly or through an account with an intermediary;
>
> (ii) it is capable of being subject to a right of control, enjoyment or use, regardless of whether such rights are legally characterised as being of a proprietary, obligational or other nature;
> and
>
> (iii) it is capable of being transferred from one party to another, including by way of voluntary disposition.

Though general, such an approach has the advantage that it applies to different categories of digital assets that may be stored, displayed, transferred, and administered on or through platforms or databases, or blockchain, cloud service, or otherwise.

In line with these definitions, UIHJ in its Comonex first of all makes a distinction between the identification, tracing, and seizure of digital assets. Each might be governed by different applicable laws.

Regarding the applicable enforcement law, Comonex distinguishes between:[57]

- Identified and accessible digital assets: regardless of where these assets are located, such assets will be seized in accordance with the applicable law of their

[55] Comonex, Arts 63–65.

[56] The writer of this chapter is the co-reporter of this ELI project. See www.europeanlawinstitute.eu/projects-publications/publications/eli-principles-on-the-use-of-digital-assets-as-security.

[57] Comonex, Art 45.

location, while respecting the international principles of sovereignty and territoriality of enforceability (*lex rei sitae*).

- Unidentified and/or inaccessible digital assets: such assets are subject to the applicable law of the State that controls or ordered enforcement (*lex fori*).

Another question regarding applicable law is about the competence of the enforcement agent. Such competence of an enforcement agent to identify digital assets and the place where they can be accessed is determined by the debtor's place of residence.[58] In this respect, I also want to point to the following. Digital assets are not bound by geographical boundaries. Even more than in the case of an attachment of traditional assets, in the case of a seizure of digital assets, cooperation between enforcement agents (across borders!) is of eminent importance. In that respect, Article 42 Comonex recommends states to provide for a mechanism of cooperation between enforcement agents: if enforcement agents of one state request support from enforcement agents of another state, the latter should have an obligation to cooperate. Moreover, Comonex recommends that states cooperate by exchanging the information they hold concerning debtors.[59]

J. Attachment of Digital Assets

For the upcoming years, the attachment of digital assets will be one of the major challenges. In the opinion of UIHJ, only enforcement agents authorised by national law, whatever their status, should be able to have access to such digital assets of a person for the purpose of executing an enforceable title recognised by the applicable law.[60]

Regarding the legal status and regulatory framework of the enforcement of digital assets, a whole new area of law is developing, but there are considerable gaps and inconsistencies between the various sector-specific and nationally diverging solutions. Considering the international characteristics of such assets, international cooperation and coordination for the development of a legislative framework is an absolute necessity. In this legislation, as Comonex proposes, it is important that the different categories and legal nature of digital assets are defined.[61] As much as possible, for the attachment of digital assets, mechanisms that draw on existing enforcement procedures should be used. To safeguard the rights of a creditor who does not have an enforceable title, national law should provide that the judge can order provisional and interlocutory measures also regarding digital assets. In particular, the judge should have the power to order the transfer of the private key, to suspend access to digital assets, or to create an escrow account. When the

[58] ibid, Art 46.
[59] ibid, Arts 42 and 66.
[60] ibid, Art 72.
[61] ibid, Arts 71 and 73.

creditor has an enforceable title, judicial officers or enforcement agents should be able to proceed with a provisional or interlocutory measure without authorisation from the judge.[62]

i. Prior Service or Notification of the Enforcement Order

In accordance with Article 8 Comonex, any enforcement measure should be preceded, on pain of nullity, by the service or notification of the enforcement order on the debtor in accordance with the procedures provided for by national law. This service or notification should contain an obligation for the debtor to declare his assets, including digital assets.[63] Taking into consideration (see also section III.F.) the global character of digital assets, I can imagine that special attention is given to e-service of such an enforcement order.

ii. Access to Information on the Digital Assets

In the ideal situation, and in most cases hypothetical, the debtor cooperates and is willing to share information on the digital assets with the enforcement agent. In such a case, the debtor will hand over the relevant information, such as the private key to the enforcement agent and the digital assets, such as crypto assets, can be liquidated.

Closer to reality is the situation in which the enforcement agent will need to start a search for the digital assets of the debtor. In section III.H., I already mentioned the importance of access to information on the assets of the debtor. In the ideal situation, there exists a national cryptocurrency registry with a declaration obligation for the owners of that cryptocurrency. For the purposes of enforcement, the enforcement agent has access to such register.[64]

In case such a register does not exist, law should provide for an obligation on the part of the debtor to declare the crypto-currency or anyone who owns or manages digital assets.[65] In such a case, the question arises if the current sanction system provides sufficient sanctions (eg, penalties) in case the debtor refuses cooperation. Comonex proposes, beside financial sanctions,[66] also to introduce

[62] ibid, Art 75.

[63] ibid, Arts 8 and 81.

[64] ibid, Art 82. This is also in line with Regulation (EU) 2023/1114 of the European Parliament and of the Council of 31 May 2023 on markets in crypto assets, and amending Regulations (EU) No 1093/2010 and (EU) No 1095/2010 and Directives 2013/36/EU and (EU) 2019/1937 [2023] OJ L150/40 Art 75 para 2:

> Crypto asset service providers providing custody and administration of crypto assets on behalf of clients shall keep a register of positions, opened in the name of each client, corresponding to each client's rights to the crypto assets.

[65] Comonex, Art 83.

[66] Such extension is necessary. For example, according to Dutch law, based on the Benelux Convention providing a uniform law on penalty payments (Convention Benelux portant loi uniforme relative à l'astreinte, The Hague, 26 November 1973), for a monetary claim no penalty can be imposed.

far-reaching alternative sanctions such as temporary withdrawal of documents such as passports, driving licences and, if this is in accordance with national legislation, civil imprisonment. National law should further consider that the debtor's refusal to cooperate in the enforcement constitutes an element of criminal offence of organising his insolvency.[67]

In the case of crypto assets, unlike banks, there is no counterparty. The transactions in cryptocurrencies take place through exchange platforms, which require the intervention of a third party (the custodian) or are stored in a 'bank account', the wallet. The wallet has different appearances: a simple piece of paper with the private key on it; a hardware wallet: a USB stick (or similar) in which the cryptocurrency is stored; a desktop or mobile wallet (a piece of software on the computer or mobile phone for storing the cryptocurrency) or an online wallet. In such a case, the law should provide that enforcement agents can access cryptoassets on all computer media held by the debtor wherever they are located, if necessary, with the assistance of a computer expert.[68]

iii. The Attachment of Digital Assets

With regard to the seizure of cryptocurrencies, Comonex distinguishes between:

1. Digital assets such as crypto assets which are stored on exchange platforms.
2. Crypto assets stored in a wallet which is in the hands of the debtor.

Ad 1: Digital Assets such as Crypto Assets which are Stored on Exchange Platforms

As mentioned, with regard to the attachment of digital assets, as much as possible, the mechanisms that draw on existing enforcement procedures should be used. For digital assets, such as crypto assets held by a third party (ie, the custodian), the rules of garnishment are followed. The enforcement agent serves the garnishment order on the custodian, thus attaching the digital assets held by this third party on behalf of the debtor. The service or the notification of the garnishment order makes the digital assets unavailable under penalty of sanctions defined by the applicable national law.[69]

Within a reasonable period of time, as defined by law, the custodian is obliged to declare to the enforcement agent whether or not he holds digital assets for the debtor, under penalty defined by the applicable law for a refusal to report or for incomplete or false reporting. The statement of the third party entails a list of assets, including cryptoassets, held according to their nature and legal status, as well as their access codes (public key, private key) and any previous seizures or security interests or guarantees on the property. In the case of cryptoassets,

[67] Comonex, Art 2.
[68] ibid, Art 88.
[69] ibid, Art 84.

the third party should detail them sufficiently to allow their seizure.[70] The debtor is informed of the attachment and the possibility of objecting to the attachment within the time limit set by law.[71] To ensure security, the enforcement agent stores the cryptocurrency in a secure wallet.[72]

Ad 2: Crypto Assets Stored in a Wallet which is in the Hands of the Debtor

As mentioned, the wallet on which the cryptocurrency is located has different appearances. It is important that the enforcement agent has access to the wallet, regardless of whether it is on a computer, mobile phone, USB stick, or similar. Comonex therefore stipulates that the enforcement agent has jurisdiction over all (computer) media in the possession of the debtor, regardless of where such (computer) media are located. If necessary, the enforcement agent can be assisted by a computer expert.[73]

The writ of attachment of the crypto assets, which renders the crypto assets unavailable, is served on the debtor.[74] The writ of attachment, in addition to the mandatory information relating to the documents of enforcement agents, in the case of crypto assets, contains the following information:[75]

- A summons obliging the debtor to give them the necessary information to access the cryptoassets, under penalty provided for by law.
- A reference to judicial authorisations when necessary.
- The information that the debtor can no longer dispose of the cryptoassets under criminal penalty provided for by law.
- The report of the seizure of the carrier.
- The possibilities for the debtor to challenge the seizure and the time limits for taking such action.
- The statement of the sequestration of the seized cryptoassets.

iv. Enforcement of the Seized Crypto Assets

With regard to the enforcement of the seized crypto assets, there are several possibilities:[76]

- The cryptocurrencies are transferred to the creditor as payment.
- The cryptocurrencies are sold by the enforcement agent through an exchange platform approved by the competent authority over the enforcement agents

[70] ibid, Art 85.
[71] ibid, Art 87.
[72] ibid, Arts 86 and 9.
[73] ibid, Art 88.
[74] ibid, Art 89.
[75] ibid, Art 90.
[76] ibid, Art 91.

(ie the Ministry of Justice or the Chamber of enforcement agents). In this case, the enforcement agent orders the third party (platform) to proceed with the sale of the cryptoassets by providing such third party a certificate of no dispute or the judge's decision rendered on the dispute and authorising the sale.

- The cryptocurrency will be sold through a public sale.[77]

IV. Conclusion

It is often said that new technologies will eliminate the role of trusted third parties, such as notaries or enforcement agents. The enforcement agent is subject to public evaluation and criticism in a way that can never be replaced by technology. Especially with the technological changes, it is important that fairness and due process are guaranteed. In that respect, UIHJ supports innovation. Such innovation needs to be shaped by a secure framework. Protection of parties in the enforcement process and integrity of the enforcement agent are important, especially with advancing digitisation. The aim of Comonex is to make clear that legal certainty benefits from a clear (legal) framework. It enables to adapt enforcement procedures to current economic and social concerns, balancing the creditor's rights and the protection of fundamental rights of the debtor, in line with the principles of the rule of law and the need to protect weaker parties. The enforcement agent will continue to be needed to ensure a fair balance between all those involved in the (digital) enforcement: the necessary 'human factor'!

[77] ibid, Art 91.

6

The Proper Procedure for the Enforcement of Money Claims in Digital Assets

DOMINIK SKAURADSZUN

I. Introduction

In enforcement law, digital assets are a relatively new form of asset. When the respective enforcement acts were drafted, the legislative process typically did not include enforcement provisions concerning digital assets. But trading of such assets has now become somewhat routine over the last couple of years.[1] Yet, there is still enormous potential for further developments and a higher market share when it comes to these assets. There is an ongoing dynamic around this new form of investment, as one might see, inter alia, from the development of the Markets in Crypto-assets Regulation (MiCAR[2]). In this respect, recent advances in technology have led to the creation of a wide array of digital assets. Prominent examples include crypto assets, electronic securities, and crypto securities. All of these digital assets are becoming increasingly important in the Decentralised Finance (DeFi) sector.

Due to these developments, it is increasingly likely that a debtor affected by enforcement proceedings regarding a money[3] claim will hold digital assets. This intensifies the need for a functional and coherent procedure concerning the enforcement of money claims in digital assets. At this stage, this need is not satisfied.[4] Existing enforcement legislation often lacks customised provisions

[1] See UNIDROIT, 'Principles on Digital Assets and Private Law' (Doc C.D. (102) 6, UNIDROIT, 2023) 6: 'These types of digital assets are frequently the subject of commercial transactions.'

[2] Regulation EU/2023/1114 of the European Parliament and of the Council of 31 May 2023 on markets in crypto-assets, and amending Regulations (EU) No 1093/2010 and (EU) No 1095/2010 and Directives 2013/36/EU and (EU) 2019/1937 (MiCAR) [2023] OJ L150/40.

[3] Money claims may also be called 'monetary claims'. Differences in wording in different national laws does not indicate a different meaning.

[4] Due to the lack of provisions covering the enforcement of digital assets, the question as to whether further work on these issues is feasible and desirable is raised by HCCH-UNIDROIT, 'Digital Assets and Tokens Joint Project: Scope Paper' (HCCH, 2023) 7.

covering digital assets such as crypto assets, electronic securities, and crypto securities in case of enforcement proceedings.[5] There could be a regulatory gap concerning the legal treatment of digital assets in this regard. This magnifies the challenges involved in these proceedings.

This is not ideal. A legal review from an enforcement law perspective appears inevitable. There is a need in terms of practical relevance, but also regarding the state's enforcement monopoly:[6] if a state claims an enforcement monopoly and therefore prohibits the creditor from self-enforcement, the state must ensure that the enforcement law is efficient and that the creditor can enforce its money claim even against modern assets. The European legislator was presumably aware of this and has addressed creditors' rights and protection by drafting the new MiCAR. The trouble with the MiCAR is, on the one hand, that it mainly sets out prudential requirements that have no direct impact on individual enforcement. On the other hand, regardless of the MiCAR, the European legislator has not created any provisions on substantive enforcement law so far.[7] As a consequence, national enforcement law is applicable and faced with the task of covering digital assets.[8]

This is a challenging task. Digital assets are often hardly comparable to other assets, even other assets commonly associated with the financial market.[9] At the EU level, a digital asset in the sense of a crypto asset is defined as a digital representation of a value or of a right that is able to be transferred and stored electronically using distributed ledger technology or similar technology (MiCAR, art 3(1)(5)).[10] Crypto assets are neither issued nor guaranteed by a central bank

[5] See, therefore, for a proposal how enforcement law could be designed de lege ferenda L Fritsche, *Die Zwangsvollstreckung in Token* (Baden-Baden, Nomos, 2023) 169 ff. Some of the national laws at least allow enforcement measures in respect of certain digital assets, eg, the Austrian Enforcement Code (Exekutionsordnung) allows enforcement measures in respect of 'virtual currencies' (Austrian Enforcement Code, s 326(1) sentence 2). J Meier and A Schneider and F Schinerl, 'Staking-fähige Kryptowerte in der Insolvenz des Intermediärs' [2023] *Recht Digital* 257, 259 seem to understand this provision as broad enough to cover crypto assets in general.

[6] K Grechenig and M Kolmar, 'The State's Enforcement Monopoly and the Private Protection of Property' (2014) 170 *Journal of Institutional and Theoretical Economics* 5.

[7] Regulation 1215/2012/EU of the European Parliament and of the Council of 12 December 2012 on jurisdiction and the recognition and enforcement of judgments in civil and commercial matters (Brussels I) OJ L351/1 may assist in enforcing judgments in other Member States but does not answer the question if and when digital assets may be subject to an attachment, how to realise seized digital assets and how to involve intermediaries properly.

[8] Which is why certain adaptions may be advisable, see UNIDROIT (n 1) 6.

[9] This can be seen by a comparison of financial instruments – even if based on DLT – that are covered by MiFID II (Directive 2014/65/EU of the European Parliament and of the Council of 15 May 2014 on markets in financial instruments and amending Directive 2002/92/EC and Directive 2011/61/EU OJ L173/349) and cryptocurrencies: where the first are based on some sort of contractual obligation, owners of cryptocurrencies typically do not seek to be legally bound or enter into legal relations with other people. See D Skauradszun, 'Crypto-assets in Enforcement and Insolvency' in DM Vicente and DP Duarte and C Granadeiro (eds), *Fintech Regulation and the Licensing Principle* Lisbon, EBI, 2023) 90, 96.

[10] UNIDROIT (n 1) 6 on the other hand defines digital assets as 'an electronic record which is capable of being subject to control'. An electronic record is defined as 'information which is (i) stored in an electronic medium and (ii) capable of being retrieved'.

or public authority and do not have the legal status of currency or money. Digital assets such as crypto assets are usually based on distributed ledger technology (DLT),[11] which enables distribution based on disintermediation. The best-known form of DLT is the blockchain technology.[12] The popular cryptocurrencies Bitcoin, Ether, Stellar and Ripple are all DLT-based. This short overview of a few digital assets, however, only scratches the surface. There are many different forms of digital assets. This chapter will not cover all of them. It will instead focus on digital assets such as crypto assets, electronic securities and crypto securities in general. It will also share some thoughts on possible new constellations currently emerging and how money claims can be enforced in these emerging constellations. This analysis is based on the assumption that the creditor has an enforceable money claim against the debtor. Additionally, the debtor's assets include digital assets. These assets are to be enforced.

II. National Enforcement Law and its Integration Task Regarding Digital Assets

Based on the aforementioned assumptions, how should the issue of enforcement of digital assets be dealt with? There is no specific legal framework addressing this either at the EU level and – in the case of some European Member States – the national level. Due to the fact that enforcement proceedings are conducted by the state and invasive by nature, they require a legal basis. This legal basis can – as of now – only be found in existing provisions in national law dealing with enforcement proceedings in general.[13] These provisions are then tasked with integrating digital assets into an established system of enforcement proceedings initially designed to encompass other assets.[14]

A. Which Category of Enforcement – If any – Fits Like a Glove?

At a general level, two types of enforcement proceedings can be distinguished: immovable property and enforcement against movable property. The starting

[11] The European legislator defines the DLT as 'a technology that enables the operation and use of distributed ledgers', which means 'an information repository that keeps records of transactions and that is shared across, and synchronised between, a set of DLT network nodes using a consensus mechanism', see art 3(1)(2) and (3) MiCAR.

[12] See for the blockchain technology, inter alia, M Belotti et al, 'A Vademecum on Blockchain Technologies: When, Which and How' (2019) 21 *Institute of Electrical and Electronics Engineers* 3796; A Antonopoulos, *Mastering Bitcoin*, 1st edn (Sebastopol, O'Reilly, 2014) 163.

[13] This also applies to those national laws that mention certain digital assets but not all of them. See n 5 for an example from Austria on virtual currencies.

[14] Similar sentiments in UNIDROIT (n 1) 70 and 73.

point of this analysis is to determine which category appears more fitting to encompass the enforcement of digital assets. The idea of the provisions covering enforcement against *immovable* property being more suitable for digital assets can be swept aside decisively. From a legal – even an intuitive – standpoint, it does not appear sensible to handle a plot of land and crypto assets similarly in enforcement proceedings.[15] This also applies to crypto assets registered in a supervised register, even though such a register may share some similarities with land registers. However, the mere fact that a plot of land always has a unique location (*situs*) and can never be physically reallocated, whereas crypto assets based on a blockchain are often spread around the world and can quickly be reallocated to another blockchain address, shows the fundamental differences. Instead, finding a solution within the provisions covering enforcement against movable property appears to make more sense. Within enforcement against movable property, it can be distinguished between the enforcement of physical objects, claims and other assets. However, even though this appears as a suitable solution at first glance, it raises new problems. Considering the existing enforcement rules of some Member States of the European Union, digital assets appear as a bulky element within the system of traditional categories of movable property. These traditional categories include physical objects and claims. None of these are understood in a way that could encompass important digital assets such as crypto assets, electronic securities, and crypto securities.[16] This is even true if the crypto asset at hand gives rise to claims, as is the case with security tokens. Even in such a case, the crypto asset as a comprehensive asset and the claim arising from it have to be assessed separately. Still, using the provisions covering the enforcement against movable property has its benefits: the category of 'other assets' as it is known in some enforcement acts[17] could be interpreted broadly and therefore cover digital assets. Could this category of enforcement fit like a glove?

B. Enforcement of Other Assets within Movable Property as a Basis for the Enforcement of Digital Assets

Applying the provisions dealing with the enforcement of 'other assets' calls for an elaborate explanation. To fall under the category of 'other assets', digital assets must be suitable for satisfying the money claims of the creditor. For this, there are certain criteria to be met. First of all, it requires the particular digital asset to have a value that can be achieved when realising the asset against the debtor's will (see II.B.i.).[18] In contrast to this, a digital asset that is not realisable in this sense is

[15] Skauradszun (n 9) 99.

[16] D Skauradszun, 'Elektronische Wertpapiere in der Zwangsvollstreckung' (2022) 135 *Zeitschrift für Zivilprozess* 479, 484 ff.

[17] See, eg, German Code of Civil Procedure, s 857.

[18] See as an example the Austrian Enforcement Code, s 326(1) sentence 1 permits enforcement against 'vermögenswerte[n] Rechte', meaning that the asset must have a realisable value.

not suitable for enforcement proceedings to satisfy a money claim of the enforcing creditor. Second, the digital asset must be transferable or at least exercisable by a third party who pays money for the use of the asset (see II.B.ii.). Regarding the digital assets discussed in this analysis, it will be demonstrated that these requirements for being enforced appear to be met by most digital assets.

i. Do Digital Assets have a Value that can be Achieved in Case of Enforcement?

The digital assets covered in this analysis typically embody an asset value. This becomes clear when observing trade activity concerning – for instance – crypto assets at crypto exchanges. Trade involving these crypto assets only takes place because the market attributes a value to the crypto asset. Otherwise, it would not be rational for trade to even take place to begin with. The mere desire of a buyer in the market to acquire these crypto assets proves the value of this category of digital assets. This allows for a general conclusion to be drawn: crypto assets that are subject to trading activities embody an asset value. But this alone is not sufficient. Even though it is obvious that most digital assets do have a value, another requirement for digital assets to fall into the category of 'other assets' is an existing possibility to determine the value of these assets. Even though digital assets are not governed by a central bank, this is the case via trading platforms. Therefore, these preconditions for digital assets to fall into the category of 'other assets' are normally met. They are therefore *suitable for satisfying* money claims of the creditor.[19]

ii. Are Digital Assets Transferable?

In some states, there is also a requirement that the 'other assets' are transferable assets.[20] This requirement is more difficult to assess. The legal definition of crypto assets within the MiCAR[21] mentions that crypto assets are 'able to be transferred'. But the definition only describes a characteristic and does not establish the transferability by virtue of law. Besides, the definition is a European provision in the field of financial regulation. As a result, it does not provide any further insight as to how crypto assets are to be dealt with in national enforcement law, especially if and how they may be transferred.

Though national law might not offer a legal mechanism for the legal transfer of crypto assets, the answer might be found in the normative power of the factual. In many cases, digital assets – in particular crypto assets – are traded on a daily basis. For this to take place, they necessarily need to be transferable, even if the legal

[19] Skauradszun (n 16) 490.

[20] Eg, German Code of Civil Procedure, ss 857(1), 851(1). See for the definition of a transfer of a digital asset the understanding of UNIDROIT (n 1) Principle 2(5).

[21] See I.

basis might still be unclear.[22] The factual feature of being transferable is without a doubt the case.

iii. Conclusion: Other Assets Include Digital Assets

Based on the explanations above, digital assets in the form of intrinsic crypto assets such as cryptocurrencies,[23] extrinsic crypto assets such as asset-referenced tokens, electronic securities and crypto securities constitute 'other assets' in the category of enforcement of movable property.[24]

C. The Need for a Catch-all Provision

Although this is a convincing outcome, the fundamental issue remains. The legal basis for treating digital assets as 'other assets' in the sense explained above is rather shaky. This is still the case, even though lately, some actions by the European legislator have strengthened the arguments presented above. Rather recent amendments of the MiFID II[25] by the DLT pilot regime[26] have widened the term 'financial instruments'. This term, as defined by MiFID II now covers financial instruments, including such instruments issued by means of distributed ledger technology. This indicates DLT-based financial instruments are generally to be considered financial instruments. Accordingly, they should be treated similarly when it comes to enforcement. Based on this, there seems to be no reason to understand DLT-based financial instruments as *improper* for enforcement and therefore *excluded* from enforcement. On the contrary, the aforementioned developments point in the opposite direction.

Regardless, the European and national legislators still have to think about a sufficient legal basis for enforcement in those financial instruments. Especially in the context of enforcement – a particularly invasive procedure directly affecting the debtor's property rights, ownership rights, or proprietary rights – there is a strong need for legal certainty regarding the applicable provisions. This, in turn, emphasises the need for adequate provisions dealing with digital assets. Being able

[22] See for a review of potential legal transfer mechanisms under German law at length D Skauradszun, 'Kryptowerte im Bürgerlichen Recht' (2021) 221 *Archiv für die civilistische Praxis* 353, 371 ff.

[23] For German law see A Bauer, *Die effektive Einzel- und Gesamtvollstreckung von Blockchain-basierten Kryptowährungen* (Berlin, Duncker & Humblot, 2023) 1, 150 ff.

[24] D Skauradszun, 'Durchbruch bei der Pfändung und Verwertung von Kryptowerten' [2021] *Zeitschrift für Wirtschafts- und Bankrecht – Wertpapier-Mitteilungen* 1229, 1232 ff; Skauradszun (n 16) 487.

[25] Directive 2014/65/EU of the European Parliament and of the Council of 15 May 2014 on markets in financial instruments and amending Directive 2002/92/EC and Directive 2011/61/EU [2014] OJ L173/349.

[26] Regulation 2022/858/EU of the European Parliament and of the Council of 30 May 2022 on a pilot regime for market infrastructures based on distributed ledger technology, and amending Regulations (EU) No 600/2014 and (EU) No 909/2014 and Directive 2014/65/EU [2022] OJ L151/1.

to coherently allocate their enforcement within the category of enforcement in movable property alone is not sufficient in this regard. A proper legal stipulation dealing with this issue remains desirable. The ideal solution would be a well-thought-out catch-all provision to encompass other assets that are neither physical objects, immovable property, nor claims.[27]

D. The Ideal Design of a Catch-all Provision

As the field of digital assets is still very dynamic, this catch-all provision need not and should not explicitly define the individual digital assets.[28] The established generic terms, such as crypto assets, electronic securities, and crypto securities, cover different variants. They will continue to do so, despite potential new developments brought forth by technology. Such future developments should be kept in mind whilst drafting the proposed catch-all provision.

The EU legislator has acted wisely when it comes to this topic. Within the MiCAR,[29] the European legislator has opted for a broad definition of crypto assets. The definition of distributed ledger technology is also rather broad. This ensures a lack of regulatory gaps, even if there are new developments in the field of digital assets that cannot be foreseen at this point. There is no need for these provisions to be adjusted frequently. This is a desired outcome for a new catch-all provision in the context of enforcement proceedings. A legislator – be it the European legislator or a national legislator – will hardly be able to keep up with new technological developments in the field of digital assets. This should be taken into consideration and emphasises the need for an all-encompassing catch-all provision.

E. Conclusion: A Catch-all Provision is Necessary

Considering all the arguments above, a conclusion can be drawn. There is indeed a need for a catch-all provision covering digital assets. This, however, is only the first necessary step in developing a coherent system for the enforcement of digital assets. It could be argued that this is merely the basis for an enforcement procedure. The second step is to differentiate the enforcement – as usual – between the attachment and the realisation. Both of these phases have peculiar characteristics. These peculiarities pose new challenges when it comes to enforcing digital assets. This will be discussed in the following part.

[27] See for German law Skauradszun (n 24) 1232 ff; Skauradszun (n 16) 487; regarding blockchain-based cryptocurrency Bauer (n 23) 150 ff.

[28] This is not necessarily required in enforcement law, see Skauradszun (n 24) 1232 ff.

[29] See recital 9 MiCAR: 'Union legislative acts on financial services should be guided by the principles (…) of technology neutrality.'

III. Involvement of Intermediaries

One peculiarity of enforcement against the above-mentioned digital assets is the possibility of further parties being involved in the enforcement proceedings. This starts off with a rather counterintuitive realisation: despite the general idea behind the distributed ledger technology and digital assets – especially cryptocurrencies – based on it,[30] such assets or the respective private keys are increasingly being placed in custody. This has even become an important business model. The financial businesses engaging in this type of business are called crypto custodians. As some digital assets may be issued by the issuer, effecting a registration in an electronic (crypto) register, there could also be a registrar entity[31] involved. This is, for instance, necessary in the case of electronic securities under the German Electronic Securities Act which also covers crypto securities.[32] In those scenarios, the enforcement against digital assets might involve intermediaries in the form of crypto custodians and registrar entities.

This adds another actor to the original three-person relationship between debtor, creditor, and third-party debtor. Consequently, it establishes a four- or even five-person relationship.[33] This multiple-person relationship leads to further frictions. National enforcement law regularly allows enforcement measures against a third party such as the third-party debtor. In many cases though, there is a noticeable lack of a legal basis to include intermediaries.[34] Once again, a variety of challenges ensue.

Major challenges are connected to procedural issues arising in a multiple-person relationship. This is rooted in the fact that many national enforcement laws have not envisioned the scenario of a four- or even five-person relationship.

A. First Challenge: Service of Court Orders

The multiple-person relationship raises questions in the context of service, such as the service of court orders.[35] At first sight, there is no clear answer to the question

[30] The original idea of cryptocurrencies and DLT was to achieve decentralisation by eliminating the need for intermediaries and the need to trust a central authority. 'Recordkeeping has always been a centralised process that requires trust in the record keeper. The most important innovation of DLT is that control over the ledger does not lie with any one entity but is with several or all network participants – depending on the type of DL', H Natarajan, S Krause and H Gradstein, *Distributed Ledger Technology (DLT) and Blockchain* (World Bank Group, 2017) 1, 5; see also for the crypto asset Bitcoin M McDermott, 'The Crypto Quandary: Is Bankruptcy Ready?' (2021) 115 *Northwestern University Law Review* 1921.

[31] Also known as registry administrator.

[32] See German Electronic Securities Act, ss 12(2) and 16(2).

[33] See for the German Electronic Securities Act Skauradszun (n 16) 506 ff.

[34] Eg, German Code of Civil Procedure, s 829(2) sentence 1.

[35] FT Yalabık and İ Yalabık, 'Anonymous Bitcoin v enforcement law' (2019) 33 *International Review of Law, Computers & Technology* 34, 38.

as to whom the court orders are served. But general principles of enforcement proceedings can help in determining this.

If enforcement law permits enforcement measures against a third-party debtor, it will also stipulate obligations to inform the third-party debtor of the enforcement. In addition to this, it will prohibit the third-party debtor from continuing to perform in relation to the debtor.[36] This seems to be a basic requirement suitable for being applied in a multiple-person relationship: if a fourth or even fifth person is in some way affected by enforcement measures, there is the necessity to inform and instruct said person.[37] Otherwise, enforcement measures could potentially end up being of no avail since the intermediaries will be needed to change the register or attribute the asset to a new person. As a result, a legal basis is needed to allow the court the service of court orders and, therefore, to instruct the intermediaries, namely the crypto custodian or registrar entity.[38] And such instructions are desperately needed. The intermediaries have to be prohibited from carrying out certain acts or from conducting these acts in a particular way contradicting the enforcement. This can only be achieved by involving the intermediary, which is only possible if the intermediary is informed of the enforcement measures and the instructions, eg, to no longer change the register on demand of the debtor but to change it when being instructed by an enforcement authority or the enforcing creditor. This involvement is initiated by serving the court orders for the attachment and realisation of digital assets to the intermediaries.

The problem remains that a legal basis for this may not exist in some national enforcement laws. However, service to the third-party debtor will normally be recognised, and a provision or established practice for this will usually exist. This might allow for these provisions to be applied *mutatis mutandis*. According to their wording, these provisions usually do not cover a fourth or even fifth person, however, they allow the service in a similar situation and, because of the unintentional legal lacuna and the comparable situation, can be applied by analogy.[39] This application by analogy allows for three major objectives of enforcement law to be achieved: first, to inform the affected party, in the case at hand, the intermediary; second, to instruct the affected party; and third, to protect the affected party that is acting in good faith. Intermediaries following the court orders are permitted to trust in the validity of the court orders and can, therefore, rightly claim to be protected if the court order has been lifted at a later time.[40] This appears to be a viable solution.[41]

[36] See, for an example, German Code of Civil Procedure, s 829(2) sentence 1.

[37] In case of a registry administrator under the German Electronic Securities Act, see Skauradszun (n 16) 493 ff.

[38] See UNIDROIT (n 1) 73.

[39] For electronic securities under German law see Skauradszun (n 16) 493 ff.

[40] See for a protecting provision under German law German Code of Civil Procedure, s 836(2).

[41] Some adaptions to national law are also considered advisable by UNIDROIT (n 1) 73.

B. Second Challenge: Involvement of the Debtor and Intermediary in the Enforcement of Digital Assets

Whereas the first challenge presented concerns serving the fourth or even fifth person, the second challenge relates to the fact that the debtor and the fourth or even fifth person will have to be involved in the enforcement proceedings. The debtor needs to be involved to even commence the enforcement proceedings, as this part of the analysis will demonstrate. Additionally, there may be digital assets for which realisation – such as an amendment to an entry of the assets on the blockchain or a change in another electronic register – requires the involvement of an intermediary, such as a registrar entity or crypto custodian. This is based on the common structure of enforcement proceedings. As already mentioned above, they can basically be divided into two different steps: first, the attachment of assets, and second, their realisation in order to settle the enforced money claim.[42] In both of those steps, some issues are problematic:

i. Attachment of Digital Assets – An Instance of Auxiliary Attachment

Enforcement of digital assets requires a change of ownership, which does not necessarily mean a change of property or proprietary rights in the traditional sense, but a kind of reallocation of the digital asset. By nature, enforcement proceedings will take place against the debtor's wishes. It is therefore reasonable to assume that the debtor will not be willing to support the enforcement of its assets. Accordingly, the enforcement will have to take place without the debtor being involved. Instead, the intermediary will have to be involved in some capacity. Whether and how a change of ownership can be enabled *without the debtor* but with the intermediary involved depends on the underlying technology. In the case of DLT-based digital assets, a change of ownership by the intermediary is usually not technically possible or not legally permitted.[43] In order for a change of ownership to occur, the debtor needs to provide information concerning their digital assets. Typical information required by the creditor to initiate state conducted enforcement proceedings involves the International Securities Identification Number (ISIN) of the electronic or crypto security, the name of the crypto custodian, the name of the registrar entity, the blockchain address (wallet) and, most commonly, the private key to the crypto assets.

[42] See Skauradszun (n 16) 500 ff.

[43] Because transactions on the Blockchain regularly require knowledge of the private key. In detail about the Blockchain-Technology see M Fromberger and P Zimmermann, 'Technische und rechtstatsächliche Grundlagen' in P Maume and L Maute (eds), *Rechtshandbuch Kryptowerte* (Munich, CH Beck, 2020) § 1 para 1 ff.

Essentially, the debtor will need to grant access to the wallet and private key. This also applies in cases in which the debtor keeps their private key with an intermediary such as a crypto custodian. This information is basically part of the enforcement proceedings.[44] And for this reason, it also needs to be attached. This scenario, in which information and access data (such as private keys) must also be attached and enforced, can be called auxiliary attachment.[45] But despite this possibility, there is still a looming, underlying problem. The mere possibility of auxiliary attachment does not automatically mean there is a way to practically obtain the information. To that extent, the debtor still needs to cooperate. Given the fact that the debtor will likely be unwilling to do so, this information needs to be obtained without their consent.[46]

This raises the question as to how this can be achieved. The debtor's behaviour could potentially be a severe hindrance to the enforcement proceedings. This needs to be overcome. For this, two possibilities come to mind. There could either be a coercive fine imposed on the debtor or they could be put into coercive detention.[47]

Even though 'detention' would imply a sort of punishment being imposed on the debtor, this is not the case. Instead, coercive fines as well as coercive detention intend to force the debtor to deliver the required information.[48] But even though these measures are not punitive by nature, they are still restricted. There are certain criteria to be met if the state wants to use such invasive measures. Namely, the state has to comply with the principle of proportionality when enforcing coercive measures.[49] To comply with this principle, the state has to balance a conflict of objectives. On the one hand, the state must ensure that its enforcement authorities can realise seized digital assets. This is in the interest of the creditor who initiated the enforcement proceedings. It is also in the interest of the state and, as such, the greater good: if the state monopolises enforcement proceedings, it needs to make sure they function properly. Otherwise, there is no justification for the state to prohibit enforcement proceedings from being conducted by a state's citizens.

On the other hand, the non-compliance with enforcement orders should not lead to measures being taken that are usually associated with criminal offences, unless this is absolutely necessary. A Solomonic approach would be to limit coercive fines in terms of the amount being fined and coercive detention in the maximum duration. Additionally, it seems just to make use of coercive fines first. If this does not lead to the debtor's compliance, coercive detention may be the next step. If coercive detention does not lead to the debtor complying, there is no more

[44] See UNIDROIT (n 1) 73.

[45] Yalabık and Yalabık (n 34) 41.

[46] This issue is also identified in UNIDROIT (n 1) 73.

[47] Skauradszun (n 24) 1236 ff; see in general under German law UP Gruber, 's 888' in W Krüger and T Rauscher (eds), *Münchener Kommentar zur Zivilprozessordnung*, 6th edn (Munich, CH Beck, 2020) para 1 ff.

[48] Skauradszun (n 24) 1236 ff.

[49] For German law, *cf* Gruber (n 46) para 27.

leeway to gather the necessary information. This is an unfortunate outcome, which the state will have to accept regardless. The enforcement of seized digital assets fails in this case.

ii. Realisation of Digital Assets – Involvement of the Intermediary

Besides the aforementioned (auxiliary) attachment, there is also a need to *realise* the digital assets to actually enforce the money claim. As explained above, the debtor will be reluctant to partake in this. But the success of the enforcement cannot depend on the willingness of the debtor in this regard. Accordingly, as soon as a creditor has successfully obtained an enforceable court order, a possibility to enforce this order must exist, even without the debtor partaking or giving their consent. This must be ensured by national enforcement law.

This calls for a way to substitute the debtor's involvement. The debtor's necessary part is to instruct the intermediary to act in accordance with the enforceable court order. Even though this is something that will have the greatest effect when coming from the person whose digital assets are affected by the court order, it seems possible to skip the debtor's involvement in this situation. There should be a way for the competent authority involved in the enforcement proceedings to directly address the intermediary and give instructions on how the enforcement proceedings should take place. Thereby, the involvement of the debtor can be substituted. But a stipulation dealing with this needs to grant the right to give legally binding orders to the intermediary. This is the only way to ensure enforcement proceedings are conducted effectively.[50] If the intermediaries were free to act at their own discretion when it comes to following the orders, they might not do so. This may be due to them fearing any sort of liability potentially arising in such a scenario. It may also be because they generally do not want to compromise their customers' trust by being too open towards any sort of governmental interference in their handling of crypto assets. In turn, the potential lack of cooperation by the intermediary would render enforcement proceedings inefficient. This is an undesirable outcome. Therefore, the orders given by the competent authority have to be legally binding.

Having said this, the issue is complex. If a measure taken by the competent authority is legally binding, the problem is not entirely resolved. There may be cases in which the intermediary refuses to participate in the enforcement proceedings. This brings up the question as to how the intermediaries' compliance with respect to the attachment or realisation order can be ensured.[51] The answer to this lies in the field of regulatory law. Wherever European regulatory law or national regulatory law places the service of the intermediaries under the supervision of

[50] There might be the need for a freezing order or an order transferring control of the digital assets to an authority in order to stop the digital assets from being transferred, see UNIDROIT (n 1) 74.

[51] This is also mentioned in UNIDROIT (n 1) 73.

competent supervisory authorities, regulatory law might be an instrument to pressure intermediaries into complying with court orders concerning the attachment or realisation of digital assets. An intermediary's board of directors that fails to comply with court orders will give the impression of being unreliable. Reliability is a key requirement for directors of supervised intermediaries (eg, MiCAR, art 68(1)). This requirement not being met by the directors is reason enough for the intermediary to revoke the director's appointment. From a German perspective, this approach appears suitable when it comes to crypto custodians, which are currently governed by European (MiCAR, art 59 et seqq.) and German law[52] and therefore supervised by the financial supervisory authority, the BaFin.

C. Enforcement is Possible Even with Intermediaries, Yet Complicated

The arguments presented above would suggest enforcement proceedings remain possible, even within a multiple-person relationship. The analysis still goes to show to what extent the involvement of an intermediary complicates enforcement proceedings. To solve all the above-mentioned problems, it has to be ensured that the intermediaries are served the court orders and have said orders be legally binding for them. This is the only way to ensure effective enforcement. The same train of thought applies to the issue of the change in ownership. It has to be possible for this to happen without the debtor being involved. The technology involved in the case at hand will play a prominent role in this. In general, European and national supervisory law may be helpful to ensure an effective enforcement proceeding.

IV. Conclusion

Digital assets pose new challenges and issues for many areas of law. This is particularly true regarding enforcement proceedings of money claims involving digital assets. The frictions associated with this are difficult to reduce. An attempt to reduce these frictions should be based on a thorough analysis of the possibility of applying existing enforcement laws to digital assets and what such an application could look like. In many national enforcement law systems, digital assets may very

[52] German Banking Act (KWG), s 1(1a) sentence 1, sentence 2 no 6, (1b). See for the reliability requirement under German law KWG, s 25c(1) and the potential instruction by the supervisory authority to revoke the managing director's appointment KWG, s 36(3) sentence 1 no 1. In the near future, crypto custodians in Germany will be subject to the Crypto Markets Supervision Act (Kryptomärkteaufsichtsgesetz – KMAG). This legislation serves to ensure the effective application of MiCAR in Germany. See for non-compliance with an instruction as a reason for measures by the supervisory authority, D Linardatos, 's 23' in D Skauradszun and D Linardatos (eds), *Kryptomärkteaufsichtsgesetz*, 1st edn (Baden-Baden, Nomos, 2025, forthcoming) para 7.

well fall under the category of other enforceable assets. This is an example of existing provisions still being suitable to deal with digital assets, which only need to be assisted by a catch-all provision to erase legal uncertainties.

A similar approach appears possible when it comes to the existing stipulations on the service of court orders. This constellation leads to entirely new legal questions, which may not be adequately answered by national law in many instances. A key issue here is the four- or even five-person relationship often arising when digital assets are involved. National enforcement law is not always designed to encompass these multiple-person relationships and specific characteristics of digital assets in general. But they can be applied within a four- or even five-person relationship by analogy and cover service to intermediaries as well. This will ensure the service procedure fulfills its purpose.

Furthermore, obtaining the information necessary for the required change of ownership can be achieved by means of an auxiliary attachment. In case the debtor refuses to provide this information, there is the possibility of coercive measures being taken. In this regard, the general principles of law, such as the principle of proportionality, have to be respected. When it comes to ensuring compliance of the intermediary, utilising measures located in the field of supervisory law appears sensible. Through this approach, it is ensured that the intermediary will follow and oblige court orders. Its cooperation is thus likely. This chapter outlines that although the existing stipulations within the field of enforcement law are often not tailored to digital assets, effective enforcement may still be achieved. But nonetheless, to avoid remaining legal uncertainties and to further stabilise the legal foundation for these enforcement proceedings, the European and national legislators should act to introduce further legal provisions, thereby ensuring a well-thought-out legal framework covering all digital assets – both already existing digital assets and digital assets still to be developed in the future – in enforcement proceedings.

7

How to Find Digital Assets of the Debtor – A View from Practice of Insolvency Administration

ANNA K WILKE

I. Introduction

Digital assets have been increasingly pushing their way into the focus of experienced, but also inexperienced investors for several years now. They are intangible assets that are created, traded, and stored in a digital format. Digital assets include crypto tokens and electronic securities. The following chapter discusses how the insolvency administrator can track down the debtor's digital assets under German law, as well as how seizure and realisation can occur.

II. Crypto Tokens

A. General Facts

Crypto tokens are digital units of value that are transferred via a decentralised network, called the blockchain.[1] A blockchain is a database like a register,[2] in which all transactions that a user has ever carried out are stored and remain verifiable.[3] In the blockchain network, the peer-to-peer principle applies.[4] The

[1] M Fromberger, L Haffke and P Zimmerman, 'Kryptowerte und Geldwäsche: Eine Analyse der 5. Geldwäscherichtlinie sowie des Gesetzesentwurfs der Bundesregierung' [2019] *Zeitschrift für Bank- und Kapitalmarktrecht* 377.

[2] ibid.

[3] F Boehm and P Pesch, 'Bitcoins: Rechtliche Herausforderungen einer virtuellen Währung: Eine erste juristische Einordung' [2014] *Zeitschrift für IT-Recht und Recht der Digitalisierung* 75, 76.

[4] M d'Avoine and P Hamacher, 'Kryptowährungen im Insolvenzverfahren' [2022] *Zeitschrift für Wirtschaftsrecht* 6.

participants in the network (peers) have equal rights.[5] In contrast to the usual money systems, where intermediaries such as banks are interposed, a transaction within the blockchain takes place directly between the individual peers.[6] All transaction information is stored in blocks and strung together.[7] The blocks are encrypted and thus concatenated. The data is not stored on a central computer, but on each individual computer in the network. The data stock is thus protected from local damage events.[8] Participation in blockchain transactions requires two cryptographic keys, the public key and the private key. The public key is comparable to an account number and is used to determine the payment recipient.[9] The public key makes it possible for everyone within the network to see who owns the current crypto asset.[10] By using the public key, the transaction procedure is also pseudonymised.[11] The private key enables the user to transfer his own tokens to the recipient's public key. It is comparable to the PIN code of a debit card.[12] It ensures that only the owner can use his crypto value and that others are excluded from access. The private key is stored in a crypto wallet. Crypto wallets come in the form of websites or apps (software wallets). But there are also devices that store the private key and are not permanently connected to the internet (hardware wallets). Storing crypto assets in a self-managed wallet entails certain risks.

If you forget the private key or third parties get hold of the private key, for example, through hacker attacks, access to the crypto assets can quickly become impossible forever.[13] According to a 2020 study by Cane Island Alternative Advisors, LLC, 4 percent of available Bitcoin is lost each year because, for example, private keys are forgotten or hardware wallets are lost.[14] Large investors in particular therefore feel the need for professional storage of their crypto assets. In recent years, many companies have developed a crypto custody business within the meaning of Section 1 para 1a sentence 2 no. 6 of the German Banking Act (KWG). Crypto custody business includes the safekeeping, administration and securing of crypto assets or private cryptographic keys for the purpose of holding, storing or disposing of crypto assets for others. The peer-to-peer principle, which is typical for blockchain technology, is softened by the interposition of these custodians as intermediaries.[15] In crypto custody, crypto assets are transferred to wallets of

[5] ibid.
[6] Boehm and Pesch (n 3) 75.
[7] d'Avoine and Hamacher (n 4) 7.
[8] ibid.
[9] Fromberger, Haffke and Zimmermann (n 1) 378; d'Avoine and Hamacher (n 4) 7.
[10] Fromberger, Haffke and Zimmermann (n 1) 378 et seq.
[11] M Fromberger and P Zimmermann in P Maume and L Maute (eds), *Rechtshandbuch Kryptowerte* (Munich, CH Beck/Vahlen, 2020) ch 1, 6.
[12] d'Avoine and Hamacher (n 4) 7.
[13] S Schröder and I Triantafyllakis, 'Kryptowerte in der Insolvenz des Kryptoverwahrers: Massebefangen oder aussonderbar?' [2023] *Zeitschrift für Bank- und Kapitalmarktrecht* 12, 13.
[14] Cane Island Alternative Advisors, LLC, 'There Will Never Be More Than 14 Million Bitcoins, Research Note', 2020, 3, available at: static1.squarespace.com/static/5d580747908cdc0001e6792d/t/5e98dde5558a587a09fac0cc/1587076583519/research+note+4.17.pdf.
[15] Schröder and Triantafyllakis (n 13) 12.

crypto custodians (custodial wallet, provider-dependent wallet). The advantage of professional custody is that the custodian companies specialise in securing crypto assets and comply with the latest security standards to protect them from hacker attacks, for example. The custodian may only dispose of the tokens in custody based on an instruction from the customer.[16]

Crypto tokens can be divided into three different types. Currency tokens function as a means of payment.[17] Utility tokens embody a claim and can be compared to digital vouchers.[18] These tokens are issued by an emitter and can be redeemed with the emitter for the service owed.[19] Investment tokens are also issued by an emitter. With this type of token, the ownership includes, for example, participation rights in the issuer's profits, payment claims, and co-determination rights.[20] The cryptocurrency Bitcoin had a value of $68,000 in 2021 and now has a value of around $25,000.[21] The reason for the high value of Bitcoin is partly because many people want to invest their assets in a 'safe' way and exclude outside access. However, if the goal is to store one's assets in such a way that no one else can access them, what is the situation in insolvency proceedings? Does the insolvency administrator have access to the debtor's digital assets, and how can they be located?

B. Crypto Tokens as Objects of the Insolvency Estate

The purpose of German insolvency proceedings is the equal satisfaction of creditors, which is to be achieved by the best possible realisation of the debtor's assets, Section 1 German Insolvency Code (InsO). In this context, the insolvency administrator may liquidate all assets that form part of the insolvency estate. Pursuant to Section 35 InsO, the insolvency estate includes the assets belonging to the debtor at the time of commencement of the proceedings and whatever he acquires during the proceedings. Although the InsO speaks of 'all assets', this only refers to the part of the debtor's assets for which he is liable.[22] For digital assets to be part of the insolvency estate at all, they must be subject to foreclosure, Section 36 para 1 sentence 1 InsO.[23]

[16] ibid 15.

[17] Fromberger and Zimmermann (n 11) ch 1, 20; U Kleinert and V Mayer, 'Elektronische Wertpapiere und Krypto-Token: Aktuelle Rechtslage und die Blockchain-Strategie der Bundesregierung vom 18.9.2019' [2019] *Europäische Zeitschrift für Wirtschaftsrecht* 857, 858.

[18] Fromberger and Zimmermann (n 11) ch 1, 20; Kleinert and Mayer (n 17) 858.

[19] ibid.

[20] Fromberger and Zimmermann (n 11) ch 1, 20.

[21] On 10 November 2021: $68,763, available at: www.finanzen.net/devisen/bitcoin-dollar-kurs/historisch.

[22] H Hirte and JP Praß, 's 35 InsO' in H Hirte and H Vallender (eds), *Uhlenbruck Insolvenzordnung*, 15th edn (Munich, Franz Vahlen, 2019) para 13.

[23] ibid.

i. Foreclosure for Monetary Claims

It is disputed in the literature according to which provisions of the German Civil Procedure Code (ZPO) can be enforced for monetary claims in crypto tokens.[24] There is an agreement that a seizure of property pursuant to Sections 808 et seq. ZPO is ruled out because tokens are not physical objects pursuant to Section 90 German Civil Code (BGB) due to their lack of physical separability.[25] It is also not possible to seize and transfer currency tokens according to Sections 829, 835 ZPO. Currency tokens are not monetary claims. Electronic money is characterised by the fact that it establishes a claim for conversion into cash against a central body. Within the decentralised blockchain network, however, there is no such central body against which a corresponding claim could be directed.[26] Moreover, there is no obligation to accept currency tokens as 'money' in Section 245 ZPO.[27] When joining the blockchain network, the participants do not want to enter into a contractual obligation from which such claims can be derived.[28] They lack a corresponding intention to be legally bound.[29] Section 1 para 11 sentence 4 KWG also stipulates that currency tokens are not to be equated with money. Investment and utility tokens give rise to claims, but they are more than just claims.[30] Moreover, the claims they embody are only covered by Sections 829 et seq. if they are monetary claims.

One may think of the classification of cryptocurrencies as other property rights, which are attachable pursuant to Section 857 para 1 ZPO. In the case of crypto tokens, this would have to be a different property right.[31] There is broad agreement that currency tokens do not represent relative rights.[32] However, it is disputed whether absolute rights exist in crypto tokens. The data set describing a token is not software within the meaning of Section 69a of the Copyright Act (UrhG).[33] Moreover, no other enumerative ancillary copyrights under the UrhG are relevant for crypto tokens.[34] Only absolute immaterial legal right *sui generis* comes into consideration. Representatives of such an absolute right consider the necessary requirements to be fulfilled. By assigning a token to the public key of the holder, a token can be assigned to a specific person. Only the holder can dispose of the token with his private key. Free use of the token by the holder and

[24] M Strauch and B Handke in P Maume and L Maute (n 11) ch 2, 266.

[25] Strauch and Handke (n 24) ch 2, 266; D Skauradszun, 'Kryptowerte im Insolvenzverfahren des Anlegers oder Emittenten' [2021] *Zeitschrift für Wirtschaftsrecht* 2610, 2612.

[26] Strauch and Handke (n 24) ch 2, 267.

[27] ibid.

[28] Skauradszun (n 25) 2612.

[29] F Boehm and I Bruns, 'Digitale Währungen am Beispiel Bitcoin' in P Bräutigam and D Rücker, *E-Commerce* (Munich, CH Beck, 2017) 974–88; Strauch and Handke (n 24) ch 2, 267.

[30] *cf* Strauch and Handke (n 24) ch 2, 270–71.

[31] Strauch and Handke (n 24) ch 2, 267; Boehm and Bruns (n 29) 977; Skauradszun (n 25) 2613.

[32] Skauradszun (n 25) 2612; L Maute in P Maume and L Maute (n 11) ch 2, 114.

[33] Boehm and Bruns (n 29) 977.

[34] Strauch and Handke (n 24) ch 2, 267.

the possibility of excluding others from using it are guaranteed by the private key. The necessary conditions for an absolute right – allocation, use and exclusion[35] – are fulfilled. This argues for currency tokens to qualify as other property rights.[36] In order for the 'other property right' within the meaning of Section 857 para 1 ZPO to be seized, the requirement of transferability pursuant to Section 851 ZPO must be met due to the reference to the provisions on the enforcement of claims.[37] However, since 1 January 2020, this has not been a problem because the introduction of the legal definition of crypto assets in Section 1 para 11 sentence 4 KWG has stipulated that they are transferable. A counter-opinion rejects an absolute immaterial legal right in relation to crypto-tokens.[38] According to case law, new absolute rights must in principle be created by the legislator.[39] In exceptional cases, absolute rights can be derived on the basis of fundamental rights or the synopsis of legal valuations, for example, the general right of personality.[40] However, for such a further development of the law, a regulatory gap is required.[41] Such a gap does not exist in the case of crypto tokens, since the purpose of an absolute right – protection against impairment of integrity – is already guaranteed by blockchain technology.[42] The blockchain technology binds possibilities of influence and excludes negligent impairments of integrity.[43] As long as the blockchain is operated, the integrity of a token is guaranteed.[44] If one rejects the classification of crypto tokens as absolute rights, an analogous application of Section 857 ZPO comes into consideration. Both a direct and a corresponding application of Section 857 ZPO lead to the fact that Section 829 ZPO must also be applied accordingly.[45] This is because there are no relative rights within the blockchain network related to currency tokens. Therefore, there is no third-party debtor within the meaning of Section 829 ZPO. It is problematic that the blockchain system is

[35] G Wagner, 's 823 BGB' in FJ Säcker et al. (eds), *Münchener Kommentar zum Bürgerlichen Gesetzbuch*, 8th edn (Munich, CH Beck, 2020) para 303.

[36] G Spindler and M Bille, 'Rechtsprobleme von Bitcoins als virtuelle Währung' [2014] *Zeitschrift für Wirtschafts- und Bankrecht* 1357, 1363; L Shmatenko and S Möllenkamp, 'Digitale Zahlungsmittel in einer analog geprägten Rechtsordnung: A bit(coin) out of control – Rechtsnatur und schuldrechtliche Behandlung von Kryptowährungen' [2018] *Zeitschrift für IT-Recht und Recht der Digitalisierung* 495, 498 et seq; D Linardatos, 'Der Mythos vom "Realakt" bei der Umbuchung von Bitcoins – Gedanken zur dinglichen Erfassung von Kryptowährungen' in E Beyer et al. (eds), *Privatrecht 2050 – Blick in die digitale Zukunft* (Baden-Baden, Nomos, 2020) 181, 205; D Skauradszun, 'Kryptowerte im Bürgerlichen Recht' [2021] *Archiv für die civilistische Praxis* 353, 369 et seq.

[37] J Flockenhaus, 's 857 ZPO' in HJ Musielak and W Voit (eds), *Zivilprozessordnung mit Gerichtsverfassungsgesetz*, 20th edn (Munich, Franz Vahlen, 2023) para 1; F Krüger, 'Bitcoin (BTC) und andere Kryptowährungen als verwertbare Insolvenzmasse' [2022] *Zeitschrift für das gesamte Insolvenzrecht* 1261, 1264.

[38] Maute (n 32) ch 2, 125.

[39] *cf* BGH, NJW 2005, 3353; Maute (n 32) ch 2, 117.

[40] BGH, NJW 1954, 1404.

[41] Maute (n 32) ch 2, 121.

[42] ibid.

[43] ibid.

[44] ibid.

[45] Strauch and Handke (n 24) ch 2, 268.

based on the fact that every acquisition of tokens by means of a private key is effective. The *inhibitorium* brought about by the seizure is therefore not intended to lead to the relative invalidity of a right in the seized token vis-à-vis the execution creditor.[46] A restriction of the marketability of the tokens by means of seizure liens would simply not be accepted by the blockchain participants and would also hardly be implementable in practice.[47]

Furthermore, a corresponding application of Sections 808 et seqq. for the compulsory enforcement of tokens due to monetary claims can be considered.[48] Currency tokens are comparable to money.[49] In the case of seizure of property pursuant to Sections 808 et seq., seizure prevents the debtor from preventing the enforcement purpose by using the asset. The transfer of the tokens to a wallet of the insolvency administrator is equivalent to such a taking of possession.[50] All views conclude that crypto tokens are subject to enforcement for monetary claims.

ii. Foreclosure of Titles Directed to Tokens

For the enforcement of titles directed to crypto tokens, Sections 887 et seq. ZPO are applicable. An analogous application of Sections 883 et seq. ZPO is out of the question because there is no regulatory gap, as the possibility of enforcement according to Sections 887 et seq. ZPO exists.[51] If the title is directed to the surrender of certain individual tokens, only the holder of the private key can transfer them. There is no fungible act, and Section 887 ZPO is relevant.[52] If the title is directed to the surrender of a credit balance of tokens, a third party may also make a corresponding transfer of tokens to the execution creditor at the debtor's expense. In this case, there is a fungible act, and Section 888 ZPO is relevant.[53] Overall, it can be stated that tokens are subject to foreclosure. Crypto tokens are therefore part of the insolvency estate (Section 36 InsO).

C. Acquisition of Knowledge

Before the insolvency administrator can take possession of crypto tokens (Section 148 para 1 InsO), he must have knowledge of these assets. The insolvency application forms do not yet contain any specific query about crypto assets. Difficulties in determining crypto assets may arise if the debtor does not provide voluntary information.

[46] ibid.

[47] DO Effer-Uhe, 'Kryptowährungen in Zwangsvollstreckung und Insolvenz am Beispiel des Bitcoin' [2018] *Zeitschrift für Zivilprozess* 513, 517; Strauch and Handke (n 24) ch 2, 268.

[48] Strauch and Handke (n 24) ch 2, 269.

[49] ibid.

[50] ibid.

[51] ibid 272.

[52] ibid 271–72.

[53] ibid 271–72.

i. Problems with the Anonymity of the Blockchain

The first step of the insolvency administrator in the initial meeting is to ask the debtor whether he is in possession of digital assets of any kind. In principle, the debtor is obliged to provide information on all circumstances relating to the proceedings, Sections 97 para 1, 101 InsO. In this context, information must be provided on assets located both in Germany and abroad. Particularly in the case of crypto assets, however, there is the difficulty that they entail a certain anonymity. Within the network of crypto tokens, all participants can track transactions, which are stored in the blockchain. The blockchain represents a kind of decentralised cash book to which every user has online access.[54] There is no central administration to document transactions. Each participant has his own cash book with all transactions of all participants, which he must maintain himself. A block is the documentation of all transactions of a certain period of time. The blocks are cryptographically linked to each other. By chaining the blocks in a certain order, it is excluded that a manipulation of the transactions can take place, because an intervention would require a recalculation of all transactions, which is considered technically impossible.[55] The problem is that only the pseudonyms of the users are stored in the blockchain.[56] So everyone can see the pseudonym, but it is not so easy to determine which identity is hidden behind it.

Tracking blockchain transactions can be made almost impossible by using so-called tumblers.[57] Here, tokens are first transferred to the public key of the tumbler service. The service has several public keys of its own. The tokens are transferred under these public keys and mixed with tokens of other users of the tumbler service.[58] Afterwards, the corresponding number of tokens is transferred to the recipient. In this way, the recipient receives the correct number of tokens, but the sender's public key can no longer be found out. This anonymity of the blockchain may tempt the debtor not to disclose information about his crypto assets.[59] In order to enforce the debtor's obligations to cooperate, the insolvency administrator has the measures pursuant to Section 98 InsO at his disposal. Pursuant to Section 98 para 1 sentence 1 InsO, the insolvency administrator may apply to the insolvency court for the debtor to affirm in lieu of an oath that, to the best of his knowledge and belief, he has provided the information requested correctly and in full. The affirmation in lieu of an oath is punishable by law. In addition, the insolvency administrator can obtain information on the debtor's bank accounts via Sections 98 para 1a InsO, 802l para 1 sentence 1 ZPO.[60] The insolvency court

[54] H Wilsch, 'Die Blockchain-Technologie aus der Sicht des deutschen Grundbuchrechts' [2017] *Deutsche Notar-Zeitschrift* 761, 762.

[55] E Sixt, *Bitcoins und andere dezentrale Transaktionssysteme* (Wiesbaden, Springer Gabler, 2017) 30.

[56] Krüger (n 37) 1265.

[57] Working draft of the Federal Ministry of Finance, Kryptowertetransferverordnung, status 11 May 2021, 6; Krüger (n 37) 1265.

[58] Fromberger, Haffke and Zimmermann (n 1) 379.

[59] D'Avoine and Hamacher (n 4) 9 ff.

[60] A Forbriger, 's 802l BGB' in T Rauscher and W Krüger (n 35) para 28.

may have the debtor brought before it by force and order compulsory detention for a maximum of six months if the debtor fails to comply with his duty to provide information (Sections 98 para 2 and 3 InsO in conjunction with 802g para 2, 802h and 802j para 1 ZPO). Should the debtor endure the period of detention, further coercive measures under the InsO are not available. To persuade the debtor to provide information, the insolvency administrator should point out to him that the violation of duties to cooperate pursuant to Sections 300 para 3, 290 para 1 No. 5 InsO may result in the denial of residual debt discharge if the debtor is a natural person.

ii. 'Local' Data of the Debtor

Pursuant to Section 22 para 3 sentence 2 InsO, the preliminary insolvency administrator has the right to inspect the debtor's books and business papers. The powers of the preliminary insolvency administrator also apply to the 'normal' insolvency administrator.[61] Furthermore, the business books belong to the insolvency estate pursuant to Section 36 para 2 No. 1 InsO. The power of disposal over invoices, cash vouchers, payrolls[62] etc, is therefore vested in the insolvency administrator pursuant to Sections 21 para 1, 22 in the preliminary proceedings and Section 80 para 1 InsO. Since these are now stored in digital form, the insolvency administrator has the right to access corresponding data on the debtor's data carriers, for example, PC or mobile devices.[63] A look at the bookkeeping under the asset item 'other assets' could provide information about crypto assets in current or fixed assets if the bookkeeping is in order. A look at tax returns or notices can also be helpful.

iii. Communication Data

If no information about crypto assets is found in the debtor's records, it may be necessary to check the debtor's communications for relevant references. The debtor's communication data is protected by the basic communication rights pursuant to Article 10 para 1 of the German Constitution, the 'Grundgesetz' (GG).[64] The general purpose of insolvency law does not yet justify any encroachment on these fundamental rights.[65] Access to the debtor's communication data is only justified under Article 10 para 2 GG if there is a sufficiently clearly formulated legal

[61] M Jaffé, 's 148 InsO' in R Stürner, H Eidenmüller and H Schoppmeyer (eds), *Münchener Kommentar zur Insolvenzordnung*, 4th edn (Munich, CH Beck, 2019) para 67.

[62] K Jungmann and S Zündorf, 'Insolvenzrechtliche "Postsperren" im Zeitalter digitaler Kommunikation' [2021] *Zeitschrift für Insolvenzrecht* 513, 516.

[63] O Spiekermann, 'Ermittlungsmethoden des Sachverständigen und des vorläufigen Insolvenzverwalters im Insolvenzantragsverfahren' [2022] *Neue Zeitschrift für Insolvenz- und Sanierungsrecht* 841, 844; Jungmann, Zündorf (n 62) 516.

[64] Jungmann and Zündorf (n 62) 517.

[65] ibid.

basis.[66] Such a basis – at least for communication by post – is the postal block pursuant to Section 99 InsO. According to this, the insolvency court can order, upon application or ex officio, that the companies carrying out postal traffic must forward all mail addressed to the debtor to the insolvency administrator. In relation to crypto assets, communication with the various parties involved is likely to be almost exclusively through electronic means. Whether Section 99 InsO can also be applied to electronic communication such as emails or communication via messenger services like 'WhatsApp' and Co, is questionable.[67] Section 99 InsO contains the concept of transmission. This means that once the postal block has been ordered, the insolvency administrator will be the new recipient of all mail sent to the debtor. The debtor will therefore no longer receive any mail, which will instead be forwarded to the administrator. It is questionable how this principle can be technically implemented.

The applicability of Section 99 InsO to emails is widely affirmed in the literature.[68] This is because, for example, in the case of email traffic, a practical implementation of the concept of transmission is conceivable by obliging providers to forward emails to the insolvency administrator.[69] In the case of messaging services, however, the principle of forwarding leads to communication coming to a standstill.[70] This is because, according to the principle of transmission, the insolvency administrator is the new recipient of the messages instead of the debtor. Since he has no possibility to reply, a typical two-way communication via messaging services will come to a standstill relatively quickly. Moreover, the operators, most of whom are based abroad, will be reluctant to cooperate. The Federal Constitutional Court of Germany ('Bundesverfassungsgericht') has ruled that the freezing of emails stored in the domain of a provider (for the purposes of criminal proceedings) must be measured against Article 10 para 1 GG.[71] In doing so, it established that the communication process protected by this Article does not end when the mail arrives on the provider's server. Nowadays, emails are usually no longer downloaded to one's own local server. When emails are stored on an external provider server, they are not 'local' data. Because the communication process has not been completed, the data is still subject to the protection of Article 10 para 1 GG. Therefore, the insolvency administrator cannot obtain information solely based on Sections 80, 148 InsO, and Sections 97, 101 InsO.[72]

It is questionable whether the insolvency administrator can access emails stored on external provider servers via Section 99 InsO. Because the communication

[66] ibid 535.

[67] ibid 525.

[68] H Zipperer, 's 99 InsO' in H Hirte and H Vallender (n 22) para 6; G Stephan, 's 99 InsO' in R Stürner, H Eidenmüller and H Schoppmeyer (n 61) para 20; M Lojowsky, 's 99 InsO' in E Braun (ed), *Insolvenzordnung (Inso)*, 9th edn (Munich, CH Beck, 2022) para 3.

[69] Jungmann and Zündorf (n 62) 524; Stephan (n 68) para 20.

[70] Jungmann and Zündorf (n 62) 525.

[71] BVerfG, NJW 2009, 2431.

[72] Jungmann and Zündorf (n 62) 535.

process has not yet ended, the scope of Section 99 InsO is open. According to the case law of the 'Bundesverfassungsgericht', when mails are stored on external servers, the communication process can, in case of doubt, continue indefinitely.[73] By analogous application of Section 99 InsO, the insolvency administrator could access email correspondence that existed long before the mail block was ordered. However, Section 99 of the Insolvency Code only covers email that was 'sent' after the postal blocking order was issued.[74] Access to 'older' emails is not covered by Section 99 InsO.[75] As an interim result, it should be noted that the insolvency administrator can access 'local' data within the debtor's sphere of control based on his power of disposal pursuant to Sections 80, 148 InsO. Communication data stored on external servers can only be accessed via Section 99 InsO if they were sent to the debtor after the postal blocking order. The insolvency administrator has a right of access to data other than communication data stored in the cloud by virtue of his power of disposal under Sections 80, 148 InsO, since the protection of Article 10 para 1 GG does not require an extra basis for intervention here.[76]

iv. Possibilities for a New Version of Section 99 InsO

Crypto tokens are highly fungible assets that can be quickly liquidated in the market. The tracing of crypto assets by the insolvency administrator must be done as quickly as possible, because some debtors will be inclined to transfer their crypto assets in order to make them inaccessible to the insolvency administrator. To provide the insolvency administrator with an effective means of quickly tracking down crypto assets, Section 99 InsO should be adapted to today's technical realities. The term 'mail' should be changed to a term that covers all types of electronic communication.[77] 'Companies' within the meaning of Section 99 InsO must not only be postal service providers. Rather, all types of providers must be included.[78] Considering the urgency of tracking down crypto assets of the debtor, a new version of Section 99 InsO should distance itself from the concept of transmission. The insolvency administrator should not have to wait for coincidence but should have a claim for information against the provider.[79]

v. Transaction Data in Crypto-transactions

Since 1 October 2021, the so-called 'Travel Rule' of the Financial Action Task Force (FATF) has been implemented in Germany by the Ordinance on Increased Due

[73] M Martini, 'Art 10 Grundgesetz' in A Kämmerer and M Kotzur (eds), *von Münch/Kunig Grundgesetz-Kommentar*, 7th edn (Munich, CH Beck, 2021) para 76; Jungmann and Zündorf (n 62) 532, 535.

[74] Jungmann and Zündorf (n 62) 538.

[75] ibid 539.

[76] ibid 542.

[77] ibid 545.

[78] ibid.

[79] ibid 546.

Diligence for the Transfer of Crypto Assets (KryptoWTransferV) of the Federal Ministry of Finance.[80] The FATF is an international institution that sets standards for combating money laundering and terrorist financing. Recommendation 16 of the FATF requires states to create a system for collecting information on the identity of principals and recipients of crypto transactions (Travel Rule). The KryptoWTransferV implements the Travel Rule only for transactions between a crypto value service provider and a further obligated party pursuant to Section 2 No. 1 KryptoWTransferV. Crypto value service providers include wallet providers, crypto custodians or crypto exchanges.[81] If the further obligated party is also a crypto value service provider, the obligated parties must apply Articles 4 and 6 as well as 7, 8 and 9 of Regulation (EU) 2015/847[82] accordingly in the case of a transaction pursuant to Section 3 KryptoWTransferV. This means that for a transaction of crypto assets, information about the name of the principal, his public key, and address, as well as the number of an official document or the birthday/place of birth of the principal, the name of the recipient and his public key must be transmitted. This information must be verified and stored by the recipient (Article 7 paras 3, 4, 5 Regulation [EU] 2015/847). If a crypto value service provider is only active on one side of the transaction, obligated parties must assess the risk of abuse of the transaction for money laundering and terrorist financing purposes and take appropriate measures (Section 4 paras 1, 2 KryptoWTransferV). In particular, this includes the collection, storage and verification of the name and address of the transaction participant for whom no crypto value service provider is acting.

Inspection of this data would make it much easier for the insolvency administrator to track down crypto assets of the debtor. However, this hardly seems possible with the existing legal situation. The KryptoWTransferV says nothing about the conditions under which the collected data may be forwarded by the obligated parties. However, the method of using the KryptoWTransferV to transfer crypto values into the scope of Regulation (EU) 2015/847 suggests that the provisions of Regulation (EU) 2015/847 must also be applied regarding the further treatment of the data. If Article 14 of Regulation (EU) 2015/847 is applied accordingly, only the competent authority for anti-money-laundering and counterterrorism of the respective Member State may access the transaction data. In Germany, this is the Financial Intelligence Unit (FIU) according to Section 27 of the Money Laundering Act (GwG). This authority may only pass on the transaction data to other agencies in certain cases (Section 32 GwG). The disclosure to a bailiff or insolvency administrator is explicitly not regulated. The same problems are likely to exist if the CryptoWTransferV expires pursuant to Section 7 para 2

[80] K Hirzle and J Hugendubel, 'Die Entwicklung des Kryptorechts im Jahr 2022' [2022] *Zeitschrift für Bank- und Kapitalmarktrecht* 821, 828.

[81] A Patz, 'Überblick über die Regulierung von Kryptowerten und Kryptowertedienstleistern' [2021] *Zeitschrift für Bank- und Kapitalmarktrecht* 725, 731.

[82] Regulation (EU) 2015/847 of the European Parliament and the Council of 20 May 2015 on information accompanying transfers of funds and repealing Regulation (EC) No 1781/2006 [2015] OJ L141/1.

CryptoWTransferV when the new version of Regulation (EU) 2015/847 enters into force. The then applicable new version of Regulation (EU) 2015/847, which also includes crypto assets and implements the Travel Rule, does not establish any substantively different rules, at least in the current draft.[83]

A regulation in Section 32 GwG similar to Section 93 para 8 sentence 3 of the German Tax Code (AO) would be desirable. Section 93 AO regulates that the Federal Central Tax Office retrieves and passes on account information according to Section 93b paras 1, 1a AO upon request in cases determined by law. Such a statutory provision is found in Section 802l para 1 sentence 1 no. 2 ZPO.[84] Section 802l ZPO could be supplemented by a number authorising the bailiff to request the FIU to retrieve transaction information of the debtor from obligors within the meaning of the KryptoWTransferV. An extension of this provision to the effect that the insolvency administrator can obtain information on whether and which public keys are assigned to the debtor is desirable. This would make it much easier to find out whether the debtor has crypto assets.

vi. Other Measures

The insolvency administrator may search the debtor's tax records for evidence of digital assets. In its decisions of 30 August 2012[85] and 17 October 2012,[86] the Berlin Administrative Court ruled that the insolvency administrator has a claim for information against the tax office regarding the debtor's tax data under section 3 para 1 sentence 1 of the Berlin Freedom of Information Act. In most cases, the insolvency administrator will have such a claim for information under the respective freedom of information laws of the federal states, which is enforceable through administrative law.[87] In federal states that do not have their own Freedom of Information Act, such claims can only be asserted on the basis of the principle of the rule of law in conjunction with the fundamental right of freedom of occupation (Article 12 para 1 GG) as well as the fundamental right of process (Article 19 para 4 GG).[88] The insolvency administrator may learn of the debtor's crypto assets through filings to the table of claims related to crypto transactions.[89] The insolvency administrator can write to possible wallet holders to learn about digital assets of the debtor. Most established crypto custodians can be contacted via a support request on their website (eg, Coinbase, Bitcoin Suisse, Gemini). He can also request the debtor's

[83] Hirzle and Hugendubel (n 80) 829.

[84] B Rätke, 's 93 Abgabenordnung' in F Klein and G Orlopp (eds), *Abgabenordnung einschließlich Steuerstrafrecht*, 16th edn (Munich, CH Beck, 2022) para 96.

[85] VG Berlin, NZI 2013, 413 ff.

[86] VG Berlin, ZIP 2018, 1508 ff.

[87] For North Rhine-Westphalia, for example OVG Münster, NZI 2011, 915; D Eisolt, 'Nutzung der Informationsfreiheitsgesetze für Auskunftsansprüche des Insolvenzverwalters gegen das Finanzamt – Aktueller Stand der Rechtsprechung' [2013] *Deutsches Steuerrecht* 439, 443.

[88] Eisolt (n 87) 443.

[89] D'Avoine and Hamacher (n 4) 9.

account statements to examine them for past transactions.[90] These must be examined for transactions to or from known crypto marketplaces or exchanges.[91] If the debtor uses a custodial wallet, he usually has to set up a bank account at a credit institution corresponding to the public key.[92] This serves as a digital exchange. For example, the crypto custodian 'Bison' opens an account with 'Solarisbank AG'. If this bank account is known, a connection to existing crypto assets can be established. Attention should be paid to recurring bookings in the sense of savings plans. Further means of taking note are a look in the electronic securities register or research in the circle of creditors.

D. Taking Possession of Crypto Tokens

Once the insolvency administrator has become aware of the debtor's crypto tokens, the next problem is how to take possession and secure them. Above all, the insolvency administrator must act quickly, because otherwise there is a risk of mass reduction if the debtor transfers his crypto assets to third parties.[93] As long as the debtor has access to the private and public keys, the holder can manage the assets.[94] In principle, it is advisable to transfer the tokens to the insolvency administrator's own wallet as quickly as possible.[95] This prevents the debtor from accessing the tokens, as his private key is then no longer of any use to him.[96] However, the debtor's private key is required to transfer the tokens to the wallet of the insolvency administrator. If this is stored in a hardware wallet, the insolvency administrator can have it seized pursuant to Section 883 ZPO.[97] An enforceable copy of the order opening the insolvency proceedings shall serve as the title (Section 148 para 2 InsO).[98] In the case of software wallets, it depends on whether the debtor uses a provider-dependent or provider-independent wallet. Provider-dependent wallets store the private key after a user account has been created.[99] The user then has access to the private key via the account login and can carry out transactions. If the debtor has his wallet at such a crypto custodian, the insolvency administrator must get the login data for the account.[100] The (preliminary) insolvency administrator can request information from the custodian. If the debtor refuses to disclose his login credentials, the insolvency administrator can request new login

[90] ibid.
[91] ibid.
[92] ibid.
[93] ibid 10 et seq.
[94] Krüger (n 37) 1266 ff.
[95] Strauch and Handke (n 24) ch 2, 275.
[96] ibid 269.
[97] ibid 272.
[98] ibid 275.
[99] Fromberger, Haffke and Zimmermann (n 1) 378.
[100] D'Avoine and Hamacher (n 4) 12 ff.

credentials.[101] This is also possible without the debtor's assistance. In the case of crypto custody, the insolvency administrator may also directly instruct the custodian by virtue of its power of disposition to transfer the tokens to the insolvency administrator's public key.[102] Provider-independent wallets do not store private keys.[103] In order to carry out transactions, the private key itself must always be entered. In the case of a provider-independent account, the insolvency administrator is dependent on the debtor providing him with the public and private keys. If the debtor does not surrender his private key contrary to his duty to cooperate under Section 97 InsO, the insolvency administrator is left with the measures of Section 98 InsO. He may also attempt to enforce execution against the tokens. For the enforcement of the transfer of tokens to a wallet of the insolvency administrator, Section 887 or Section 888 InsO is relevant, depending on the title.[104]

E. Liquidation of the Tokens

After the report date to all creditors pursuant to section 156 InsO, the tokens are realised without delay. Section 159 InsO does not allow waiting until a possible price increase. Due to the high volatility of crypto tokens, such waiting is very risky and may be relevant for the liability of the insolvency administrator. With regard to the type of liquidation, the insolvency administrator has discretion. However, the most favorable and efficient method of liquidation must be chosen.[105] As a rule, private sale brings the best proceeds, whereby the crypto tokens are offered at the market price on trading platforms.[106] An auction will usually not be worthwhile, as higher costs are incurred and buyers will not pay more than in the case of a private treaty sale due to the possibility of acquiring the tokens on the market at the market price.[107] The prices for the different types of tokens vary between the different trading platforms. The administrator can obtain information on the current prices and the trustworthiness of the trading platforms on online comparison portals such as 'Coinmarketcap' or 'Cryptoradar'. In the end, the platform with the highest rating while still being trustworthy should be chosen.[108]

III. Electronic Securities

In addition to the abovementioned crypto-tokens, electronic securities also count as digital assets.

[101] ibid.
[102] Skauradszun (n 25) 2616.
[103] Fromberger, Haffke and Zimmermann (n 1) 378.
[104] Text to n 51.
[105] BGH, NJW-RR 2006, 1273, 1274.
[106] Effer-Uhle (n 47) 530; Strauch and Handke (n 24) ch 2, 277.
[107] Strauch and Handke (n 24) ch 2, 277.
[108] ibid.

A. General Facts

There are two types of electronic securities. On the one hand, there are electronic traditional securities of the German commercial code (HGB). These include the note of lading, warehouse warrant and bill of lading. On the other hand, there are the electronic securities of the Electronic Securities Act (eWpG).[109] These will be dealt with in more detail below. Electronic securities under the eWpG are bearer bonds within the meaning of Section 793 BGB. They include bonds, participation certificates, warrants, certain commercial papers, investment certificates, asset-backed securities, collateralised debt obligations, convertible bonds, and profit participation bonds.[110] Pursuant to Article 95 para 1 of the German Investment Code (KAGB), shares in investment funds may also be issued as electronic bearer share certificates. Pursuant to section 95 para 3 KAGB, a large part of the provisions of the eWpG shall apply to these accordingly, unless the KAGB prescribes more specific provisions. Shares, on the other hand, are not covered by the eWpG, as they securitise membership rights and not claims.[111] Nowadays, classic securities are not held in paper form in a safe at the holder's premises. Securities are held in collective safe custody centrally with a custodian. This is done either in the form of a collective securities deposit pursuant to Section 5 para 1 sentence 2 of the Act on the Custody and Purchase of Securities (DepotG)[112] or by means of a global certificate pursuant to Section 9a para 2 DepotG.[113] The debtor has fractional ownership of the collective securities deposit or the global certificate pursuant to Section 6 DepotG.[114]

Electronic securities do not require physical documents at all. Instead of one or more certificates being held in custody by a securities clearing and deposit bank, the securities are entered in a register. There are two types of registers for electronic securities. On the one hand, there are central registers, which are kept by a custodian or the securities clearing and deposit bank, Section 12 para 2 eWpG. On the other hand, there are decentralised crypto securities registers, which can even be kept by the issuer, Section 16 para 2 eWpG. Section 95 para 3 KAGB only provides for the possibility of issuing electronic fund units in centrally held registers. However, section 95 para 5 provides for a regulation authorising the issuance of electronic fund units in decentralised registers as well. This authorisation was used so that the Ordinance on Crypto Fund Units (KryptoFAV) came into force on 18 June 2022. According to this ordinance, electronic fund shares can now also be

[109] D Saive and M Essmer, 'Verpfändung und Vollstreckung bei elektronischen Wertpapieren' [2022] *Neue Juristische Wochenschrift* 3038.

[110] S Omlor, 'Elektronische Wertpapiere nach dem eWpG' [2021] *Recht Digital* 371.

[111] M Habersack, 's 793 BGB' in FJ Säcker et al (n 35) para 11.

[112] U Gruber, 's 808 ZPO' in T Rauscher and W Krüger (eds), *Münchener Kommentar zur Zivilprozessordnung mit Gerichtsverfassungsgesetz und Nebengesetzen*, 6th edn (Munich, CH Beck, 2020) para 4.

[113] Saive and Essmer (n 109) 3038.

[114] ibid.

issued via decentralised registers. Electronic securities can be kept in the register as a collective registration or as an individual registration in accordance with the collective custody.

B. Securities as Objects of the Insolvency Estate

In order for electronic securities to be part of the insolvency estate, they must be subject to compulsory execution, Section 36 InsO. When it comes to the question of compulsory enforcement in electronic securities, a distinction must be made between securities with collective entry and securities with individual entry. In principle, the same applies to electronic securities with collective registration as to classical securities in collective custody, Section 9 para 1 sentence 1 eWpG.[115] The object of enforcement is the co-ownership share in the collective holding of the securities or in the global certificate. This is attachable according to Sections 857, 828 et seq. ZPO. The possibility of an attachable claim for surrender against the custodian pursuant to Section 7 of the DepotG may also be considered. However, this appears problematic with regard to the question of how a surrender of electronic securities should be possible. In the case of the individual registration of electronic securities, attachability according to Section 808 ZPO comes into consideration. Pursuant to Section 2 para 3 eWpG, electronic securities are deemed to be objects within the meaning of Section 90 German Civil Code (BGB). Seizure under Section 808 ZPO is affected by the bailiff taking custody of the property. In the case of electronic securities in the central register, it is not possible to speak of a seizure even if the bailiff is entered as the new owner. Seizure via Section 808 ZPO is therefore ruled out.[116] The situation is different for electronic securities in a crypto securities register. The register is decentralised. Therefore, no custody of the electronic securities can be attributed to the registrar. Access to the securities in a decentralised register takes place via a private key, as in the case of cryptocurrencies. Such access by means of a private key is partly considered as taking possession. Accordingly, seizure would be possible via Section 808 ZPO. In any case, even in the case of an individual entry, an attachment according to Section 857 in connection with Sections 828 et seqq. ZPO is possible.[117] It can be stated that electronic securities are subject to execution and thus form part of the insolvency estate.

C. Acquisition of Knowledge

The same obligations of the debtor to cooperate pursuant to Section 97 InsO shall apply. The insolvency administrator's investigation options and problems are

[115] ibid 3039.
[116] ibid 3041.
[117] ibid 3038.

similar to those that also exist for crypto tokens. After the opening of proceedings, the insolvency administrator may commission a bailiff to obtain relevant information from the Federal Central Tax Office and credit institutions pursuant to Sections 4, 148 InsO and 802l ZPO.[118] In the opening proceedings, such an order is made by the insolvency court (Section 20 para 1 sentence 2 InsO).

D. Taking Possession and Liquidation

Especially in the case of electronic securities in decentralised crypto securities registers, problems can arise with regard to obtaining private keys. When the insolvency administrator has gained access to the electronic securities, they will be liquidated.

IV. Conclusion

Dealing with digital assets is difficult for insolvency administrators, but unavoidable. Digital assets are part of the insolvency and liability estate. From a purely logical point of view, crypto assets must also be attachable and realisable, because otherwise the insolvent debtor could transfer his assets into digital assets and protect them from realisation in the insolvency. However, the method of realisation as well as attachment and protection still pose some technical and factual hurdles. It is important to exhaust all sources of information. It would be desirable to adapt the investigation rights and the right of information of the insolvency administrator and the bailiff to the current state of the art, because at present bailiffs and insolvency administrators are dependent on the assistance of the debtor. The position of the insolvency administrator needs to be strengthened for creditors. A regulatory regime for cryptocurrencies could help with the fundamental issues.

[118] M Vuia, 's 80 InsO' in R Stürner, H Eidenmüller and H Schoppmeyer (n 61) para 96k.

8

Interim Remedies in Crypto Fraud Cases

NIK YEO

I. Introduction

The courts of England and Wales[1] have for many decades been willing to grant interim relief to a claimant to protect assets of a defendant against whom the claimant would want to enforce a judgment, where there was a risk that the defendant would dissipate those assets prior to any attempt to enforce.[2] This used to be colloquially known as a '*Mareva* injunction' but is now referred to as a 'freezing injunction' or 'freezing order' or, even more colloquially still, a 'freezer'. This jurisdiction has been regularly used by victims of crypto fraud to seek to recover crypto assets from wrongdoers.

II. Freezing orders

A. Domestic FOs

The jurisdiction of the Court to make a freezing order was found in section 45 of the Supreme Court of Judicature (Consolidation) Act 1925, now section 37(1) of the Senior Courts Act 1981 (previously known as the Supreme Court Act 1981). Section 37(3) of the Senior Courts Act puts the freezing jurisdiction on a statutory footing:

> 37 Powers of High Court with respect to injunctions and receivers.
>
> (1) The High Court may by order (whether interlocutory or final) grant an injunction or appoint a receiver in all cases in which it appears to the court to be just and convenient to do so.

[1] Scottish courts are governed by a fundamentally different legal system which is far more civilian-based.

[2] *Nippon Yusen Kaisha v Karageorgis* [1975] 1 WLR 1093 and *Mareva Compania Naviera SA v International Bulkcarriers Ltd* [1975] 2 Lloyd's Rep 509.

(2) Any such order may be made either unconditionally or on such terms and conditions as the court thinks just.
(3) The power of the High Court under subsection (1) to grant an interlocutory injunction restraining a party to any proceedings from removing from the jurisdiction of the High Court, or otherwise dealing with, assets located within that jurisdiction shall be exercisable in cases where that party is, as well as in cases where he is not, domiciled, resident or present within that jurisdiction.

However, this is a power given to the High Court of England and Wales (including the Circuit Commercial courts) and cannot be exercised by a lower court, such as the county courts.

The power can be used to freeze all or an identified category of the defendant's assets. As section 37(3) makes plain, the defendant does not itself have to be within the jurisdiction; rather the injunction is based on the fact that the assets are in the jurisdiction. That gives rise to complexities when it comes to identifying the location (or *situs*) of crypto assets, which is beyond the scope of this chapter.[3]

B. WFOs

The power of the courts of England and Wales to make freezing orders has been extended to prevent defendants over whom the court can exercise personal jurisdiction from dissipating assets, wherever those assets are located. Again, the jurisdiction is found in the general wording of section 37(1) of the Senior Courts Act.[4] This is colloquially known as a 'worldwide freezing order' or 'WFO'.

This extends to permitting an English court exercising its personal jurisdiction over a defendant to order that defendant to transfer assets held overseas from one jurisdiction to another.[5]

[3] Briefly, English courts have coalesced around the suggestion that crypto assets are situated where their beneficial owner is resident or (if a company) where it has its central management and control: *Tai Mo Shan Limited v Persons Unknown* [2024] EWHC 1514 (Comm) [9]; *Tulip Trading Ltd v Bitcoin Association for BSV* [2022] EWHC 667 (Ch), [142]-[152]; *cf Ion Science v Persons Unknown* (21 December 2020, unreported) Comm, [13] and *Fetch.AI Limited v Persons Unknown* [2021] EWHC 2254 (Comm), [14], both of which spoke in terms of domicile, although there was no difference in either case between domicile and residence. What is more notable is that this approach looks in effect to the physical place of the claimant (who typically will be the one asserting that they are beneficially entitled to the assets), and so is very claimant-friendly. Professor A Dickinson, whose writings are cited in *Ion Science v Persons Unknown* (21 December 2020, unreported) Comm, *Fetch.AI Limited v Persons Unknown* [2021] EWHC 2254 (Comm), and *Tulip Trading Ltd v Bitcoin Association for BSV* [2022] EWHC 667 (Ch), in fact suggests that situs is an unsatisfactory touchstone: D Fox & S Green (eds), *Cryptocurrencies in Public and Private Law* (Oxford, OUP, 2019) para 5.109. The Law Commission of England and Wales are currently considering what the *situs* rules should be for crypto assets.

[4] *Derby & Co Ltd v Weldon (Nos 1 & 2)* [1990] Ch 48 (CA) 58G.

[5] *Derby & Co Ltd v Weldon (No 6)* [1990] 1 WLR 1139 (CA) 1151. See also the discussion on *Law* below.

C. Broad Idea Injunctions

Since the freezing orders referred to above (whether domestic or worldwide) are interim relief, designed to 'hold the ring' pending resolution of the substantive dispute, there must be some underlying substantive proceedings between the claimant and the defendant. Initially, the courts of England and Wales only granted freezing orders in favour of English proceedings. However, it is now recognised that courts will grant a free-standing injunction in support of substantive proceedings by the claimant against the defendant in foreign courts, or in an arbitration, so long as the English court has personal jurisdiction over that defendant.[6]

It is not necessary that such proceedings (whether intended to be commenced in the jurisdiction or elsewhere) are already on foot by the time of the application for interim relief,[7] but if not, then typically the English court will require an undertaking from the claimant to commence them within a certain (typically short) time.[8]

Furthermore, English courts will grant such interim relief against a third party who is not intended to be a substantive defendant at all – what is colloquially called a 'non-cause of action defendant' – so long as there is a good arguable case[9] that the asset held by the third party could be used to satisfy any eventual judgment against the actual defendant: in effect, where it appeared that those who hold assets do so on behalf of the defendant.[10]

The non-cause of action defendant must, of course, itself be subject to the personal jurisdiction of the English courts.[11]

The last two extensions can be combined into what is sometimes called, rather aptly, a '*Broad Idea* injunction':

> Once it is accepted that an interlocutory injunction can be granted (i) where substantive proceedings are taking place abroad and (ii) against a 'non-cause of action defendant', there is no reason why it should not be granted in an appropriate case where both circumstances are combined. Furthermore, the examples given earlier of third party disclosure orders, Bankers Trust orders[[12]] and website blocking orders show that there is no principle or practice which prevents an injunction from being granted in

[6] *Channel Tunnel Group Ltd v Balfour Beatty Construction Ltd* [1993] AC 334 (HL) 341, 343, 362.

[7] *Broad Idea v Convoy Collateral* [2022] 2 WLR 703 (SC), [95].

[8] *Tai Mo Shan Limited v Oazo Apps Limited* (20 February 2023 and 6 March 2023, unreported) see para 4 of Sch A to the Order of 20 February 2023 which is available at iapps.courts.state.ny.us/nyscef/ViewDocument?docIndex=QyLFt1iB0IcRNAIjmaIv1g==.

[9] The precise standard of proof required to establish interim relief is discussed in detail below.

[10] *TSB Private Bank International SA v Chabra* [1992] 1 WLR 231.

[11] *Broad Idea v Convoy Collateral* [2022] 2 WLR 703 (SC), [82]; also Civil Jurisdiction and Judgments Act 1982, s 25 (1), if the substantive proceedings (i) have been or are to be commenced in a 2005 Hague Convention State (s 25(1)(a)) and (ii) fall within the scope of the 2005 Hague Convention (s 25(1)(b)), which applies to 'international cases to exclusive choice of court agreements concluded in civil or commercial matters'.

[12] Discussed below.

appropriate circumstances against an entirely innocent party even when no substantive proceedings against anyone are taking place anywhere.[13]

D. Test for Freezing Orders (Including Broad Idea Injunctions)

The principles governing the making of freezing orders generally[14] were summarised by Haddon-Cave LJ in *Lakatamia Shipping Company Limited v Morimoto* [2019] EWCA Civ 2203:

> 33. The basic legal principles for the grant of a WFO are well-known and uncontroversial and hardly need re-stating. It nevertheless is useful to remind oneself of the succinct summary of the test by Peter Gibson LJ in Thane Investments Ltd v Tomlinson (No 1) [2003] EWCA Civ 1272 at [21] where he stated that, before making a WFO, the court must be satisfied that:
>
> … the applicant for the order has a good, arguable case, that there is a real risk that judgment would go unsatisfied by reason of the disposal by the defendant of his assets, unless he is restrained by the court from disposing of them, and that it would be just and convenient in all the circumstances to grant the freezing order.'
>
> 34. I also gratefully adopt (as the Judge did) the useful summary of some of the key principles applicable to the question of risk of dissipation by Mr Justice Popplewell (as he then was) in Fundo Soberano de Angola v dos Santos [2018] EWHC 2199 (Comm) (subject to one correction which I note below):
>
> (1) The claimant must show a real risk, judged objectively, that a future judgment would not be met because of an unjustified dissipation of assets. In this context dissipation means putting the assets out of reach of a judgment whether by concealment or transfer.
> (2) The risk of dissipation must be established by solid evidence; mere inference or generalised assertion is not sufficient.
> (3) The risk of dissipation must be established separately against each respondent.
> (4) It is not enough to establish a sufficient risk of dissipation merely to establish a good arguable case that the defendant has been guilty of dishonesty; it is necessary to scrutinise the evidence to see whether the dishonesty in question points to the conclusion that assets [may be] dissipated. It is also necessary to take account of whether there appear at the interlocutory stage to be properly arguable answers to the allegations of dishonesty.
> (5) The respondent's former use of offshore structures is relevant but does not itself equate to a risk of dissipation. Businesses and individuals often use offshore structures as part of the normal and legitimate way in which they deal with their assets. Such legitimate reasons may properly include tax planning, privacy and the use of limited liability structures.

[13] ibid.

[14] Mention is made of WFOs or 'worldwide freezing orders' in this quote but it applies also to domestic freezing orders. WFOs are discussed in more detail below.

(6) What must be threatened is unjustified dissipation. The purpose of a WFO is not to provide the claimant with security; it is to restrain a defendant from evading justice by disposing of, or concealing, assets otherwise than in the normal course of business in a way which will have the effect of making it judgment proof. A WFO is not intended to stop a corporate defendant from dealing with its assets in the normal course of its business. Similarly, it is not intended to constrain an individual defendant from conducting his personal affairs in the way he has always conducted them, providing of course that such conduct is legitimate. If the defendant is not threatening to change the existing way of handling their assets, it will not be sufficient to show that such continued conduct would prejudice the claimant's ability to enforce a judgment. That would be contrary to the purpose of the WFO jurisdiction because it would require defendants to change their legitimate behaviour in order to provide preferential security for the claim which the claimant would not otherwise enjoy.

(7) Each case is fact specific and relevant factors must be looked at cumulatively.

The sixth of these principles is worth emphasising. As said in *Vneshprombank LLC v Bedzhamov* [2019] EWCA Civ 1992:

> 57. … As is clear from numerous statements of principle, a freezing order is not intended to provide a claimant with security for its claim but only to prevent the dissipation of assets outside of the ordinary course of business in a way which would render any future judgment unenforceable. While the disposal of assets outside of the ordinary course of business is prohibited as being contrary to the interests of justice, payments in the ordinary course of business are permitted even if the consequence will be that the defendant's assets are completely depleted before the claimant is able to obtain its judgment. This has been clear since the decision of Robert Goff J in The Angel Bell [1981] 1 QB 65. Moreover, so long as the payment is made in good faith, the court does not enquire as to whether it is made in order to discharge a legal obligation or whether it represents good or bad business on the defendant's part.

The claimant must also show that its underlying claim against the defendant presents a 'serious issue to be tried' (which is the phraseology to be preferred over 'good arguable case', although the two tests are essentially the same). It does not require the claimant to show at this interim stage that it is likely to win at trial, that it has 'a better than fifty per cent chance of success', or that it has the 'better of the arguments'. It is sufficient for a claimant to show that its case is 'more than barely capable of serious argument', that its case is 'more than merely arguable and carries some degree of conviction'.[15] To protect then against the risk that the interim injunction is subsequently shown at trial to have been wrongly granted, a claimant will typically have to give an undertaking (or 'cross-undertaking') to compensate the defendant (or any affected third

[15] *Ninemia Maritime Corporation v Trave Schiffahrtsgesellschaft mbH (The Niedersachsen)* [1983] 2 Lloyd's Rep 600; considered recently in *Dos Santos v Unitel International Holdings BV* [2024] EWCA Civ 1109, [96], [100], [106], [122], [126], [128], [131].

party) for losses caused by the wrongful grant of interim relief (as distinct from losses caused by the proceedings themselves).[16]

Where, as is common, the freezing order is sought at a hearing listed without notice having been given to the respondent, then the claimant is under further obligations in relation to how the application for a freezing order is presented. For convenience, this is discussed separately below, since those principles apply to any 'without notice' application.

III. Proprietary Injunctions

Although sometimes referred to under the umbrella term 'freezing order', a proprietary injunction is different. First, it requires the claimant to be able to assert a proprietary interest (discussed below), and second the test for granting such an injunction is different to that of a freezing order (discussed under the next sub-heading).

If a fiduciary, for example, an agent, trustee, or company director, disposes of assets of the fiduciary's principal, beneficiary or company (as applicable) in breach of fiduciary duty, then that other party will retain an equitable property interest in the assets in the hands of the recipient, unless the recipient is a bona fides purchaser for value without (actual or constructive) notice of the breach of fiduciary duty.[17] If the recipient has transferred those assets to third parties then the claimant will need to show that it can satisfy the rules of 'equitable tracing' to retain its equitable proprietary interest in the assets down the line.[18]

Where the claimant can maintain a proprietary claim to assets held by another, then a court of England and Wales can grant an interim proprietary injunction over those assets to prevent them being disposed of or otherwise dealt with pending determination of the claimant's proprietary claim. Typically, such claims are based on an equitable proprietary right. However, crypto assets give rise to an unresolved question as to what it is to have *legal* title to crypto assets.

A. When you Own Crypto

Under English law, it is presently unclear whether a person can be said to 'own' crypto assets (eg, have legal ownership) if the person does not control the relevant

[16] *Dos Santos v Unitel International Holdings BV* [2024] EWCA Civ 1109, [130]; *Tharros Shipping Co Ltd v Bias Shipping Ltd* [1994] 1 Lloyd's Rep 577, 582.

[17] *Foskett v McKeown* [2001] 1 AC 102, 108.

[18] Those rules are beyond the scope of this chapter but see generally (eg) *Snell's Equity*, 34th edn (London, Sweet &Maxwell, 2022) paras 30-051–30-066.

private key. If a person can do so, then that creates the possibility of a claimant asserting a legal right to crypto assets where a third person controls the private key.

This arises from the question as to whether anyone can 'own' crypto assets if no one has control over the relevant private key. That was to be determined as a preliminary issue in *Tulip Trading Ltd v Bitcoin Association for BSV*:[19] the claimant claimed that he 'owned' crypto assets even though the private key had been corrupted and no one could apparently use it. However, those proceedings have now been discontinued[20] and so the question must await another occasion.

If such ownership could be established, then it calls into question the technique commonly used to destroy (or 'burn') crypto assets, by transferring them to a public address to which there is no (or no known) corresponding private key. Someone could then claim ownership of crypto assets even after they had been burnt.[21] Also, it would then seem difficult to distinguish between the situation where (as in *Tulip* (n 3)) the claimant asserts that no one controls the private key and a situation where the claimant asserts (legal) ownership where someone else controls the private key.

In practice, however, it is more likely that a claimant will wish to rely merely on an equitable proprietary right, rather than a legal proprietary right, since equitable tracing rules are more flexible than common law tracing rules.[22]

B. Test for Proprietary Injunctions

This is different from the test for freezing orders, and somewhat easier to satisfy. As a result of the claimant having a proprietary claim to the assets sought to be frozen, the Court will simply apply the same test as for any (non-freezing) interim

[19] Jurisdictional issues dealt with at [2022] EWHC 667 (Ch) and [2023] EWCA Civ 83.

[20] See *Crypto Open Patent Alliance v Wright*; *Tulip Trading Limited v Bitcoin Association for BSV* [2024] EWHC 1809 (Ch), [3]. At [243], J Mellor commented: 'It is not without significance that the TTL claim was discontinued just a few days before the deadline for disclosure. If TTL had been required to give disclosure, it is highly likely that it would have contained some documents which I found to be forged in my Main COPA Judgment (see [2024] EWHC 1198 (Ch)), and likely to have included yet further forgeries, as pleaded.'

[21] There is a practical issue of course as to whether the claimant could ever recover such burnt assets, however *Tulip Trading* claimed that it was possible to modify the Bitcoin blockchain code to allow access to crypto assets without controlling the private key: *Tulip Trading Ltd v Bitcoin Association for BSV* [2023] EWCA Civ 83, [38].

[22] See *Snell* (n 18), although the general rule that mixing stymies tracing or following at common law may not apply to crypto tokens if the issuer maintains a record of each and every token's location, as was suggested was the case with Tether (USDT) in *D'Aloia v Persons Unknown* [2024] EWHC 2342 (Ch), [209], [210], [212]. However, even here the judge recognised that the law may well develop an 'innocent recipient' defence – that is, extending the '*bona fide* purchaser without notice' defence that applies to extinguish pre-existing equitable title so that such a purchaser also takes free of any pre-existing legal title to crypto ([2024] EWHC 2342 (Ch), [211]), just as happens currently with fiat currency: if you receive stolen banknotes in change when paying for a purchase, so long as you are not aware of the prior theft you take full legal and beneficial title to those stolen banknotes.

injunction. That is known as the *American Cyanamid* test;[23] namely whether: (a) there is 'a serious issue to be tried' on the merits; (b) in the absence of an injunction, the claimant would be liable to suffer prejudice that is not readily compensable in damages; and (c) the balance of convenience favours the grant of the injunction.

The 'serious issue to be tried on the merits' threshold has recently been confirmed by the Court of Appeal to be applicable to both freezing orders and other interim injunctions, such as proprietary injunctions.[24] Again, a claimant will typically have to give a cross-undertaking in damages.

Nevertheless, the test for a proprietary injunction is easier to satisfy than the test for a (non-proprietary) freezing order because there is no need to show a risk of dissipation.

IV. Effect on Third Parties

A freezing order or proprietary injunction will typically be endorsed with the following words at their outset:

> If you [xx] disobey this order you may be held to be in contempt of court and may be imprisoned, fined or have your assets seized.
>
> Any other person who knows of this order and does anything which helps or permits the respondent to breach the terms of the order may also be held to be in contempt of court and may be imprisoned, fined or have their assets seized.

The effect is that a claimant, having got such an order, can serve it on third parties, such as a UK-based regulated bank with whom the defendant (respondent) is known to maintain an account containing funds, which are the subject of the freezing order or proprietary injunction, and the bank is then put on notice that if it permits its customer to withdraw such funds, it exposes itself to contempt proceedings. In practice, this has proved an effective mechanism to enforce the freezing order or proprietary injunction over moneys held in such banks. Contempt proceedings for breach of a freezing order are not unknown.[25]

Although cryptocurrency exchanges do not tend to be based in the UK or regulated by UK authorities, many do still take cognisance of such orders and freeze user's accounts on the exchange's platform upon receipt of such orders.

If the victim did not wish simply to rely on an exchange freezing a user's account upon being served with a freezing order or proprietary injunction obtained against a wrongdoer, the victim could seek an order directly against the exchange as a non-cause of action defendant (utilising the procedure endorsed in *Broad Idea*).

[23] Named after *American Cyanamid Co v Ethicon Ltd* [1974] AC 396. See *Polly Peck International v Nadir (No 2)* [1992] 4 All ER 769 (CA), 784.

[24] See n 15 above.

[25] eg, *Wang v Darby* [2024] EWHC 1394.

However, in a number of cases, claimants have gone further and sought to establish a cause of action against an exchange – eg alleging that the exchange holds stolen crypto assets as a constructive trustee for a victim whose accounts have either been hacked or (more typically) who have been tricked into transferring assets to the fraudster (commonly known in the fiat fraud world in the UK as an 'authorised push-payment' (or APP) fraud[26]). Such a claim requires showing that the victim can trace into the crypto assets transferred by the exchange's user to the exchange. That itself requires that (if common law tracing is relied on) there has been no mixing of the victim's crypto assets in any wallet prior to or on receipt by the exchange.[27] If equitable tracing is relied on, it requires showing that the equitable tracing rules are properly applied through each wallet in the chain between the victim and the exchange, and that none of the intermediate recipients or the exchange itself is a bona fide purchase for value without notice.[28] If that can be shown, then, if a proprietary injunction is granted, the exchange will need to freeze the user's account. However, the same result might be able to be achieved simply by serving a freezing order or proprietary injunction on the exchange as a third party or obtaining such an order against the exchange as a non-cause of action defendant.

In practice, a victim's motivation for bringing proceedings against a cryptocurrency exchange itself is usually because the user's account has already been depleted and the victim seeks to make the exchange personally liable for crypto assets that the exchange had, on the instructions of its customer, transferred out of the exchange's wallets. Victims have sought to bring a personal claim in restitution (although that requires showing that the exchange received crypto assets, which can be traced *at law* – not in equity – to the exchange) or for the equitable wrong of 'knowing receipt'.[29] However, such claims are difficult to get off the ground.[30]

[26] Examined in detail in *Barclays Bank UK PLC v Philipp* [2024] AC 346.

[27] Typically, crypto exchanges receive crypto assets into a wallet address generated specifically for that customer's transfer, but those wallets are then often swept into an 'omnibus' or 'pooled' (hot) wallet, and there may well be further sweeps from such hot wallets to cold wallets, so that various customers' crypto assets are mixed with one another: see *Piroozzadeh v Persons Unknown* [2023] EWHC 1024 (Ch), [8], [41]. Therefore, other than (perhaps) where the particular crypto token's issuer keeps a record of the whereabouts of each token (see n 22 above), such mixing will stymie common law tracing. An exchange may also be able to rely on an 'innocent recipient' defence (see n 21 above).

[28] See N Yeo 'Crypto Exchanges: The Basics' [2023] *Journal of International Banking & Financial Law* 459. Equitable tracing is not necessarily confined to traditional rules such as 'first in-first out' and 'pari passu', but may extend to other methods 'provided that it treated all innocent claimants and potentially claimants comparably and was properly evidenced': *D'Aloia v Persons Unknown* [2024] EWHC 2342 (Ch), [221].

[29] *D'Aloia v Persons Unknown* [2024] EWHC 2342 (Ch), [343]-[345]; *D'Aloia v Persons Unknown* [2024] EWHC 895 (Ch); *Byers v Saudi National Bank* [2024] 2 WLR 237. See also N Yeo '*Byers v Saudi National Bank*: Bona Fide Purchase, Knowing Receipt and Crypto Litigation' [2024] *Journal of International Banking & Financial Law* 83.

[30] See the failed cases of *Piroozzadeh v Persons Unknown* [2023] EWHC 1024 (Ch) (the claimant subsequently discontinued) and *D'Aloia v Persons Unknown* [2024] EWHC 895 (Ch) (strike out); [2024] EWHC 2342 (Ch) (trial).

V. Orders and Injunctions against Persons Unknown

It is possible to sue an unidentified defendant in the English courts. Such a defendant or defendants will be referred to as 'person(s) unknown'. (This is not a unique jurisdiction: the New York State courts, for example, permit proceedings to be commenced against 'John Does'.[31])

However, under English court procedure, in order for a defendant to appear and defend a claim, it is necessary for it to identify itself to the court and to the claimant,[32] reflecting the principle of 'open justice'.[33] A party (including a defendant) can always seek an order that their names be redacted.[34] But that presupposes that the court and the party's opponent already knows of their identity.[35]

Hence, when serving proceedings 'by NFT' (in effect, the transmission of an NFT to a blockchain wallet where there is sufficient evidence that it is controlled by the unknown wrongdoer, with the NFT's 'artwork' containing a hyperlink to a website from which the documents to be served can be downloaded),[36] English courts have permitted the claimant to require that the defendants identify themselves sufficiently in order to receive a password to access the documents to be served on that website.[37]

It is presently unclear what ultimate orders could be made against 'persons unknown' if they do not take part in the proceedings, therefore do not identify themselves, and so the claimant seeks to proceed to final judgment (either as a judgment in default of the defendant participating, or as a summary judgment[38]). There are two recent conflicting first instance decisions, one of which held that the

[31] See, eg, *Tai Mo Shan Limited v John Does Nos 1-100* (judgment 26 March 2024, Supreme Court of the State of New York, No 651017/2023).

[32] Civil Procedure Rules ('CPR'), r 10.5 (when filing an Acknowledgement of Service) or r 11 (if challenging the Court's jurisdiction); see *Persons Unknown v Wright* [2023] EWHC 2292 (Ch), [4], [29].

[33] *Persons Unknown v Wright* [2023] EWHC 2292 (Ch), [32].

[34] CPR, r 39.2(4); see *Persons Unknown v Wright* [2023] EWHC 2292 (Ch), [11].

[35] *Persons Unknown v Wright* [2023] EWHC 2292 (Ch), [42].

[36] A process sanctioned by the English Courts under CPR, r 6.37(5)(b)(i) in *Osbourne v Persons Unknown* [2023] EWHC 39 (KB), [45]–[48], even though this was going to be the sole method of service, since there was no other available methods of service.

[37] *Osbourne v Persons Unknown* [2023] EWHC 2974 (KB), [21]–[24]; *Tai Mo Shan Limited v Persons Unknown* [2024] EWHC 1514 (Comm), [18]. However, it is surely right that a claimant should not be permitted to password-protect those documents to be served which would be readily available to the public from the Court file (such as the Claim Form, Particulars of Claim, Defence and Reply), and so password protection, and the requirement for persons unknown to identify themselves in order to obtain that password, should only apply to other documents not readily available from the Court file: *Tai Mo Shan Limited v Persons Unknown* [2024] EWHC 1514 (Comm), [18].

[38] English courts are sympathetic to a claimant's desire to have a final judgment enforceable in other jurisdictions where default judgments may not be readily enforceable, and so will entertain an application for summary judgment, even though it is anticipated that the defendant will not appear and so the claimant would be entitled to a default judgment. Indeed, a default judgment for a specified amount of money, for an amount to be decided by the court, or for delivery of goods, could be obtained simply by filing a request for an administrative action by the court: CPR, r 12.4(1).

court has no power to make final orders for personal remedies against 'persons unknown' while they remain unnamed[39] and the other which held that there is no such restraint, so long as the court has jurisdiction over the 'persons unknown'.[40] Until this is determined by the Court of Appeal, claimants and first instance courts are likely to adopt the narrower approach – meaning that relief granted upon a default judgment or summary judgment against 'persons unknown' will in practice be restricted to proprietary relief.

VI. Ancillary Information Orders

A freezing order or proprietary injunction often also contains obligations on the defendant to provide information about assets, whether they fall within the scope of the order or injunction, or outside it.[41] So, for example, in *Wang v Darby* [2024] EWHC 1394, [15],[42] the freezing order required the defendant to identify precisely what crypto assets were held and where they were '*located*'.

There are also a number of free-standing bases for obtaining information about assets from third parties who are not actual or intended defendants, even if those third parties are outside the jurisdiction.[43]

The *Norwich Pharmacal* jurisdiction is that:[44]

> (…) if through no fault of his own a person gets mixed up in the tortious acts of others so as to facilitate their wrongdoing he may incur no personal liability but he comes under a duty to assist the person who has been wronged by giving him full information and disclosing the identity of the wrongdoers (…) justice requires that he should co-operate in righting the wrong if he unwittingly facilitated its perpetration.

The conditions to be satisfied for the court to exercise its power to grant *Norwich Pharmacal* relief are that:[45]

- A wrong must have been carried out, or arguably carried out, by an ultimate wrongdoer.

[39] *Boonyaem v Persons Unknown* [2023] EWHC 1380 (Comm), [30], [34]. See also *Tai Mo Shan Limited v John Does Nos 1-100* (judgment 26 March 2024, Supreme Court of the State of New York, No 651017/2023).

[40] *Mooij v Persons Unknown* [2024] EWHC 814, [44]. See also *Jones v Persons Unknown* [2022] EWHC 2543 (Comm), where summary judgment was given against 'persons unknown' for the personal claim of damages for deceit and unjust enrichment).

[41] CPR, r 25.1(1)(g): 'an order directing a party to provide information about the location of relevant property or assets or to provide information about relevant property or assets which are or may be the subject of an application for a freezing injunction'.

[42] The earlier substantive judgment in the same case is at *Wang v Darby* [2021] EWHC 3054 (Comm).

[43] Service out of the jurisdiction is sanctioned by CPR, PD 6B 3.1(25) (commonly known as 'gateway 25'). See also CPR 31.16 (pre-action disclosure from a likely party) and CPR 31.17 (disclosure of documents against a non-party).

[44] *Norwich Pharmacal Co v Customs and Excise Comrs* [1974] AC 133, at 175.

[45] *Ramilos Trading Ltd v Buyanovsky* [2016] EWHC 3175, [11].

- The standard of proof is that of a 'good arguable case'.[46]
- There must be the need for an order to enable action to be brought against the ultimate wrongdoer. In identifying the necessity for an order, the cases emphasise the importance of flexibility and discretion.[47]
- The person against whom the order is made must (a) be mixed up in so as to have facilitated the wrongdoing; and (b) be able or likely to be able to provide the information necessary to enable the ultimate wrongdoer to be sued.

The separate, but overlapping, *Bankers Trust* jurisdiction allows a court to order a third party to provide information concerning the nature and location of assets against which the claimant asserts a proprietary claim.[48] A *Bankers Trust* order is available where there is a prima facie,[49] or arguable,[50] case of fraud giving rise to potential tracing claims.

VII. 'Without Notice' Hearings

The courts of England and Wales are able to entertain submissions for interim relief from a claimant without the presence of the defendant (respondent), and without the claimant even notifying the defendant (respondent) that the hearing is to take place, if there are 'good reasons' for doing so.[51] Such an application used to be called an '*ex parte*' application, but now it is known as a 'without notice' application. The claimant must typically show both that it is urgent and that there is a risk that the defendant might act to prejudice the effectiveness of the interim relief (eg, by dissipating it). If the matter is urgent but not secret, then at least informal notice is expected to be given.[52]

Importantly, if the matter is heard without the other side having been notified (or if only informal notice is given and even if the other side turn up), then the claimant has an obligation to be full and frank with the court and draw the court's attention to such defences and objections to the relief sought that the defendant could reasonably be expected to make itself.

[46] ibid at [27].

[47] *Ashworth v MGN Ltd* [2002] 1 WLR 2033 per Lord Woolf CJ at [57]: 'New situations are inevitably going to arise where it would be appropriate for the jurisdiction to be exercised where it has not been exercised previously. The limits which apply to its use in its infancy should not be allowed to stultify its use now that it has become a valuable and mature remedy. That new circumstances for its appropriate use will continue to arise as illustrated by the decision of Sir Richard Scott V-C in P v T Ltd [1997] 1 WLR 1309 where relief was granted because it was necessary in the interests of justice, albeit that the claimant was not able to identify without discovery what would be the appropriate cause of action.'

[48] *Bankers Trust Co v Shapira* [1980] 1 WLR 1274 and *Arab Monetary Fund v Hashim (No 5)* [1992] 2 All ER 911.

[49] *Kalmneft v Denton Wilde Sapte* [2002] 1 Lloyd's Rep 417, [14].

[50] *Miles Smith v Barclays* [2017] EWHC 3338 (Ch), [28].

[51] CPR, r 25.3(1).

[52] CPR, PD 23A 2.4 and 2.8.

Any interim relief granted at a 'without notice' hearing will simply be for a short time, until a 'return date' hearing is listed of which the defendant has notice. A claimant's failure at the 'without notice' hearing to be full and frank is likely to be challenged at the 'return date' hearing and may lead to the interim relief being discharged (although if there are still grounds for the interim relief notwithstanding the failure to be full and frank, then it may be continued or regranted).

The most notable example of a failure to be full and frank in crypto litigation was in the recent case of *Piroozzadeh v Persons Unknown* [2023] EWHC 1024 (Ch), where the judge pointed out:

> [T]he duty is on the legal representatives as well as the claimant to identify and anticipate likely defences. If as a result of their involvement in other litigation the legal representatives are aware both of the way in which the eighth defendant asserted that its pooling operations functioned and the nature of the legal consequences which were said by it to flow from that, there can in my judgment be no basis for them to say that it did not occur to them that such defences were not likely to be run. [30]
>
> [T]he quid pro quo for proceeding in the absence of a respondent is that the court must be told what arguments might have been raised if the respondent were present. [36]
>
> As to culpability, while I am inclined to think that this was a case of the legal representatives adopting an overenthusiastic approach to the merits of their client's case as against the exchanges, there is some level of culpability. The reality is that a deliberate decision was made not to disclose a possible defence. [38]
>
> The duty extends not just to a fair presentation of the underlying facts (to the extent they are known or might properly be anticipated), but also the way in which those facts might reasonably be expected to support a defence. All of this needs to be properly explained in order to ensure that the presentation is fair. [39]
>
> As I have already emphasised, the duty of fair presentation is very important. Careful attention is required to ensure that every avenue is fully explored before relief of this sort is sought, more particularly where the delay from the time of the fraud and, indeed, from the time at which the investigation had started, meant that the excuse of having insufficient time to give mature consideration to the way in which the case should be put (or might be defended) would not, even if material, be available to the claimant or his legal representatives. [40]

VIII. Examples of Cryptoasset Recovery Using Interim Relief Powers of the Court

A. Seizure of Assets from Blockchain Wallet to which a Claimant has a Proprietary Claim

In the crypto asset context, this was exemplified in the successful recovery of approximately $450 million of hacked crypto assets from the well-publicised

Wormhole portal hack. In that case, persons unknown hacked the Wormhole network, a blockchain bridge enabling those with a native token on one blockchain to 'port' it to another blockchain: for instance, a holder of ETH on the Ethereum blockchain can obtain wrapped ETH ('wETH') on the Solana blockchain by locking ETH with Wormhole and then receiving wETH from Wormhole on the Solana blockchain on a 1:1 basis. Users who had received wETH could then 'redeem' that wETH for ETH on the Ethereum blockchain through Wormhole. In February 2022, a hacker exploited a vulnerability in the Wormhole protocol to create (or 'mint') 120,000 wETH on the Solana blockchain without first having locked equivalent ETH with Wormhole, and then the hacker promptly proceeded to 'redeem' much of that newly minted wETH by passing it back through Wormhole to receive ETH. That then led to a deficit of (then) approximately $320 million of ETH in Wormhole to the detriment of genuine users: if all genuine holders of wETH had then attempted to 'redeem' their wETH for ETH, there would have been a shortfall of ETH of a value of approximately $320 million, potentially leading to the collapse of the Wormhole network itself.

In order to remedy the situation, *Tai Mo Shan Limited* (TMSL) stepped in within 24 hours of the hack and deposited the shortfall of ETH into the Wormhole portal to ensure that genuine users could still 'redeem' their wETH for ETH on a 1:1 basis. TMSL had an interest in the viability of the Wormhole network as it was a user, an affiliate of a company that had created the initial version of Wormhole and an affiliate of one of the developers and 'guardians' of Wormhole.

The ETH that the hacker 'redeemed' from Wormhole remained in an Ethereum wallet for a year, before much of it was then passed through various intermediate wallets before being converted into derivative crypto assets of ETH: 'staked ETH' ('stETH'), 'wrapped staked ETH' ('wstETH') and 'rocket ETH' ('rETH'). The hacker used the wstETH and rETH as security to borrow another crypto asset called 'DAI' on the Maker defi protocol, utilising a front-end defi application, Oasis, owned and controlled by Oazo Apps Limited ('Oazo') English company.

Shortly thereafter, TMSL learnt that it would be possible, via the Oasis application, to seize assets from the Ethereum wallet controlled by the hacker which it had used in the Oasis app. TMSL therefore applied to the English courts in February 2023 for, and was granted, an interim proprietary injunction against Oazo, as a non-cause of action defendant, compelling Oazo to take steps to seize those crypto assets and transfer them out of the hacker's Ethereum wallet to a wallet whose private key was controlled by TMSL's English solicitors, to prevent the dissipation of those assets subject to resolution of substantive proceedings which TMSL intended to bring against the hacker. Shortly thereafter, TMSL brought proceedings in the New York State courts against the hacker (as 'John Does', identified as being the controllers of that Ethereum wallet and the wallets through which the stolen ETH had been passed). TMSL's claim was based on a number of causes of action arising under New York law, including claims based on the assertion that TMSL was entitled by equitable subrogation to claim the amounts it used, making good the loss to the genuine users of Wormhole.

To be clear, while the stolen assets (or their derivatives) were being held by TMSL's English solicitors, TMSL had no access to them. Rather, those solicitors were holding them pursuant to undertakings to the English court given by those solicitors personally (as offices of the English court) that it 'shall not dissipate or deal in any way, either directly or indirectly, with [the crypto assets transferred to that wallet] subject to any order of this Court to the contrary (...) and shall not (...) transfer them from the [identified wallet controlled by those solicitors], subject to any order of this Court to the contrary'.[53] In effect, those solicitors were holding those crypto assets in what is colloquially known as a 'stakeholder' capacity.

TMSL prosecuted its claim against the hacker in the New York State court and obtained a default judgment that it was entitled to the assets being held in their English solicitors' Ethereum wallet.

TMSL then commenced separate proceedings in the English courts against the hacker, as 'persons unknown', for recognition and enforcement of that New York judgment, which was granted on 16 July 2024, and the crypto assets held by its English solicitors were ordered by the English court to be transferred to TMSL (those solicitors' undertakings to the English court then being released).[54] In this way, interim relief against a non-cause of action defendant in England, in support of proceedings in New York, led to the successful recovery of a huge quantity of hacked crypto assets.

B. Seizure of Assets from Exchange Account to which a Claimant has a Personal Claim

In *Law v Persons Unknown*,[55] the claimant had obtained judgment against unidentified wrongdoers, obtaining both an order that the contents of one account maintained by the wrongdoers on a cryptocurrency exchange based outside the jurisdiction was the claimant's property, and also an order for various personal remedies against the wrongdoer.[56] After judgment, the claimant obtained a WFO against the 'persons unknown' defendant. The exchange was joined as a defendant, but the WFO did not extend to it. The judgment here was to obtain orders against the exchange to enable the earlier proprietary and personal relief to be enforced.

Crypto assets in the exchange account mentioned above were traceable proceeds of the fraud, in respect of which the claimant had a proprietary claim. The court therefore had no difficulty ordering the exchange to transfer the contents of that account to the claimant.

[53] *Tai Mo Shan Limited v Oazo Apps Limited* (20 February 2023 and 6 March 2023, unreported), see paras 1 & 2 of Sch B to the Order of 20 February 2023 which is available at apps.courts.state.ny.us/nyscef/ViewDocument?docIndex=QyLFt1iB0IcRNAIjmaIv1g==.

[54] *Tai Mo Shan Limited v Persons Unknown* [2024] EWHC 1514 (Comm), [2024] EWHC 2532 (Comm).

[55] *Law v Persons Unknown* (26 January 2023, unreported) London Circuit Com Ct.

[56] This was before articulation of the potential problem with final personal orders against persons unknown, as articulated in *Boonyaem* (n 39).

There was a second account maintained by the 'persons unknown' on the exchange that had a larger quantity of crypto assets credited to it. The claimant acknowledged, however, that he was not able to trace his stolen crypto assets into that second account. Nevertheless, the court recognised that if that account were maintained with a bank in the jurisdiction, then the claimant could enforce a personal monetary order against that account. Since the account was maintained outside the jurisdiction, the court ordered the exchange to do one of two things:

- either itself convert the crypto assets into fiat currency, transfer that fiat currency to England and Wales and then pay it either directly into court[57] or pay it to the claimant's solicitors who would then pay it into court [9], [24]; or
- transfer the cryptocurrency into a wallet maintained by the claimant's solicitors, who would then themselves convert it into fiat currency, transfer it to their client account or to pay it into court directly [24].

That was all to enable the claimant to make an application to obtain a 'third party debt order' so as to enforce his personal claims against such assets paid into court or held by their solicitors in its client account.[58] However, there was no certainty that such an application would be successful, and so the court recognised that the claimant might be required to return the funds held in court to the original exchange wallet. The court therefore required the claimant to give an undertaking to the court, if the funds had to be returned to the 'persons unknown', to compensate the 'persons unknown' for any fluctuation in value since conversion into fiat currency.[59] Such exposure could be very significant, given the fluctuations of crypto asset prices.

Although this case only involves reaching into an account maintained on a cryptocurrency exchange platform,[60] rather than (as in *Tai Mo Shan*) reaching into a blockchain wallet, it again demonstrates the remedial flexibility of the courts of England and Wales when faced with crypto asset recovery issues, including ordering third parties to transfer crypto assets to others for safekeeping.

[57] The courts of England and Wales are willing and able to accept fiat currency to hold pending the outcome of disputes between the parties, however they do not (currently at least) maintain any cryptoasset wallet and so cannot receive crypto assets in the same way.

[58] Pursuant to CPR, r 72.10.

[59] *Law v Persons Unknown* (26 January 2023, unreported) [2023] WLUK 577, [29].

[60] Often referred to as a 'wallet', but strictly it is an off-chain contractual (and possibly proprietary/trust) relationship between exchange and its customer.

PART III

Insolvency and Digital Assets

9

Digital Assets in Insolvency Law's Maze: Key Issues and Possible Solutions

MATTHIAS LEHMANN

I. Introduction

Insolvency is the point of collision between the world of digital assets and the world of state law. It is at this point that the privately created assets must prove their value. No wonder, then, that the relationship between insolvency and digital assets is fraught with difficulties.[1]

The main source of these difficulties lies in the digital assets' peculiar nature. They are rivalrous, in the sense that they cannot be used without diminishing their value.[2] Their holder can exclude others from their use. And digital assets can be subject to control, which allows to transfer them to other parties or to use them as collateral. All these characteristics resemble those of traditional, tangible assets. Yet by nature, digital assets are incorporeal. They have no bodily, tangible reality. In this, they are akin to other intangible assets, in particular claims, which lack the digital assets' capacity to be controlled.[3]

This hybrid nature makes characterising digital assets for purposes of insolvency law so problematic. At the same time, the exact characterisation is essential, given that insolvency law typically draws a strict line between rights in tangible assets on the one hand and claims on the other.

[1] From the nascent literature on these problems, see, eg, M Haentjens et al., 'The Failed Hope of Disintermediation: Crypto-Custodian Insolvency, Legal Risks and How To Avoid Them' [2020] *Singapore Journal of Legal Studies* 526; J Sarra and L Gullifer, 'Crypto-claimants and bitcoin bankruptcy: challenges for recognition and realization' [2019] *International Insolvency Review* 233.

[2] On the concept of rivalrousness, see E Ostrom, 'Beyond Markets and States: Polycentric Governance of Complex Economic Systems' in DH Cole and MD McGinnis (eds), *Elinor Ostrom and the Bloomington School of Political Economy – A Compendium of Key Statements, Collaborations, and Reactions, Volume 1: Polycentricity in Public Administration and Political Science* (Lanham, Lexington Books, 2014) 115.

[3] See, eg, English Law Commission, *Digital assets: Final report* (Law Com No 412, 2023) paras 5.9– 5.12.

These problems are compounded by the functioning of the blockchain. Distributed ledger technology is designed to exclude double-spending and make the ledger tamper-proof. For this reason, any change of the ledger is excluded once a block has been added to the chain, resulting in the 'immutability' of the blockchain.[4] This may conflict with particularities of insolvency proceedings, eg, the power of the insolvency court or administrator to avoid, ie, to retroactively invalidate, specific transfers or transactions. Moreover, decentralised applications ('DApps') are running on a fully automated basis, without virtually any possibility of human intervention. This again may clash with the principles of insolvency law, which typically require a sudden halt in payments once insolvency proceedings are opened or an application for such proceedings has been filed.

All of this goes a long way in explaining the complexity of the relationship between digital assets and insolvency law. This chapter maps the main problems of this relationship. The notion of 'insolvency' will be understood in a wide sense – similar to 'bankruptcy' – as covering all collective proceedings, whether they aim at liquidation or reorganisation.[5] Pre-insolvency proceedings, such as restructurings, are not covered specifically; yet many of the considerations of this chapter may apply to them *mutatis mutandis*.

From the outset, the readers must curb their expectations. This chapter neither provides an exhaustive account nor detailed solutions to all the riddles in the relation between digital assets and insolvency law. It will merely provide an analysis of pervasive issues that plague every legal system and some suggestions for their solution. The study of this chapter thus does not spare the reader from analysing the situation of a specific legal system. Insolvency is, first and foremost, a matter of national law. It is up to every state to decide whether to take up the suggestions made or not.

The rest of this chapter will be structured along the timeline of insolvency proceedings. First, it will discuss issues arising until insolvency proceedings are opened (II). Then, problems in determining whether digital assets belong to the insolvency estate and the rights of the holders of such assets will be analysed (III). Thereafter, the focus will be on the realisation of the rights of the creditors or third-party holders of digital assets (IV), before the chapter concludes (V).

II. Pre-insolvency Phase and Effect of Opening

This part discusses the particular issues that are created in the period up until the opening of insolvency proceedings, including the moment of opening itself.

[4] On the functioning of blockchains and immutability, see RD Taufick 'Block Change: The Fallacy of Blockchain Immutability and Cartel Governance' [2020] *Notre Dame Journal on Emerging Technologies*, 307, 315 et seq.

[5] See UNCITRAL, Model Law on Cross-Border Insolvency, Art 2 (a); UNCITRAL, *Guide to Enactment and Interpretation of the UNCITRAL Model Law on Cross-Border Insolvency* (2014), Part 2, 38–39, paras 65, 66.

Insolvency law already has some effects in the pre-insolvency phase. Many of them will apply retroactively once the proceedings have been formally opened, which may create particular issues for digital assets.

A. Suspension of the Debtor's Power of Disposition – Effects on Blockchain Transfers

One effect of the insolvency proceedings is that the insolvency estate is constituted. As a consequence, the debtor loses the power to dispose of the assets, which now belong to the insolvency estate. The precise moment when this will happen varies. Some national laws put the moment of the insolvency estate's constitution at the time of the opening of the insolvency proceedings, while others refer to the time when the application for insolvency is filed.[6]

The constitution of the insolvency estate and the simultaneous disposition of the debtor may interfere with pending payments or transfers, which the debtor initiated before the relevant point in time, but which are perfected only thereafter. The key word here is 'finality'. Where a transfer is considered as being final, the transferred asset belongs to the recipient, who does not have to care about the subsequent insolvency of the transferor. On the other hand, where a transfer is not 'final', the asset in transfer belongs to the insolvency estate. This concept was first developed for payment settlement systems.[7] Later, it was extended to securities settlement systems.[8] Finality also could play a key role for transfers on the blockchain or other electronic networks.

When exactly a payment or transfer is final is ordinarily determined by the law governing such payment or transfer.[9] However, under the conditions of the blockchain, finding such a law is highly complex. Typically, the applicable law has not been chosen, and the parties to such transactions as well as their location are unknown. While attempts have been made to determine the law governing digital assets,[10] there has as of yet been little discussion of the rules governing transfers

[6] UNCITRAL, *Legislative Guide on Insolvency Law* (2005), Part 2, p 81, para 22.

[7] See NR Nelson, 'Settlement Obligations and Bank Insolvency' [1990] *Business Lawyer (ABA)* 1473, 1478 (on the introduction of settlement finality in the Clearing House Interbank Payments System [CHIPS]); see also B Geva, 'Payment Finality and Discharge in Funds Transfers' [2008] *Chicago-Kent Law Review* 635–648 (discussing payment finality and discharge of the debtor's obligation for debit and credit transfers as well as cheques).

[8] On the finality of transfers within payment and securities settlement systems under EU law, see K Löber, 'The Changing Legal Landscape for Clearing and Settlement in the European Union' [2005] *Uniform Law Review* 155, 163–165.

[9] See, eg, Art 10 Directive 98/26/EC of the European Parliament and of the Council of 19 May 1998 on settlement finality in payment and securities settlement systems [1998] OJ L166/45.

[10] See in particular the UNIDROIT, *Principles on Digital Assets and Private Law* (2023) Principle 5; see also ss 12–107 of the US Uniform Commercial Code (UCC); s 32 of the German Electronic Securities Act (*Gesetz über elektronische Wertpapiere*).

on the blockchain.[11] One possibility would be to consider the whole blockchain as a transfer system and treat it analogously to payment and securities settlement systems.[12] However, this approach is yet to be adopted by any state. Moreover, there are perennial difficulties in establishing the law that would govern such a system.[13]

Instead of assessing finality from a legal perspective, one could choose a technological approach and identify finality with the immutability of the blockchain. Under such an approach, the transfer would be final when the block containing the information about the specific transfer could no longer be changed. Yet it turns out that this point cannot be easily determined either. As Hossein Nabilou shows in his contribution to this book, this is because blockchains are not 'deterministic', but rather 'probabilistic': based on the ledger, it is impossible to say definitely that a block has become immutable; one can only speak about the probability that it will stay as is.[14] Hence, the code does not provide the law, not in relation to finality nor to other questions.

Against this background, it would perhaps be better to return to the law. An alternative legal approach would be to determine the point of finality by fiction. For instance, one could adopt a rule, either by statute or by case law, under which transfers in the Bitcoin network are deemed to be final after, say, six rounds of confirmations. To be sure, this would not inhibit any technological change of the blockchain ledger in the seventh or later round. Yet such a change would be ignored for purposes of insolvency law. Any transfer having survived six rounds of confirmations would be deemed final, meaning that the transferred asset belongs to the recipient and not to the estate, even if it were to be corrected or annulled by a later round of confirmations.

The advantage of such a rule would be that it guarantees legal certainty. Although it may be in tension with technological reality, it may be used as an anchor for the participants in the crypto economy by shaping perceptions about when a transfer is considered to be final. This, in turn, may inform practices in the crypto space, which might evolve around the legally certain – though fictitious – point in time.[15] In that regard, a healthy dialogue between the tech community and the lawyers may evolve.

[11] But see B Yüksel Ripley, 'Cryptocurrency Transfers in Distributed Ledger Technology-Based Systems and their Characterisation in Conflict of Laws' in J Borg-Barthet et al (eds), *From Theory to Practice in Private International Law: Gedächtnisschrift for Professor Jonathan Fitchen* (London, Hart Publishing, 2024) 109.

[12] On blockchains as settlement systems in the sense of the EU Finality Directive, see M Lehmann, 'Art 12: Payment systems and financial markets' in G Cuniberti and A Leandro (eds), *The European Insolvency Regulation and Implementing Legislations* (Cheltenham, Edward Elgar Publishing, 2024) para 12-001.

[13] C Wendehorst, 'Proprietary Rights in Digital Assets and the Conflict of Laws' in A Bonomi et al (eds), *Blockchain and Private International Law* (Leiden, Brill, 2023) 101, 121 et seq.

[14] See H Nabilou, ch 15 in this volume.

[15] For a more pessimistic view, see H Nabilou, ch 15 in this volume.

B. Avoidance of Suspicious Transfers on the Blockchain

Many national laws allow an insolvency court or administrator to overturn actions or transactions taken by the debtor in the run-up to insolvency. The goal is to ensure the integrity of the insolvency estate and the equal treatment of all creditors (*par conditio creditorum*).[16] Typically, avoidance is possible for transfers that took place within a certain period before a specified start date, such as the filing of an insolvency application or opening of insolvency proceedings.[17] The criteria for determining suspicious transactions vary from country to country. The EU Commission recently submitted a proposal for a directive providing, inter alia, for a minimum harmonisation of rules on avoidance actions.[18] The effect of the avoidance provisions is that the transfer is either void or voidable (vis-à-vis the creditors).[19] In the last case, the insolvency practitioner needs to bring an action declaring the transaction as being void. Crucially, in both cases, the avoidance will have retroactive effect.

How can such an effect be guaranteed on a blockchain, which by design cannot be changed by a decision of an insolvency court or practitioner? The answer is relatively simple. While the blockchain cannot be changed by a judgment or administrative measure, the insolvency court or practitioner can order a so-called 'reverse transfer'. By such an order, the recipient is obliged to send back the assets it has received. If they find themselves unable to do so, e.g. because they have already transferred it to another party, they may have to restitute a digital asset of the same type or pay the value. In any case, there is no reason to consider the immutability of the blockchain as an obstacle to the carrying out of insolvency proceedings, or of avoidances of pre-insolvency transactions.

C. Insolvency Safe Harbour for Digital Asset Claims?

A last problem that shall be briefly discussed here is whether the insolvency harbour for close-out netting is available for transactions on a blockchain. Close-out netting is a mechanism through which all outstanding obligations between the parties are upon a certain event reduced and replaced by a single obligation, representing the aggregate value of the combined obligations.[20] The purpose of close-out netting is to reduce insolvency risks. Parties to such a mechanism do not have to bear the full insolvency risk of their counterparty. This spares them from having to use costly collateral, excludes domino effects of individual insolvencies, and thereby increases the stability of the whole financial system. For this reason,

[16] UNCITRAL, *Legislative Guide on Insolvency Law* (2005), Part 2, 136, para 151.

[17] ibid, Part 2, p 135, para 150.

[18] Proposal for a Directive of the European Parliament and of the Council harmonising certain aspects of insolvency law, COM(2022) 702 final.

[19] UNCITRAL, *Legislative Guide on Insolvency Law* (2005), Part 2, 146–147, paras 186–187.

[20] UNIDROIT, *Principles on the Operation of Close-Out Netting Provisions* (2013) Principle 2.

many insolvency laws around the world recognise the validity of close-out netting mechanisms and their effects by a specific safe harbour.[21]

In the literature, it was denied that these safe harbours were also available for obligations to be paid in Bitcoin.[22] Everything depends on the specific wording: 1. of the close-out netting arrangement; and 2. of the insolvency safe harbour for these types of arrangements. However, many of the latter use terms like 'pay' or 'payment', and do not seem to be limited to official or 'fiat' currency.[23] In some states, Bitcoin or other cryptocurrencies have started to become accepted as means of payment. In one state – El Salvador – they are even an official means of payment as they have obtained legal tender status.[24] Also from a policy perspective, there is little reason to discard such obligations from close-out netting mechanisms and the safe-harbours protecting them. Creditors of Bitcoin claims run similar counterparty risks as creditors of claims to be paid in fiat money, and financial stability could be affected if these creditors are not paid and therefore must declare bankruptcy. These micro- and macroeconomic risks could be avoided by a broad interpretation of the safe harbours. Whether this is possible depends, of course, on the convertibility of the cryptocurrency into the currency used for netting. At least for cryptocurrencies with an established market like Bitcoin, this is possible. In sum, there are good reasons to argue that the insolvency safe harbour for close-out netting should be extended to obligations in digital assets.

III. Determination of Rights and Assets

Once insolvency proceedings are opened, it is important to determine the exact composition of the insolvency estate and the rights of the creditors. Again, the nature of digital assets may render this task complex.

A. Digital Assets as Part of the Estate

Perhaps the most benign difficulties exist regarding the composition of the insolvency estate. There should be no shadow of a doubt that the debtor's digital assets

[21] For a comparative overview, see P Paech, 'Systemic Risk, Regulatory Powers and Insolvency Law – The Need for an International Instrument on the Private Law Framework for Netting' (03/2010), *Institute for Law and Finance Goethe-Universität Frankfurt am Main Working Paper Series No. 116*, 18–23 www.ilf-frankfurt.de/fileadmin/_migrated/content_uploads/ILF_WP_116.pdf.

[22] Sarra and Gullifer (n 1) 258 (emphasising that it is unlikely that bitcoin would count either as money or as foreign currency in the context of a close-out netting arrangement).

[23] See, eg, the insolvency safe harbour in the Financial Collateral Directive (Directive 2002/47/EC of the European Parliament and of the Council of 6 June 2002 on financial collateral arrangements [2002] OJ L168/43) Art 7, and the definition of the term close-out netting provision in its Art 2 para 1 lit n.

[24] See El Salvador, Legislative Decree No. 57 'Ley Bitcoin', 9 June 2021 (Salvadorian Official Record No. 110, Vol 431). The Central African Republic has also briefly recognised Bitcoin as legal tender, but quickly withdrew this status.

belong to the estate. This is independent of whether the legal system governing the insolvency proceedings, the *lex fori concursus*, recognises property rights in digital assets. Even where it does not, the digital assets will become part of the estate. The simple reason is that every asset and other interest of the debtor, whether it is property or merely a claim, belongs to the insolvency estate. This is a consequence of the right of creditors to receive the fullest satisfaction possible for their claims.[25] Thus, the debtor loses the power of disposition over his digital assets at the latest when the insolvency proceedings are opened.

There remains a practical problem for the insolvency practitioner: How to identify and access the debtor's digital assets? Due to their intangible nature, the cryptographic methods used, and the pseudonymity reigning on the blockchain, it will often be difficult to trace digital assets of the debtor. Even after their existence is known, the insolvency court or practitioner may have problems in seizing them. For this, they need information, such as the private key of the digital asset or the password for a wallet in which it is stored. Finally, even if it is possible to locate and seize the digital assets, it is unsure how the estate should deal with them. Moving them into a separate address may create its own risk, such as those of a hack, with a potential liability of the insolvency administrator looming large.

In this context, it must first be stressed that concealing an asset from the insolvency court or administrator is subject to criminal sanctions in numerous states.[26] Moreover, in many jurisdictions the debtor has a duty to disclose pro-actively all of his assets. Finally, the insolvency court or practitioner has broad investigative powers, which it can use to find digital assets that belong to the debtor. Still, this does not solve all problems, since debtors may be uncooperative or outrightly hide their assets. The cryptographic methods and the global nature of the blockchain make this particularly easy. They make it necessary to search and chase digital assets worldwide.

To increase transparency, it has been suggested to establish a database or register of digital assets with a reporting obligation on the part of the person concerned.[27] However, it may be doubted that this solution will work. The high volume of daily trading in virtual assets makes it unlikely that any register could truly reflect the current ownership. Moreover, a recalcitrant debtor who does not want to cooperate with the insolvency court or practitioner will also refuse to provide the necessary information to the database or register.

[25] See, eg, 9th Appellate Court of Moscow, 15 May 2018, *Tsarkov*; on this decision, see, eg, A Jeffrey and I Kokorin, 'When Bitcoin meets insolvency: Is Bitcoin property? Dutch and Russian responses', *LexisNexis Blog* (8 June 2018) blogs.lexisnexis.co.uk/randi/when-bitcoin-meets-insolvency-is-bitcoin-property-dutch-and-russian-responses/ (reporting that the court ruled it would be arbitrary and deprive creditors of their right to fullest satisfaction of their claims if an economic value would be excluded from the insolvency estate).

[26] Sarra and Gullifer (n 22) 255 (for Canada and UK).

[27] M Schmitz (ed), *Code Mondial de l'Exécution digitale/Global Code of Digital Enforcement* (Brussels, Bruylant, 2021) Art 48 para 1.

Another proposal is to 'legitimise' virtual asset trading by conferring legal status to them.[28] It is hoped that this would allow existing traditional financial and commercial institutions to bring the technology into their frameworks and thereby reduce the use of dubious offshore entities.[29] Again, it is doubtful that this approach will bear any fruits. Introducing digital assets to the traditional financial sector will certainly make it more attractive for some users. However, it is more than likely that there will remain some who will shun the transparency that comes with banks and other regulated service providers.

A more promising route seems to be to impose duties on custodians. The vast majority of digital assets are today held in custody.[30] This creates points of centralisation, which offer ample opportunities for tracing, locating, and seizing assets. Requests of information could be issued to custodians by courts and enforcement agents.[31] These could even be addressed to custodians established in other countries.[32] If the custodian answers positively or in parallel with the disclosure order, it could be sent an injunction, requiring it to freeze a particular asset.[33] Finally, the custodian could also be tasked with the realisation of the asset, through an order to sell the asset at the highest possible market price.

Of course, this solution only works for those digital assets that are held in custody. Even if these are by far the most, there will inevitably be some that are held directly and for which the insolvency estate needs to take different, more cumbersome measures. However, this divergent treatment is not unique to digital assets. Money, for instance, is also traced, seized and realised in very different procedures, depending on whether it is held in a bank account or as cash. The practice of insolvency cannot ignore the particular characteristics of the novel phenomena. Nor can these characteristics be eliminated via special insolvency rules. It is insolvency law that needs to adapt to reality, not the other way around.

B. Treatment of Holders as Owners or Creditors

The biggest, and at the same time the thorniest, question is how digital assets are to be treated within insolvency proceedings. Are those who hold bitcoins or

[28] M Bayliss, 'Virtual Assets, Real Insolvency Issues' [2020] *Banking & Finance Law Review* 107, 115.

[29] *cf* ibid.

[30] M Lehmann et al., 'Staking Your Crypto: What are the Stakes?' [2023] *Journal of Business and Technology Law* 53, 63.

[31] See also Art 49 phrase 2 Global Code of Digital Enforcement (n 27), which provides a disclosure obligation of everyone who 'manages digital assets'. Although the wording is unclear, this may be a reference to custodians.

[32] Indeed, English courts are already issuing such requests worldwide with their disclosure orders, see, eg, *Ion Science Ltd and Duncan Johns v Persons Unknown, Binance Holdings Limited, Payward Limited and Mirriam Corp LP* (28 January 202[2], unreported), Com Ct; *LMN v Bitflyer Holdings Inc* [2022] EWHC 2954, Com Ct; *Sally Jane Danisz v Persons Unknown and Huobi Global Ltd* [2022] EWHC 280, QB. See in detail Yeo, ch 8 in this volume.

[33] See again the practice of the English courts, eg, *Ion Science Ltd and Duncan Johns v Persons Unknown, Binance Holdings Limited, Payward Limited and Mirriam Corp LP* (28 January 202[2], unreported), Com Ct; *LMN v Bitflyer Holdings Inc* [2022] EWHC 2954, Com Ct; *Sally Jane Danisz v Persons Unknown and Huobi Global Ltd* [2022] EWHC 280, QB.

other digital assets to be regarded as owners, who can demand the restitution of their property? Or are they merely creditors, with the consequence that they will have to register a claim in the insolvency proceedings and risk receiving merely a fraction?

First a terminological issue: The term 'holder' is used here provisionally to designate those who exercise control over the asset, in particular by virtue of the private key that allows to transfer such assets. It will be necessary to refine the definition of the term later when the specific relationship between the custodian and the customer is discussed.[34]

The question of how holders of digital assets are to be treated in insolvency has haunted insolvency practitioners and has led to litigation around the world.[35] It depends on how these assets are to be characterised – as property or something else. Some courts have rejected the property characterisation by stressing the intangible nature of digital assets, which would not allow to consider them as objects of ownership or other proprietary rights.[36] Other courts, however, have found little difficulty characterising digital assets as property.[37] It was argued, for instance, that bitcoins have a defined subject matter allowing them to be isolated from other assets; that they are identifiable for third parties; that they are capable of assumption; and that they have some degree of permanence and stability.[38]

In line with the general approach of this contribution, the question of how digital assets and their holders are to be treated in insolvency shall be answered here from a policy perspective and independent of the particularities of a specific legal system. On the one hand, one could argue that those who have invested in Bitcoin and similar digital assets should be taken by their words: They have bought 'cryptocurrencies', thus private money, and should receive the same treatment as money creditors. On the other hand, this view would ignore that Bitcoin is a special type of money: it is conceived as operating independently of any intermediary, allowing direct peer-to-peer transfers.[39] To achieve this purpose, it is necessary to consider the holders of these assets as being their owners until their transfer is final. Otherwise, the digital assets would have no owner at all! Clearly, those who invest in Bitcoin believe, and are led to believe, that they

[34] See II.B.

[35] For an overview, see L Pascoe, 'Digital currency exchanges, ICOs and insolvency: the story so far' [2019] *Insolvency and Restructuring International* 5. Further discussion by Bayliss (n 28); Sarra and Gullifer (n 22); E Inacio, 'Digital assets in insolvency and restructuring' [2018] *Eurofenix Spring* 12–13.

[36] See, eg, Tokyo District Court, Civil Division 28, 5th August 2015 (Year of Heisei 27), Mt Gox, Heisei 26 (Year of 2014), (Wa)33320, for a full translation of the judgment, see Megumi Hara et al. www.law.ox.ac.uk/sites/files/oxlaw/mtgox_judgment_final.pdf.

[37] See, eg, High Court of New Zealand, *Ruscoe v Cryptopia Limited (in liquidation)* [2020] NZHC 728, at para 120 (ruling that cryptocurrencies may be considered as property in insolvency proceedings under the Common law and statutory law in New Zealand).

[38] ibid, para 114–119 (relying on the definition of property by Lord Wilberforce in *National Provincial Bank Ltd v Ainsworth* [1965] AC 1175 (HL), at 1242–1249).

[39] S Nakamoto, 'Bitcoin: A Peer-to-Peer Electronic Cash System' www.bitcoin.org/bitcoin.pdf.

acquire proprietary rights. The Bitcoin White Paper says as much since it repeatedly employs the term 'ownership'.[40] Of course, this belief may be deemed wrong from a legal perspective. Yet denying digital assets property status in insolvency would mean denying investment protection, disappointing investors, and pulling the rug from under the feet of an entire industry. At the same time, it would provide a windfall to other creditors, who have done little to deserve a share in the value of digital assets that others have acquired.

The better policy reasons speak thus in favour of recognising rights in digital assets. This concerns not only ownership, but also limited rights *in rem*, such as liens, pledges or mortgages. This also is the position adopted by international soft law, namely the UNIDROIT Principles on Digital Assets and Private Law, which were adopted in 2023, and call for the recognition of 'proprietary rights' in digital assets.[41] States should adapt their law accordingly and treat digital assets as objects of proprietary rights. This can be achieved either via legislation or court decisions. Where statutes stand in the way, they should be amended; where it is old case law, it should be overruled.

C. Property Rights of Digital Asset Custodians or Customers?

The plea for the recognition of proprietary rights in digital assets still leaves open the question to whom such rights should belong. This problem is particularly salient in the custody context. Is the custodian to be regarded as the owner, or the client for whom the custodian holds the digital assets?

Before trying to answer this question, two points must be addressed. First, certain countries that do not recognise property rights in digital assets and, for this reason, do not acknowledge any rights of the customer have found another way to protect the customer. Instead of granting a substantive right, they have devised a procedural mechanism. This mechanism will be discussed later.[42]

Second, it is necessary to come back to the definition of the term 'holder', which depends on the exercise of control. In the custody situation, either the custodian or the customer can be considered the 'holder' of the digital asset. In many cases, the custodian has the exclusive access to the private keys and thus exercises control over the assets. It is thus the 'holder'. However, it holds these keys on behalf and/or in the interest of the customer. In other words, it exercises control *for* the customer, which may justify considering the latter as being their owner. The determination who 'holds' the digital assets is thus not necessarily conclusive for answering the question who owns them.

[40] ibid.

[41] UNIDROIT *Principles on Digital Assets and Private Law* (2023) Principle 3 (1) and commentary, paras 3.1.–3.4. On the effects of such proprietary rights in insolvency, see Principle 19 paras 19.1.–19.12.

[42] See III.C.

In analysing whether the digital assets belong to the custodian or its customer, particular emphasis has been laid on the terms of the custody agreement.[43] It has been meticulously studied, for instance, whether the terms employ expressions such as 'your assets', 'trust' or similar words that may be indicative of the distribution of property rights between the custodian and the customer. It is true that the terms of the agreement have some value in this respect. In particular, they are decisive for the question of whether there is custody *at all* or a different arrangement. For instance, customers often administer the digital assets themselves, with the intermediary or platform only providing ancillary services, such as the protection of access to the private keys.[44] In this case, it is difficult to speak of custody. There is hardly any doubt that such an arrangement does not impinge upon the distribution of title. Hence, the digital assets remain with the customers.

Beyond the question of the nature of the agreement, however, one should not place too much emphasis on the terms and conditions. More often than not, they are drafted in an ambiguous way.[45] Further, their content is exclusively determined by the custodians, who naturally favour their particular interests when drafting them. Moreover, the terms and conditions often contain technical language, which is poorly understood by their users. Most of all, users normally do not read terms and conditions, but merely accept them by 'ticking the box'. And even if they would read and understand them, they hardly have any chance to influence their content due to their inferior bargaining position. The rights of the customer should not depend on a document that either does not clearly decide the issue or in a way is detrimental to the user, who is generally unaware of it and cannot influence its content.

Instead of leaving this decision to a detailed study of the terms and conditions, the state should intervene, either via the legislator or the courts. In order to secure legal certainty, a general policy decision is necessary. Do customers deserve to be protected in the event of insolvency of their custodian as having proprietary rights to the digital assets held in their name? Asked this way, there cannot be any doubt that the answer to this question must be affirmative. In the conflict between custody customers and general creditors, the first clearly deserve priority over the latter. Most customers believe they would not worsen their legal status by using a custodian; otherwise, they would simply not use one. The state also has an

[43] See, eg, M Haentjens et al., 'The Failed Hopes of Disintermediation: Crypto-Custodian Insolvency, Legal Risks and How to Avoid Them' [2020]) *Singapore Journal of Legal Studies* 526, 535–538 (examining the terms and conditions of Coinbase and Gemini); Sarra and Gullifer (n 22) 240 (examining the terms and conditions of Coinbase and Freewallet).

[44] An example for this type of service are the so-called 'non-custodial wallets', see, eg, GM Nori and M Girolametti, 'International Insolvency Law and Cryptocurrencies' in Bonomi et al. (n 13) 417, 443 (defining non-custodial wallets as those for which the intermediary does not take custody and control over the private keys of the user).

[45] For a comprehensive analysis of custody agreements, see D Zetzsche and A Nikolakopoulou, ch 11 in this volume.

interest in encouraging and protecting this expectation. If even established and trusted custodians were not considered as protecting customers' rights, the latter would have even fewer incentives to keep their assets directly or use shady offshore intermediaries. Custody of digital assets is a socially useful activity, which serves an important purpose, namely securing and protecting the wealth of the customers. A protection of customer rights in custody has also been provided by legislators and courts in the case of securities custody. Today, it would simply be unimaginable that the title of investors in shares or bonds should depend on the terms and conditions of the custodian. Instead, they are clearly and uniformly regulated by legislation.[46] The custodians are not necessarily disfavoured by such protection. On the contrary, it increases the trust in the whole industry if their customers' rights are safeguarded in the event of their insolvency. That they do not guarantee such protection themselves via their terms and conditions can only be explained by the – not uncommon – mistake of ignoring a public good for private, short-term goals.

Tightly interwoven with the problem of customer rights is how digital assets are stored. Some custodians create unique blockchain addresses for each individual customer. In this case, the customers' proprietary rights can be acknowledged without any problems, as the assets can be easily attributed to specific individuals. Other custodians, however, store digital assets in so-called omnibus addresses, where they are lumped together with those of other investors.[47] In this case, the assets cannot be attributed to an individual, but only to a community of investors. This does not necessarily exclude property protection, though. Omnibus accounts are also used by custodians of securities in the financial industries. It has been recognised that their customers enjoy collective rights in the assets, such as co-ownership or securities entitlements.[48] Of course, this approach runs into problems where there are insufficient assets for all of the custodian's customers. But a shortfall can be made up by holding the custodian liable; and if the custodian is insolvent and does not have sufficient assets, the loss can be distributed pro rata among the customers of the omnibus account.[49] This still serves investors better than having no property protection at all. Therefore, the way in which the assets are held is not determinative for the recognition of property rights of the customers.

[46] In the US, see Art 8 of the US Uniform Commercial Code (UCC); in the EU, see Regulation (EU) No 909/2014 of the European Parliament and of the Council of 23 July 2014 on improving securities settlement in the European Union and on central securities depositories OJ L257/1.

[47] Haentjens et al. (n 43) 535 and 537 (juxtaposing the omnibus addresses used by Coinbase and the segregated addresses used by Gemini).

[48] See, eg, T Keijser and CW Mooney Jr., 'Intermediated Securities Holding Systems Revisited: A View Through the Prism of Transparency' in L Gullifer and J Payne, *Intermediation and Beyond* (Oxford, Hart Publishing, 2019) 309.

[49] See, eg, Art 26 para 2 lit b UNIDROIT Convention on Substantive Rules for Intermediated Securities (Geneva, 9 October 2009; Geneva Convention).

However, the protection of property rights fails where the custodian has transferred all customers' assets to third parties in good faith or mixed them with its own assets. In this case, there is no other way for the customers than to register a claim in the insolvency proceedings. Yet, the situation is here no different than in other cases of fraudulent custodians. The customer can only avoid this risk by carefully selecting her contractual partner.

Some authors suggest that the protection of customers may be achieved via regulation.[50] Yet regulation cannot make up for private property rights in insolvency. Regulatory rules, however stringent, may be violated by the custodians. Customers would thus be left high and dry in the event of an insolvency, and the tightest net of regulatory duties thrown over intermediaries would not help them.

However, there are some states that do not recognise property rights in intangible assets.[51] They have to search for other ways of protecting the customer. A very original solution has been found in Switzerland. Swiss law does not recognise ownership in digital assets apart from those representing a claim or other asset.[52] In order to protect customers of crypto custodians, the Swiss legislator introduced a special procedural mechanism in its Debt Enforcement and Bankruptcy Law.[53] This mechanism applies if a custodian had the obligation to keep crypto-based assets (*kryptobasierte Vermögenswerte*) for a client available at all times, and if there is a sufficient nexus between the client and the respective assets of the estate. The sufficient nexus exists if either of two conditions is met: a) the crypto-based asset can be individually allocated to the client (eg, because it is held in an individual blockchain address or because it is allocated to him in the internal recordings of the custodian); or b) the crypto-based asset is allocated to a community of clients, but the individual share of the client is evident.[54] These conditions resemble closely those that exist in other laws for the recognition of property rights. And indeed, their effects are the same: The insolvency practitioner (or insolvency court, as the case may be) is obliged to make an order for the restitution of the crypto-based assets. Nevertheless, the procedural mechanism cannot fully substitute the recognition of proprietary rights. To give just two examples, it is unable to explain how persons obtain title to digital assets, and how collateral rights in such assets can be created.

To sum up, investors in digital assets deserve protection in insolvency, regardless of whether they hold these assets directly or through a custodian. This protection is best ensured by recognising substantive proprietary rights in such assets.

[50] D Zetzsche and A Nikolakopoulou, ch 11 in this volume.

[51] See, eg, on Japanese law T Morishita, ch 14 in this volume.

[52] On those so-called registered values (*Registerwerte*), see ss 973d–973i Swiss Code of Obligations (*Obligationenrecht*).

[53] S 242a Swiss Debt Enforcement and Bankruptcy Law (*Schuldbeitreibungs- und Konkursgesetz* – SchKG).

[54] See on the draft of this provision B Maurenbrecher and U Meier, 'DLT Draft Law – Insolvency Law Aspects' *2020/03 CapLaw* www.caplaw.ch/2020/dlt-draft-law-insolvency-law-aspects/.

The importance of granting proprietary rights in digital assets is also recognised by international soft law.[55] States should adapt their law accordingly to respond to the special risks of the new asset class.

IV. Realisation of Rights

After it has been decided to whom the digital assets belong – whether to the estate, the direct holder, the custodian, the customer, or another party – the story is far from over. It now becomes crucial how these rights can be realised. In this context, one must distinguish between three situations: In the first, the digital assets do not belong to the estate but to some other person, eg, a customer of the insolvent custodian or a third party to whom they have been transferred; in this case, the question is how the assets will be restored to them. In the second situation, a person has a claim for digital assets, for instance, a creditor of the insolvent debtor; in this case, it may be necessary to assess the value of the assets. In the third situation, digital assets are part of the insolvency estate; in this case, they must be sold off for the benefit of the creditors. In all of these situations, particular issues may arise due to the nature of digital assets.

A. Restitution of Digital Assets to Holder

Where digital assets are controlled by the insolvency court or administrator, but belong to another person, they must be restituted to that person. This is of particular significance in the event of insolvency of an intermediary who holds digital assets for its customers.[56] These customers must be able to recover 'their' assets. But it may also be relevant in other situations, for instance, where the insolvent debtor has received digital assets under a contract that turns out to be void.

The simplest and safest way to allow for such recovery is to acknowledge a right *in rem*, or proprietary right, of the customer in the digital assets.[57] An alternative is to provide for a procedural right to restitution.[58] But how are digital assets actually restituted? This is easier said than done.[59] Since they have no corporeal reality, digital assets cannot just be handed over. Theoretically, the private key could be recorded on a piece of paper or on a USB key, which would then be delivered to the customer. Yet this would not only be very cumbersome but also very risky.

[55] See above n 41.
[56] See above III.B.
[57] See above III.C.
[58] See above III.C on Swiss law.
[59] See also Swiss Federal Council (Schweizerischer Bundesrat), 'Botschaft zum Bundesgesetz zur Anpassung des Bundesrechts an Entwicklungen der Technik verteilter elektronischer Register' (27 November 2019), BBl 2020 233, 263 et seq., 291 et seq.

One option is to transfer the digital assets to another custodian. But this again entails certain risks, as the assets could be lost during the transfer or by the receiving custodian. What is more, this method also creates transfer fees, which may be significant. Furthermore, it is not easy to select the proper custodian. This selection could be done by each customer, who would be allowed to designate a custodian of choice. But in this case, the administrative burden for the insolvency practitioner is very high. An alternative is to transfer all digital assets to one and the same custodian. This seems especially appropriate where all assets are held together in an omnibus account; but also, assets held in individual blockchain addresses by the insolvent custodian could be transferred to a successor institution. A downside of this approach is that the customer will have no say over the selection of the new institution, although it will have to deal with it from now on.

Another option is to send the private keys to a public address of the customer. As a result, the customers would hold the assets themselves. An advantage of this solution is that the customer would not have to deal with a new intermediary. She would also have direct control over her assets. But a negative is that the transfer would generate fees. Moreover, it would not only be very risky but also quite cumbersome for the intermediary to send the assets to each customer's individual address.[60] Finally, some customers may not have sufficient technological knowledge to manage their digital assets themselves.

The best option seems to be to leave the holder the choice between both options. This is almost inevitable when the digital assets are owned by a third party who has not entrusted them to the insolvent debtor. In such a case, the third party has an unfettered right to receive the digital assets, and it should be able to decide on the way in which they are returned. But the customer of an insolvent custodian should also have the right to choose the preferred option of restitution. True, fulfilling the customer's wishes may generate costs, in form of transfer fees and administrative burdens. But such costs could be charged to him, especially where they are higher than absolutely necessary.[61] The customer may have a contractual or tort claim against the debtor for the compensation of these expenses, which he can register in the insolvency proceedings.

B. Valuation of Digital Assets (Claims)

A subject that has attracted considerable attention is the question of how to assess the value of digital assets in the context of insolvency.[62] This issue can come up

[60] To illustrate, in one case – Voyager – in-kind distribution of digital assets to 120,000 customers was rejected due to its complexity and the risks involved, see T Kostoula, 'Valuation of cryptoassets in EU insolvency: Challenges and prospects' [2023] *International Insolvency Review* 8, 29.

[61] See also s 242a para 4 Swiss Debt Enforcement and Bankruptcy Law (obliging the party requesting restitution to bear the costs).

[62] See, eg, Bayliss (n 28); Kostoula (n 60).

in two different ways: First, there may be a need to determine the value of the digital assets themselves, for instance when calculating the value of an estate that comprises such assets, or when assessing whether the debtor is solvent or insolvent. Second, it may be necessary to determine the value of claims for digital assets that have been registered in the debtor's insolvency proceedings. Among these two issues, the second stands out, as the problem of calculating the value of claims is particularly urgent and determinative for individual rights.

One can often hear or read the complaint that the valuation of digital assets would create special problems.[63] The primary reason cited is their high volatility, which would make it difficult to assess their value correctly and ensure the best possible outcome for creditors.[64] These problems are typically illustrated by various cases. The most famous is the case of Mt. Gox, once the leading exchange for Bitcoin, which filed for insolvency in 2014.[65] The subsequent spike of the Bitcoin price caused the Japanese insolvency court to replace the pending bankruptcy proceedings with 'rehabilitation proceedings'.[66] These proceedings, which promise a better return for creditors, are not available in most jurisdictions. Another frequently cited case is *Hashfast*,[67] where the defendant allegedly owed the bankruptcy estate bitcoins after the avoidance of a transfer. Here again, the spectacular rise in Bitcoin's value during the proceedings created an issue. The defendant's lawyer applied to the bankruptcy court to characterise Bitcoin as a currency, which would have fixed the value of the claim to that at the time of the transfer.[68] A different issue arose in the *Envion* case, which concerned a token issuer over whom insolvency proceedings had been opened in Switzerland. Some of the creditors had claims for Ether, the native asset of the Ethereum network, against the debtor. Under the rules of Swiss bankruptcy law, these claims had to be converted into fiat money. Again, the volatility of the crypto market created the question of which time should be used for the conversion. From cases like these, it is generally concluded that special rules regarding the valuation of digital assets in insolvency would be needed.[69]

Although the volatility of digital assets is undeniably very high, this does not in and of itself require and justify an entirely new approach to valuation. Similar valuation problems also exist for other volatile assets, eg, options, futures, or contracts for difference, whose value may be completely extinguished in a matter of seconds. That is precisely the reason why a fixed point in time is needed for

[63] Bayliss (n 28) 110–116; Kostoula (n 60) 16–18.

[64] ibid.

[65] On this case, see Morishita, ch 14 in this volume.

[66] ibid.

[67] *Hashfast Technologies LLC v Lowe* (*In re Hashfast Technologies, LLC*), Case No. 14-30725-DM (Bankr. N.D. Cal. Feb. 22, 2016).

[68] See *In Re Hashfast Technologies LLC*, Case No. 14-30725-DM, Defendant Dr. Marc A. Lowe's Opposition to Motion for Partial Summary Judgment, Summary available at www.georgiabankruptcy-blog.com/files/2016/02/Bitcoin-Def-Brief.pdf.

[69] Bayliss (n 28); Kostoula (n 60) 21 (suggesting that international standards could benefit from a re-examination because they were not drafted with cryptoassets in mind); Pascoe (n 35) 7 (reminding that the conversion of crypto assets to fiat currency may prove important in a volatile market).

their valuation. Such a fixed point in time is indispensable to ensure the ordered and smooth running of the insolvency procedure. It would create insurmountable complexities and inequities if the valuation could be challenged later when the value of the asset had developed favourably.

The precise moment can be, eg, the time of opening of the insolvency proceedings, or the time when the insolvency application is filed. Necessarily, there is some arbitrariness in this fixing. And undoubtedly, the accompanying rigidity may cause hardship for investors in digital assets. If these are to be avoided, the best method is to recognise a right of investors to segregate their assets from the debtor's estate.[70] In this way, they can claim the restitution of the *asset* itself, sparing them the risk of an unfavourable or deficient valuation of the asset at the start of the insolvency proceedings. At the same time, this also safeguards the estate from the danger of a precipitous fall in value of the digital assets during the course of the proceedings. The solution to the valuation conundrum thus does not lie in a reform of the valuation methods, but in the granting of *in rem* or procedural rights for investors in digital assets.

Admittedly, not all investors in digital assets can receive such a right. For example, such a right cannot be granted to those who have ordered digital assets from the debtor and transferred fiat money or cryptocurrencies to that effect, but whose order has not yet been executed. In this case, there are simply no digital assets which could be restituted to the creditor. Another case is where digital assets have been 'stolen' from an exchange or custodian by a hacker. In cases such as these, it is unavoidable to assess the value of the claim, and thus of the digital assets which are its object. How should this be done?

One possibility is to use general accounting rules, such as the International Valuation Standards (IVS) or the International Financial Reporting Standards (IFRS).[71] However, most of them do not contain specific provisions for digital assets. Instead, they contain pre-existing categories, which would have to be applied, such as 'financial instruments' or 'intangible assets'. For others, an adequate category is lacking, eg stablecoins.

For this reason, a whole plethora of new approaches have been suggested, such as referring to the cost of production, the future returns of the digital asset, or the size of the network.[72] All of these factors seem highly speculative and fail to reflect the true present value of the digital assets. The cost of production, for instance, says nothing about the demand for a certain asset; the future returns remain often highly improbable; and the size of the network only provides a weak indication about the value of the assets traded on it.

Consequently, the only remaining option is to use classical methods of valuation. The first of them is the market approach: Many digital assets are traded on

[70] See above III.B.
[71] Kostoula (n 60) 19–20.
[72] ibid 23–25 (referring to the cost of production, equation of exchange and network value to transaction ratio).

exchanges or through other service providers. These publish or offer specific prices for the digital assets, which can be used to determine their value. Where there are price differences between several exchanges, one can use a median value or refer to the exchange with the highest trading volume.

Where a digital asset is not traded on a crypto exchange, but generates a future income, for instance a utility token, one can use the discounted cash flow approach. Under this approach, the future revenue will be calculated and then discounted to achieve a present value of the returns. This approach can only be used where the future returns are certain, eg, in cases where the right to receive preexisting goods or to use a certain service, the provision of which is ensured, is represented by a utility token.

For tokens for which there is no liquid market and which do not create any income, such as Non-Fungible Token (NFT), it has been suggested to follow a cost approach.[73] This approach is based on cost of a property of equal utility.[74] However, for NFT or similar digital assets, there is no object of equal utility in the real world. It will therefore be necessary to find out if there are other, similar digital assets that have been sold for value, and use their price for appraisal purposes. If not, the only remaining option is to value the digital asset at zero.

In sum, it is not necessary to reinvent the wheel in order to determine the value of digital assets. The traditional and time-honoured methods that are applied in other areas, such as the market approach or the discounted cash flow approach, can be used for this purpose. These methods should not be applied depending on a particular category to which the digital asset belongs, such as cryptocurrency, stablecoin or utility token. Rather, one should apply them following a waterfall: where a market for a digital asset exists, the price on this market indicates the value; where no such market exists, but the digital asset generates a guaranteed revenue in the future, one should use the discounted cash flow method; failing that, one must look for substitute digital assets with a price tag. Where none of these methods is available, one must assign the digital asset zero value.

C. Sale of Estate or Digital Assets

A very different issue, and one that must be carefully distinguished from the valuation of the claims of investors, is how the value of the digital assets belonging to the insolvency estate shall be realised. In accordance with the general goal of insolvency proceedings, it is necessary to maximise the value of such assets, for the benefit of the registered creditors.

The ideal solution in such cases is a reorganisation, in which the whole business is sold. An example would be the sale of a crypto exchange or other service

[73] ibid 22.

[74] Tegova, European Valuation Standards (2020), 152, para 4.7 www.tegova.org/static/72fa037473e198cbd428e465158bcfdb/a6048c931cdc93_TEGOVA_EVS_2020_digital.pdf.

provider to a competitor. This allows to realise the business' value as a going concern. Still, a buyer for the whole business needs to be found in the first place. In addition, reorganisation requires in many countries a plan, which needs to be approved by the creditors. Even if they agree, competition authorities may still halt the deal where it would create or increase a dominant market position.

Where reorganisation is impossible or disallowed, it is necessary to proceed to liquidation, ie the sale of individual assets. For some digital assets, this may be especially challenging.

Little difficulties are presented by those digital assets that are traded on crypto exchanges. These exchanges can be used to sell off the digital assets belonging to the estate. Where the debtor itself is such an exchange, the assets have to be sold on competing exchanges. Typically, crypto exchanges are highly liquid, meaning they provide a sufficiently large pool of digital assets or fiat money that is necessary for the quick execution of orders to buy or sell such assets.[75] They also publish prices for digital assets that facilitate the search for the appropriate moment of a sale.

One particular problem, however, is that the sale of large chunks of a specific type of digital assets on these exchanges may depress its market price. This problem emerged in the insolvency of Mt. Gox, where the sale of significant amounts of Bitcoin created a bear market, ultimately depriving the investors of some value that could otherwise have been realised.[76] To avoid such a situation, the insolvency practitioner should tread carefully when selling digital assets of the estate.

For digital assets that are not traded, it is necessary to find individual buyers. This could be done, for instance, through an auction. But some digital assets have no secondary market or individual party that would be interested. In that case, a realisation is not possible.

V. Conclusion

Digital assets create a number of specific problems in insolvency. The reason is their intangible and cryptographic nature, which makes it difficult to trace and locate them and to assess their value. However, it is important to not overstate the difficulties. Most of them can be solved by using the existing legal rules, techniques and instruments. These need to be adapted to the specific context of digital assets. Above all, in order to protect investors in the event of insolvency, it is necessary that states recognise proprietary rights in digital assets. Otherwise, the investors in such assets will be faced with unsurmountable difficulties in realising their rights.

[75] On the notion of liquidity, see R Veil (ed), *European Capital Markets Law* (Oxford, Hart Publishing, 2022) § 9 para 6 et seq.

[76] Pascoe (n 35) 6 (recounting that the trustee of Mt. Gox was criticised for creating a Bitcoin bear market by selling large quantities of the cryptocurrency).

10

Digital Assets in Enforcement and Insolvency from a Liechtenstein Legal Perspective

THOMAS NÄGELE AND MARKUS STELZL

I. Introduction

Blockchain technology has arrived in the middle of society and is becoming increasingly relevant to more and more areas of daily life. As such, crypto assets may lead to questions in case a natural person or a company becomes insolvent or in case a person intends to enforce its rights with crypto assets being involved. Are digital assets part of the insolvency estate? Is it possible for a creditor to enforce, eg, a pledge over digital assets, and how is the procedure? The following article is intended to shed some light on such questions and give an overview of the legal implications of digital assets in enforcement and insolvency from a Liechtenstein legal perspective.

II. Short Introduction to the Liechtenstein Blockchain Act (TVTG)

The Principality of Liechtenstein is one of the first countries worldwide to introduce a law specifically dealing with digital assets. The so-called Token and TT Service Provider Act (TVTG)[1] was first published on 1 January 2020 and covers civil law as well as supervisory law aspects of the token economy in the Principality of Liechtenstein. The TVTG, together with the enactment of uncertificated securities in the final section of the Law on Persons and Companies (SchlT PGR),[2] enables

[1] Gesetz vom 3. Oktober 2019 über Token und VT-Dienstleister (Token und VT-Dienstleistergesetz; TVTG).

[2] Personen- und Gesellschaftsrecht vom 20. Januar 1926 (PGR).

the tokenisation of certain rights.[3] The digital representation of rights in a token by means of trustworthy technologies[4] is described as 'tokenisation'.[5] Tokenisation thereby comprises the technical design and the legal connection between the token and the right represented in the token.[6] When reading the TVTG, one will notice that the legislative authority of the Principality of Liechtenstein intentionally used technology-neutral terms instead of 'Blockchain' or 'Distributed Ledger Technology' and avoided using other terms due to possible terminological and technological changes in the future.[7] The TVTG is therefore ready for potential future changes in technology or terminology.

A. Token Pursuant to the TVTG

A token[8] can be described as a 'container' that can be 'filled' with certain rights.[9] The so-called 'Token-Container-Model'[10] has been created by *Nägele*[11] and is the pinpoint of the TVTG.

As mentioned above, a token can, but does not necessarily have to represent any right. Therefore, two types of tokens can be distinguished, the so-called 'intrinsic' and 'extrinsic' tokens.[12] Intrinsic tokens are – in terms of the TVTG – empty containers that do not represent a right and therefore do not derive their value or any benefits from external rights.[13] A popular example of an intrinsic token for purposes of the TVTG is Bitcoin, because Bitcoin is a token ('empty container') pursuant to the TVTG, but it does not represent any right against an issuer or anyone else. Extrinsic tokens, in comparison, are containers that

[3] T Nägele, *Die Rechtsnatur von Token* (Vaduz, DLT Media, 2021) 9, 84; M Stelzl and T Feldkircher, 'Die Verpfändung von Krypto-Assets – Ein (Aus)Blick nach Liechtenstein und das Regime der Verpfändung von Wertrechten' [2022] *Zeitschrift für das Recht der digitalen Wirtschaft* 330.

[4] TVTG 2020, Art 2 para 1 lit a) defines 'Trustworthy Technology (TT)' as: 'Technologies through which the integrity of Tokens, the clear assignment of Tokens to TT Identifiers and the disposal over Tokens is ensured.'

[5] Bericht und Antrag der Regierung an den Landtag des Fürstentums Liechtenstein betreffend die Schaffung eines Gesetzes über Token und VT-Dienstleister (Token- und VT-Dienstleister-Gesetz; TVTG) und die Abänderung weiterer Gesetze (BuA) No 54/2019, 58. See also Nägele (n 3) 35.

[6] Nägele (n 3) 9.

[7] BuA No 54/2019, 59.

[8] TVTG 2020, Art 2 para 1 lit c) defines 'Token' as 'a piece of information on a TT System which (i) can represent claims or rights of memberships against a person, rights to property or other absolute or relative rights; and (ii) is assigned to one or more TT Identifiers'.

[9] BuA No 54/2019, 58 et seq; see also T Feldkircher and M Stelzl, 'Sustainable Finance: Nachhaltigkeit durch Tokenisierung?' [2021] *Zeitschrift für das Recht der nachhaltigen Entwicklung* 381.

[10] On the 'Token Container Model', T Nägele and N Xander 'De lege ferenda: Überblick über das "Token Container"-Modell im TVTG' in C Piska and O Völkel (eds), *Blockchain rules* (Vienna, MANZ, 2019) 394 et seq.

[11] Nägele (n 3) 9, 84.

[12] S Möllenkamp and L Shmatenko, 'Blockchain und Kryptowährungen' in T Hoeren, U Sieber and B Holznagel (eds), *Handbuch Multimedia-Recht*, 58th edn (Munich, C.H. Beck, 2022). See also Nägele (n 3) 89 et seq.

[13] Nägele (n 3) 91.

contain rights.[14] An example of an extrinsic token would be a token that represents the rights of a shareholder of a company limited by shares (*Aktiengesellschaft*). The definition of a token pursuant to the TVTG is very wide and includes any category of token, including what is often referred to as crypto coins or cryptocurrency. MiCAR,[15] for instance, distinguishes between 'asset-referenced token', 'electronic money token' and 'utility token'. All of these categories fall within the definition of a token pursuant to the TVTG, but the TVTG does not provide for any categories of tokens.

A notable particularity of the Liechtenstein blockchain law is that with the linking of the TVTG to Section 81a para SchlT PGR, it was made legally possible to create uncertificated securities.[16] Accordingly, a debtor may issue rights with the same function as securities as uncertificated securities or replace fungible securities by uncertificated securities, provided that certain conditions are met. This means that every right capable of being securitised is also capable of being represented by uncertificated securities, since the legislator has placed uncertificated securities on an equal footing with certified securities. Any right securitised in an uncertificated security can also be represented in a token within the meaning of the TVTG. This opens up the possibility to create (uncertified) security tokens pursuant to the TVTG.

B. Trustworthy Technology

As already briefly introduced, the TVTG uses the term Trustworthy Technology (TT) and TT Systems[17] to describe the technological basis in a technology neutral way. The current technological basis of the TVTG is blockchain technology. Blockchain technology has a specific technological structure, which makes it almost impossible for individuals to change information in their favour and without authorisation. If this applies to a system, the technological structure of the system can prevent misuse by design. The systems structured in this way are classified as TT and TT systems.[18] From this inevitably follows that not necessarily all blockchains fall under the scope of the TVTG. If a blockchain does not fulfil the quality criteria necessary to qualify as a TT system within the meaning of the TVTG, it falls out of scope and a service provider not using a TT system cannot register as a TT service provider pursuant to the TVTG.

[14] Nägele (n 3) 92.

[15] Regulation (EU) 2023/1114 of the European Parliament and of the Council of 31 May 2023 on markets in crypto-assets, and amending Regulations (EU) No 1093/2010 and (EU) No 1095/2010 and Directives 2013/36/EU and (EU) 2019/1937 [2023] OJ L150/40.

[16] Stelzl and Feldkircher (n 3) 330 to 335.

[17] TVTG 2020, Art 2 para 1 lit a) defines 'TT Systems' as 'Transaction systems which allow for the secure transfer and storage of Tokens and the rendering of services based on this by means of trustworthy technology'.

[18] Nägele (n 3) 67.

C. Rules for Disposal of Tokens

The TVTG provides for specific rules for the disposal of tokens, which are, in particular, laid down in Articles 6 and 7 TVTG.

Whereas Article 6 TVTG defines what a disposal over a token is and specifies the requirements for a valid disposal, Article 7 para 1 TVTG establishes the principle that a disposal over the token results in the disposal over the right represented by the token. However, the principle of Article 7 para 1 TVTG is to be read restrictively and in consideration of Article 7 para 2 TVTG. Taking this into account, Article 7 para 1 TVTG only takes effect if the legal effects – ie, the transfer of the right represented by the token in the case of technological transfer of the token – occur by operation of law.[19] Consequently, synchronisation between the analogue and digital worlds only takes place if the applicable civil law actually provides for this legal consequence for the respective right represented in the token.[20]

Legal relationships in the analogue world are governed by the applicable Liechtenstein law. Therefore, depending on the right represented in the token – in addition to the transfer of the right to dispose of the token taking place at the digital level – the legal requirements and conditions for the transfer of the tokenised right pursuant to general principles of Liechtenstein law have to be met for a legally effective disposal of the token.[21] If, for example, the right of ownership to a watch is tokenised, in simplified terms, in addition to the transfer of the right of disposal of the token at the digital level, the conclusion of a purchase agreement and the physical transfer – or a permissible transfer surrogate (*Übergabesurrogat*) – of the watch to the purchaser are also necessary for the transfer of ownership right at the analogue level. Only if both, the digital transfer of the token and the analog transfer of the watch, are legally and factually effected, the right represented in the token is transferred.

D. TT Service Providers

In addition to the civil law section, the TVTG contains a supervisory law section that in particular provides for a registration obligation for various TT Service Providers.[22] The TVTG provides for registration duties for the services provided by a total of eleven categories of TT Service Providers, including, eg, a Token

[19] BuA No 54/2019, 168 et seq; Nägele (n 3) 89; Stelzl and Feldkircher (n 3) 330 to 335.

[20] T Feldkircher and U Wegstein, 'Die Tokenisierung von Eigentumsrechten im Fürstentum Liechtenstein' [2021] *Zeitschrift für das Recht der digitalen Wirtschaft* 177; Stelzl and Feldkircher (n 3) 330 to 335.

[21] SL Wild, *Zivilrecht und Token-Ökonomie in Liechtenstein. Eine Analyse der zivilrechtlichen Bestimmungen des TVTG unter Berücksichtigung des Wertrechts* (Vienna, Verlag Österreich, 2020) 65; Stelzl and Feldkircher (n 3) 330 to 335.

[22] TVTG 2020, Art 2 para 1 lit i).

Issuer,[23] TT Key Depository[24] or TT Exchange Service Provider.[25] All TT service providers have in common that they provide a service to a third party, with the exception of the token issuer, which may also be required to register under the TVTG, if it issues tokens in its own name. A so called 'self-issuer' is however only subject to the registration obligation if tokens in the amount of CHF 5 million or more are issued within a period of 12 months.

III. Short Introduction to Liechtenstein Enforcement Law

Liechtenstein enforcement law is set out in the Liechtenstein Enforcement Act (EO).[26] This act provides for the enforcement of a claim of the creditor determined in an enforceable title against its debtor. A condition for any enforcement is therefore a legally enforceable title. An enforcement title is a formal document issued in a formal procedure that confers enforceability of a claim.[27] The different enforcement titles are set out in Article 1 EO. This may, for instance, be a payment order (*Zahlungsbefehl*), judgment (*Urteil*) or order (*Beschluss*) of a domestic court in the Principality of Liechtenstein.

To initiate enforcement proceedings, the creditor has to file for the opening of the enforcement procedure by way of a formal enforcement application.[28] The competent court is the District Court of Vaduz, and the relevant judge usually grants enforcement without prior hearing, but only if the relevant claim of the creditor is already due. Besides an appeal (*Rekurs*), the debtor may defend himself by way of opposition action (*Oppositionsklage*)[29] or impugnation action (*Impugnationsklage*).[30] The opposition action (*Oppositionsklage*) is an objection against the claim itself, whereas the impugnation action (*Impugnationsklage*) is an objection against the enforcement grant. Third parties may also have a right to defend themselves by way of action for segregation (*Aussonderungsklage*),[31] which aims for the segregation of assets, eg, owned by third parties.

[23] TVTG 2020, Art 2 para 1 lit k) defines 'Token Issuer' as 'a person who publicly offers the Tokens in their own name or in the name of a client'.

[24] TVTG 2020, Art 2 para 1 lit n) defines 'TT Token Depositary' as 'a person who safeguards Token in the name and on account of others'.

[25] TVTG 2020, Art 2 para 1 lit q) defines 'TT Exchange Service Provider' as 'a person, who exchanges legal tender against Tokens and vice versa and Tokens for Tokens'.

[26] Gesetz vom 24 November 1971 über das Exekutions- und Rechtssicherungsverfahren (Exekutionsordnung; EO).

[27] Marxer & Partner Rechtsanwälte (eds), *Liechtenstein Business Law* (Vienna, MANZ, 2021) 406 et seq.

[28] EO 1971, Art 33.

[29] EO 1971, Art 18.

[30] EO 1971, Art 19.

[31] EO 1971, Art 20.

Once the creditor has an enforceable title, enforcement may be initiated by way of an enforcement application. The creditor seeking enforcement has various means of enforcement set out in the EO at his disposal. The EO distinguishes between: (i) enforcement for monetary claims; and (ii) enforcement for the purpose of obtaining acts or omissions. Within the enforcement for monetary claims, a further distinction is made by law between enforcement on immovable assets and enforcement on movable assets. The enforcement on movable assets includes the enforcement against movables (*körperliche Sachen*), receivables (*Geldforderungen*), claims for the delivery of tangible assets (*Ansprüche auf Herausgabe und Leistung körperlicher Sachen*) and against other pecuniary rights (*andere Vermögensrechte*) of the debtor.

IV. Enforcement and Token

A. Statutory Rules

There are no specific statutory provisions in the EO in relation to the enforcement of tokens. The TVTG, however, provides for certain clarifications. Article 7 para 3 TVTG states the following:

> The disposal over a Token is also legally binding in the event of enforcement proceedings against the transferor and effective vis-à-vis third parties, if the transfer:
>
> was activated in the TT system prior to the commencement of the legal proceedings, or
>
> was activated in the TT the system after the initiation of the legal proceedings and was executed on the day of the proceeding's openings, provided that the accepting party proves that he was without knowledge of the proceedings openings or would have remained without knowledge upon the exercise of due diligence.

This statutory provision shall, in case of an enforcement proceeding, clarify at which point in time the transfer of a token is legally valid. This provision, in particular para b, is important, because it makes clear that the focus for the transfer is on the triggering of the transfer and not on the actual enforcement, as the transaction may technically take a longer period of time, detached from the triggering.[32]

Article 25 para 1 TVTG states the following:

> Tokens held on a fiduciary basis or in the name of the customer shall be deemed third-party assets in proceedings to secure rights or in the case of compulsory enforcement and insolvency proceedings of the TT Service Provider and shall be segregated in favour of the customer, subject to all claims of the TT Service Provider against the customer.

Article 25 para 2 TVTG states the following:

> TT Keys[33] which a TT Service Provider holds or keeps in safe custody for a customer in its own name or in the name of a third party shall be deemed third-party assets

[32] BuA No 54/2019, 202 et seq.

[33] TVTG 2020, Art 2 para 1) lit e) defines 'TT Keys' as 'a key that allows for disposal over Tokens'.

> in proceedings to secure rights or in the case of compulsory enforcement and insolvency proceedings of the TT Service Provider and shall be segregated in favour of the customer, subject to all claims of the TT Service Provider against the customer.

Article 25 para 4 TVTG states the following:

> In the event of enforcement against the user's TT Service Provider, the user may raise an objection under public law (article 20 of the EO) if the enforcement relates to the Tokens secured in accordance with (1) or the TT Keys secured in accordance with (2).

These provisions set out in Article 25 TVTG have to be read against the background that a TT service provider has to make sure that the assets of the customers are segregated from its own assets in case the TT service provider holds assets of the customers as fiduciary or in the name of the customer.[34] Tokens can therefore, for purposes of the protection of customers, not be subject of an enforcement proceeding over the assets of a TT service provider in such a case.[35] Paragraph 4 of Article 25 TVTG in particular grants a customer of a TT service provider, with regard to the tokens or TT keys held on trust or in the name of a customer by that TT service provider or held in custody by the TT service provider on behalf of the customer, the right to file an opposition action (*Oppositionsklage*) or an action for the discontinuance of enforcement pursuant to Art 20 EO against the person seeking enforcement against the TT service provider. Any customer whose tokens or TT keys are wrongly attributed to the assets of the TT service provider and included in an enforcement action can use this action to obtain a cessation of the enforcement.[36]

As there are no specific rules for enforcement of tokens in the EO, the general provisions and principles of the EO have to be applied. As a general principle, enforcement pursuant to the EO in the Principality of Liechtenstein requires that assets of the debtor exist in the Principality of Liechtenstein. Article 4 TVTG states that if Liechtenstein law is applicable, tokens are to be considered as domestically located assets. This means that any token that is subject to the TVTG may be subject to enforcement proceedings in the Principality of Liechtenstein.

B. Tokens as Part of the Enforcement Procedure

These clarifications in the TVTG lead to the conclusion that it has been the intention of the lawmaker in the Principality of Liechtenstein that tokens shall be part of the enforcement procedure. Furthermore, the Liechtenstein enforcement law is based on a reception of the Austrian enforcement law.[37] Austrian literature argues that crypto assets (tokens) are subject to enforcement,[38] which further clarifies that

[34] BuA No 54/2019, 264 et seq.
[35] BuA No 54/2019, 264.
[36] BuA No 54/2019, 268.
[37] BuA No 52/2018, 8 et seq.
[38] A Meisinger, 'Einführung in die Gesamtreform des Exekutionsrechts' and A Frauenberger, 's 326 EO' in A Deixler-Hübner (ed), *Exekutionsordnung – Kommentar* (Vienna, LexisNexis ARD ORAC, 2019).

this principle also applies in the Principality of Liechtenstein. Tokens are therefore subject to enforcement in the Principality of Liechtenstein.

C. Enforcement Measures

In contrast to Austrian law,[39] tokens are not to be qualified as movable property (*Sache*) from a Liechtenstein property law perspective.[40] However, with the civil law part of the TVTG, a special property law, applicable to tokens, has been created, without interfering with the existing property law applicable to movable assets (*Sachen*).[41] As a result thereof, the provisions of the EO on the enforcement of movable property may be applied to tokens by analogy.

Even if one would not allow such an analogous application, the result of the enforcement would remain the same. According to Article 4 TVTG, tokens constitute domestic assets. Thus, enforcement of tokens is possible according to the provisions on enforcement on 'other property rights' pursuant to Article 241 et seq EO. The tokens constitute alienable property and could therefore be realised by a court by way of public auction pursuant to Article 243 EO. Since this public auction is governed by the provisions on the public auction of seized movable property, the same rules apply to the public auction as for movable property.

The rules for the disposal of tokens pursuant to Article 6 and 7 TVTG, in particular Article 7 para 2 TVTG, must also be observed in the case of such a public auction in enforcement proceedings in relation to tokens. If a third party acquires the tokens in the course of the public auction, the legal requirements and conditions for the transfer of the tokenised right pursuant to general principles of Liechtenstein law are also applicable and have to be met. In the case of the tokenisation of the right of ownership to a watch, not only the token itself must be transferred to the TT Identifier[42] of the acquirer (Article 6 TVTG). It is further necessary that the watch is physically given to the acquirer pursuant to Liechtenstein property law. Otherwise, the ownership right represented in the token is not transferred to the acquirer.

In addition to a court enforcement, in certain cases, also an out-of-court enforcement of a token may be permissible. This would, for instance, be the case if a token is pledged to a pledgee pursuant to a token pledge agreement and the parties have agreed that the pledgee may enforce the pledge by way of private sale (*freihändiger Verkauf*) of the tokens. Depending on the actual token, also in this case Article 7 para 2 TVTG has to be observed.

[39] O Völkel, 'Virtuelle Währungen als Sachen im Sinne des § 285 ABGB' in C Piska and O Völkel (eds), *Blockchain rules* (Vienna, MANZ, 2019) 63 et seq.

[40] BuA No 54/2019, 62 et seq, 201; Nägele (n 3) 40 et seq.

[41] BuA No 54/2019, 62 et seq; Stelzl and Feldkircher (n 3) 330 to 335.

[42] TVTG 2020 Art 2 para 1 lit d) defines TT Identifier as 'an identifier that allows for the clear assignment of Tokens'.

V. Short Introduction to Liechtenstein Insolvency Law

Liechtenstein insolvency law is set out in the Liechtenstein Insolvency Act (IO).[43] Any insolvency proceeding presupposes the material insolvency of a debtor. A material insolvency of a debtor is given if the debtor is either: (i) unable to pay their debts (*Zahlungsunfähigkeit*) within the meaning of Art 8 IO; or (ii) overindebted (*Überschuldung*) within the meaning of Art 9 IO. As a general principle, it can be noted that as soon as the insolvency proceeding has been initiated, the insolvency estate of the debtor will be used to satisfy all of its creditors equally.

For insolvency proceedings in the Principality of Liechtenstein, the District Court of Vaduz is competent. The condition for the opening of any insolvency proceeding is that it can be expected that there are enough assets of the debtor to cover the costs of the insolvency proceedings (start-up costs) pursuant to Article 6 IO. If this condition is not met, the court does not open the insolvency proceedings. Both the debtor as well as any creditor may file for the opening of the insolvency proceedings. Pursuant to Article 5 IO, the insolvency proceedings shall extend to all the debtor's assets subject to enforcement or forming the subject matter of an action for avoidance that belong to the debtor at the time of opening of the insolvency proceedings or that the debtor acquires during the insolvency proceedings (*insolvency estate*).

The IO defines three specific types of proceedings (for companies):

1. Reorganisation proceedings with the debtor in 'control' (*Sanierungsverfahren mit Eigenverwaltung*). The debtor itself retains, generally and subject to certain restrictions, control over the insolvency estate's assets;
2. Reorganisation proceedings (*Sanierungsverfahren*) without the debtor in 'control'. An insolvency administrator is appointed and takes the control; and
3. Bankruptcy proceedings (*Konkursverfahren*). A court-appointed insolvency administrator takes control of the task of selling the insolvency estate's assets at a maximum value. Any proceeds made are paid to the creditors.

For all three types of proceedings set out above, claims are classified and ranked in the following order of priority:

1. Secured Creditors

Secured creditors can be segregated into: (i) creditors that have a claim to separation of assets (*Aussonderungsanspruch*); and/or (ii) creditors that have a claim to segregation (*Absonderungsanspruch*). An example of a creditor with a claim to separation of an asset (*Aussonderungsrecht*) is the owner of an asset which is (for any reason) with the insolvent debtor, whereas a pledgee (*Pfandnehmer*), as example for a claim to segregation (*Absonderungsanspruch*), would have a claim

[43] Gesetz vom 17. Juli 1973 über das Insolvenzverfahren (Insolvenzordnung; IO).

to separation to receive proceeds of enforcement from a specific pledged asset. Secured creditors are, however, subject to the restraint that no secured claim can be paid within six months from the opening of insolvency proceedings if such a claim might jeopardise the business continuity of the insolvent debtor.[44]

2. Estate Claims

Estate claims (*Masseforderungen*) are to be satisfied prior to other insolvency claims. This could be for instance costs of the insolvency proceedings, the expenses of management and administration of the insolvency estate, labour claims and the costs of the insolvency administrator. All these claims are shared on a pro rata basis.

3. Insolvency Claims

Insolvency claims (*Insolvenzforderungen*) are claims of unsecured creditors and may be filed with the competent court within a certain time period after the opening of insolvency proceedings. Those insolvency creditors who filed a claim that was not contested by the insolvency administrator also share in such claims on a pro rata basis.

Last, there may also be subordinate claims resulting from an agreement (eg, a subordinated loan agreement with the debtor as the borrower) with a creditor to subordinate a claim or from statutory provisions. Subordinate creditors are only satisfied by any surplus available for distribution after the insolvency proceedings.

VI. Insolvency and Token

A. Statutory Rules

The IO does not specifically provide for any rules on the insolvency status of tokens. The TVTG however provides for certain clarifications in relation to tokens and insolvency:

Article 25 para 4 TVTG provides in particular for a right of separation (*Aussonderungsrecht*) of users' tokens in case of the opening of insolvency proceedings in relation to a TT service provider. That means that a customer of a TT service provider is treated like an owner of the tokens for purposes of the insolvency proceedings of such TT service provider by law. Tokens are subject to a unique position and do not fall in the insolvency estate of the TT service provider in such case.[45] In addition, reference is made to Article 25 para 1, 2 and 4 TVTG described above.

Because there are no specific rules in the IO on the insolvency in relation to tokens, the general provisions and principles of the IO have to be applied.

[44] IO 1973, Art 91.

[45] BuA No 54/2019, 264.

Also, other jurisdictions do not yet have specific legal rules dealing with insolvency and tokens.[46]

B. Tokens as Part of the Insolvency Estate

Pursuant to Article 5 IO, all the debtor's assets subject to enforcement or forming the subject matter of an action for avoidance are insolvency estates (*Insolvenzmasse*). Legal literature states however that only assets that do have a value may form part of the insolvency estate.[47] This means that, eg, any personal rights are not part of the insolvency estate.[48]

As regards tokens, it is possible to determine a price for them, and tokens are generally assets which can be subject to enforcement.[49] A price for a token, such as Bitcoin, may be determined by using a website such as www.coinmarketcap.com, which provides prices for a huge number of different tokens. With the possibility to determine a price, tokens do have a certain value, which makes it possible to consider them as part of the insolvency estate.

If tokens are held on a fiduciary basis or in the name of the customer by a TT service provider, these tokens are not subject to enforcement against the TT service provider and do not fall in the insolvency estate of such TT service provider pursuant to Article 25 TVTG. These tokens would however be part of the insolvency estate of the customer of such TT service provider, if such customer would become insolvent.

In addition, it can be taken from the explicit reference in the TVTG to insolvency proceedings that tokens within the meaning of the TVTG were intended to form part of the insolvency estate.

C. Realisation of Tokens in Insolvency Proceedings

With the opening of the insolvency proceedings, the insolvency administrator shall realise the assets belonging to the insolvency estate and invest cash fruitfully pursuant to Article 71 IO. The insolvency administrator therefore also has to realise tokens which belong to the insolvency estate.

[46] For Germany for example P Scherer, *Blockchain im Wertpapierbereich* (Tübingen, Mohr Siebeck, 2020) 141.

[47] G Kodek, 's 2 IO' in C Koller, E Lovrek and M Spitzer (eds), *Kommentar zur Insolvenzordnung* (Vienna, Verlag Österreich, 2019) para 30; M Trummer, 'Insolvenzrechtliche Hypothesen zu Krypto Assets und Smart Contracts' [2022] *Zeitschrift für Insolvenzrecht & Kreditschutz* 94.

[48] OGH (Austria) 8 Ob 593/86.

[49] M Werner, 'Zivilverfahrens- und Vollstreckungsrecht' in S Omlor and M Link (eds), *Kryptowährungen und Token* (Frankfurt am Main, dfv Mediengruppe, 2021) 305, 352; Trummer (n 40) 94.

One practical problem of an insolvency administrator could be whether they will be able to get knowledge of any tokens of the debtor.[50] Generally, a debtor is obliged to provide a detailed asset register (*Vermögensverzeichnis*) and if the debtor has not already done so before the opening of the insolvency proceedings, the insolvency court shall order to produce an asset register without delay pursuant to Article 59 IO. Therefore, if the debtor also provides a full list of all tokens, wallets and/or TT keys in the asset register, the insolvency administrator will have an overview and will be able to act.

Assuming that the insolvency administrator has an overview of the tokens of the debtor, the insolvency administrator (with certain exceptions) has to realise the assets belonging to the insolvency estate. Liechtenstein insolvency law states that pursuant to Article 72 para 2 IO, assets belonging to the insolvency estate shall be sold by the court at the request of the insolvency administrator unless there is a more advantageous method of realisation. By stating that a sale by the court may only be made unless there is a more advantageous method of realisation, the IO prioritises a realisation out of court, a so called 'voluntary sale' or 'private sale' of the insolvency estate.[51]

This is understood as the realisation of the insolvency estate's assets using the possibilities of the civil law.[52]

The insolvency administrator may therefore realise tokens (which are part of the insolvency estate) by way of private sale. The tokens may be sold: (i) to a third party by way of a purchase agreement in exchange for a cash payment of the current price of the tokens, (ii) if listed at a crypto exchange, by selling the tokens there in exchange for cash at the price the tokens are listed there, or (iii) any other crypto marketplace, such as a decentralised exchange.[53]

From a Liechtenstein legal perspective, the insolvency administrator has to adhere to the rules for the disposal of tokens pursuant to the TVTG, in particular Article 7 TVTG, if they want to dispose of the tokens. Therefore, depending on the actual token, the transfer procedure might differ. If the token is qualified as an intrinsic token, the transfer can be affected by way of technological transfer of the token. This would be applicable to, eg, Bitcoin or other cryptocurrencies. If the token is to be qualified as an extrinsic token (and therefore represents a right), the insolvency administrator has to check which right the token represents. Depending on the represented right, not only the technical transfer of the token has to be made, but also the legal requirements and conditions for the transfer of such right pursuant to general principles of Liechtenstein law have to be met (see example of the transfer of a tokenised watch above).

[50] M d'Avoine and P Hamacher, 'Kryptowährungen im Insolvenzverfahren' (2022) *Zeitschrift für Wirtschaftsrecht* 9 et seq.

[51] W Jelinek and S Zangl and C Jaufer, *Taschenkommentar zur Insolvenzordnung* (Vienna, MANZ, 2020) 159; W Jelinek, 's 119 IO' in Koller, Lovrek and Spitzer (n 41) para 5 (with further references).

[52] Jelinek, 's 119 IO' in Koller, Lovrek and Spitzer (n 41) para 42.

[53] D'Avoine and Hamacher (n 44) 10 et seq.

Tokens, in particular crypto currencies, are often highly volatile. A realisation of such should therefore be done without culpable hesitation by the insolvency administrator,[54] to avoid that, eg, the price of the token drops drastically. If the insolvency administrator does not act fast, this may even be a reason for a liability, because the insolvency administrator is responsible to all parties involved in the insolvency proceedings for any pecuniary disadvantages caused to them by the improper performance of his duties.[55] The potential volatility will most likely make a sale by the court impossible, because this will take longer than the out of court sale by the insolvency administrator and is therefore potentially disadvantageous.

VII. Conclusion

Tokens can be part of enforcement proceedings and insolvency proceedings from a Liechtenstein legal perspective. Since there are no specific legal rules set out in the applicable enforcement law or insolvency law, the general principles have to be applied. In addition, in particular the rules of the TVTG for the disposal of tokens have to be met, as otherwise the transfer of the token and the transfer of the right represented in the token may fall apart. While it would be useful to include certain clarifications in the existing legal frameworks for enforcement and insolvency, it is not necessary to overregulate as the challenges may be solved with the existing legal framework. It would for instance be useful to clarify which enforcement measures may be used in relation to tokens. As there is not much experience with the enforcement in relation to tokens or an insolvency involving tokens, the enforcing party and/or court as well as the insolvency administrator may face practical challenges. Existing enforcement law and insolvency law, if read together with the TVTG, provide a solid legal framework for the enforcement and insolvency proceedings in the Principality of Liechtenstein, but more experience will show potentially necessary adjustments in applicable law.

[54] D'Avoine and Hamacher (n 44) 10 et seq.
[55] IO 1973, Art 4 para 4; D'Avoine and Hamacher (n 44) 10 et seq.

11

Crypto Custody in Insolvency: An Empirical View

DIRK ZETZSCHE AND ARETI NIKOLAKOPOULOU*

I. Introduction

This chapter which summarises the results of the authors' earlier research,[1] analyses the terms and conditions (T&Cs) of providers of crypto custody and wallet services. These contractual clauses were at the heart of large-scale crypto insolvencies and asset misappropriations of crypto firms culminating in the FTX failure, now dubbed collectively the 'Crypto Winter'.[2] The events occurring throughout the Crypto Winter have significantly undermined investors' trust in the modus operandi of many crypto asset service providers (CASPs) and sparked an increasing demand for investment-grade custody solutions that safeguard clients' assets effectively. Even at the time of writing, news about crypto custodians suddenly disappearing with users' funds is all over the internet.[3] Hence, despite a more recent rebound of crypto asset markets and increasing institutionalisation of the former,[4] the need for a sophisticated crypto custody framework is apparent.

By looking at a hand-selected dataset of T&Cs available on the websites of crypto providers in the period of May 2023/24, we provide insights into crypto custody practices and identify trends, patterns, as well as potential contradictions

* This research was funded in whole, or in part, by the Luxembourg National Research Fund (FNR), grant reference NCER22/IS/16570468/NCER-FT.

[1] See DA Zetzsche and A Nikolakopoulou, 'Crypto Custody and Crypto Wallets – An Empirical Assessment' (2024), ▪___ *Journal of Financial Regulation* ▪___ (submitted).

[2] For a detailed analysis of the 'Crypto Winter' see D Arner et al., 'The Financialization of Crypto: Lessons from FTX and the Crypto Winter of 2022–2023' (2024) *Computer & Security Review*, available as (2023) UNSW Law Research Paper no 23–31, 19, 6 ff, ssrn.com/abstract=4372516 accessed 18 June 2024.

[3] BluShark Media, 'BitForex Disappears With Millions, Prompting Outrage and Investigations' (*Medium*, 27 February 2023) blusharkmedia.medium.com/bitforex-disappears-with-millions-prompting-outrage-and-investigations-1a632baa952f accessed 18 June 2024; G Jenkinson, 'CoinEx hack: Compromised private keys led to $70M theft' (*Cointelegraph*, 19 September 2023) cointelegraph.com/news/coinex-compromised-private-keys-behind-70-million-hack accessed 18 June 2024; S Shukla, 'Crypto Exchange HTX Hit by $258 Million Outflow After Hack' (*Bloomberg*, 11 December 2023) www.bloomberg.com/news/articles/2023-12-10/justin-sun-linked-crypto-exchange-htx-sees-258-million-outflow-after-hack accessed 18 June 2024.

[4] See Zetzsche and Nikolakopoulou (n 1).

and divergences across the crypto industry, and seek to assess the level of client and customer protections that prevails in the crypto custody industry. As a regulatory benchmark for assessing the quality of client protection, we use the custody requirements of the EU Regulation of Markets in Crypto assets (MiCAR).[5]

The remainder of this chapter is divided into three parts. II summarises our approach to data collection, while III presents our results on crypto custody practices; and IV concludes.

II. Analytical Approach and Data Sample

For an assessment of the prevailing custody practices, we collected and analysed a sample of T&Cs used by a sample of custodial wallet providers, including some of the most prominent and largest, and scrutinised that sample to ascertain which rights and positions the T&Cs grant to clients.

A. Sample Composition

Our sample includes 88 T&Cs of 110 custody providers from 48 jurisdictions made available online on the websites of prominent custody providers in the period between May 2023/24.

As for the choice and size of the sample, we lack reliable estimates, both on the overall number of crypto custodians *and* on their importance as measured by number of assets held in custody or number of clients.

B. Selection Criteria

For that reason, the sample's composition follows three criteria, which we believe together amount to meaningful coverage of the crypto custody market.[6]

First, given the lack of disclosure requirements for the crypto assets held by the custody providers, only a limited number of wallet providers, in particular certain leading centralised exchanges (CEXs), disclose the assets held in their custody on a regular basis. Our sample of 110 providers includes the largest 20 providers that disclose their holdings.

Second, CEXs are important custody providers, given that they offer custodial wallets to their clients in order to facilitate trading activities. Of the sample of

[5] *cf* Regulation 2023/1114/EU of the European Parliament and of the Council of 31 May 2023 on markets in crypto-assets, and amending Regulations (EU) No 1093/2010 and (EU) No 1095/2010 and Directives 2013/36/EU and (EU) 2019/1937 (MiCAR), [2023] OJ L150/40.

[6] For sources and references, see See Zetzsche and Nikolakopoulou (n 1).

110 providers, 70 are leading CEXs. Among them, 20 CEX disclose their holdings and thus overlap with the first category.

The third criterion is qualitative in nature. We searched for websites listing 'top crypto custody providers' and similar rankings. Of the 110 providers selected, 40 were listed in these rankings. These 40 were on top of the 70 custody providers we identified as being linked to a CEX.

C. Sample vs Size of the Market

Based on their proof of reserves (PoR) and similar (rare) disclosures about the assets under their custody, those that disclose these data among the selected custodians hold a share of at least 9.03 per cent of the entire crypto asset market[7] by USD value. Figure11.1 lists the top 10 CEX custodians by assets under custody (AuC) disclosed in our sample, revealing significant market concentration, with Binance being by far the most dominant provider.

Figure 11.1 Top 10 CEX Custodians by AuC[8]

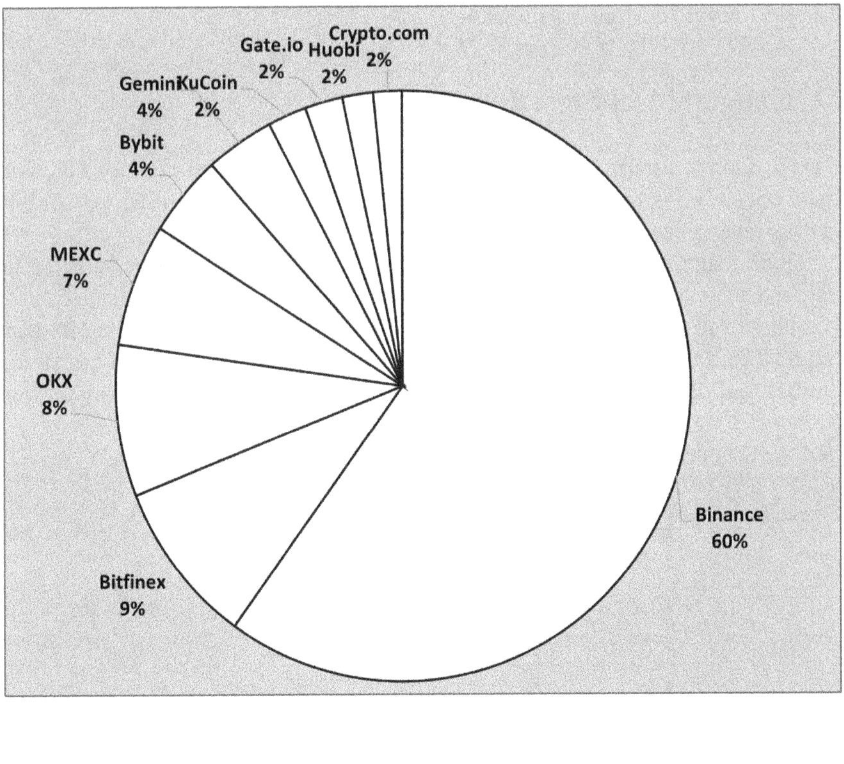

[7] Data on the entire crypto market industry as of CoinMarketCap 21 March 2024.
[8] Data on the AuC of the custodians as of CoinMarketCap 21 March 2024.

Figure 11.2 Number of CEXs by AuC[9]

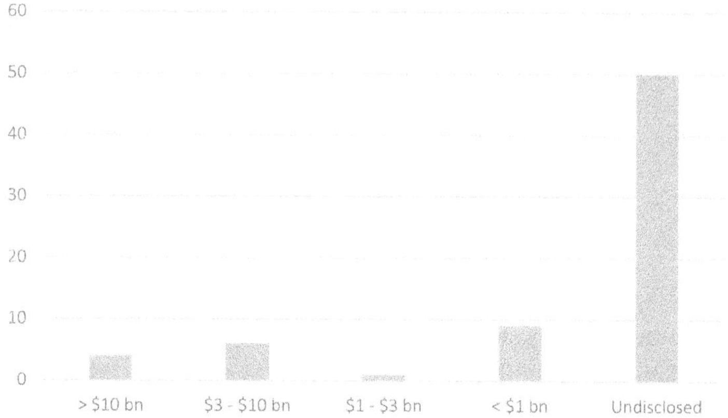

According to data on AuC disclosed, Binance holds a much larger AuC amount in custody than all of the other CEX custodians collectively. Note that we lack similar data on AuC held in wallets provided by the prominent – based on qualitative criteria – crypto custodians altogether.

D. Geographical Breakdown

For our sample comprising 88 T&Cs we rely on custodians that disclose T&Cs on their websites. Figure 11.3 shows the jurisdictions of their registered seat and/or crypto-related licence or registration as per their website disclosures.

Since many custodians belong to a group with multiple entities residing or licensed in several jurisdictions simultaneously, we include in the geographical breakdown all those jurisdictions that we could identify on their websites. In turn, the 88 T&Cs correspond, to sample custodians that have in total, 197 registered entities and/or crypto licences. Often it remains unclear to which entity a given licence belongs, or whether a given entity is licensed. Yet, both the registered seat *and* the licence give some indication on the regional scope of activities.

Figure 11.3 Breakdown of Sample by Region

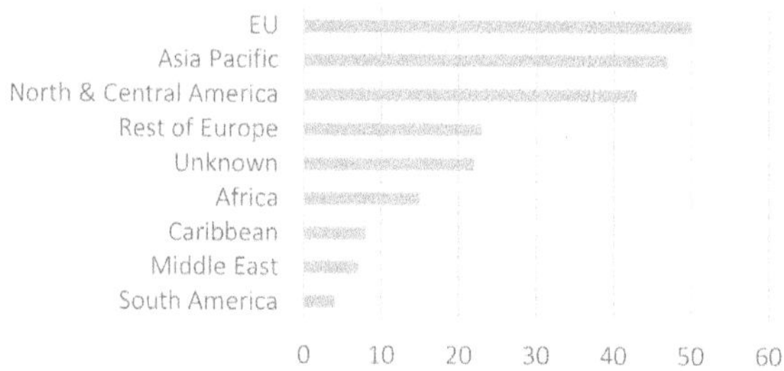

[9] ibid.

Figure 11.4 displays the top jurisdictions by the same measure (registered seats and/or licence) as follows: the US (31); Singapore (12); Lithuania (12); Australia (11); Switzerland (10); UK (9); Seychelles (9); Canada (8); Poland and Hong Kong (6 each); and Italy, France (5 each), Germany, BVI, Cayman Islands, Indonesia, South Korea (4 each).

Figure 11.4 Breakdown of Sample by Jurisdiction

III. Crypto Custody Practices Shown in the Dataset

A. Safekeeping

In financial legislation related to the custody of financial instruments, the notion of safekeeping plays a pivotal role.

The common denominator of safekeeping duties[10] in financial legislation is as follows: for financial assets that can be held in custody, safekeeping's core

[10] It shall be noted that the safekeeping *lato sensu* includes more duties that complement each other and eventually ensure the safeguarding of the clients' rights over the assets held in custody, such as the asset segregation, insolvency protection.

notion and *conditio sine qua non* is the mere fact of holding those assets in custody under the custodian's name on behalf of the client. Thus, safekeeping traditionally englobes the following two different cases: (i) for tangible assets that can be physically delivered to the custodian (eg, a painting or a piece of art), the custodian shall be in a position to physically control and retrieve the assets; and (ii) for financial instruments that can be registered in a financial instruments account, the custodian shall properly register those in such an account opened in the custodian's books under the name of the client.

The crypto assets practice has disrupted this established dichotomy and introduced the notion of custody and safekeeping in the form of holding and controlling *the means of access* to such assets by way of private cryptographic keys.

Therefore, as a first step in our research, we attempt to ascertain whether the service providers in our sample T&Cs undertake crypto asset safekeeping duties by explicitly stipulating in their terms that they provide a custody solution for crypto assets of their clients, offer (custodial) wallets, safeguard or safekeep assets, or somehow hold, store or control the client's assets and/or the cryptographic keys or other similar expressions.

Our sample reveals that, despite their custodial activity declared on their website, only 62 (71 per cent) of our sample T&Cs mention that they offer a type of custodial, safekeeping service related to their clients' crypto assets. Meanwhile, 23 (26 per cent) lack any relevant reference,[11] while three (3 per cent) deny[12] the provision of a wallet service and/or custody to their clients.

Figure 11.5 Safekeeping

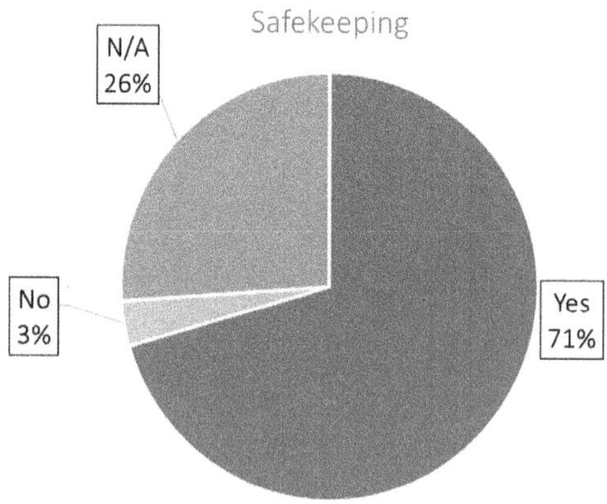

[11] In the N/A category that lacks any reference on safekeeping we also include three sample T&Cs that mention nothing on the custody service except a mere sentence that any provider's custodial services are governed by a different agreement, which was not accessible to us. Furthermore, one T&Cs describing only a semi-custodial and/or non-custodial service where the service provider does not hold enough keys to perform a transaction without the client's cooperation is also part of the N/A category. For our taxonomy on semi-custodial and self-custodial solutions *cf* DA Zetzsche, J Sinnig and A Nikolakopoulou, 'Crypto Custody' (2024) 19 *Capital Markets Law Journal* 207, 214 ff.

[12] One out of those service providers denied wallet provision in their T&Cs but mentioned safekeeping in their custody statement.

We observe that well-established crypto custodians seem to be reluctant to subscribe to the same custodial safekeeping obligations in their legally binding documents that custodians of financial instruments would ordinarily subscribe to, by avoiding clear obligations. Either there is ambiguity with regard to what crypto custody and safekeeping entails, or providers are seeking to optimise their legal position by avoiding commitments. We understand both to be hindrances to the achievement of legal certainty.

B. Key Storage

The Crypto Winter demonstrated that the custodians, and especially exchange-linked wallet providers, prefer to use so-called 'hot storage' of private keys of multiple clients in order to gain liquidity for their transactions in the short term.[13] In the use of hot wallets, it is implied that the cryptographic keys associated with the clients' assets are generated and stored online (eg, on the custodian's servers (for custodial hot wallets), or on the client's browser or mobile app data store (for self-custodial hot wallets). These key storage tools are constantly connected to the internet, to ensure time and cost efficiency. Yet they come with downsides: hot wallets have been referred to as 'an attractive "honey pot" for hackers'[14] and are technically vulnerable.[15] On the contrary, cold wallets which generate and store the private keys offline (eg, on devices not connected to the internet like a USB stick or hard drive device) are considered the safer variant of crypto custody.[16]

Thus, from a client's perspective, it is important to know whether their assets are being held in hot or cold storage. In a similar vein, Article 75(1) of MiCAR mandates crypto custodians to disclose their custody policies and the risks associated therewith in their custody agreement.

Against this background, we find that an astonishing 69 (79 per cent) of our sample T&Cs omit any reference to hot or cold storage, one (1 per cent) admitted to hot storage. Only two (2 per cent) admit to the use of a cold storage mechanism and another 16 (18 per cent) employ a combined hot and cold storage mechanism.

[13] D Zetzsche et al., 'Remaining Regulatory Challenges in Digital Finance and Crypto assets after MiCA', (2023) Study requested by the ECON Committee (European Parliament), 46–47 ssrn.com/abstract=4487516 accessed 18 June 2024.

[14] P Bains et al., 'Regulating the Crypto Ecosystem: The Case of Unbacked Crypto Assets' (September 2022) 7 *Fintech Notes*, 22 www.imf.org/en/Publications/fintech-notes/Issues/2022/09/26/Regulating-the-Crypto-Ecosystem-The-Case-of-Unbacked-Crypto assets-523715 accessed 18 June 2024.

[15] For an analysis of the multiple hot wallet hacks of prominent custodians during the Crypto Winter *cf* Zetzsche, Sinnig and Nikolakopoulou (n 11).

[16] *cf* A Antonopoulos, *Mastering Bitcoin: Programming the Open Blockchain* (2nd edn, O'Reilly Media, 2017). ch 13.

Figure 11.6 Key Storage Transparency

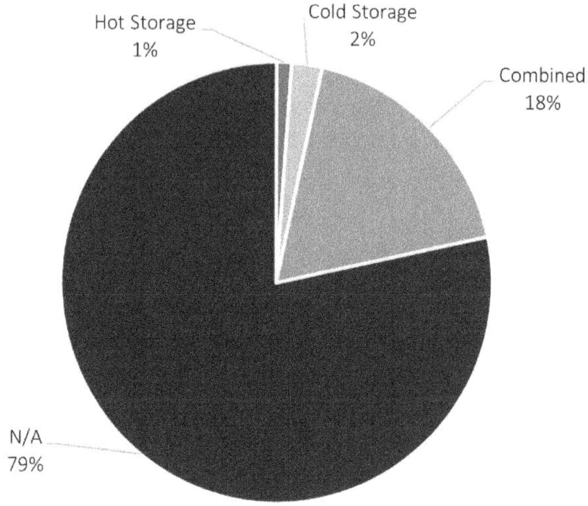

C. Asset Segregation, Omnibus Wallets, and Outsourcing to Third Parties

Custodial arrangements for financial assets are divided into two broad categories: omnibus or individually segregated accounts. Individual accounts show each client's individual rights, while omnibus accounts present all clients' assets collectively in one account.

Traditional finance (TradFi) regulation balances cost and client protection considerations. A custodian at the first level of the custody chain (eg, a custodian entering into a contractual relationship with the client) has the legal obligation to provide a fully segregated account for each of their clients individually and to properly record the assets of each client in the books and registers of the custodian.[17] This two-pronged obligation ensures the ringfencing of each client's assets against insolvency risks.

TradFi regulation provides, further, that if the custodian outsources safekeeping to a third party, this third-party is entitled to operate omnibus accounts. This commingling at the second level is a technical necessity to avoid the undesirable situation where, in a hierarchical set-up of the custody chain, all client data must be forwarded to, and reconciled with, the delegate. Even then, an omnibus account

[17] *cf* AIFMD, Art 11(d); UCITSD, Art 22a(3); Commission Delegated Regulation (EU) 2018/1618, Art 2(1)(d).

operated by the third-party shall exclude the proprietary assets of the delegating custodian, the proprietary assets of the third-party, as well as the assets of the third-party's other clients.

With regard to on-chain storage of crypto assets, those belonging to multiple users can be either segregated by means of assigning each user's assets to an individually segregated wallet address on the blockchain or, alternatively, can be pooled in one collective or omnibus wallet address.[18]

Omnibus wallets can leave a client exposed to risks stemming from the other clients of the custodian, whose assets are pooled inside the same wallet.[19] In the event of a wallet hack or the insolvency of client B, the loss allocation and the attribution of the commingled assets between clients A, B, and C will depend on their agreed entitlements. Client A's entitlement over the crypto assets (whatever its legal form, depending on the forum and the applicable law[20]) will depend on whether the entitlement is: (i) properly accounted for in the custodian's accounts, and (ii) recognisable and separable from other crypto assets. In principle, the custodian's orderly accounted-for internal records may serve as evidence of the client's entitlement, yet in many crypto insolvencies the precondition for this legal presumption – orderly bookkeeping – has not been fulfilled.[21]

Furthermore, while on-chain we can either have segregated or omnibus/collective wallet addresses, it is a legal necessity to somehow segregate assets off-chain as well to identify which assets belong to each user at any time. There is, however, ambiguity as to what off-chain segregation constitutes in that sense. What we saw in many of the T&Cs and what is derived by the International Swaps and Derivatives Association (ISDA)[22] is that off-chain segregation means merely that the custodian maintains in its books and records a segregated account for each client, therefore ensuring proper record-keeping of each client's assets at any time via its accounting ledger.

[18] For the notion of wallet address see Zetzsche and Nikolakopoulou (n 1).

[19] On omnibus wallets regarding crypto assets see the transparency requirements in International Organization Of Securities Commissions, 'Final Report, Policy Recommendations for Crypto and Digital Asset Markets' (November 2023), Recommendation 14, www.iosco.org/library/pubdocs/pdf/IOSCOPD747.pdf accessed 18 June 2024.

[20] The legal nature of rights in crypto assets is subject to an intense debate: may have the legal nature of proprietary right (probably *ab indiviso*-undivided property) or a contractual claim. See J Woxholth et al., 'Competing Claims to Crypto assets' (2023) 2 *Uniform Law Review* 226, 230 ff; I Tirado and L Gullifer, 'Proprietary Rights and Digital Assets: A "Modest Proposal" from a Transnational Law Perspective' (2024) 84 *Law and Contemporary Problems* (in press).

[21] For the implications of inaccurate books and records in case of crypto exchanges *cf* AJ Levitin, 'Not Your Keys, Not Your Coins: Unpriced Credit Risk in Cryptocurrency' (2022) 101 *Texas Law Review* 877, 929 ff ssrn.com/abstract=4107019 accessed 18 June 2024.

[22] International Swaps and Derivatives Association (ISDA), 'Navigating Bankruptcy in Digital Asset Markets' (2023) 16–17 www.isda.org/a/CrLgE/Navigating-Bankruptcy-in-Digital-Asset-Markets-Digital-Asset-Intermediaries-and-Customer-Asset-Protection.pdf accessed 18 June 2024.

While the segregated book-keeping obligation is essential in all cases, its efficiency in protecting the clients hinges on two qualifications. First, special attention must be paid to cases where omnibus or collective accounts[23] are maintained in the books and records of the custodian and/or of the third-party safekeeping the assets, similarly to TradFi. We assume that the provision of separate accounts per client off-chain in their books and records is a logical necessity for custodians so that they can identify the account balance for each client. However, from a client protection perspective, we consider that the reference in the T&Cs to a client account and record keeping of the account balance is not of significance because this client account may ultimately also be part of an omnibus clients' account on custodian's or any third-party safekeeping's level, posing the same risks we analysed above.

Second, where custodians claim to practice 'off-chain segregation', another interpretation of such a commitment may include that the custodian stores the *public and private keys* to the wallet address in a segregated manner.[24] The latter meaning follows deductively for anyone familiar with TradFi custody, yet may not be realistic where only one set of private keys exists for the entire omnibus wallet.

For these reasons, client protection rests on: (i) who holds the asset on behalf of clients (custodian of choice vs any third-party safekeeping), (ii) what the custodian segregates or commingles on-chain in the wallet addresses, and (iii) what the custodian commingles off-chain in the accounts. In this regard, the T&Cs are very insightful.

i. Outsourcing to Third Parties

In total, 64 T&Cs (73 per cent) make no statement on outsourcing, while only 24 (27 per cent) provide that appointing a third party for the safekeeping of the clients' assets is permissible;[25] and among those only four provide the name of the third-party entity, while 20 provide no specification. Furthermore, out of those service providers that entitle themselves to appoint a third-party for safekeeping, eight inform their clients that there may be no sufficient protection in case of insolvency of this third-party, as discussed below.

[23] Omnibus accounts commingle clients' assets, while collective accounts commingle clients' assets with the custodian's own assets.

[24] For instance, the keys associated with client A and its wallet address A may need to be stored in a USB stick different from the keys associated with client B and its wallet address B. Additionally, the keys associated with clients' omnibus wallet address X may need to be stored in a different device from the keys associated with the custodian's own assets wallet address Y.

[25] We identified two cases where our sample service providers deny their wallet provision and/ custodial function and merely mention the appointment of a third party for the safekeeping of their clients' crypto assets.

Figure 11.7 T&Cs on Outsourcing to third-party safekeeping

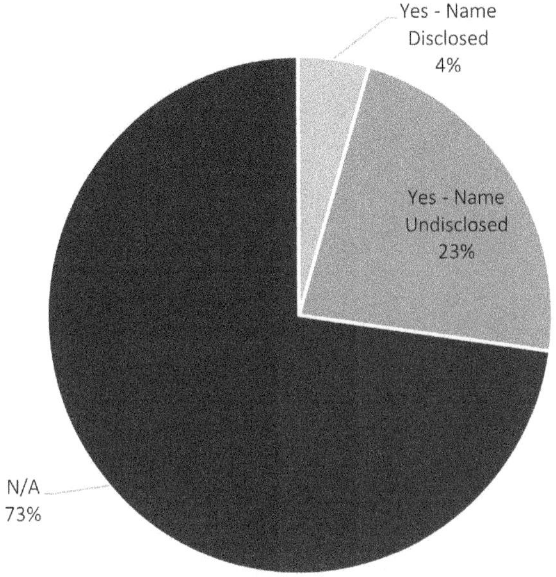

Compared to TradFi, the less hierarchical set-up of DLTs may explain the relatively low numbers here: rather than being forced to participate indirectly, by way of outsourcing, in a hierarchical custodial chain, DLTs allow all crypto custodians to function as nodes or asset-holders.

ii. On-chain Commingling/Segregation (Wallet Addresses)

Regarding the on-chain commingling, eight sample T&Cs refer to a type of shared wallet address without specifying whether these addresses commingle only clients' assets (omnibus wallet address) or whether they also include the custodian's own assets (collective wallet address).[26] In that sense, seven T&Cs refer to collective wallet addresses.[27] Meanwhile, three T&Cs stipulate that they provide omnibus wallet addresses for their clients' assets only. At the same time, five T&Cs state that they provide both commingling and segregation: on the one hand, some form of omnibus or collective wallet address and, on the other, segregated wallet addresses per client. One service provider mentions in their T&Cs the provision of segregated addresses per client. Finally, 64 omit any reference to on-chain commingling or segregation, as explained above.

[26] One of those mentions that the 'assets are not segregated'.
[27] One of those mentions that the 'assets are not segregated'.

Figure 11.8 On-chain Commingling/Segregation

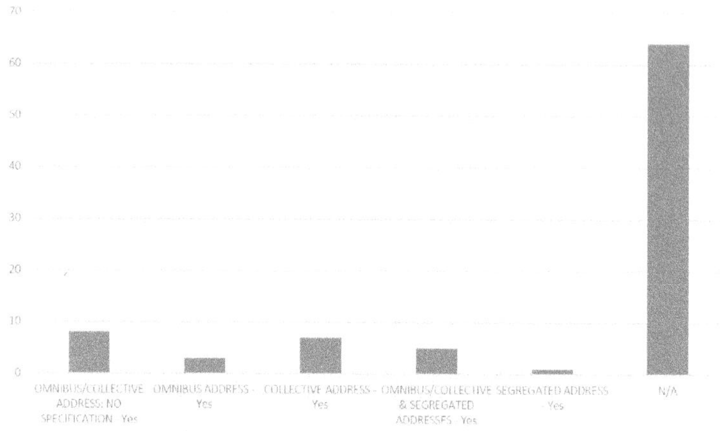

iii. Off-chain Commingling (Accounts and/ Key Storage)

Given what has been stated above, the question is whether the custodians mention in their T&Cs that they commingle the clients' assets and entitlements off-chain by employing omnibus accounts off-chain (commingling multiple clients' assets) or collective accounts (commingling the custodian's and/or any subcustodian's own assets with the clients' assets). Five T&Cs describe collective accounts in that sense, and seven T&Cs are omnibus accounts. Finally, one T&C mentions that the keys to the assets of clients are stored collectively together with the keys to the custodian's own assets. Finally, 75 T&Cs omit any reference to any off-chain commingling.[28]

Figure 11.9 Off-chain Commingling

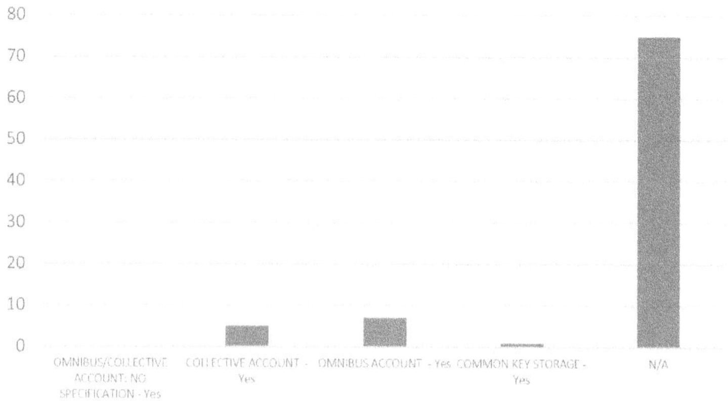

[28] We also note that segregation by means of accounting methods is mentioned: (i) when it comes to segregation from the custodian's own assets in 11 sample T&Cs, (ii) when it comes to segregation from other clients' assets in 3 sample T&Cs and lastly, for 3 sample T&Cs we couldn't identify whom the assets are segregated from.

D. Insolvency Clauses and Clients' Entitlements

The nature of clients' entitlement over crypto assets held in custody is the key factor determining the former's position in insolvency.[29] On the one hand, the client may have a proprietary right over the assets. We may see this position blurred by an arrangement similar to traditional intermediated custody where the client retains the *beneficial* right only, and the custodian holds the *legal* right over the assets. On the other hand, the client may only have an (unsecured) contractual claim to receive equivalent assets based on a creditor-debtor relationship.

The holder of proprietary rights is protected in the event of insolvency because their crypto assets will typically[30] not be used to satisfy the creditors of the custodian. By contrast, the client-claimant is an unsecured creditor in the event of the custodian's insolvency, and on a similar footing to that of other creditors of the custodian. If the claims against the insolvent estate exceed the assets, these clients will lose some or all of their asset value.[31]

Note that these are only some of the pitfalls relating to the legal entitlement of the asset-holders. Given the fact that the crypto property and insolvency laws are still largely undeveloped in most jurisdictions,[32] the content of the T&Cs is of overarching importance.

An example of the significance of the contractual stipulations with respect to clients' entitlements can be seen in the *Celsius*[33] case, where the court ruled that the T&Cs unambiguously conveyed ownership of the earned assets to the debtors based on language in the terms of use providing that account holders 'grant Celsius (…) all rights and title to such Digital Assets, including ownership rights'.[34]

[29] For details *cf* Tirado and Gullifer (n 20); Woxholth et al (n 20) 230ff; K Bruce, CK Odinet and A Tosato, 'Stablecoins in Bankruptcy' (2022) 42 *Bankruptcy Law Letter* 1, 10ff.

[30] The misconceptions and misleading practices concerning the omnibus or segregated wallets can lead to legal uncertainty or obstacles in the identification and recovery of the assets even for clients retaining proprietary rights.

[31] Inter alia ISDA (n 22) 16; L Gullifer, H Chong and H Liu, 'Client-Intermediary Relations in the Crypto asset World' in PS Davies and T Cheng-Han (eds), *Intermediaries in the Commercial World* (Oxford, Hart Publishing, 2022) 213–234; Y Yadav and R Stark, 'The Bankruptcy Court as Crypto Market Regulator' (2024) ▪__ *Southern California Law Review* ▪__ (forthcoming), ssrn.com/abstract=4601575 accessed 18 June 2024; J Bernbrock, J Nassiri and P Almasi, 'Ownership Issues in Crypto Cases' (2023) 42 *American Bankruptcy Institute Journal*; E Micheler, 'Custody Chains and Asset Values: Why Crypto-Securities are Worth Contemplating' (2015) 74 *CLJ* 505.

[32] *cf* Woxholth et al (n 20), 230 ff. For an argument that streamlining of crypto insolvency laws is a priority, *cf* Zetzsche et al (n 13), 91.

[33] *Re Celsius Network LLC*, Case No 22-10964 (MG), 2023 Bankr LEXIS 2 (Bankr SDNY 4 January 2023).

[34] J Wacholder and D Lowenthal, 'Bankruptcy Court Issues Ruling on Ownership of Celsius Account Assets', (*Patterson Belknap* 31 January 2023) www.pbwt.com/bankruptcy-update-blog/bankruptcy-court-issues-ruling-on-ownership-of-celsius-account-assets accessed 18 June 2024.

i. Clients' Entitlements to the Crypto Assets

Wording which refers to proprietary rights, title and ownership of the clients in relation to the custodied assets is mentioned explicitly in 17 T&Cs, while two T&Cs deny the clients' proprietary rights, and 69 T&Cs lack any such stipulation. Beneficial ownership and trust arrangements for the custodied assets are mentioned in ten T&Cs, while 78 T&Cs lack any stipulation thereon. Finally, eight T&Cs indicate explicitly that the client may have an (unsecured) claim in relation to the custodied assets against the custodian and/or any third-party safekeeping, while 80 T&Cs omit any stipulation on this matter.

Figure 11.10 Clients' Entitlements

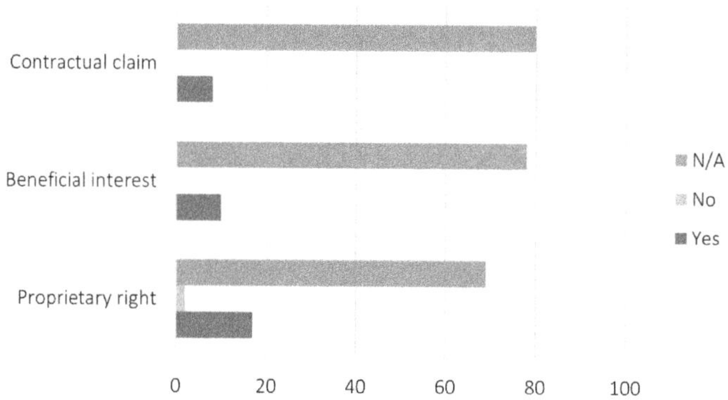

Given its importance in determining the protection of assets, the large number of T&Cs lacking detailed stipulations is surprising. While, elsewhere on their websites, most of those service providers use wording indicating that the clients' 'own' their assets, when it comes to the client's position in relation to the custodied crypto assets in their legal agreement, only 17 T&Cs mention that the title and ownership over the crypto assets remain with the client and ten mention beneficial holdings. In turn, depositing assets with the crypto custodians in our sample comes with uncertainty as to the clients' entitlements, and may even impair them outright. Given the cross-border nature of many client relationships and the associated conflicts of law therein, we find this situation worrying.

For instance, we have encountered clauses of CEXs stating that the client assigns all of their rights to all on-exchange assets to the CEX and agrees that their rights in relation to any on-exchange asset are limited to a contractual obligation against the custodian.[35] Furthermore, even if the client is mentioned as having a

[35] '[…] your rights in relation to any On-Exchange Assets are limited to a contractual obligation for Crypto.com to provide an equivalent amount and type of On-Exchange Assets […], Crypto.com, 'Exchange Terms and Conditions' (*Crypto.com*, 15 January 2024) crypto.com/exchange/document/tnc accessed 18 June 2024.

proprietary right, in five T&Cs, it is still mentioned that they bear the risk of insolvency of the custodian or the third-party safekeeping the assets.

Finally, even in cases of T&Cs containing a clause mentioning that the title and property remain with the client, this can only guarantee the protection of the clients when taking into account the other clauses of the T&Cs, for instance the segregation of the clients' assets, the prohibition of reuse of their assets by the custodian, or any outsourcing of safekeeping arrangements. If the other clauses do not move conceptually in the same direction, the mere reference that title and property remain with the client or similar wording may become a vague expression that is contradicted by the custodian's overall practice.

ii. Insolvency Protection Clause

In the event of the custodian's insolvency, six T&Cs stipulate that their clients' crypto assets are protected, six T&Cs state that there may be no such protection (eg, insolvency may lead to total loss of the clients' assets and/or that the clients may only have an unsecured claim), while one T&Cs provides for two different wallet types where one ensures protection in case of insolvency and the other not – 75 T&Cs are silent on the matter.

In the event of the insolvency of the third-party safekeeping, no T&Cs stipulate that the clients' assets are protected, while eight T&Cs mention that such protection may be lacking (eg, that the insolvency may lead to total loss of the clients' assets and/or that the clients may only have an unsecured claim), while 80 T&Cs remain silent on the issue.

Figure 11.11 Insolvency Protection

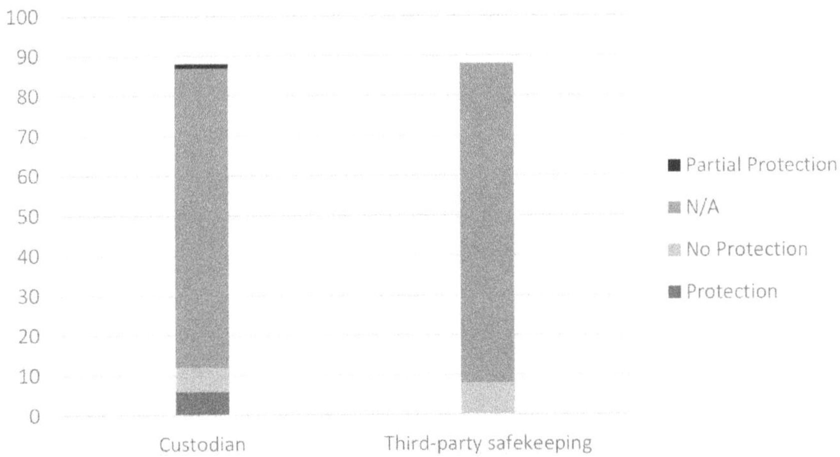

The very essence of the custody as a service and its safekeeping is at odds with the situation presented in the T&Cs observed.

IV. Conclusion

This chapter has provided an overview of the rights and obligations assigned by crypto custodians in their T&Cs to their clients.

Our empirical analysis supports a number of conclusions. To begin with, most custodians are unwilling to assume explicitly, in their legally binding documents, responsibility when safekeeping their clients' assets; some even hesitate to publish their T&Cs on the website even though they attract new clients this way. Moreover, the lack of transparency regarding the custody policies, and in particular the key storage mechanism, is a widespread practice in collective custody that carries serious risks for investors. Furthermore, when referring to asset segregation and collective custody, our observations highlight legal uncertainties surrounding these concepts that lead to inconsistent practices or practices that are inaccurately presented. Moreover, in certain cases, the clients' legal entitlements vis-a-vis their crypto assets deteriorate when the clients appoint a crypto custodian, and even more so when safekeeping is appointed to a third-party.

To date, crypto has been characterised by an absence of meaningful mandatory regulation and a large degree of contractual freedom. This has resulted in a bifurcated industry: on the one side, we observe some investor-oriented T&Cs, but on the other we see a large sample of T&Cs, including some T&Cs used by the largest custody providers, which serve primarily to shield the crypto custodian from any meaningful accountability, contrary to what the words 'safekeeping' or 'custody' entail.

If regulators are interested in achieving a mature crypto industry, financial regulation will be crucial to increase or maintain investors' confidence in crypto. Moreover, our sample suggests that financial regulation could bring the benefit of merit-based competition across providers.

12

Crypto Assets in Insolvency – Rights of Crypto Asset Holders under Austrian Law

OLIVER VÖLKEL

I. Preamble: Let's not Get Lost in Technology

At the time of writing this chapter, crypto assets have a 15-year history behind them. By their very nature, lawmakers as well as legal scholars are always one step behind when it comes to new technologies. Any new phenomena must first reach a certain critical mass to even be noticed in legal circles. If you don't hear about it, you don't think about it. Then, an understanding of the new phenomenon must mature. Only those who have a practical understanding of what they talk about can dare to tackle the legal side of the matter. And finally, a common language must be found in the collective discourse of the new phenomenon. Only then can one build on the insights of the other.

The phenomenon of crypto assets has obviously reached the necessary critical mass. The blockchain, or distributed ledger technology (DLT) is undoubtedly revolutionary. Understanding it is also crucial for its legal assessment. Nevertheless, one should avoid attaching more importance to technological aspects than they deserve in legal discussion.

The fact that such a risk exists is illustrated by the simple example of the transfer of a Bitcoin in return for payment: For the acquirer, it is important that the Bitcoin comes under his or her control; for the transferor, that they receive payment. From the perspective of the involved parties, this suggests a simple purchase. If one shifts the legal analysis to the technical level, the transferor must enter a new transaction into the blockchain, which in turn leads to the recipient's further power of disposal over the Bitcoin. Viewed from this perspective, what matters is the bringing about of a certain result, which suggests a contract for work.

The respective conclusions are not right or wrong per se, but the result of different levels of abstraction in the legal analysis. In this context, the quite perceptible tendencies to solve legal issues around crypto assets on the technological level are remarkable. Previous developments of the Internet age were rightly not legally discussed on a technological level. Understanding TCP/IP is not necessary to recognise that parties can exchange declarations of intent over the Internet, or that an animation on a screen can be copyright infringement. Even those who find a convincing counter-argument based on data transfer via TCP/IP must ultimately fail with it. It is simply an inadmissible level of abstraction.

Time and again, however, the legal discussion of crypto assets commits precisely this error. A detailed understanding of DLT and blockchain technology is necessary to see why the parties involved behave as they do. At this point, however, the influence of technology in legal discourse must end. Further analysis must tie in with human behaviour, and must tie in with how individuals interact with the technology and one another. This is the substance of the law. Let's not get lost in technology.

II. Introduction: Tackling the Question

Although the title of this chapter sounds innocent and simple, it is all but. In order to even identify where questions of insolvency can arise, first, we need to make a distinction between public (decentralised) blockchains such as Bitcoin or Ethereum, where anyone can join the consensus mechanism, and private (centralised) blockchains, where nodes are operated by one or a small number of parties and therefore can rather easily be controlled or shut down by whoever is in control. We shall call any such entity in control of a private blockchain the '**operator**'. Second, we must distinguish between crypto assets that do not represent rights vis-à-vis another party, such as, again, Bitcoin or Ethereum, and crypto-assets that serve as the carrier medium for such rights. Where a contractual counterparty exists, we shall call it the '**issuer**', even if it may be a bit unprecise in edge cases. When it comes to tokenisation, ie, the process of linking DLT-based tokens to real-world assets, we must also consider cases where '**asset custodians**' are part of the picture, holding these real-world assets on behalf of token holders. Lastly, we have to take into account parties that serve as '**crypto custodian**' holding crypto assets on behalf of others. Examples are custody providers for crypto assets or operators of trading platforms. Anyone being in a contractual relationship with one or more of the aforementioned entities shall be called a '**holder**' of crypto assets.

Depending on: (a) the type of blockchain used (public or private), (b) the type of crypto asset (issuer or issuer-less), (c) the question of whether real-world assets are being tokenised (asset custodian present or not) and (d) the type of custody of the crypto asset itself (crypto custodian present or not), a number of different parties may have to be considered for insolvency purposes.

Further, in order to make any statements as to how crypto assets are to be treated in the case of insolvency of any of the aforementioned parties, one must analyse where in the present legal framework this phenomenon fits.

III. Public Blockchains in Austrian Law

A. No Contractual Relationship Among Miners or Validators

The core aspect of public blockchains is their decentralisation. This means that: (i) no central authority adds new data to the blockchain; and (ii) no central authority determines who is to take over this task next. This is achieved by agreeing on a consensus mechanism, which allows consensus to be reached, in a decentralised fashion, on the selection of the next person responsible for this task. From the perspective of Austrian private law, the interesting questions are how agreement on the consensus mechanism is formed and how it is to be qualified legally.

i. Agreeing to a Consensus Mechanism not a Legal Declaration of Intent

The question of how the consensus mechanism is agreed upon shall only briefly be discussed for the two most relevant consensus mechanisms (ie, Bitcoin's proof-of-work, and Ethereum's proof-of-stake): With respect to proof-of-work, mining requires the use of highly specialised hardware that follows the consensus mechanism that has been programmatically established beforehand.[1] Those who use such hardware in a way that becomes apparent to other miners conclusively declare to agree on the consensus mechanism. With respect to proof-of-stake, when operating validators, units of the respective virtual currency are used as a stake to affirm one's own adherence to the consensus rules. Anyone who takes the technically necessary steps to set up a validator, and who is thereby entered into a list of active validators, also conclusively declares to agree to the consensus mechanism.

As to the legal quality of such declarations and the agreements resulting from them, it is important to stress a central principle of Austrian private law: Not every agreement (*Vereinbarung*) is also a legal contract (*Vertrag*). A declaration of intent (*Willenserklärung*) in Austrian private law (such as an offer or acceptance) is more than just 'declaring one's intent'. Matching declarations of intent always lead to an agreement. However, the Austrian Civil Code does not concern agreements but legal transactions (*Rechtsgeschäfte*).

For the conclusion of legal transactions, it is necessary that the parties form legal transaction intent (*Rechtsgeschäftswillen*). To this end, the declarations of intent must be aimed at establishing, amending, or terminating rights or legal relationships.[2] The declaration of intent must aim to trigger legal consequences.[3]

[1] *cf* C Sillaber, 'Mining your own business? Betrieb dezentraler Systeme als GesbR' [2019] *ecolex* 849.

[2] P Rummel, 's 863 ABGB' in P Rummel and M Lukas (eds), *ABGB*, 4th edn (Vienna, MANZ, 2023) para 6 et seq.

[3] Known as *Rechtsfolgentheorie*, W Flume, *Das Rechtsgeschäft*, 3rd edn (Berlin, Springer, 1979) 51 et seq; F Bydlinski, *Privatautonomie* (Vienna, Springer, 1967) 7.

If the declaration aims merely at triggering social or economic consequences, there is no legal transaction intent.[4] Whether the declarant has intended legal consequences must be assessed from the perspective of the recipient of the declaration.

This distinction makes it possible to differentiate between legal transactions and transactions that are not intended to trigger legal consequences. The question of whether legal transaction intent exists is not determined by the true intention of the declarant, but rather by the recipient's understanding in accordance with the 'theory of trust' (*Empfängerhorizont nach der Vertrauenstheorie*).[5] The declaration is deemed to have been made in the manner in which it could be understood by a reasonable recipient. Therefore, the contours of a declaration of intent shall not be determined by the actual existence of legal intent, but by the objective understanding of the declaration.[6]

How does the declaration, or agreement, to adhere to a consensus mechanism fit into this private law framework? Considering the block reward,[7] anyone who adds a new block with transactions to the Bitcoin or Ethereum blockchain creates new Bitcoins or Ether for themselves. This is also the central economic incentive to act as a miner or validator in the Bitcoin or Ethereum network in the first place. The concrete design of the consensus mechanism can therefore have far-reaching economic consequences.

However, as pointed out above, a declaration must be aimed at more than triggering economic consequences to be considered showing legal transaction intent under Austrian law. And the objective meaning of the declarations made when conducting mining or operating a validator is not directed at the creation, modification or cancellation of rights or legal relationships. The declaration, whether explicit or conclusive, to comply with the consensus mechanism of a given blockchain does therefore not constitute a declaration of legal transaction intent.

The agreement of, or consent to, a consensus mechanism, which concerns the question of who will generate the next block and therefore also who may obtain the block reward (and transaction fees), does not lead to the conclusion of a contract pursuant to section 861 of the Austrian Civil Code. The creation of a block does not concern the establishment, modification or cancellation of rights or legal relationships. The necessary legal transaction intent for the conclusion of a contract is lacking.

[4] Known as *Grundfolgentheorie*, eg, T Mayer-Maly, *Einführung in die allgemeinen Lehren des österreichischen Privatrechts* (Graz, Leykam, 1984) 39; O Lenel, 'Parteiabsicht und Rechtserfolg' in R von Jhering (ed), *Jahrbücher für die Dogmatik des heutigen römischen und deutschen Privatrechts XIX* (Jena, Fischer, 1881) 154; against F Bydlinski, 'Verträge über ärztliche Leistungen' in WH Rechberger and R Welser (eds), *Festschrift für Winfried Kralik zum 65. Geburtstag* (Vienna, MANZ, 1986) 345, 352.

[5] A Riedler, 's 863 ABGB' in M Schwimann and G Kodek (eds), *ABGB Praxiskommentar*, 4th edn (Vienna, LexisNexis, 2014) para 1.

[6] R Bollenberger, 's 863 ABGB' in H Koziol, P Bydlinski and R Bollenberger (eds), *Kurzkommentar zum ABGB* 5th edn (Vienna, Verlag Österreich, 2017) para 3.

[7] As for transaction fees, see below.

The decentralised nature of public blockchains means that the mere fact that people are mining, or operating validators does not imply the existence of a legal relationship between miners or validators.[8] Such a relationship does not exist without special circumstances (eg, in cases where miners/validators contract to form a mining pool).

How does this insight fit with the fact that miners or validators obtain Bitcoins or Ether for themselves with the block reward? Bitcoins are at least subject to property rights in a broader sense under Austrian law (*Eigentumsrecht im weiteren Sinn*).[9] In the absence of a central authority, it is also clear that the process of obtaining the block reward must be based on an original form of ownership acquisition (*originärer Eigentumserwerb*). Mining or staking is therefore not completely without legal consequences. After all, a new property right in Bitcoins or Ether is created when obtaining the block reward. However, this is not because of the agreement of the consensus mechanism, but rather a result of its execution by the respective miner or validator.

ii. Executing the Rules of the Consensus Mechanism as a Real Act

Thus, the last question to be discussed is how compliance with, or execution of, the consensus mechanism is to be classified in terms of legal transactions under Austrian law. How is it to be assessed when a miner in the Bitcoin network (or generally, in the case of proof-of-work) or a validator in the Ethereum network (or generally, in the case of proof-of-stake) transfers a block to other miners or validators? Looking at Bitcoin, the miner has provided the proof-of-work; looking at Ethereum, the validator was selected in the proof-of-stake process. In this situation, the next step is to submit the new block to the other miners or validators, who will hopefully accept it as valid so that it becomes part of the blockchain. The word 'hopefully' must be emphasised, because, in the absence of a contractual relationship, miners or validators on public blockchains have no legal claim against one another, allowing them to force the acceptance of a new block. Instead, there are only economic incentives to do so.

How should the transfer of a new block then be assessed? The miner or validator wants to change a factual state, namely that the new block becomes part of the blockchain and that they receive the block reward (and transaction fees). The miner/validator submits the block to the other miners or validators

[8] O Völkel, 'Zur Bedeutung der Dezentralität von Blockchains im Privatrecht' [2019] *Zeitschrift für Finanzmarktrecht* 601, 602.

[9] *cf* H Koziol, 'Sache, Eigentum und persönliche Sachenrechte: vernachlässigte dogmatische Schätze des österreichischen ABGB' in HC Grigoleit and J Petersen (eds), *Privatrechtsdogmatik im 21. Jahrhundert. Festschrift für Claus-Wilhelm Canaris zum 80. Geburtstag* (Berlin, De Gruyter, 2017) 1087; regarding Bitcoin *cf* A Vonkilch and M Knoll, 'Bitcoins und das Sachenrecht des ABGB' [2019] *Juristische Blätter* 139; L Fleißner, 'Eigentum an unkörperlichen Sachen am Beispiel von Bitcoins' [2018] *Österreichische Juristenzeitung* 437; O Völkel, 'Privatrechtliche Einordnung virtueller Währungen' [2017] *Österreichisches Bankarchiv* 385.

precisely because they want to achieve this outcome. Put in legal terms, the miner/validator takes a de facto action, which is linked to a legal intention. The described constellation neatly fits the concept of a real act (*Realakt*) under Austrian private law.

The legal qualification as a real act leads to appropriate results. The legal consequences of a real act occur independently of the legal capacity of the person performing the act.[10] In terms of mining and staking, this means that miners and validators can acquire ownership in newly created Bitcoins and Ether, without it being necessary to examine legal capacity in an individual case. The miner or validator who lacks legal capacity, eg, because of age, therefore also acquires the Bitcoins mined by themselves.

B. Transaction Requests are not Contractual Offers but Public Offers of a Reward

In the case of public blockchains, it follows from their decentralised nature that a transaction request is not handled centrally by one single miner/validator, but in principle in parallel by everyone participating in the network. The fact that the person who publicly transmits a transaction request to the network is indifferent to who ultimately confirms the transaction in a block is essential for the further legal assessment. All that matters to the user is that his or her transaction is taken into account in a block. It is the same with the transaction fee: it does not matter to the user at all which miner or validator ultimately receives it. It is only the result of recording the user's transaction request in a block that counts.

When sending a transaction request, the user promises a reward to the person who ultimately records the transaction in a block. Whoever confirms the transaction request should receive the transaction fee. The consequence of this is that the user's declaration of intent is not an offer within the meaning of section 861 of the Austrian Civil Code, as this would require that it be made to a specific person. The declaration of intent is therefore to be characterised differently under Austrian private law. Specifically, it could fall under the legal category of the public offer of a reward (*Auslobung*). A public offer of a reward becomes binding through the public announcement.[11] Essential to the public offer of a reward are four elements:[12]

- the intention to commit oneself which must be expressed in the respective declaration;
- the exchange purpose, ie, the reward for bringing-about a result;

[10] A Riedler, 's 859 ABGB' in Schwimann and Kodek (n 5) para 6.
[11] Völkel (n 8) 604.
[12] W Kolmasch, 's 860 ABGB' in M Schwimann and M Neumayr (eds), *ABGB Taschenkommentar*, 4th edn (Vienna, LexisNexis, 2017) para 2.

- the public announcement; and
- the indeterminate group of addressees.

The first two elements have been discussed above, and their existence has been established. The law does not impose any particular requirements on the manner of the public announcement. A public notice or publication in the media or on the Internet has been considered sufficient.[13] It is essential, however, that the announcement can actually reach the addressed group. This is ensured in the case of public transaction requests within the respective blockchain network. After all, the transaction request propagates through the entire network of the respective blockchain and is known to all miners or validators after a short time.

Lastly, the public offer of a reward must be directed at an indeterminate group of addressees. A restriction to a certain or definable larger group of persons (ie, miners or validators) does not lead to a different legal assessment.[14] The declaration results in an effective self-commitment of the user towards miners or validators.[15]

The consequence of this legal view is that there is no corresponding obligation to perform on the part of any specific miner or validator. In other words, miners or validators are not obligated to provide a service to users of the blockchain. Each miner or validator is free to execute or ignore transaction requests. If a miner or validator decides to include a transaction in a block, however, this miner or validator is entitled to the transaction fee, ie, the reward promised by the user.

IV. Crypto Assets on Public Blockchains in Austrian Law[16]

A. Crypto Assets are not Receivables

Austrian private law distinguishes between real property rights (*dingliche Sachenrechte*) and personal property rights (*persönliche Sachenrechte*; section 307 of the Austrian Civil Code). Only at first glance does the characterisation of

[13] R Bollenberger, 's 860 ABGB' in Koziol, Bydlinski and Bollenberger (n 6) para 4; Kolmasch (n 12) para 2.

[14] OGH 11. 1. 1989, 9 ObA 516/88.

[15] For details, see H Koziol, 'Freiwillige Selbstverpflichtung von Banken gegenüber der Öffentlichkeit' [2013] *Österreichisches Bankarchiv* 91.

[16] The following assessment applies to coins (ie, native tokens on a given blockchain, eg, Bitcoin on the Bitcoin blockchain, Ether on the Ethereum blockchain) and (non-native) tokens insofar as the programming of the respective smart contract does not grant other persons a possibility to dispose of tokens against the will of another person.

crypto assets as personal property rights seem obvious. Book money, ie, a claim against a credit institution, is counted among the personal property rights. However, the decisive difference between crypto assets on the one hand and book money on the other is that the coin or token does not represent a claim against a third party. The mere fact that a person has the private key to a certain amount of crypto assets does not constitute a claim against any other person. As pointed out above, in particular, there is no claim against miners or validators. Only if there exists another agreement, eg, between the holder and an issuer, the crypto asset may represent a claim against another party. This representation of a claim by a token must be distinguished from the token itself, however.

B. Possession of Crypto Assets

Austrian legal literature unanimously qualifies Bitcoin and comparable crypto assets as things (*Sachen*) within the meaning of section 285 of the Austrian Civil Code.[17] For justification, reference is usually made to the broad definition in the Civil Code. A certain minimum degree of controllability is required for a phenomenon to be qualified as a thing.[18] Completely uncontrollable phenomena such as free air and flowing water,[19] but also ideas or concepts are not recognised as things. These phenomena are not controllable at all and consequently not things in the sense of the law.

The question arises as to why controllability should be the decisive factor and what exactly is meant by controllability in the case of Bitcoin, for example. The answer to the first question can be derived from the concept of assignment (*Zurechnungsgedanke*) in Austrian property law:[20] Without controllability, an assignment of legal goods to legal subjects is not conceivable. In the case of crypto assets, it is the immutability of the blockchain and the necessity of a private key that make the phenomenon controllable.

For the following discussion, a precise understanding of the term 'incorporeal thing' (*unkörperliche Sache*) is decisive. 'Incorporeal thing' refers to things that do not have a physical form (section 292 Civil Code). This is interpreted as spatial delimitability in solid, liquid, or gaseous state.[21] In addition, the law expressly states that all rights belong to the category of 'incorporeal things' and mentions as an example the rights to hunt or to fish (section 292 Civil Code). It follows that rights form only a subgroup of incorporeal things. Besides rights, the Civil Code recognises other things that do not have a physical form as a form of 'other

[17] Vonkilch and Knoll (n 9) 139; Fleißner (n 9) 437; M Aigner, 'Das Pfandrecht und die Blockchain' [2019] *Österreichisches Bankarchiv* 819.

[18] C Holzner, 's 285 ABGB' in Rummel and Lukas (n 2) para 5 with further references; N Hofmann, 's 285 ABGB' in Schwimann and Kodek (n 5) para 3.

[19] ibid.

[20] Hofmann (n 18) para 1.

[21] G Kodek, 's 292 ABGB' in Schwimann and Neumayr (n 12) para 1.

incorporeal thing'. As an example, legal literature mentions sound waves or electromagnetic waves.[22]

On the basis of the framework presented above, it can be examined whether the civil law provisions on possession (*Besitz*; sections 309 ff Civil Code) are also applicable to crypto assets. According to Austrian law, possession is the actual dominion (*custody, power*) over a thing, with the will to have it as one's own (section 309 Civil Code). The object of possession can be all corporeal and incorporeal things that can also be an object of legal transactions (section 311 Civil Code). Since crypto assets are the object of commercial and legal transactions, the provisions on possession apply.

In contrast to corporeal things, incorporeal things are taken into possession by using them in one's own name (section 312 Civil Code). In the case of such unilateral[23] acquisition of possession, third-party possession must be recognisably excluded; the specific requirements are based on the prevailing view of the involved parties (*beteiligte Verkehrskreise*).[24] Accordingly – *not your keys, not your coins* – third-party possession is only recognisably excluded if crypto assets are held at one's own address on the blockchain knowing the associated private key.

The Austrian Civil Code regulates the loss of possession expressly only with regard to tangible things (section 349 Civil Code), immovable property (section 350 Civil Code) and relative rights (section 351 Civil Code). There is no express provision on the category of other incorporeal things, to which crypto assets belong according to the view defended here.

With regard to the quasi-physical quality of crypto assets, it can be argued that the provision for tangible things can be applied *mutatis mutandis* to crypto assets. Accordingly, possession is lost if the thing 'is lost without hope of being found again [1st case]; if it is voluntarily abandoned [2nd case]; or comes into the possession of another [3rd case]'.

An object is lost if it is removed from custody of the possessor without their will and without the acquisition of possession by a third party.[25] Whether there is a loss of custody is to be judged according to the perception of the involved parties.[26] The element 'without hope' is to be understood objectively as the absence of a reasonable prospect of recovery in the foreseeable future; temporary inaccessibility, however, does not mean loss of possession.[27]

In the case of crypto assets, again, the view of the relevant parties must be considered: *Not your keys, not your coins* means that possession is lost if knowledge

[22] E Helmich, 's 292 ABGB' in A Kletečka and T Schauer (eds), ABGB-ON, edn 1.04 (Vienna, MANZ, online via www.rdb.at) para 4; B Eccher and O Riss, 's 292 ABGB' in Koziol, Bydlinski and Bollenberger (n 6) para 1.

[23] OGH 24. 6. 1976, 2 Ob 520/76.

[24] G Kodek, 's 312 ABGB' in Kletečka and Schauer (n 22) para 1.

[25] C Holzner, 's 349 ABGB' in Rummel and Lukas (n 2) para 1.

[26] ibid.

[27] Holzner (n 25) para 2.

of the private key is lost. The temporary inability to dispose of crypto assets, on the other hand, does not lead to a loss of possession, for example because there is no access to the Internet for a certain period of time.

The question of the transfer of possession of other incorporeal things such as Bitcoin or Ether is dealt with below because of the factual connection with a transfer of ownership.

C. Ownership of Crypto Assets

Everything that belongs to a person, all his corporeal and incorporeal things, is called his property (section 353 Civil Code). The object of the right of ownership can therefore both be corporeal and incorporeal things. The prevailing view is that the right of ownership is not fully applicable to claims (incorporeal things).[28] Therefore, a distinction is made between the property right in a narrower sense and in a wider sense (also called 'legal competence', *Rechtszuständigkeit*), whereas only corporeal things should be objects of the property right in the narrower sense.[29]

The question of the ownership of crypto assets has been addressed in Austrian legal literature, especially in connection with Bitcoin. There is at least a consensus that Bitcoins, and probably also comparable crypto assets, can be the subject of a property right in the wider sense.[30]

Fleißner[31] affirms the possibility of an acquisition of property in a narrower sense. She emphasises that the concept of ownership according to the wording of section 353 Civil Code is not limited to tangible objects. *Vonkilch/Knoll*[32] deal with the question of the necessity of a special act of transfer. The authors point out exceptions to the principle of tradition (*Traditionsprinzip*), according to which the transfer by declaration is also to be recognised in the case of crypto assets analogous to section 428 Civil Code. They also argue that the property law provisions of the Civil Code are largely tailored to tangible, actually controllable objects; thus, it can only be decided on the basis of the relevant valuations of the individual property law provisions whether they are applicable to crypto assets. *Aigner*[33] argues, following section 354 Civil Code, for an analogous application of the property law provisions to all digital assets. *Diwok/Gritsch*[34] point out the problems arising from the understanding of crypto assets as incorporeal things when acquiring ownership. *Dafinger* argues that characteristics of property,

[28] Vonkilch and Knoll (n 9) 139 et seq.

[29] A Illedits, 's 354 ABGB' in Schwimann and Neumayr (n 12) para 1.

[30] Völkel (n 8) 385; Fleißner (n 9) 440 et seq; Vonkilch and Knoll (n 9) 139; Aigner (n 17) 816.

[31] Fleißner (n 9) 440 et seq.

[32] Vonkilch and Knoll (n 9) 139.

[33] Aigner (n 17) 816.

[34] G Diwok and D Gritsch, 'Bitcoin, Monetary Terms and Means of Payment' [2020] *Zeitschrift für Finanzmarktrecht* 68.

namely the power to exclude and the power to control, are present in crypto assets such as Bitcoin applying ownership rules in the narrower sense would be possible by means of analogy.[35]

Crypto assets on public blockchains are not based on a relative right. Thus, they belong to the category of other incorporeal things under section 292 Civil Code, such as radiation or sound waves. Due to their particular controllability, crypto assets have a pronounced quasi-physical character. Therefore, one should agree with *Fleißner* that despite their incorporeality, property rights in the narrower sense can be acquired in crypto assets. *Vonkilch/Knoll*[36] correctly point out that the property law provisions of the Civil Code are tailored to objects that can actually be controlled; however, as elaborated above, crypto assets are in no way inferior to tangible objects with regard to their controllability. The fact that most property law provisions are based on actual controllability[37] therefore serves as an argument for the applicability of the property law provisions also to crypto assets.[38]

It must be pointed out once again that not every crypto asset can be controlled in the same way. If the necessary minimum degree of control cannot be exercised over a particular crypto asset, the considerations made above do not apply. Smart contracts whose programming allows third parties to intervene in the position of control over tokens, ie, enables transfers without the consent of the authorised party, for example, or grants third parties the possibility of preventing transfers, are not suitable for conveying positions of ownership.

Whether sufficient dominion can be exercised over a particular crypto asset is a preliminary question for deciding whether this crypto asset is subject to the provisions of Austrian property law in a narrower sense. In the case of Bitcoin and comparable digital assets, this preliminary question can be answered in the affirmative.

D. Derivative Acquisition of Ownership

i. Physical Handover from 'Hand to Hand'

The basic case for the transfer of ownership in movable objects – which also includes crypto assets[39] – is the 'corporal transfer from hand to hand' (*körperliche Übergabe von Hand zu Hand*; section 426 Civil Code). Corporeal transfer is understood as the procurement of the actual custody in favour of the

[35] F Dafinger, 'Kryptowährungen und der Modus beim Eigentumserwerb in Österreich' [2022] *Recht Digital* 17.

[36] Vonkilch and Knoll (n 9) 139.

[37] Hofmann (n 18) para 1.

[38] *cf* G Kogler, 'Non Fungible Tokens und Sachenrecht' [2021] *Juristische Blätter* 685.

[39] Fleißner (n 9) 440.

transferee.[40] A thing is brought into a situation, by which it is actually under the control of the transferee.[41] The decisive factor is the possibility of exclusive influence, not necessarily a 'corporeal touching' of the thing and also not the change of location.[42]

'Hand to hand' is therefore not to be taken literally. What matters is the establishment of a close relationship which is sufficient to indicate that the acquirer is in possession of the thing.[43] Even if the law speaks of a 'corporeal transfer', this does not necessarily imply a restriction to corporeal objects. Also, incorporeal things can be 'corporeally' transferred from hand to hand if they can be controlled in a way comparable to corporeal things. In this respect, hand-to-hand transfer is possible in the case of crypto assets pursuant to section 426 Civil Code.

As was discussed above, crypto assets have a highly quasi-corporeal character. Despite their incorporeality, they can be controlled in (for incorporeal things) previously unknown intensity. Possession (control, dominion) is held by whoever knows the private key associated with the crypto assets. Therefore, the transfer on the blockchain leads to the transfer of possession from hand to hand according to section 426 Civil Code if it is made to an address whose associated private key is known to the acquirer.

ii. Transfer by Sign (Zeichen)

In the case of such movable objects, which by their nature do not permit a physical handover, the handover by means of a sign is permissible (section 427 Civil Code). If the transferor hands over the private key to the crypto asset to the transferee, for example, in the case of the transfer of a physical wallet, this would be an example of a transfer by sign. Disclosure of the private key is therefore a sufficient form of handover.[44] It is not necessary to ensure that neither the transferor himself nor a third party continues to have knowledge of the private key. Procuring sole possession is not mandatory for an effective handover by sign. If the transferee wants to ensure that they obtain sole possession, they must transfer the crypto assets to another address in their sole possession.

iii. Transfer by Declaration

Finally, a thing can be handed over by declaration (section 428 Civil Code). With respect to crypto assets, transfer by declaration is also permissible.[45] Transfer by

[40] B Eccher and O Riss, 's 426 ABGB' in Koziol, Bydlinski and Bollenberger (n 6) para 1 with further references.

[41] T Klicka and A Reidinger, 's 426 ABGB' in Schwimann and Kodek (n 5) para 1.

[42] Eccher and Riss (n 40) para 1 with further references.

[43] OGH 12. 3. 1996, 10 Ob 2035/96d.

[44] Fleißner (n 9) 441.

[45] Vonkilch and Knoll (n 9) 139.

constitutum possessorium, a shorthand transfer or handover *brevi manu* as well as instructions of possession (*Besitzanweisung*) are therefore also acceptable forms of handover in the case of crypto assets.

The prerequisite for this in the case of *constitutum possessorium* is that the person who has knowledge of the private key will in future hold the crypto assets to be transferred in the name of the transferee. In the case of shorthand transfer, the prerequisite for this is that the person who newly forms the corresponding will to possess certain crypto assets already had knowledge of the private key. Prerequisite for the instruction of possession is that the person instructed has knowledge of the private key.

E. Original Acquisition of Ownership

Ownership can be acquired originally (*originär*) in things that cannot be distinguished by individual characteristics (fungible objects) by blending, without good faith being required for the acquisition (section 371 Civil Code). Blending is present if the fungible things can no longer be distinguished from each other. Not only in the case of money and bearer instruments, but also in the case of other fungible things, acquisition of ownership by blending is possible.[46] If, for example, cash is still available in a distinguishable form, ie, if it has not been mixed with funds belonging to another person, ie, if it is separable and clearly distinguishable, it can be the subject of a property action and give rise to a right of segregation in insolvency proceedings.[47] However, if this cash can no longer be clearly allocated to a person and has been mixed with other assets of another person, this other person has acquired original ownership. Since crypto assets are fungible things, an original acquisition of ownership according to section 371 Civil Code is also possible. What is required is an indistinguishable commingling on an address on the blockchain.

V. Private Blockchains in Austrian Law

In addition to public blockchains such as Bitcoin or Ethereum, there are also private and centralised systems to consider. These private blockchains are characterised by the fact that only one person or a select group of people operate the infrastructure. These persons thus have control over the functioning and continuation of the system. Such a structure can be found in 'permissioned' blockchains, where these systems require the consent of one or more other persons to participate in the mining process or validation of blocks.

[46] T Klicka and A Reidinger, 's 371 ABGB' in Schwimann and Kodek (n 5) para 5.
[47] P Schulyok, 's 44 IO' in A Konecny (ed), *Insolvenzgesetze* (Vienna, MANZ, 2021) para 15.

The conclusions presented above for public blockchains are only applicable to private DLT networks in exceptional cases. Take, for example, the case of a blockchain whose entire infrastructure is operated by only a single person (natural or legal). In such a case, one person makes their technical infrastructure available to other persons. The relationship between operator of a private blockchain and the user is best described as the provision of software as a service by the operator.

From a purely technical point of view, also in this example a transaction request is still a validly signed and technically correctly structured instruction to transfer crypto assets or to interact with a smart contract. However, the legal classification of the transaction request is different from that of the public blockchain. In contrast to public blockchains, where the user does not care which person from an undefined group of miners or validators ultimately confirms the transaction request in a block, this is not the case in our example. In fact, there is only one person who can include the transaction request in a block, namely the operator of the respective blockchain. As a declaration of intent by the user, the transaction request is thus not a public offer of a reward, because these must be addressed to an undefined group of addressees. Instead, it is a regular contractual offer that can be accepted by fulfilment by the operator of the private blockchain. Acceptance results in the conclusion of a contract that might be governed by terms of service provided by the operator; or that instead might be governed by implied terms if no explicit terms of service exist. A transaction request in such a centralised private blockchain is therefore merely an offer by the user to the operator of the blockchain to record the transaction. In such systems, contracts are concluded between the users and the operator on an ongoing basis. If the user offers a transaction fee to the operator of the blockchain infrastructure in return for recording the transaction request in the blockchain, a contract for consideration is formed.

How does a permissioned DLT system fit into the picture, where, in contrast to the example discussed above, several different people each operate a node? Can such a system be qualified as 'decentralised' in the above discussed sense, resulting in the qualification of transaction requests as public offers of a reward? The answer depends on whether the parties operating the DLT infrastructure (as miners or validators, or in other roles) are contractually bound to one another in such a way that they form a (eg, civil law) company. If this is the case, it could be argued that the user interacts with only one entity, ie, the company formed by the miners or validators. In such a case, the user's transaction request remains a regular contractual offer. The situation may be different in case the operators of the permissioned DLT infrastructure do not form such a company but are rather bound to one another on the basis of non-corporate agreements. In such a case, as with other decentralised systems, the transaction request might still be regarded as a public offer of a reward. Unfortunately, no generally applicable answer can be given; rather, it depends on the specifics of a given permissioned DLT system.

Further, the considerations made when qualifying crypto assets on public blockchains do not apply when it comes to private blockchains. While the legal relationship between operator and user in its entirety (as personal property) is to be qualified as a thing (*Sache*) within the broad meaning of section 285 of the Austrian Civil Code,[48] it is doubtful that a crypto asset, as part of this legal relationship, can be viewed as constituting a separate and distinguishable thing. The considerations justifying this result in respect of crypto assets on public blockchains are simply not present. In particular, transactions on private blockchains in the sense here discussed are not immutable. While this question has not been settled in Austrian legal literature definitively, it seems reasonable to reject crypto assets on private blockchains as separate and distinguishable legally protected interests (*Rechtsgüter*).

VI. Crypto Assets in Insolvency

As discussed above, depending on: (a) the type of blockchain used (public or private), (b) the type of crypto asset (issuer or issuer-less), (c) the question of whether real-world assets are being tokenised (asset custodian present or not), and (d) the type of custody of the crypto asset itself (crypto custodian present or not) a number of different parties have to be considered for insolvency purposes. Based on the legal considerations also discussed above, the following first conclusions can be drawn. A detailed discussion of every single possible permutation of the identified matrix components must be reserved for other publications. The following should therefore only be understood as a first indication as well as an invitation to further legal discussion.

A. Insolvency Estate and Claims for Segregation

The insolvency estate encompasses all assets subject to execution which belong to the debtor at that time of, or which it acquires during, the insolvency proceedings (section 2(2) Austrian Insolvency Act). The total assets subject to execution include all assets belonging to the debtor at the time of commencement of the proceedings and which it otherwise acquires during the further course of the proceedings.[49]

The insolvency estate includes all movable and immovable assets of the debtor, such as shares in real property, including co-ownership shares, claims such as claims for damages, claims for rent, tenancy rights, virtual currencies, and

[48] Vonkilch and Knoll (n 9) 139; Fleißner (n 9) 56; Aigner (n 17) 819.

[49] G Feuchtinger and M Lesigang (eds), *Praxisleitfaden Insolvenzrecht*, 3rd edn (Vienna, Linde, 2010) 47.

the like.[50] Crypto assets are thus assets subject to execution either as virtual currencies or otherwise as movable property, unless exceptional circumstances apply. They are also part of the insolvency estate unless they are objectively unusable. In addition, they may be excluded from the insolvency estate if the crypto assets cannot be used for economic purposes and do not generate any income. Otherwise, they must be included in the inventory by the insolvency administrator, and the associated private keys and public addresses must be disclosed by the debtor. Crypto exchange platforms can be forced to provide information about debtor accounts with a protective order of the insolvency court.[51]

Pursuant to section 44 para 1 Austrian Insolvency Act, a right is granted to reclaim items that are part of the insolvency estate but which do not belong to the debtor in whole or in part. Anyone who can show that they have a right *in rem* or a personal right to an object is entitled to such segregation.[52] The person entitled to segregation is a third party who pursues a real property right or personal property right to which they are entitled independently of the insolvency proceedings. Whether such a third party is entitled is to be assessed exclusively in accordance with the general principles of property law.[53] The claim for segregation relates to things in the broader sense,[54] ie, it also covers crypto assets within the limitations discussed above. The most frequent reason for segregation is ownership[55] or co-ownership.[56]

B. Insolvency of the Operator

The possibility of an insolvency of the operator of a blockchain only needs to be considered in the case of a private blockchain. The insolvency of a miner or validator (as 'operator' in a broader sense in the case of a public blockchain) does not have an impact on the legal situation whatsoever. This is because, as pointed out above, holders and miners/validators are not in a contractual relationship with one another. Conversely, in cases where the legal relationship between holder and operator of a private blockchain constitutes the provision of software services, segregation claims (as discussed below) with respect to crypto assets are excluded.

In cases of crypto assets having an issuer, ie, in cases where a legal relationship between issuer and holder exists, an insolvency of the operator of a private

[50] ibid.

[51] M Lutschounig, 'Virtuelle Währungen in der Insolvenzmasse' [2022] *Österreichische Jurist:innenzeitung* 1179.

[52] Schulyok (n 47) para 2.

[53] ibid para 3.

[54] F Mohr, *Insolvenzordnung*, 11th edn (Vienna, MANZ, 2012) s 44 IO para 408.

[55] Schulyok (n 47) para 7.

[56] F Mohr (n 54) s 44 IO para 409.

blockchain has an impact on the legal situation only insofar as the means to represent the legal relationship (ie, the crypto asset) no longer exists. This does not invalidate the legal relationship between issuer and holder, however. In such a case, the holder and issuer will have to agree to substitute the crypto asset used to represent the legal claims by another crypto asset (or by other means).

In the case of crypto assets representing tokenised real-world-assets, with respect to the legal relationship between holder and issuer, the same conclusion can be drawn, based on the same legal arguments. Instead of the crypto asset used up until insolvency of the operator, a new form of representing instructions to the custodian must be agreed on.

Self-custody vis-à-vis third-party custody might have legal implications insofar as it may determine which person has to file a claim in insolvency proceedings. Whether the service provider or the holder is entitled to file the claim must be determined on the basis of their contractual relationship, ie, by answering the question: Who does the claim against the operator belong to?

C. Insolvency of the Issuer or the Asset Custodian

The possibility of an insolvency of the issuer of a crypto asset mostly needs to be considered in cases where a contractual relationship is formed between an issuer and a holder, and for the most part in cases where this contractual relationship comprises a continuing obligation (*Dauerschuldverhältnis*) as opposed to a specific obligation (*Zielschuldverhältnis*). An example of a continuing obligation is the promise of the issuer to redeem the crypto asset in the future or to make payments on it. In contrast, the mere sale of a crypto asset that can be used to interact with already existing smart contracts (and which do not need to be maintained by the issuer to operate properly) would constitute a specific obligation. Specific obligations can be relevant in an insolvency context in case one side has fulfilled their end of the contract but not the other. In the case of continuing obligations, this is the case by default.

When it comes to tokenised real-world-assets, an insolvency of the issuer may give rise to segregation claims vis-à-vis that issuer (in case the issuer also acts as custodian for said real-word-assets) or vis-à-vis a third-party asset custodian. Also, the insolvency of the asset custodian itself must be considered. Whether or not a segregation claim exists depends – in both cases – on the contractual relationship formed, in particular, whether or not the contract provides the crypto asset holder with ownership claims to the tokenised real-world assets.

D. Insolvency of the Service Provider (Crypto Custodian)

The possibility of an insolvency of a crypto asset service provider must be considered in cases where crypto assets are not held in self-custody by the holder, but rather are held by a service provider (crypto custodian). Whether a right to segregation exists in the event of insolvency depends not only on the contractual agreement, but also on the correct safekeeping of the crypto assets.

With regard to the specific contractual agreement, two cases must be distinguished from one another. The customer's claim against the service provider can, for example, be directed toward receiving back a certain quantity of crypto assets, but the claim does not relate to specific individual pieces. The claim is then merely of debt nature, comparable to the claim of an account holder vis-à-vis a bank for the surrender of the credit balance. Just as the bank account holder has no claim to segregation against the insolvent bank, the customer also has no claim to segregation against the insolvent crypto asset service provider in such cases. Only in case the agreement between service provider and customer relates to the custody of specific crypto assets, a right to segregation can exist.

With regard to the correct safekeeping of the crypto assets, in order not to jeopardise the customer's claim to segregation in the event of the insolvency of the service provider, care must be taken to ensure that the customer (in case of a purchase from the service provider) acquires ownership in the crypto assets from the service provider and that the customer's ownership is not lost at a later point in time, eg, through commingling of assets. In the opposite case, when the customer deposits crypto assets with the service provider, care must be taken to ensure that the customer's original ownership is not lost in the course of the transfer to the service provider (or later), again, for example through commingling.

VII. Conclusion

When considering rights of crypto asset holders under Austrian law in the event of insolvency, care must be taken to identify which parties are involved, and exactly what claim is made against which other party. Further, any insolvency considerations must be based on a thorough understanding and clear categorisation of the different types of crypto assets in the private law framework. Only if both conditions are met, a clear picture of the legal ramifications can emerge.

13

Protection of Holders of Crypto Assets under French Law

HUBERT DE VAUPLANE

The question of the level of protection afforded to digital asset owners under French law has so far not been the subject of much comment.[1]

However, the work undertaken by the *Haut Comité Juridique de la Place de Paris* in connection with the measures to adapt French law to the entry into force of the MiCA Regulation[2] has highlighted the following points.

First, to date, France has not had to suffer any cases where a digital asset intermediary has failed to protect its customers' assets. There have been cases of fraud where intermediaries have been criminally prosecuted, but to our knowledge there has never been a case where, following the bankruptcy of a digital asset platform, the holders of these assets have been unable to dispose of their assets. To put it another way, there has been no bankruptcy of a French digital asset platform.

Second, French law – prior to the entry into force of MiCA – does not provide for any specific regime on this subject, unlike in the case of securities. Thus, French law is silent on the question of who owns customers' digital assets held with a digital service intermediary registered with the AMF.

Consequently, the regime applicable in the event of default by a French intermediary depends: (i) on the legal nature of the digital assets; and (ii) on the type of default. Implementation of the MiCA Regulation will bring changes to the French law currently applicable (iii).

[1] *cf* however, H de Vauplane, 'La revendication d'actifs numériques' [2019] *Revue trimestrielle du droit financier* 55.

[2] Regulation (EO) 2023/1114 of the European Parliament and of the Council of 31 May 2023 on markets in crypto assets, and amending Regulations (EU) No 1093/2010 and (EU) No 1095/2010 and Directives 2013/36/EU and (EU) 2019/1937 [2023] OJ L150/40.

I. Legal Nature of Digital Assets under French Law before MiCA

French legal scholars and practitioners agree that digital assets are intangible movable property, naturally fungible and 'consumable', even if the parties may stipulate otherwise in their contractual relations on the last two points.

Digital assets can represent:

1. A claim against the token issuer (this is the case for most utility tokens, but also for *Electronic Money Token* and *Asset Referenced Token* as defined by MiCA);
2. A value (for digital assets without an issuer).

It is now generally accepted that the solutions developed by legal doctrine and case law for French book-entry securities can be transposed, *mutatis mutandis*, to digital assets, even though there are differences with securities. This is particularly the case where the transfer of ownership regime is concerned.

It can thus be argued that digital assets represent rights or values, which are the subject of property rights. The registration of a digital asset on a blockchain in the name of an investor presumes the investor's ownership of the digital asset.

However, as French law currently stands, holders of digital assets are not expressly qualified as owners, in the same way as holders of financial securities, as set out in article L. 211-4 of the French Monetary and Financial Code.[3] Article L. 552-2 of the Monetary and Financial Code stipulates that a token is an 'intangible asset representing, in digital form, one or more rights that can be issued, registered, retained or transferred by means of a shared electronic recording device enabling the owner of said asset to be identified, directly or indirectly'. It should be noted that this article will disappear when French law is brought into line with MiCA, and that this reference to ownership will also disappear.

Article L. 552-2 of the French Monetary and Financial Code does not state that digital assets must be registered in the name of their owner, but that a digital asset makes it possible to identify the owner of the token. This is already a positive element, as there is a strong presumption that the holder of the token is the owner. But can we still consider that holders of digital assets are protected in the same way as owners of securities as long as the existence of this property right is not clearly stated in the law? It's doubtful.

It is generally agreed by scholars and practitioners in France that the holder of a digital asset that is held with an intermediary only has a 'restitution claim'

[3] Code monétaire et financier (CMF), L 211-4:

> The securities account is opened, or registration in a shared electronic recording system is made, in the name of one or more holders who are the *owners of* the financial securities registered therein (emphasis added).

against the intermediary, due to the qualification of the digital assets as an 'irregular deposit or an 'irregular loan'.[4]

This is the logical consequence of its legal classification as intangible fungible property.

II. Types of Restitution of Digital Assets

We need to distinguish between the situation of an intermediary placed under an insolvency regime, an intermediary who makes a mistake in his custody of financial securities, an intermediary who suffers fraud and an intermediary who participates in fraud.

In the first case, French law does not provide for any particular and specific regime derogating from common law for intermediaries, whether regulated or not, who are custodians of their customers' digital assets. As a result, and due to the fungible nature of these digital assets, digital asset holders have a simple claim for equivalent restitution. Their situation may be even less protected if, in their contract with their intermediary, they have authorised the latter to dispose of their digital assets (eg, stacking operations), which amounts to the intermediary becoming the owner by virtue of the qualification of irregular deposit or irregular loan.

In the second case, the intermediary may be held contractually liable in the event of non-compliance with its custodial obligation under the custody agreement. French case law imposes an absolute obligation on the custodian of financial securities to return the securities, even in the event of fraud, taking the view that the custodian's 'custodial' role[5] and the obligations incumbent upon it are a matter of public policy.[6] On this point, French law applicable to digital assets differs from the solution applicable to securities. Under French law, a custodian of digital assets has no obligation to return the digital assets themselves, but merely to return the 'means of access' to the digital assets,[7] provided that the disappearance of the digital assets cannot be attributed to the custodian.[8]

[4] *cf* T. com. Nanterre, 6th ch, Feb. 26, 2020, no. 2018F00466, SDE Bitspread Ltd c/ SAS Paymium. Under French law irregular deposit or irregular loan are certain types of agreement. They are valid and enforceable. The word 'irregular' is used to point out it shows to fungible assets.

[5] Cass com, March 10, 2015, no 14-11.046, F-D.

[6] Cass com, May 4, 2010, three rulings: No 09-14.187, Société générale, FS-P+B (N° Lexbase: A0776EXZ); No. 09-14.975, Société RBC Dexia Investor services bank France, FS-P+B (N° Lexbase: A0792EXM) and No. 09-14.976, FS-D (N° Lexbase: A0793EXN).

[7] AMF General Regulations, Art 722-1, 6°:

> [the custodian] ensures that the necessary means are in place to return the means of access to the digital assets mentioned in 1° of article D. 54-10-1 of the Monetary and Financial Code. Except in the case of events not attributable, directly or indirectly, to the digital asset service provider, it returns control of the means of access to the digital assets to the customer as soon as possible. If it is impossible to restore control of these means of access, the digital asset custodian compensates in money its customer.

[8] 'Events not attributable to the digital asset custodian include, in particular, any event that it can demonstrate is independent of its operation, including a problem inherent in the operation of the

If the intermediary has been *hacked* or defrauded by a third party in relation to the digital assets it holds in safekeeping, the intermediary's liability will then be that of a custodian of fungible intangible property, and of the manner in which it has implemented its obligation to 'safekeep' the assets. The classic case law on deposit contracts will apply.

If the intermediary has participated in the fraud, either as an author or as an accomplice, he may be prosecuted for breach of trust or fraud.[9] Conversely, if the intermediary is the victim of the actions of one of his employees, he may be compensated for breach of trust.[10]

III. The Post-MiCA Situation under French Law

For its part, the MiCA Regulation introduces new elements that do not appear as such in French law or in nearby European law, ie MiFID.

Article 70 of the Regulation states that

> Crypto asset service providers that hold crypto assets belonging to clients or the means of access to such crypto assets shall make adequate arrangements to safeguard the ownership rights of clients, especially in the event of the crypto asset service provider's insolvency, and to prevent the use of clients' crypto assets for their own account.

This article therefore expressly mentions the existence of customer property rights, and from this point of view is to be welcomed.

Nevertheless, it would be preferable, in order to ensure continuity of legal reasoning and application of case law and doctrine in France with regard to book-entry securities, to specify explicitly in the French Monetary and Financial Code that holders of crypto assets are the owners of these crypto assets, along the lines of article L. 228-1, para 6 of the French Commercial Code[11] or article L. 211-4, para. 1 of the French Monetary and Financial Code.[12]

This being said, the MiCA Regulation does not specify the conditions under which regulated providers must ensure the protection of their clients' property

shared electronic recording device or in an automated computer program ("smart contract") that may rely on a shared electronic recording device that it does not control'.

[9] Cass. crim., May 30, 1996, n° 95-82.427 (N° Lexbase: A7201CLB), Bull crim, n° 224, in the 'Tuffier' case, named after the stockbroker in question, where the judge considered that there was a deposit to qualify the facts as a breach of trust.

[10] Crim. March 19, 2014, n°12-87.416, so-called Kerviel case.

[11] CMF, L 228-1, para 6:

> Securities, whatever their form, must be registered in an account or in a shared electronic recording system *in the name of their owner* (…) (emphasis added).

[12] CMF, L 211-4, para 1:

> The securities account is opened, or registration in a shared electronic recording system is made, in the name of one or more holders who are the *owners of* the financial securities registered therein (emphasis added).

rights in crypto assets. The practical way to effectively ensure this protection lies in the segregation of accounts between crypto assets belonging to clients and crypto assets belonging to the intermediary itself.

This is indeed the meaning of article 75.7 of the MiCA Regulation, which stipulates that intermediaries carrying out the business of custody and administration of crypto assets 'shall segregate holdings of crypto assets on behalf of their clients from their own holdings and ensure that the means of access to crypto assets of their clients is clearly identified as such. They shall ensure that, on the distributed ledger, their clients' crypto assets are held separately from their own crypto assets'. The same article states in a separate paragraph that 'Crypto asset service provider shall ensure that the crypto assets held in custody are operationally segregated from the crypto asset service provider's estate'. Nothing more is said about this functional separation, and no implementing regulation on this point is planned by the commission. It is therefore during the application process for licensing with its regulator that the service provider will have to detail the operational conditions of this segregation. However, the operation of segregation in the field of crypto assets is not currently harmonised in practice, either from an operational or technical point of view. For example, should this segregation be reproduced only in the 'cold wallet' in place at the intermediary level, or also in the 'hot wallet' within the blockchain? Similarly, should this segregation be carried out within a specific timeframe? Should segregation take place at least once a day? Several times a day? In real time? In other words, should intra-day *pooling of* crypto assets between proprietary and third-party accounts be prohibited?

Furthermore, the same Article 75.7, in another paragraph, states that regardless of the law applicable to the custody agreement,

> crypto assets held in custody shall be legally segregated from the crypto asset service provider's estate in the interest of the clients of the crypto asset service provider in accordance with applicable law, so that creditors of the crypto asset service provider have no recourse to crypto assets held in custody by the crypto asset service provider, in particular in the event of insolvency.

This provision is important in that it can be considered a rule of European ordre public.[13] This is all the more remarkable given that an equivalent provision in securities law does not exist at European level in the MiFID regulation, nor does it exist in French law. This represents a real advance in European law to protect customers' ownership of crypto assets, notwithstanding the law applicable to the contract with their custodian.

On the other hand, unlike securities, and given the technical characteristics of crypto assets, according to which there are technically no shortfalls in transactions involving digital assets, it seems unnecessary to draft an article equivalent

[13] A Jeauneau, *L'ordre public en droit national et en droit de l'Union européenne. Essai de systématisation* (Paris, LGDT, 2015); cf also C Picheral and F Sudre, *L'ordre public européen. Droit communautaire et droit européen des droits de l'homme* (Paris, Documentation française, 2001); T Corthaut, *EU Ordre public* (Alphen aan den Rijn, Kluwer Law International, 2012).

to Article L. 211-10 of the French Monetary and Financial Code.[14] This article provides, on the one hand, for the verification of the balance and accounting of assets with the CSD (since this function does not exist in blockchain) and the proportional distribution of assets actually existing with the CSD to holders in the event of a discrepancy with the position held by the financial intermediary; it also provides for the possibility for holders of financial securities to transfer to another regulated intermediary once the above-mentioned proportional distribution has been restored. On the other hand, and in view of the way blockchain works, clarification is required on one particular point: intermediaries offering a crypto asset custody service generally have an internal 'position-keeping' register for each customer, in addition to registering crypto assets in wallets in the name of each customer. This is because crypto asset transactions are not 'transcribed' into blockchains in real time, but after a 'certain amount of time', even if this, in practice, does not exceed one day. It seems necessary that French law – like every national law – should provide for the situation in which the total number of crypto assets recorded on the intermediary's internal register for all its customers, and as communicated to those customers, does not correspond to the total number of crypto assets actually recorded on the blockchain.

In order to take into consideration the legal consequence of MiCA on substantial law and to protect the owners of crypto assets, a report by the *Haut Comité Juridique de la Place de Paris* ('HCJP') commissioned by the AMF and published in March 2024 recommends creating an ad hoc legal regime for crypto assets.[15]

The aim of this ad hoc regime is to assert the existence of a full right of ownership for the benefit of holders of crypto assets, thereby ruling out any possibility of creditors of the defaulting custodian laying claim ('*revendication*') to the crypto assets of the custodian's customers. This right of ownership would thus be the best protection for crypto asset holders in the event of default or insolvency by their custodian service provider.

First at all, this ad hoc regime would stipulate that all crypto assets within the meaning of the MiCA Regulation are tradable and transferable ('*négociables*') as for securities. Consequently, this regime would be applicable to all crypto assets

[14] CMF, L 211-10:

> In the event of the opening of receivership or liquidation proceedings against an intermediary mentioned in article L. 211-3, the court-appointed administrator or liquidator, together with the provisional administrator or liquidator appointed, where applicable, by the Autorité de contrôle prudentiel et de resolution (Bank of France entity), verifies on a financial security-by-financial security basis that all the financial securities held in an account with a central depository or another intermediary in the name of the defaulting intermediary, whatever the nature of the accounts opened with these intermediaries, are in sufficient number to enable the intermediary to fulfil its obligations to account holders.
>
> In the event of a shortfall in the number of such securities, a proportional allocation is made among the account holders concerned on a security-by-security basis, who may have the securities returned to them transferred to a securities account held by another intermediary or by the issuer.

[15] www.hcjp.fr/nouvelles-technologies-financieres.

regardless of their nature. More specifically, crypto assets representing legal claims would not have to follow the assignment of claims regime from the code civil.

Second, the transfer of ownership of these crypto assets would take place through the registration of these crypto assets 'in favour of the purchaser' (and not in the name of the purchaser due to the pseudonymity of crypto assets). For an operational point of view, it is proposed that the AMF's General Regulations will determine the registration to be taken into account for the effective transfer of ownership (registration in the distributed register or in the register of opposition maintained by the intermediary).

Third, this ad hoc regime will transpose the rule in French law governing the protection of purchasers acting in good faith, as set out in article 2276 of the French Civil Code, to the situation of purchasers of crypto assets. However, the possibility of a *revendication* action in the event of loss or theft (as provided for in article 2276 of the French Civil Code for tangible assets) should be ruled out, due to the potential knock-on effects on successive transactions.

Fourth, the report recommends the introduction of an article equivalent to the aforementioned Article L. 211-10 of the French Monetary and Financial Code, which allows assets to be transferred to another custodian after being allocated to the owner according to the pro rata rule in the event of insufficient crypto assets to the custodian.

Last, this ad hoc regime expressly provides that crypto assets held by a MiCA-regulated service provider providing custody and administration services on behalf of clients cannot be seized by the service provider's creditors. This applies even if the crypto assets are under the control of the service provider (eg within an omnibus wallet under its control/in its name). In addition, it applies to crypto assets held directly within a DLT or with another custody service provider in a chain of sub-custodians.

This report adopts different responses to those set out in the UNIDROIT Principles on Digital Assets. It considers that the notion of control, provided for in the UNIDROIT Principles, is not relevant to French law, insofar as French law recognises the possession of intangible movable property. Above all, the HCJP report considers that the legal regime for intermediated cryto-assets (ie, crypto assets that are registered in a wallet with a regulated custodian intermediary) should be as close as possible to the legal regime applicable to intermediated financial securities, in order to ensure the best possible protection for crypto asset holders.

If adopted, this regime would assimilate crypto assets to financial securities in terms of the legal principles of property law.

The conclusions of this report are to be studied by the government with a view to amending French law in 2024.

It should also be noted that the provisions relating to the securities or cash deposit guarantee scheme are not applicable to crypto assets; as a result, and given that only a restitution claim exists as this is a fungible asset, holders of crypto assets in France are not protected in the same way as owners of securities, covered by the deposit guarantee scheme.

14

Insolvencies of Crypto Exchanges: Experiences of Japan

TETSUO MORISHITA

I. Introduction

Japan is a country where crypto asset transactions are under strict regulations to protect customers and investors. According to the record published by the Japan Virtual and Crypto Assets Exchange Association, which is a self-regulatory organisation, the number of active user accounts was 5.4 million in January 2024.[1]

The Japanese Regulation of Crypto Asset Exchanges cannot be considered in isolation from crypto asset exchange insolvency. The insolvency of Mt Gox in 2014 was one of the reasons why Japan introduced the new regulation of cryptocurrency exchange ahead of the world. Also, the litigations related to the Mt Gox bankruptcy provide important materials for examining various legal issues of crypto assets. The recent FTX bankruptcy proved that the regulation of crypto asset exchanges in Japan has worked well for customer protection.

This chapter first provides an overview of the regulations on crypto asset exchanges, by focusing on key provisions important for customer protection in the event of insolvency of crypto asset exchanges. Then, the legal issues raised in the insolvencies of Mt Gox and FTX will be examined.

II. Overview of the Regulations on Crypto Asset Exchanges

The regulation regarding crypto asset transactions has developed in three stages. Crypto assets first gained significant public attention in Japan with the collapse of Mt Gox in February 2014, which was then the world's largest cryptocurrency exchange. Mt Gox was incorporated under Japanese law and had its head

[1] jvcea.or.jp/cms/wp-content/themes/jvcea/images/pdf/statistics/202401-KOUKAI-01-FINAL.pdf.

office in Tokyo. The insolvency of Mt Gox raised various legal issues and triggered the introduction of new regulations on crypto assets.

In 2016, to address the concern of customer protection caused by Mt Gox insolvency, a new chapter on the regulation of cryptocurrency exchanges was added to the Payment Services Act (PSA). The cryptocurrency exchange was defined as an entity who carries out: (i) purchase and sale or exchange of crypto assets, (ii) intermediary, brokerage or agency services of purchase and sale or exchange of crypto assets, or (iii) management of customers' money in connection with the above (i) and (ii) in the course of its business.[2] The 2016 version of the PSA has made the registration to the Prime Minister necessary to conduct cryptocurrency exchange business in Japan. To protect customers cryptocurrency exchanges are required to keep customers' information secure, to provide necessary information to customers and to segregate customers' assets from the assets of the exchange itself.[3]

In January 2018, CoinCheck, a deemed crypto currency exchange, suffered unauthorised access and the crypto currency called NEM that was worth 58 billion Yen was stolen. In addition, in September 2018, Bitcoin and Monacoin that were worth seven billion Yen were stolen from Zaif, another crypto currency exchange. Although the crypto asset exchanges in these cases did not go bankrupt, they raised serious concerns about the protection of customers' assets. To respond to these incidents and to address the emergence of ICOs, the substantial enhancement of the regulation was made in 2019, which is the second stage.

The 2019 version not only strengthens the regulation of crypto asset exchanges but also newly introduced regulation of certain types of security tokens, crypto currency derivatives, and unfair transactions. Regarding the regulation of crypto asset exchanges, the 2019 version of PSA has added custody business which is defined as the management of crypto assets on behalf of others as business to the definition of crypto asset exchange business,[4] and significantly strengthen measures to protect customers' assets from the hacking and insolvencies of crypto asset exchanges.

The current PSA has the following set of rules to protect customers' assets.

1. Customers' money and crypto assets must be managed separately from those of the crypto asset exchange.[5] The money must be entrusted to trust companies.[6] The crypto assets must be managed in the method to clearly divide the customers' crypto assets and the exchange's own crypto assets

[2] The 2016 version of PSA, art 2(5). English translations of Japanese statutes are available at Japanese Law Translation (www.japaneselawtranslation.go.jp/).

[3] On the regulation of cryptocurrencies introduced in May 2016, see T Morishita, 'Recent Developments of Japanese laws and regulations on FinTech' in DW Arner et al. (eds), *Research Handbook on Asian Financial Law* (Cheltenham, Edward Elgar Publishing, 2020) 454, 465ff.

[4] Art 2(15)(iv) of the current version of PSA.

[5] PSA, art 63-11(1)(2); The Guideline for Supervision of Crypto-Asset Exchange Service Providers, II-2-2-3 (The Guideline is a FSA's internal guideline for its officers for their performance of administrative functions, but it has the nature of de facto regulations).

[6] PSA, art 63-11(1); Cabinet Office Order on Cryptoasset Exchange Service Providers, art 26.

and in the manner wherein each customer's crypto assets can be identified immediately.[7] More specifically, the customers' crypto assets must be managed in a separate wallet from the wallet that manages the crypto assets of the exchange.[8]

2. Customers' crypto assets must be managed in mediums that are not constantly connected to the internet (cold-wallet), except to the minimum extent necessary for the smooth operation of the business (at most 5 per cent of the total value).[9]
3. To protect customers from the risk of hacking, crypto asset exchanges must hold the crypto asset of the same type and same volume as the customer' crypto assets held in a medium that is constantly connected to the internet (hot-wallet), and such crypto assets shall be kept as their own crypto assets but in separate wallets from the wallets where their own crypto assets are kept (such crypto-assets are called 'performance-guarantee crypto asset', because they are kept to ensure the performance by crypto asset exchanges even when customers' crypto assets kept in hot-wallet are stolen by hackers). The performance guarantee crypto assets must be kept in cold-wallet.[10]
4. Customers have a kind of lien (right to receive payment in priority) over the crypto assets segregated for the customers and the performance-guarantee crypto assets in respect of their claim for the transfer of crypto assets against their crypto asset exchanges.[11]
5. With respect to crypto assets deposited by customers and performance guarantee crypto assets, crypto asset exchanges must reconcile the balance of

[7] PSA, art 63-11(2); Cabinet Office Order on Cryptoasset Exchange Service Providers, art 27(1).

[8] Guideline for Supervision of Crypto-Asset Exchange Service Providers, II-2-2-3-2 (3). English translation of the guideline is available at www.fsa.go.jp/common/law/guide/kaisya/e016.pdf.

[9] PSA, art 63-11(2); Cabinet Office Order on Cryptoasset Exchange Service Providers, art 27(2)(3). Electronic devices that have been connected to the Internet even once cannot be 'cold-wallet'. (Guideline for Supervision of Crypto-Asset Exchange Service Providers, II-2-2-3-2(3)(v).)

[10] PSA, art 63-11-2; Cabinet Office Order on Cryptoasset Exchange Service Providers, art 29.

[11] PSA, art 63-19-2 (1) stipulates 'A person who has concluded a contract for the management of crypto assets with a cryptoasset exchange service provider has the right to receive, in preference over other creditors, payments with regard to a claim for the transfer of crypto assets that the person holds against the cryptoasset exchange service provider, for the return of the regulated crypto assets (meaning the crypto assets of the users of the cryptoasset exchange services that the cryptoasset exchange service provider manages separately from its own crypto assets pursuant to the provisions of Article 63-11, paragraph (2) and the performance-guarantee crypto assets)'. As discussed later, the legal nature of crypto assets and the rights of customers who have deposited crypto assets with crypto asset exchange service providers under private law are not clear under Japanese law. However, under the Payment Services Act, it is considered that customers at least have the right to instruct cryptocurrency exchange service providers to transfer the cryptocurrency they have deposited to themselves or to a third party, and the article is worded to give them priority in relation to 'claim for the transfer of crypto assets that the person holds against the cryptoasset exchange service provider'. However, PSA, art 63-19-2 (2) stipulates 'The provisions of Article 333 of the Civil Code (Act No. 89 of 1896) apply mutatis mutandis to the right referred to in the preceding paragraph', and Japanese Civil Code, art 333 stipulates 'Statutory liens may not be exercised against the movables that are the subject matter of the same after the obligors have delivered those movables to third party acquirers.' Therefore, if crypto assets are transferred to third parties, customers lose their priority rights.

> crypto assets on their books with the amount of crypto assets on the blockchain or other network every business day. If the balance of crypto assets on the blockchain is less than the balance of crypto assets on the books, they must analyse the cause of the deficiency and the deficiency must be resolved within five business days.[12]

As the third stage, in 2022, the regulation of issuers and intermediaries of stablecoins was introduced. Before 2022, crypto assets denominated in fiat currency were not subject to the regulation of crypto assets under the Payment Services Act. However, the 2022 version of the regulation has added stablecoins into the regulatory framework of the Payment Services Act, while the issuance of fiat currency denominated crypto assets was considered as a kind of fund transfer business, which only banks and fund transfer serviced providers may do. Under the 2022 version of the regulation, a newly introduced category of the issuance of stablecoins using trust has made it possible for entities other than banks and fund transfer service providers to issue stablecoins,[13] and new regulations on intermediaries handling stablecoins on behalf of customers have been introduced.[14]

III. Insolvency of Mt Gox and Relevant Issues

A. Chronology of the Case[15]

On February 28, 2014, Mt Gox filed the petition for commencement of a civil rehabilitation proceeding. In the petition, it was explained that about 750K Bitcoin deposited by customers and 100k Bitcoin of Mt Gox itself were lost due to the illegal access, and the company was in the excess of debts (asset: 3.6 billion Yen, current liabilities: 6.5 billion Yen).[16] On March 14, 2014, Mt Gox filed a petition for recognition of Japan proceeding under Chapter 15 of the US Bankruptcy Code, and got a temporary order to preserve its assets in the US.[17] As explained in more

[12] Guideline for Supervision of Crypto-Asset Exchange Service Providers, II-2-2-3-2(3)(iv).

[13] PSA has introduced the new concept, 'electronic payment instrument', which corresponds to stablecoin, and 'specified beneficial interest in trust' has been defined as one of the types of electronic payment instrument (art 2(5)). 'Specified beneficial intrust in trust' is 'a beneficial interest in a money trust (limited to cases where it is indicated on a property value (limited to one that is recorded on an electronic device or any other object by electronic means) which can be transferred by using an electronic data processing system), for which the trustee manages the amount of money accepted under a trust agreement by means of deposits …' (art 2(9)).

[14] Intermediaries of stablecoin issued by banks are regulated under the Banking Act (Chapter VII-5) as 'electronic payment handling service', and other types of electronic payment instrument are regulated under PSA as 'electronic payment instrument service provider' (Chapter III-2).

[15] Various announcements and notices by the company and trustee that are useful to know the history of the case are available at www.mtgox.com/.

[16] Mt Gox, 'Announcement regarding an application for commencement of a procedure of civil rehabilitation' (28 February 2014) www.mtgox.com/img/pdf/20140228-announcement_eng.pdf.

[17] Mt Gox, 'Announcement regarding the applicability of US Bankruptcy Code Chapter 15' (14 March 2014) www.mtgox.com/img/pdf/20140314-announcement_chapter15.pdf.

detail below C, on April 16, 2014, the Tokyo District Court dismissed the petition for a civil rehabilitation proceeding and issued the temporary administration order.[18] Then, on April 24, the Court decided the commencement of a bankruptcy proceeding of Mt Gox.[19] On June 18, 2014, the US Bankruptcy Court issued an order recognising the Japanese bankruptcy proceeding as a foreign main bankruptcy proceeding.[20]

Since the commencement of the bankruptcy proceeding of Mt Gox, the price of Bitcoin had skyrocketed and been raised from $557.4 at the commencement of the bankruptcy proceeding to $7,497.9 in July 2018. This rise in the price of Bitcoin meant an increase in the estate of the bankrupt. So, on November 24, 2017, a group of Mt Gox creditors filed a petition for commencement of a civil rehabilitation proceeding, believing that a civil rehabilitation proceeding would allow much more flexibility to create a rehabilitation plan that would provide for a better return to creditors in light of the increase in the price of Bitcoin. On June 22, 2018, the court stayed the bankruptcy proceeding and commenced a civil rehabilitation proceeding. It is expected that the repayment will start on October 31, 2024.[21]

B. Preservation of Assets

The bankruptcy trustee of the Mt Gox case was Mr Nobuaki Kobayashi. He wrote, 'when a trustee is appointed, the first thing to do is the preservation of assets', 'in particular, if the unauthorised loss of crypto assets is the cause of the bankruptcy, there may be a high probability that problems exist with the cryptoasset exchange's management of the crypto assets. Therefore, a trustee should promptly take over the management of the crypto assets from the cryptoasset exchange and preserve them.'[22] Lawyers are usually appointed as trustees, but lawyers do not have expertise in how to manage crypto assets. Mr Kobayashi points out that it is necessary to properly appoint outside experts, but it is also necessary to properly supervise the experts by having them mutually monitor each other using multiple outside experts, rather than blindly trusting the outside experts.[23] In case of the Mt Gox bankruptcy, immediately after the temporary administration order on April 16,

[18] Mt Gox, 'Information regarding the dismissal of the application for commencement of a civil rehabilitation procedure and the order for provisional administration' (16 April 2014) www.mtgox.com/img/pdf/20140416_001_press_release.pdf.

[19] Mt Gox, 'Bankruptcy proceedings written decision' (24 April 2014) www.mtgox.com/img/pdf/20140424_decision.pdf.

[20] Mt Gox, 'Order Recognizing Foreign Main Proceeding and Granting Related Relief by U.S. Bankruptcy Court' (18 June 2014) www.mtgox.com/img/pdf/20140618_order.pdf.

[21] Mt Gox, 'Notice Concerning Change of Repayment Deadlines' (21 September 2023) www.mtgox.com/img/pdf/20230921_announcement_en.pdf.

[22] N Kobayashi and N Takeuchi, 'Tosanji niokeru Angoshisan no Toriatsukai to Gutaitekitaio' (Treatment of crypto assets in insolvencies and concrete ways of handling), Kinsyu Shoji Hanrei, No 1611, 70 (2021) (in Japanese).

[23] ibid.

2014, the trustee secured private keys for Bitcoin addresses, in which about 200K Bitcoin held by Mt Gox were managed, and transferred the Bitcoin to his own address.[24]

C. Choice of Proceedings

There are no special insolvency proceedings for crypto asset exchanges in Japan. In the case of Mt Gox, the petition for a civil rehabilitation proceeding was dismissed, and the bankruptcy proceeding was first initiated. Then the case was transferred to the civil rehabilitation proceeding. Let us examine what the transition from the bankruptcy proceeding to the civil rehabilitation proceeding meant for creditors.

In Mt Gox's case, a petition for a civil rehabilitation proceeding was initially filed, but the petition was dismissed and a bankruptcy proceeding was initiated.[25] The detailed reason for the dismissal of the civil rehabilitation proceeding was not disclosed, but a document released by Mt Gox indicated that it was due to the fact that even after a month and a half had passed since the petition was filed, the factual investigation into the loss of crypto assets had not progressed and no sponsor had been found.[26] Another factor may have been that only about a quarter of the crypto assets entrusted to Mt Gox by its customers were kept at the company's address.[27]

Since then, however, the price of Bitcoin has risen more than tenfold. In bankruptcy proceedings, the amount of non-monetary claims such as claims for the return of Bitcoin shall be evaluated at the commencement of the bankruptcy proceeding.[28] While there was a huge increase in the value of the bankruptcy estate as a result of the rise of the price of Bitcoin, the amount of the bankruptcy claims was fixed with the conversion rate at the time of the commencement of the bankruptcy proceeding, and creditors would have received only a monetary dividend evaluated at the very low price of Bitcoin. As a result, it was expected that substantial assets would have remained even after the bankruptcy claims had been fully repaid. If so, such assets would have been received by the CEO of Mt Gox, who substantially held a large portion of Mt Gox shares. Therefore, on November 29, 2017,

[24] Report prepared by the trustee for the first creditors meeting on 23 July 2013 (Tokyo, 23 July 2013), 3ff. www.mtgox.com/img/pdf/20140723_report_en.pdf.

[25] For more details on this point, S Steele and T Morishita, 'Lessons from Mt Gox: practical considerations for a virtual currency insolvency' in DW Arner et al (eds), *Research Handbook on Asian Financial Law* (Cheltenham, Edward Elgar Publishing, 2020) 479, 483ff.

[26] Mt Gox's release on the dismissal of the petition for commencement of a civil rehabilitation procedure and the order for provisional administration on 16 April 2014 (Tokyo, 16 April 2013) www.mtgox.com/img/pdf/20140416_001_press_release.pdf.

[27] According to Mt Gox's release on the amount of Bitcoin held by Mt Gox on 20 March 2014 (Tokyo, 20 March 2014) www.mtgox.com/img/pdf/20140320-btc-announce.pdf, when Mt Gox made petition for civil rehabilitation proceedings, only 200,000 Bitcoin were held by Mt Gox, while it accepted about 750,000 Bitcoin from customers.

[28] Bankruptcy Act, art 103 (2).

some creditors filed a petition for the commencement of civil rehabilitation proceeding,[29] which was granted by the court on June 22, 2018.[30]

Let us examine more concretely. According to the report for the civil rehabilitation proceeding prepared by the trustee dated October 1, 2019, the amount of customers' approved claims for Bitcoin was 802,521.76624822 and for Bitcoin Cash was 792,296.17251283. In addition, there were monetary approved claims in various currencies, which amounted to 7,152,558,789 in Japanese Yen equivalent. On the other hand, as of September 30, 2019, the rehabilitation debtor, Mt Gox, held 141,686.35446516 Bitcoin, 142,846.35166254 Bitcoin Cash and 69,397,600,922 Japanese Yen bank deposit.[31]

As mentioned above, in bankruptcy proceedings, the amount of bankruptcy claims is converted into Yen at the market rate at the time of commencement of bankruptcy proceedings.[32] Also in civil rehabilitation proceedings, the amount of voting rights is calculated based on the amount converted into Japanese Yen at the exchange rate at the time the civil rehabilitation proceeding is commenced.[33] In the case of Mt Gox, the conversion rate for Bitcoin in the bankruptcy proceeding was 55,812 Japanese Yen per Bitcoin. In contrast, the trustee's report in the civil rehabilitation proceedings states that the approved amount of claims for Bitcoin is 802,521.76624822, while the amount of voting rights is 601,344,660,315 Japanese Yen.[34] This means that each Bitcoin was converted at 749,318.8 Japanese Yen per Bitcoin. While the amount of creditors' claims would not have increased if the bankruptcy proceeding had continued, regardless of how much the value of Bitcoin held by the debtor increased, the newly initiated civil rehabilitation proceedings would have increased the amount of creditors' claims in Japanese Yen by approximately 14 times.

Some creditors in Mt Gox's insolvency proceeding prefer to receive dividends in Bitcoin rather than in Japanese Yen. While there are divergent views on whether it is possible to pay dividends in non-monetary form in insolvency proceedings, it is generally considered possible if creditors agree to receive dividends in non-monetary form and the court approves. In fact, in Mt Gox's civil rehabilitation proceedings, creditors can choose whether to be paid in Japanese Yen, in Bitcoin or in Bitcoin Cash.[35] The legal reasoning behind the decision to allow the payment of dividends in crypto assets has not been published and is not clear. However, an article written by the trustees of Mt Gox in 2021 took

[29] Mt Gox, 'Announcement Regarding Petition for Commencement of Civil Rehabilitation Proceedings Filed by Some of the Creditors' (29 November 2017) www.mtgox.com/img/pdf/20171129_annoucement.pdf.

[30] Mt Gox, 'Announcement of Commencement of Civil Rehabilitation Proceedings' (22 June 2018) www.mtgox.com/img/pdf/20180622_announcement_jp.pdf.

[31] Report by the trustee on 1 October 2019, www.mtgox.com/img/pdf/20191001_report.pdf.

[32] Bankruptcy Act, art 103 (2).

[33] Civil Rehabilitation Act, art 87(1).

[34] Report by the trustee on 1 October 2019, www.mtgox.com/img/pdf/20191001_report.pdf.

[35] Mt Gox, Request to Select a Repayment Method and Register Payee Information (1 December 2022) www.mtgox.com/img/pdf/20221201_announcement_en.pdf.

the view that, although there are legal difficulties in calculating the dividend in crypto assets and paying out dividends in crypto assets, it is permissible to calculate the dividend in money and then pay out crypto assets to creditors who wish to receive crypto assets instead of money as substitute performance. (In this case, from the perspective of creditors' equality, it is desirable that all creditors, not only creditors who have deposited crypto-assets, can equally wish to be repaid in crypto-assets.)[36] It is presumed that this approach may have been followed in the actual Mt Gox case.

D. Nature of Customers' Rights

One of the legal issues at stake in the Mt Gox insolvency proceedings was the legal nature of Bitcoin and the nature of the rights of customers who deposited Bitcoin with the crypto asset exchange. Whether in bankruptcy or civil rehabilitation proceedings, if the customer has ownership over the Bitcoin, he can exercise his right of segregation (*torimodoshiken*) based on ownership and reclaim the Bitcoin, claiming that the Bitcoin is property belonging to him and not to the bankruptcy estate or rehabilitation debtor.[37]

This issue was disputed as a part of Mt Gox bankruptcy proceeding in the following court cases.

i. Tokyo District Court Judgment on August 5, 2015 (LEX/DB25541521)

In this case, upon the bankruptcy of Mt Gox, a customer who had deposited Bitcoins with Mt Gox brought a suit against the bankruptcy trustee, claiming that the deposited Bitcoins were owned by him and seeking restitution based on a right of segregation. According to Mt Gox's records, the balance of the Bitcoin in the plaintiff's account at Mt Gox was 458.8812618 Bitcoin when the bankruptcy proceeding was commenced. The customer argued, among other things, that the legal nature of Bitcoin as a virtual currency involved a right to segregation based on their right to ownership (*shoyūken*) of the Bitcoin. The plaintiff argued that Bitcoin should be considered as the object of ownership rights because the plaintiff had exclusive control of the certain portion of Bitcoin recorded on Mt Gox's Bitcoin address, and thus the plaintiff's Bitcoin should be returned to the plaintiff and did not form part of the bankruptcy estate.

The Court dismissed the customer's claims, finding that ownership may exist only in 'tangible things' which may be exclusively controlled. Article 206 of the

[36] Kobayashi and Takeuchi (n 21) 71ff.

[37] Bankruptcy Act, art 62 and Civil Rehabilitation Act, art 52.

Civil Code stipulates that, 'an owner has the rights to freely use, obtain profit from and dispose of the thing owned, subject to the restrictions prescribed by laws and regulations'. Article 85 of the Civil Code defines the term 'things' as used in the Civil Code, including in Article 206, as a 'tangible thing'. First, in the Court's view, a Bitcoin is not a tangible thing because it does not physically occupy any space. The Court also held that a Bitcoin may not be exclusively controlled by a person, because any transfer of that Bitcoin required a third party such as a miner to effect the transfer of the Bitcoin even if the customer holds the private key. Moreover, there is no electronic record which indicates the balance of the bitcoin associated with the relevant address; the balance of the Bitcoin for an address can only be calculated from the record of transactions on the blockchain that occurred in relation to that Bitcoin address. The Court held that the recording on blockchain was simply a history of the transactions leading up to that point, and such a record could not be the object of an ownership right. Accordingly, the Court concluded that the customers of Mt Gox were not entitled to a return of their Bitcoin or a percentage of their Bitcoin.

The Court's findings on the issue of exclusive control are controversial, however. Bitcoins held on Mt Gox's exchange were able to be sold by specific individuals who held the relevant private keys. Although transactions of Bitcoins need to be verified by a process known as mining, the person in charge of the private key still has ultimate control over the transfer of the Bitcoin. Miners are not entitled to dispose of Bitcoin themselves and are merely performing a role to verify and validate transactions.

ii. Tokyo District Court Judgment on January 31, 2018, Kinyu Shoji Hanrei No 1539, 8

A customer of Mt Gox filed an action to oppose the assessment of its bankruptcy claim by the trustee. The customer filed seven claims, but the trustee denied most of them arguing that there were no balance or accounts as claimed by the customer in the record of Mt Gox.

The Court stated, 'although the legal nature of the rights of holders of Bitcoins (electromagnetic records) is not necessarily clear, at least when Bitcoins are recognised as virtual currency, it is understood that they have aspects as claims necessary to be handled similarly as currency ('a coin claim' in the judgment naming),' and the coin claims were understood to be transferred together when Bitcoins (electromagnetic records) were transferred using an electronic data processing system. The Court concluded, if, as the plaintiff alleged, the representative of the bankrupt company withdrew the plaintiff's Bitcoins and lost them without authority, then the Bitcoins have already been transferred elsewhere and the coin claim has also been transferred elsewhere at the same time, meaning that the plaintiff did not have a coin claim against the bankrupt company at the time the bankruptcy proceedings commenced.

iii. Tokyo District Court Judgment on March 2, 2020, Kinyu Shoji Hanrei No. 1598, p. 42

A customer who had deposited Bitcoins with a virtual currency exchange claimed that the Bitcoins were stolen due to unauthorised access and sought damages for breach of a contract for bailment of Bitcoins. The court ruled that a bailment is a contract to keep a certain thing in custody, and since Bitcoin is not a tangible thing, no contract for bailment was formed.

These court decisions do not clarify the legal character of crypto assets, and there are no other court decisions that clearly state the legal character of crypto assets. The majority view in Japan on the legal character of crypto assets starts from the conventional understanding that, under Japanese law, the subject matter of property rights is limited to things, and, under Japanese law, things are limited to tangible objects; therefore, crypto assets that are not tangible objects cannot be subject to property rights such as ownership rights, as expressed in the above judgment (i). However, in the author's view, the fact that crypto assets are traded as property in real world should be respected and it is not appropriate to apply a legal treatment that deviates from the common sense of business dealings. Even if it is difficult to exclusively control intangible information and data in general in the same way as tangible things, unlike information in general, the exclusive control of crypto assets is practically possible through the use of a private key. Thus, although crypto assets are not things, they should be treated as property with economic value, and the legal principles of property rights that apply to tangible property should be applied mutatis mutandis to the attribution and transfer of crypto assets. Blockchain records are important evidence when considering the attribution and transfer of rights.

Although the rules of property law should be applied to the attribution and transfer of crypto assets, the concrete rules of property law differ depending on the nature and function of the tangible objects. Currently, most transactions of crypto assets are for investment purposes, and in such situations the same rules should apply as to the attribution and transfer of certificates (immaterial or dematerialised) of investment securities. On the other hand, if crypto assets perform the same function as currency, it is desirable to apply the same rules of ownership as those applicable to currency, ie that the person in possession of the object (a banknote) always has ownership rights over the object. The above judgment (ii) seems to imply the latter idea. However, considering that Bitcoins are mainly used for investment purposes, it is inappropriate to apply the rules of property law for currencies to Bitcoins in cases where rights of customers who have deposited Bitcoins in crypto asset exchanges are at issue.

E. Result of Hard Fork

After Mt Gox's bankruptcy proceedings started, the hard fork of Bitcoin occurred, and Bitcoin Cash was created. In Mt Gox's insolvency proceeding, Bitcoin Cash derived from Bitcoin deposited by customers is treated as belonging to the customers.[38] However, there is a case that denied customers' right on crypto assets created as a result of hard forks, the judgment of Tokyo District Court on December 20, 2019, Kinyu Shoji Hanrei No 1590, p 41. In this case, a customer who had deposited Bitcoin with a crypto asset exchange claimed that the contract between the customer and the exchange was a contract for deposit of fungibles or a contract equivalent thereto, and that Bitcoin Gold that branched off from Bitcoin as a result of the hard fork belonged to the customer because it was the same deposited property or the fruit of the same deposit as the original Bitcoin, and requested to transfer Bitcoin Gold to the customer. The Court didn't mention the legal nature of Bitcoin, but rejected the customer's claim stating that there was no express agreement between the customer and the exchange regarding how crypto assets generated as a result of hard fork should be treated, and Bitcoin Gold was not listed as the crypto assets that the exchange would deal with. Also, the judgment opined that there was no implied agreement that Bitcoin Gold should be allocated to the customer, because the exchange had not developed the necessary system to deal with Bitcoin Gold, it had not made necessary registration under PSA to deal with Bitcoin Gold, it had announced that Bitcoin Gold might not be allocated to customers when risk management was insufficient, and it was the exchange that had made decisions regarding the allocation of crypto assets created as a result of hard fork in the previous cases, such as Ethereum Classic and Bitcoin Cash.

The management of crypto assets needs certain technologies and it is difficult to require crypto asset exchanges to be equipped with technologies that can handle all crypto assets. Therefore, if it cannot reasonably be expected that crypto asset exchanges will be equipped with the technologies necessary to manage crypto assets resulting from hard forks due to cost or other constraints, it should be considered that crypto asset exchanges are not obliged to accept such new crypto assets as customers' assets. However, exchanges' profiting from such new crypto assets, while not attributing the new crypto assets to their customers, should, in principle, be considered to constitute unjust enrichment.

F. Proof of Claims

In the Mt Gox bankruptcy proceeding, most of the claims filed by customers were denied by the trustee. More concretely, as of May 24, 2016, 24,750 people had filed

[38] eg, in the judgment of Tokyo District Court on December 23, 2021, Kinyu Shoji Hanrei No 1640, 14, the lawsuit between a creditor and the trustee of Mt Gox, the judgment states as the undisputed facts, 'on 1 August 2017, a hard fork from the Bitcoin blockchain to the Bitcoin Cash blockchain (i.e. a split between the previous blockchain and a new blockchain following a change in the specifications of the virtual currency) occurred, and all persons who held Bitcoin as of that date automatically also held Bitcoin Cash at a ratio of 1 Bitcoin Cash per 1 Bitcoin (no dispute).' Also, the Report by the trustee on 1 October 2019 in the Civil Rehabilitation Proceeding of Mt Gox (www.mtgox.com/img/pdf/20191001_report.pdf) states Bitcoin Cash are kept for customers.

claims totalling an amount of 263,519,268,303,371 Japanese Yen as calculated at the time. Of those claims, the trustee accepted only claims worth 45,609,593,503 Japanese Yen; that is, only 0.0173 per cent of the amount of claims filed.[39] It is not surprising that some creditors were dissatisfied with the Trustee's denial of their claims, and there were reported cases in which customers challenged the trustee's denial of the bankruptcy claims which they had filed.

In Tokyo District Court judgment on December 23, 2021, Kinyu Shoji Hanrei No 1640, p.14, a customer filed a claim for the return of 4260.06 Bitcoin, and the trustee denied the claim, stating that Mt Gox's records showed that all Bitcoin held by the customer had already been sold. The plaintiffs disputed the credibility of Mt Gox's records, pointing out that it was the unauthorised access of a third party to the Bitcoin held by Mt Gox that led to its bankruptcy, and that the former representative of Mt Gox had illegally altered the balance on the trading system. However, the court ruled that Mt Gox's records were reliable by pointing out that its records had been investigated by a third-party organisation, which found no particular problem.

Also, in Tokyo District Court judgment on January 31, 2018, Kinyu Shoji Hanrei No 1539, p.8, the creditor claimed that s/he held up to seven accounts with Mt Gox at the time of its bankruptcy with varying amounts remaining in those accounts. However, the trustee determined that the creditor was unable to establish the existence of five out of the seven accounts, and the balance of the remaining two accounts was almost zero. The judgment opined that the trustee had taken reasonable steps to ascertain the reliability of the database, and the balance shown in the database was reliable.

Accurately ascertaining the amount of customers' claims is the first step in the insolvency proceedings of a crypto asset exchange. Especially in cases where crypto asset exchanges have been hacked or fraudulent transactions have been made, strict verification of the reliability of the records maintained by the crypto asset exchange is essential. Also, who should owe the burden of proof of the existence and balance of an account could be an important issue. Customers typically do not have their own record of their digital transactions, and it is therefore difficult for them to prove their claims.

G. Cross-border Nature

Though Mt Gox was a company incorporated under Japanese law and its headquarters were located in Japan, according to the announcement by the company, only about 0.8 per cent of around 127,000 creditors were Japanese.[40] Also, Mt Gox

[39] Mt Gox, 'Q&A Regarding Acceptance or Rejection of the Claims' (3 June 2016) www.mtgox.com/img/pdf/20160603_qa_en.pdf, Q 1-1.

[40] Material prepared by Financial Services Agency for the 4th meeting of the working group on the enhancement of payment business held on 16 November 2015, 3, www.fsa.go.jp/singi/singi_kinyu/kessai_wg/siryou/20151116/01.pdf (in Japanese).

had entered the US market in collaboration with US companies. As a result, the insolvency proceedings of Mt Gox have involved cross-border natures.[41] In the Mt Gox case, after the application of a civil rehabilitation proceeding in Japan on February 28, 2014, the company made the application for the recognition of Japan proceeding under Chapter 15 of the US Bankruptcy Code on March 10, 2014. In its announcement, Mt Gox explained that the US court immediately issued a temporary order and,

> 'This means that the effect of the Civil Rehabilitation applies now on a temporary basis to assets located in the United States, which will be preserved. Accordingly, the acceptance by the US court of the Civil Rehabilitation means that any enforcement of a judgment against MtGox Co., Ltd, any attachment of its assets, the creation of any lien against its assets or the disposition of any assets located in the United States are temporarily no longer possible.'[42]

The US bankruptcy court recognised the Japan bankruptcy proceeding as the foreign main proceeding on June 18, 2014.[43] According to the report for the civil rehabilitation proceeding submitted by the trustee on October 1, 2019, in addition to the US court, the trustee has applied for recognition and support in the UK and Canada.[44]

Given that the business of the crypto asset exchanges is conducted online and that cross-border transactions are easy, it is highly likely that international insolvency issues will arise in the insolvency of crypto asset exchanges.

IV. FTX

A. Chronology of the Case[45]

FTX Japan KK is a Japanese corporation, and FTX Trading Limited, which is an Antigua and Barbuda corporation and whose headquarters are located in the Bahamas, indirectly holds 100 per cent of its shares. The origin of FTX Japan was Quoine Ltd, which was doing its business as a registered crypto asset exchange under PSA. In 2022, FTX Trading purchased Liquid Group Ltd, a parent company of Quoine Ltd. With this purchase, Quoine has changed its name to FTX Japan.[46]

[41] On some of these elements, see A Harney and S Stecklow, 'Special Report: Twice burned – How Mt Gox's bitcoin customers could lose again' (Reuters 2017) jp.reuters.com/article/idUSKBN1DG1UA/.

[42] Mt Gox, 'Announcement regarding the applicability of US Bankruptcy Code Chapter 15' (14 March 2014) www.mtgox.com/img/pdf/20140314-announcement_chapter15.pdf.

[43] Mt Gox, 'Order Recognizing Foreign Main Proceeding and Granting Related Relief by U.S. Bankruptcy Court' (18 June 2014) www.mtgox.com/img/pdf/20140618_order.pdf.

[44] Report by the trustee on 1 October 2019, www.mtgox.com/img/pdf/20191001_report.pdf.

[45] On the chronology of events relating to FTX Japan, see material prepared by FSA for the 9th meeting of the Study group on ways to deal with digital and decentralised finance on 19 July 2023, 16, www.fsa.go.jp/singi/digital/siryou/20230421/jimukyoku.pdf (in Japanese).

[46] The website of Liquid Ltd, www.liquid.com/ja/company/ (in Japanese).

On November 8, 2022, FTX Trading suspended withdrawals of assets by customers. Then on November 9, FTX Japan suspended withdrawals of customers' assets. On November 10, FSA issued an administrative order to instruct FTX Japan to suspend its business and to hold its assets within Japan.[47] On November 11, FTX Trading filed the petition for Chapter 11 in the US for all group companies, including FTX Japan. However, on November 14, FTX Japan made an announcement about its state of holding of crypto assets, which showed that, for all types of crypto assets, the amount of crypto assets kept in cold wallets exceeded the amount deposited by its customers.[48] On December 1, 2022, FTX Japan announced that customers' assets held by FTX Japan are not subject to Chapter 11, stating 'According to the law firm representing our headquarters, it is their opinion that the cash and crypto assets entrusted to us by our clients are not included in property subject to Chapter 11, considering the manner in which these assets are deposited and maintained, as well as property rights under Japanese law.'[49] On February 21, 2023, FTX Japan has started the repayment to its customers.[50]

B. Effectiveness of Regulations

So far, there has been no insolvency proceeding on FTX Japan in Japan. No publicly available documentation explaining why FTX Japan's assets have been excluded from Chapter 11 in the US has not been available. However, in this author's view, the fact that the business of FTX Japan has been operated independently in accordance with Japanese laws and regulations must have been an important reason.

Some viewed the Japanese regulation as being too strict compared to other countries prior to the collapse of the FTX. However, by virtue of the strict regulation, FTX Japan keeps more crypto assets in cold wallets than it receives from

[47] FSA, Administrative Actions v FTX Japan, Inc (10 November 2022) www.fsa.go.jp/en/news/2022/20221111/20221110.html.

[48] FTX Japan, 'Announcement on the Status of Our Management of Customers' Assets' (14 November 2022) support-jp.liquid.com/hc/ja/articles/22371335249677-%E5%BD%93%E7%A4%BE%E3%81%AB%E3%81%8A%E3%81%91%E3%82%8B%E3%81%8A%E5%AE%A2%E6%A7%98%E3%81%AE%E8%B3%87%E7%94%A3%E3%81%AE%E7%AE%A1%E7%90%86%E7%8A%B6%E6%B3%81%E7%AD%89%E3%81%AB%E3%81%A4%E3%81%84%E3%81%A6. After this announcement, FTX Japan regularly announced the status of customers assets on its website (in Japanese).

[49] FTX Japan, 'Measures to Resume Services' (1 December 2022) support-jp.liquid.com/hc/ja/articles/22371507388813-%E3%82%B5%E3%83%BC%E3%83%93%E3%82%B9%E5%BE%A9%E6%97%A7%E3%81%AB%E5%90%91%E3%81%91%E3%81%9F%E5%8F%96%E7%B5%84%E3%81%BF%E3%81%AB%E3%81%A4%E3%81%84%E3%81%A6.

[50] FTX Japan, 'Update on the Resumption of Withdrawals by FTX Japan K.K. (21 February 2023) support-jp.liquid.com/hc/ja/articles/22219671217293-%E5%87%BA%E9%87%91-%E5%87%BA%E5%BA%AB%E3%82%B5%E3%83%BC%E3%83%93%E3%82%B9%E3%81%AE%E9%80%B2%E6%8D%97%E7%8A%B6%E6%B3%81%E3%81%AB%E3%81%A4%E3%81%84%E3%81%A6). Some of FTX Japan's customers originally traded with the Japanese entity and some originally traded with FTX's overseas entities, and there seem to be some cases where the question of which range of customers are eligible for the return of assets as FTX Japan's customers has become an issue.

its customers and will be able to return assets to all customers. From such a view point, it should be accepted that the aforementioned strict regulations for customer protection have achieved its goal.

V. Conclusion

In the insolvency of crypto asset exchanges, the private law issue of what rights customers have over crypto assets and the issue of the effectiveness of regulation for customer protection are intertwined. In the case of Japan, the former is unclear, but the latter is well developed which has resulted in the protection of customers' rights in the insolvency of crypto asset exchanges.

So far, crypto assets have yet to play a significant role in the payment system and ensuring the integrity of the payment system has not been a key issue. However, if crypto assets do play such a role in the future, regulations to ensure that the failure of some crypto asset exchanges does not affect the safety and effectiveness of the payment system will be necessary.

15

Settlement Finality and Legal Certainty in Proof-of-Work Blockchains*

HOSSEIN NABILOU

I. Introduction

Settlement risk has been one of the age-old problems in conventional payment and settlement systems. The main sources of settlement risks are counterparty default risk, operational risks, and uncertainty about the irrevocability of a transaction.[1] Since a settlement failure may result in the failure of a chain of other transactions, it may cause contagion and result in systemic risks if not properly addressed.[2] Due to its potential systemic consequences, such risks have traditionally attracted considerable legal and regulatory scrutiny towards the payment and settlement systems in general and settlement finality in particular.

Various technological, institutional, and legal mechanisms have evolved to address the potential risks stemming from settlement risk. Early examples of such legal mechanisms concern netting, which reduces the settlement risk (ie, the risk that arises when the payments are not exchanged simultaneously), and close-out

* This chapter was drafted while the author was holding the UNIDROIT – Bank of Italy Chair at the International Institute for the Unification of Private Law (UNIDROIT). The chapter has extensively benefited from the discussions with the members of the digital assets and private law group. The author is grateful to UNIDROIT for its generous funding, excellent logistical support, and enriching intellectual environment throughout conducting research on this chapter. The author is also thankful to Candida Leone for her invaluable feedback on the earlier drafts of this chapter. All errors are those of the author. This chapter is originally published in the *Business & Finance Law Review*, Volume 7, Issue 1.

[1] See D Mills et al, 'Distributed ledger technology in payments, clearing, and settlement' (2016) Finance and Economics Discussion Series www.federalreserve.gov/econresdata/feds/2016/files/2016095pap.pdf.

[2] A rather infamous example of the settlement risk is what has come to be known as the Herstatt risk, which refers to cross-currency settlement risks in deferred net settlement (DNS) systems resulting from trading across time zones. See C Bamford, *Principles of international financial law*, 3rd edn (Oxford, Oxford University Press, 2019) 87; Committee on Payment and Settlement Systems of the central banks of the Group of Ten countries, 'Delivery versus payment in securities settlement systems' (1992) 14 www.bis.org/cpmi/publ/d06.pdf; N Westernhagen et al, 'Bank failures in mature economies' (2004) BIS Working Paper No 13 www.bis.org/publ/bcbs_wp13.pdf.

netting, which reduces pre-settlement risk such as the risk of default before the settlement date.[3] More recently, various technological and institutional innovations have given rise to different forms of mechanisms that protect the counterparties against settlement risks. Such mechanisms have been largely successful in promoting financial stability. However, more recently, settlement risk has come into vogue due to the potential settlement issues in the blockchains that use Proof-of-Work (PoW) consensus algorithms.

In studying settlement risks, it is crucial to focus on the two key components of a settlement: the settlement asset (or how settlement is achieved operationally) and legal finality (or how settlement finality is achieved for legal purposes).[4] The settlement asset used in FMIs should have certain properties. It needs to be in the form of an asset bearing the least credit and liquidity risks. This is particularly important within wholesale payment systems, where an otherwise illiquid settlement asset or an asset having counterparty risk would create systemic implications for the systemically important payment systems (SIPS). For example, in Europe and the euro area, SIPS operators must ensure that the final settlements of one-sided payments in the euro are carried out in central bank money (CeBM).[5] The same requirement applies to settling two-sided payments or non-euro one-sided payments, where practicable and available. If CeBM is not used, the operator must ensure that the settlement asset for money settlements has little or no credit and liquidity risks.[6] For settlements in commercial bank money (CoBM), certain conditions are imposed on the SIPS.[7] This chapter does not study the price stability or the quality of the settlement asset (such as bitcoin in the Bitcoin Blockchain), instead, it investigates the operational and legal finality aspects of the settlement on certain PoW blockchains.

As major cryptocurrencies carry various degrees of liquidity risks in addition to price volatility, they would not be considered reliable settlement assets.[8]

[3] See R Derham, *The Law of Set-Off*, 4th edn (Oxford, Oxford University Press, 2010); PC Harding, *Mastering the ISDA Master Agreements (1992 and 2002): A Practical Guide for Negotiators*, 3rd edn (London, Pearson, 2010).

[4] See Committee on Payments and Market Infrastructures, *Distributed ledger technology in payment, clearing and settlement: An analytical framework* (2017) 15 www.bis.org/cpmi/publ/d157.pdf.

[5] Regulation of the European Central Bank (EU) No 795/2014 of 3 July 2014 on oversight requirements for systemically important payment systems (ECB/2014/28) [2014] OJ L217/16, as amended by Regulation (EU) 2017/2094 of the European Central Bank of 3 November 2017 amending Regulation (EU) No 795/2014 on oversight requirements for systemically important payment systems (ECB/2017/32) [2017] OJ L 299/11, Art 10 para 1.

[6] Regulation of the European Central Bank (EU) No 795/2014 (n 5), Art 10 para 3.

[7] Regulation of the European Central Bank (EU) No 795/2014 (n 5), Art 10.

[8] H Nabilou, Testing the Waters of the Rubicon: The European Central Bank and Central Bank Digital Currencies' [2019] *Journal of Banking Regulation* 299; H Nabilou, 'The dark side of licensing cryptocurrency exchanges as payment institutions' [2019] *Law and Financial Markets Review* 1; H Nabilou, 'Bitcoin Governance as a Decentralized Financial Market Infrastructure' [2021] *Stanford Journal of Blockchain Law & Policy* 26; H Nabilou and A Prüm, 'Ignorance, debt and cryptocurrencies: The old and the new in the law and economics of concurrent currencies' [2019] *Journal of Financial Regulation* 1; H Nabilou, 'How to Regulate Bitcoin? Decentralized Regulation for a Decentralized Cryptocurrency' [2019] *International Journal of Law and Information Technology* 266. Stablecoins may be an exception,

In addition, the use of distributed ledger technologies (DLTs) or blockchain for settlement purposes may pose various other risks, such as potential operational and security risks stemming from the use of new technology, lack of interoperability with the conventional FMIs, the potential governance issues in blockchains, and potential issues regarding tamper resistance, privacy, and data integrity.[9] From among all such risks, this chapter investigates a specific risk in the payments made by cryptocurrencies. This risk concerns the probabilistic finality of certain cryptocurrencies that use PoW blockchains, such as Bitcoin.[10] The finality of payments and settlements on the Bitcoin Blockchain is viewed as probabilistic due to the likelihood that the most recent transactions embedded in the blockchain may be undone, or bitcoins may be double-spent due to the formation of a fork.[11] The probabilistic finality of Bitcoin has been subject to criticism[12] because the fact that transactions are technically vulnerable to forking or potential unwinding is an impediment to Bitcoin's objective of becoming a payment network or a settlement layer for transactions.

Regarding settlement finality in PoW blockchains, there seem to be two main problems. First, in the arrangements relying on consensus algorithms for settlement finality, there may not be a single point in time when the settlement finality is achieved. Furthermore, the legal regime may not expressly recognise finality in such networks, even though the participants in the system may have impliedly been deemed to have agreed on a certain moment for the finality of the transfer.[13] In other words, both in legal and operational terms, difficulties may arise with respect to the finality of settlement under the current legal and regulatory frameworks around the globe.

One major limitation of this chapter is that it only discusses settlement finality in PoW blockchains. Different networks may have different mechanisms for transaction confirmation. PoW and Proof of Stake (PoS) are two main mechanisms. Within the PoW blockchains, various blockchains may use different methods of recording transactions. In general, the recording of transactions in blockchains may rely on two major models: account-based settlement and

but as the history of stablecoins has revealed, the potential flaws in the design may not constitute a great bulwark against price volatility. See JP Koning, 'End of a stablecoin' (*Moneyness*, 22 August 2016) jpkoning.blogspot.com/2016/08/end-of-stablecoin.html; B Dyson, 'Can 'stablecoins' be stable?' (*Bank Underground*, 28 March 2019) bankunderground.co.uk/2019/03/28/can-stablecoins-be-stable/.

[9] Committee on Payments and Market Infrastructures (n 4).

[10] Bank for International Settlements, 'Cryptocurrencies: looking beyond the hype' (June 2018) Annual Economic Report 101 www.bis.org/publ/arpdf/ar2018e5.pdf.

[11] Bank for International Settlements (n 10) 101.

[12] See T Swanson, 'Settlement Risks Involving Public Blockchains' (Great Wall of Numbers, 24 March 2016); ML Bech et al, 'On the future of securities settlement' [2020] *BIS Quarterly Review* 67, 75 www.bis.org/publ/qtrpdf/r_qt2003i.pdf. The uncertainty stemming from the settlement finality may be a serious obstacle for the use of certain forms of distributed ledger technologies (DLTs) in the settlement of securities. See Advisory Groups on Market Infrastructures for Securities and Collateral and for Payments, 'The use of DLT in post-trade processes' (2021) 7 www.ecb.europa.eu/pub/pdf/other/ecb.20210412_useofdltposttradeprocesses~958e3af1c8.en.pdf.

[13] Bank for International Settlements (n 10).

token-based settlement.[14] Some networks update balances in the ledger that records the positions through debits and credits, while others work based on transferring digital assets in the ledger (namely, the ledger records the transfer of ownership of a given digital asset that is native to the ledger).[15] Although PoW blockchains differ from the PoS blockchains in terms of settlement finality,[16] the method of transaction recording may have little bearing on the debate on settlement finality.[17] This chapter only deals with on-chain transactions on the blockchains that rely on the PoW consensus algorithms with probabilistic finality. Off-chain transactions, depending on the methods and the media used, are subject to the relevant rules of exchanges or payment and settlement systems.[18]

This chapter first explains the concept of probabilistic finality in cryptocurrencies relying on PoW with a special focus on the Bitcoin Blockchain. Second, it highlights the role and importance of transaction finality in traditional commercial and payment transactions. Third, it elaborates on the importance of distinguishing between *legal* finality, as opposed to *operational* finality, in private and commercial law as well as in regulatory law. Fourth, the chapter dives deeper into the underpinnings of the concept of settlement finality and its private law as well as regulatory law foundations. In doing so, in addition to discussing the concept of finality in transactions such as the sale of goods, it explores the concept of finality in payments and securities settlement systems and argues that the protections and legal mechanisms that are applicable in payment and settlement systems can also be extended to the PoW blockchain transactions. Fifth, the chapter concludes by arguing that not only PoW blockchains, but also conventional settlement systems, cannot ensure technological or operational finality in its strictest sense. Therefore, it is inevitable to rely on legal finality both in traditional payment and settlement systems as well as cryptocurrency networks, however, limitations of legal protections in the PoW blockchains should not be overlooked.

II. Transaction Processing and the Problems with Settlement Finality in the Bitcoin Blockchain

Understanding the reasons behind the probabilistic finality in the PoW blockchains requires studying the main value proposition of such networks. It seems that the main driving force behind the first cryptocurrency was censorship resistance that

[14] ACF Chan, 'UTXO in Digital Currencies: Account-based or Token-based? Or Both?' (*arxiv*, 20 September 2021) 1 arxiv.org/pdf/2109.09294.

[15] Committee on Payments and Market Infrastructures (n 4) (stating that certain other networks work based on transferring digital representation of physical asset that are held in custody off-chain).

[16] ibid.

[17] ibid.

[18] ibid.

'allows participants to transact in an environment with minimum social trust'.[19] Censorship resistance would mean that there would be no central or single entity in the system that could influence the system in any substantial manner, eg, by blocking transactions.[20] The way to achieve such censorship resistance is thought to be through decentralisation.[21] However, creating and maintaining artificial scarcity in electronic records (assets) in a decentralised manner by preventing duplication (eg, double spending) has proved to be a substantial challenge that hampered the emergence of digital assets for decades. Bitcoin as a distributed peer-to-peer ('P2P') system eventually solved the age-old double-spending problem by bringing together a decentralised P2P network (the Bitcoin Protocol), a public transaction ledger (the blockchain), a set of consensus rules for independent transaction validation and native asset issuance, and a mechanism for reaching global consensus on the valid chain in a decentralised manner, ie, the PoW algorithm.[22]

Prior to Bitcoin, even outside the virtual space, addressing the double-spending problem was delegated to trusted third parties with centralised ledgers, who verified and confirmed financial transactions and determined their legal finality.[23] Such intermediaries could, as a matter of course, exert control on the transaction within the bounds defined by law and contract.[24] Bitcoin solved this problem in a secure, *decentralised*, consensus-based, and censorship-resistant manner, without relying on centralised third parties.[25] The PoW algorithm used in the Bitcoin Blockchain appears to be a secure technique that provides a decentralised and incentive-compatible mechanism for verifying and confirming transactions, as well as securing the Bitcoin Blockchain.[26]

In the Bitcoin network, the user controlling a private key (A), which controls a specific unspent transaction output (UTXO), can send it to another user (B) through the blockchain. When A fills in the amount and fee and sends the instructions, the wallet signs the transaction using A's private key. As soon as the transaction is signed, it is propagated and validated by the network nodes. Then, the miners include the transaction in the next block which is to be mined. The miner who solves the PoW and succeeds in finding the nonce propagates the

[19] Nabilou, 'Bitcoin Governance as a Decentralized Financial Market Infrastructure' (n 8); see also N Szabo, 'Money, blockchains, and social scalability' (*Unenumerated*, 9 February 2017).

[20] Nabilou, 'Bitcoin Governance as a Decentralized Financial Market Infrastructure' (n 9).

[21] ibid.

[22] S Nakamoto, 'Bitcoin: A Peer-to-Peer Electronic Cash System' www.bitcoin.org/bitcoin.pdf; AM Antonopoulos, *Mastering Bitcoin: Programming the Open Blockchain*, 2nd edn (Beijing, O'Reilly Media, 2017) 2.

[23] Nakamoto (n 22).

[24] ibid.

[25] ibid.

[26] The proof-of-work in principle discourages a 51% attack on the network through certain incentive mechanisms which make hacking the system economically unfavorable to the hacker. See J Stark, 'Making Sense of Cryptoeconomics' (*CoinDesk*, 19 August 2017) www.coindesk.com/markets/2017/08/19/making-sense-of-cryptoeconomics/; see K Heires, 'The Risks and Rewards of Blockchain Technology' (*Risk Management*, 1 March 2016) www.rmmagazine.com/articles/article/2016/03/01/-The-Risks-and-Rewards-of-Blockchain-Technology-.

block to the network. Thereafter, the nodes verify the result and propagate the block.[27] As soon as the result was verified by the nodes, B sees the first confirmation in his wallet indicating that the amount of bitcoin sent by A is received. With each new block, new confirmations appear. Decentralisation is achieved in the sense that the network is open and permissionless and unlike traditional centralised payment systems, everyone can join the network to verify and confirm the transaction.

However, such a simplistic overview of the transaction in the Bitcoin Blockchain masks the complexity of the settlement finality in PoW blockchains. There are at least four main reasons that prevent PoW blockchains from guaranteeing the finality of individual payments. First, despite the transparency of the blockchain technology that allows the users to verify whether a specific transaction is included in the ledger or not, there can be rival versions of the ledger or chains of which the parties may not be aware. Simultaneous updates to the ledger by two parties can potentially result in the unwinding of some transactions *ex-post* in spite of the parties' perception that the transaction was final. As ultimately one of the chains or updates to the ledger will survive, the finality of the payments appended to each ledger will remain probabilistic.

The second issue originates from the famous 51 per cent attack.[28] This means that the miners who have substantial computing power can potentially manipulate the ledger, although only to a limited extent. The issue arises from the fact that at the time that a transaction is perceived to be settled, it is impossible to ensure the finality of the settlement because the attacker would only reveal the forged ledger once it is sure that its attack was successful.[29] This would have a serious implication for the finality of the settlement in the sense that the finality will remain probabilistic. Although the difficulty with which a successful attack could be performed diminishes as the subsequent updates are added to the ledger, the tamper resistance can never reach 100 per cent.[30]

The third problem with the finality of transactions may arise from forking, which happens if a subgroup of cryptocurrency users may coordinate to use a new version of the ledger or protocol, while other users insist on using the original ledger.[31] This will lead to the emergence of two sub-networks of users, resulting in network splitting.[32] Blockchains have split in several historical instances, including

[27] See, eg, as soon as the transaction is submitted to the blockchain, it is often picked up by node operators – miners who put the transaction in a block ready for confirmation. The miners confirm those blocks that adhere and conform to the consensus rules and relay them to the node operators.

[28] Although Bitcoin has never been subject to a successful 51% attack, there have been a few successful 51% attacks to perform double-spends on some cryptocurrencies such as Verge, Bitcoin Gold, and MonaCoin. See C Haan, 'Verge, Bitcoin Gold and MonaCoin Hacked' (*Crowdfund Insider*, 25 May 2018) www.crowdfundinsider.com/2018/05/133936-verge-bitcoin-gold-and-monacoin-hacked/.

[29] Bank for International Settlements (n 10).

[30] ibid.

[31] ibid.

[32] BitMEX Research, 'A complete history of Bitcoin's consensus forks' (*BitMEX Blog*, 28 December 2017) https://blog.bitmex.com/bitcoins-consensus-forks/; see also V Buterin, 'Bitcoin Network

a 2013 case whereby an erroneous upgrade to the Bitcoin protocol and its rollback via coordination between developers and miners led to a blockchain fork.[33] On 11 March 2013, there was an erroneous upgrade to Bitcoin protocol that led to two sets of miners mining legacy protocol and the updated one separately. A chain-split of at least 24 blocks occurred, with the new chain having a maximum lead of 13 blocks. However, the fork was rolled back by coordination between developers and miners who decided to *ignore the longest chain*, an apparent violation of the Nakamoto consensus.

The problem with potential coordinated reorganisations would give rise to concerns about transaction finality. For example, in the immediate aftermath of the Binance hack in 2019, there have been discussions about Bitcoin Blockchain reorganisation to reverse transactions and undo the damage. Although such discussions faced immediate and strong resistance from users and developers, leading to the concession by miners and exchanges not to pursue the proposal, such issues are likely to add further questions as to the finality of transactions on blockchains.

Fourth, since the Bitcoin block subsidy, which is allocated to the successful miner, will stop sometime in the year 2140, in the absence of such a reward, the miners will lack adequate incentives to mine bitcoin, thereby confirming transactions and contributing to the security of the blockchain. Although, in theory, this concern may be enough to prevent the Bitcoin network from functioning presently by way of backward induction, it seems that market participants anticipate that some solutions will be found for this problem through time, eg, transaction fees substituting the block reward. Thus far, various proposals for dealing with such an issue have been put forward, such as improving block space, perpetual issuance of the block reward, crowdfunding, and adapting the supply of the block space,[34] however, none have been implemented or even tested. The lack of incentive to confirm transactions on the Bitcoin blockchain – if not an existential threat to the Bitcoin network – will likely increase the time needed for the transaction confirmation and will have a significant bearing on transaction finality.

Despite such concerns, the probability of transactions being reversed, undone, or ending up in an orphan chain is a function of the block height, meaning that the probability of undoing transactions embedded in the Bitcoin Blockchain depends on how deep the transaction is recorded in the blockchain. As more and more blocks are built on the Bitcoin Blockchain, the lower the probability of undoing the embedded transactions, and as the transaction gets deeper and deeper in the blockchain, the probability becomes infinitesimal. At a certain point, this probability becomes so small that it seems that it has persuaded some authors to suggest that

Shaken by Blockchain Fork' (*Bitcoin Magazine*, 13 March 2013) bitcoinmagazine.com/technical/bitcoin-network-shaken-by-blockchain-fork-1363144448.

[33] BitMEX Research (n 32).

[34] Hasu, J Prestwich and B Curtis, *A model for Bitcoin's security and the declining block subsidy* (2019) www.lopp.net/pdf/A-model-for-Bitcoins-security-and-the-declining-block-subsidy-v1.05.pdf.

the PoW algorithm of the Bitcoin protocol[35] ensures that the extrinsic investment in expended energy would act as a 'thermodynamic guarantee of immutability'.[36]

In addition, the concerns about probabilistic finality and the absence of legal protections might be reduced as certain developments, such as the Lightning Network,[37] may significantly diminish the use of the Bitcoin Blockchain for retail (large volume, low value) transactions. However, it seems that such developments, rather than solving the problem, just transfer it to somewhere else, meaning that they may eventually increase the number of wholesale (large value, low volume) transactions on the Bitcoin Blockchain. Furthermore, most transactions in cryptocurrency exchanges take place through book entries on the books of the relevant exchange rather than using blockchains to transfer tokens. However, inter-exchange and inter-wallet transactions are likely to go through the relevant blockchain. Therefore, at the time of writing, due to transaction batching used for discharging inter-exchange liabilities, which is essentially like the deferred net settlement (DNS) systems in conventional finance, the number of transactions that settle on the Bitcoin Blockchain does not appear to be large, however, the amounts that are settled remain sizeable. In other words, these inter-exchange markets exhibit the attributes of large-value payment systems (LVPS), where systemic risks may become prevalent. If cryptocurrency markets become sufficiently large, these markets would become the Achilles heel of the cryptocurrency ecosystem due to settlement finality risks as well as the volatility and illiquidity of the settlement assets. The next section elaborates on the concept of settlement finality and its legal importance.

III. The Legal Importance and Implications of Settlement Finality

Settlement finality – defined as the exact moment in time at which the proprietary interests in the object or medium of transaction pass from one party to another party and the obligations of the parties to a transaction are discharged in an unconditional and irrevocable manner (eg, in a way that cannot be reversed even by the subsequent legal defences or actions against each other)[38] – has been one of the most intriguing questions of contract and commercial law and of immense

[35] Nakamoto (n 22); see also Antonopoulos (n 22).

[36] A Antonopoulos, *The internet of money* (Merkle Bloom LLC, 2016).

[37] See J Poon and T Dryja, *The bitcoin lightning network: Scalable off-chain instant payments* (2016) lightning.network/lightning-network-paper.pdf; A van Wirdum, 'The History of Lightning: From Brainstorm to Beta' (*Bitcoin Magazine*, 4 April 2018) bitcoinmagazine.com/technical/history-lightning-brainstorm-beta.

[38] For a similar definition, see Committee on Payment and Settlement Systems and Technical Committee of the International Organization of Securities Commissions, *Principles for Financial Market Infrastructures* (April 2012) Principle 8 www.iosco.org/library/pubdocs/pdf/IOSCOPD377-PFMI.pdf; Committee on Payments and Market Infrastructures (n 4).

practical as well as intellectual relevance.[39] In law, settlement finality often depends on the type of the contract (eg, whether the contract involves the exchange of commodities [goods], securities [including derivatives], or funds) as well as the settlement terms embedded in the contract (eg, the nature of the second leg of the transaction, what private law refers to as price). For instance, in securities transactions when the securities are delivered to the buyer and the funds to the seller, the transaction is said to be final (ie, settled). In commodity trades, depending on the specific terms of the settlement, the commodities transaction may only involve the settlement of funds, or delivery of financial instruments, other documents, or commodities themselves.[40] In derivative transactions, the settlement depends on the type of the derivative and the terms of the settlement. In such transactions, often the settlement involves settlement of funds (ie, cash settlement) and only on very rare occasions, the commodity itself.[41]

By definition, each leg of a transaction is considered final when the transfer is irrevocable and unconditional. When there are multiple legs to the transaction, the delivery vs payment (DvP), delivery vs delivery (DvD), or payment vs payment (PvP) mechanisms are often used to coordinate settlement of different legs of the transactions as well as to manage the risk of one leg settling with finality and the other failing to settle.[42] Because depending on the legal nature of the object or medium of exchange the settlement finality may vary, the determination of the nature of the settlement asset is an important consideration in determining the nature of the settlement in cryptocurrency transactions. In addition, in cryptocurrency transactions, depending on the cryptocurrencies being used as a medium of exchange or as the object of exchange, the settlement terms and methods may differ. This chapter assumes that cryptocurrencies are being used as media of exchange.

The moment of finality is of great significance in commercial and financial transactions as it provides legal certainty to the parties to a transaction as well as the interested third parties to the effect that a transaction that has cleared the moment of finality cannot be successfully challenged in a court of law. As the finality of a transaction bars many of the defences, which might otherwise be brought by the payer, transferor, or third parties against the payee or transferee to unwind a transaction, the finality of a transaction is essential to commerce as it gives parties and third parties the assurance that the transactions will not be unwound *ex-post*.

[39] As this definition suggests, the conventional concept of settlement finality is inherently a legal concept meaning that a legal definition of finality necessarily bars certain defences that would otherwise be available to the payer against the payee.

[40] This is the case, for example, in the sale of goods.

[41] JC Hull, *Options, futures, and other derivatives*, 9th edn (London, Pearson, 2018) 47.

[42] Mills et al (n 1); see generally Committee on Payment and Settlement Systems (n 38); Committee on Payment and Settlement Systems (n 2); JH Dalhuisen, *Dalhuisen on Transnational Comparative, Commercial, Financial and Trade Law Volume 1: The Transnationalisation of Commercial and Financial Law and of Commercial, Financial and Investment Dispute Resolution. The New Lex Mercatoria and its Sources*, 6th edn (London, Hart Publishing, 2016) 517.

This means that the parties can take the funds free from any claims and can use them without worrying about the potential challenges to the transactions that could result in unwinding any future transactions in which the received funds are used. In addition, as settlement finality is relied upon by the parties in updating their own ledgers and determining the amount of their assets and liabilities, it has serious implications for the balance sheets of the participants, rights of their customers and creditors, the assignment of liability to each party, and ultimately for measuring and monitoring risk.[43]

One of the major benefits of having a clear legal regime for determining the exact moment of finality manifests itself in the context of bankruptcy law, where before all the obligations are cleared and settled, the payer becomes subject to an insolvency proceeding. Under such circumstances, the question may arise as to whether the uncleared and unsettled transaction constitutes part of the estate of the insolvent party or belongs to the non-defaulting solvent party. The importance of bankruptcy regimes to transaction finality is not limited to the determination of the bankruptcy estate, as bankruptcy regimes are often intrusive, and where the benefits of finality come into conflict with the goals of bankruptcy law, often it is the former that gives way. For example, the bankruptcy estate may be able to unwind certain transactions entered into prior to the liquidation due to the transaction being identified as a transaction at an undervalue, as a voidable preference, or an extortionate credit bargain.[44]

Given its importance in terms of legal certainty, to minimise the uncertainty that may arise from potential *ex-post* legal interventions, special legal protections have been created to achieve legal transaction finality. Traditional commercial law, as well as bankruptcy law, have created similar approaches to determining the finality of commercial transactions. These mechanisms often rely on specific legal constructs such as a moment or a condition upon the realisation of which the transaction is deemed to be final, meaning that it is no longer possible to unwind the transaction. However, given the potential systemic importance of determining the moment of finality and its importance to the orderly functioning of the financial markets, regulatory law has taken a rather different approach to determining the moment of finality in the FMIs by defining the exact moment of transaction finality and moment of irrevocability of transfer orders, which will be reviewed later in this chapter.[45]

In addition to the issues that have been dealt with for centuries in conventional commercial and financial transactions regarding their finality, the advent of new payment technologies poses new challenges to determining the finality of

[43] Mills et al (n 1).

[44] A Dignam and J Lowry, *Company Law*, 7th edn (Oxford, Oxford University Press, 2012) 472.

[45] See eg, Directive 98/26/EC of the European Parliament and of the Council of 19 May 1998 on settlement finality in payment and securities settlement systems [1998] OJ L166/45, Art 3; C Murray, D Holloway and D Timson-Hunt, *Schmitthoff's Export Trade: The Law and Practice of International Trade* (London, Sweet & Maxwell, 2007) 81.

transactions and payments made using such technologies. As explained in the prior chapter, these challenges are more significant in the context of blockchains relying on the PoW consensus algorithms, as the finality on such blockchains is probabilistic rather than deterministic. In other words, in such transactions, the payer can theoretically never be sure that his payment obligations have been discharged and the payee can never be sure whether he is the rightful owner of the funds, is free of all claims against the payer, and whether subsequent legal action can reverse or unwind the transaction at hand. This means that there always remains a probability of reversibility of the transactions due to either hacks or attacks, forking that may cause the specific transaction to end up in an orphan chain, or potential legal action that might be brought against the payee by the payer or interested third parties (eg, the creditors of the payer).

Probabilistic transaction finality in PoW blockchains may have further real and legal implications depending on the specific use-cases of a given cryptocurrency. For example, if a cryptocurrency is used as collateral to secure a transaction in a Decentralised Finance (DeFi) setting, the probabilistic settlement finality might get in the way of determining the exact moment of the perfection of a security interest. One way of creating and perfecting a security interest over a crypto-asset may be that the crypto-asset should come under the *control* of the secured party. The uncertainty regarding the exact moment of the finality of the transaction may become problematic if between the time of the creation of the security interest and its perfection the debtor becomes subject to an insolvency proceeding or where there are two competing security interests that leave the court struggling to establish the priority between competing secured creditors.

Furthermore, operational settlement can become more complicated when the delivery of one asset is against the delivery of another (or against payment) such as the exchange of securities against cash or the exchange of one currency for another.[46] Under these circumstances, uncertainty about the finality of one leg of the transaction can prevent the other leg from becoming final. In the FMIs, this risk is important because of the back-to-back transactions and the fact that the counterparties may face funding constraints if their transaction happens to be unwound *ex-post*.[47]

Probabilistic settlement finality could create even more problems when both legs of financial transactions are conducted in a blockchain relying on probabilistic finality. For example, in the DvP systems, the delivery of an asset against payment for that asset is dependent upon the payment.[48] In these types of settlement systems each leg's finality is conditional on the finality of the other leg. Not only must there be a clear moment of finality for both legs of the transaction, but also each leg's finality must be conditional on the finality of the other leg. This interdependency

[46] Committee on Payments and Market Infrastructures (n 4) 15–16.
[47] Committee on Payment and Settlement Systems (n 38).
[48] See Committee on Payment and Settlement Systems (n 2).

of two sets of probabilistic finality adds more complexity if such networks become widespread as part of decentralised financial market infrastructures (dFMIs).

An even further complicating factor would be the case where the payment and delivery legs of a transaction are conducted in different networks, platforms, or blockchains, and there is no trusted third-party intermediary to provide assurances regarding the finality of settlements.[49] In case of default by a counterparty after the settlement of one of the legs of the transaction, there must be legal clarity as to the status of the transaction. To say the least, in the absence of legal clarity, counterparties should consider extra risk management measures for the risks stemming from such eventualities relating to settlement risks.[50]

Probabilistic finality in PoW blockchains may also give rise to serious systemic concerns in the case of the potential interconnectedness of conventional payment and settlement systems with DeFi. As the transaction finality cannot be ensured operationally and as the existing legal regimes may not be applicable to the transfers using cryptocurrencies to define the moment of settlement finality, the increasing interconnectedness between conventional payment and settlement systems and the payments using cryptocurrencies may increase the contagion channels between these two sectors. At the moment, it is not clear that if the cryptocurrencies became large enough, whether regulators or even central banks would be able to readily deal with such risks. Therefore, it seems that there is a need for legal intervention to define the finality in the transactions on PoW blockchains. However, before moving forward, there is a need for distinguishing two different concepts of finality, ie, legal and operational finality.

A. Legal vs. Operational Finality

What seems to be a source of major confusion in the debate about the probabilistic finality on the PoW blockchains is that the critiques of transaction finality on the Bitcoin Blockchain often confuse two different aspects of finality: technical, de facto, or *operational* finality, and de jure or *legal* finality. The operational settlement on the Bitcoin Blockchain is probabilistic, as is the operational settlement with

[49] See Mills et al (n 1).

[50] ibid. Although some authors have highlighted the use cases of the blockchain technology for the settlement systems, the analysis in this chapter shows that at least certain types of blockchains may not be very suitable for use as the settlement layer. For authors' work highlighting the use cases of the blockchain technology in settlements. See generally E Micheler, 'Custody Chains and Asset Values: Why Crypto-Securities Are Worth Contemplating' [2015] *CLJ* 505, 532; E Micheler and L von der Heyde, 'Holding, clearing and settling securities through blockchain technology creating an efficient system by empowering asset owners' [2016] *Butterworths Journal of International Banking and Financial Law* 652; DC Donald and MH Miraz, 'Restoring Direct Holdings and Unified Pricing to Securities Markets with Distributed Ledger Technology' (2019) *The Chinese University of Hong Kong Faculty of Law Research Paper*; DC Donald, 'From Block Lords to Blockchain: How Securities Dealers Make Markets' [2018] *Journal of Corporation Law* 29; P Paech, 'Securities, intermediation and the blockchain: an inevitable choice between liquidity and legal certainty?' [2016] *Uniform Law Review* 612.

cash and any other means of electronic payments, as there is always a theoretical possibility of taking the cash back by using brute force, or reversing the transaction due to a technical failure in the payment system, including that of a central bank.[51] However, the near impossibility of operational finality does not necessarily mean that the payment is not *legally* final, in the sense that legal challenges cannot invalidate the payment *ex-post*. In other words, probabilistic *operational* finality does not necessarily imply probabilistic *legal* finality and vice versa,[52] and the impossibility of operational finality does not necessarily put a question mark on the legal finality of a transaction. The difference between settlements with conventional payments vis-à-vis the settlements within a PoW blockchain with probabilistic finality is that the settlements on the conventional payment systems enjoy legal finality, whereas there is no legal protection as to the finality of the settlements on the PoW blockchains.

When the operational mechanisms for settling a transaction cannot theoretically provide 100 per cent bulletproof deterministic finality of a transaction, it would be up to the law to intervene and create presumptions for the finality of a settlement, namely, as soon as certain requirements are met, a transaction would be deemed final. This means that although in the PoW blockchains the actual transfers are not 100 per cent final and immutable, the law may want to presume a certain moment of finality provided certain conditions are met. One major role of legal presumptions has been that where reality cannot provide certainty, the law takes over and acts as a supplier of fictional certainty to meet the demand for it. Such presumptions have been developed for the sale of goods, and in the context of negotiable instruments and money, there seems to be no reason why such judicial, statutory, or regulatory presumptions cannot be developed for the transactions conducted on PoW blockchains. For example, following custom, the law may presume that after six confirmations[53] a transaction is legally final.[54]

[51] Although the cash transactions are technically reversible, ie, by taking back the possession of the cash after the payment (technical probabilistic finality), the law protects such transactions by granting strong legal protections on the settlement by cash. One such reason for the strong protections is ensuring the fungibility of banknotes. See *Crawfurd v The Royal Bank* (1749) Mor 875 (Scot.).

[52] See L Gullifer and R Hay, 'How final is final? Settlement finality, blockchains and DLT' [2020] *Butterworths Journal of International Banking and Financial Law* 8. In fact, technically speaking, in most transactions, the real world may not provide a solid 100% certainty; therefore, there is a need for the law to intervene and presume that as soon as certain requirements are met, a transaction would be deemed final. As on the Bitcoin Blockchain, similar to any other payment system, the actual transfers are not 100% final and immutable, but the law may presume that at a certain point in time a transaction becomes final. In other words, the fact that the finality on the Bitcoin Blockchain is not deterministic does not stop the law from presuming the finality of a transaction on its blockchain.

[53] Despite the fact that some merchants even accept zero-confirmation transactions for small payments, such transactions, as far as they are not included in the blockchain, carry certain levels of risks and the transferee would only accept such transactions at his own peril.

[54] Although the case law may evolve and presume settlement finality after six confirmations for private-law purposes, given the potential for systemic risk arising from the ambiguity as to the finality of payments, such issues may better be dealt with *ex-ante* within a *regulatory* framework, as is the case with conventional payment and settlement systems.

However, under the current legal framework for payments and settlements, the laws ensuring settlement finality (eg, the EU Settlement Finality Directive),[55] which require payment and settlement systems to specifically define the moment of entry and irrevocability of the orders and transactions, are not applicable to payments made by cryptocurrencies.[56] The lack of any legal protection for settlement finality in and of itself may create various legal problems for the parties to the transaction and may entail systemic implications if the cryptocurrency markets become sufficiently large, and more sophisticated products and services develop around them. The next section explores the foundation of the concept of legal finality and its emergence from private law, the influence it had on the law of payments, and the concept of settlement finality in regulatory law.

IV. Settlement Finality in Private and Public (Regulatory) Law

To understand the significance of the settlement finality, the importance of legal presumptions, and how they have come to drive a wedge between the operational aspects of finality and its legal aspects, some flashback to the roots of the concept of settlement finality in private law would be enlightening. From a private law perspective, the debate on finality is rooted in two main contractual freedoms. First, freedom to choose the method and medium of payment as a means of discharging obligations.[57] According to this principle, the parties are free to choose whatever they want as a medium of exchange. As payment is only one method of discharging obligations, the parties to a transaction may even choose to settle obligations through countertrade (eg, goods for goods, goods for services, services for goods, or services for services) or other arrangements of their own choice. In addition to the freedom to choose the method and medium of payment, from a purely private law perspective, the parties to a transaction are free to choose the moment of the finality of their transaction.[58]

[55] Directive 98/26/EC (n 45).

[56] ibid, Arts 1–2.

[57] Although the creditor is entitled to require the payment in legal currency, the parties may substitute a different obligation from that originally undertaken. See H Beale, *Chitty on Contracts*, 32th edn (London, Sweet & Maxwell, 2017) 1577. The legal tender laws should not be confused with the freedom to select a specific means of payment (which is probably an extension of the freedom of contract).

[58] 'The position is different under the laws of Netherlands, Spain, Germany, the Argentine, Brazil, Chile, and Colombia where the property passes only if the intention of parties is supported by the actual delivery of the goods.' Murray, Holloway and Timson-Hunt (n 45) 77–78. As many jurisdictions afford some flexibility on the separation of delivery and the legal construct of passing of property, certain jurisdictions afford the flexibility to parties so that they modify the applicable laws on the passing of the property in the goods sold to be modified by special arrangements between parties to a transaction. Under the UK laws, there are two fundamental principles: (1) If parties contract for the sale of unascertained goods, the property does not pass unless and until the goods are ascertained; and (2) If the contract is for the sale of specific or ascertained goods, the property passes according to

When parties choose to pay with a given medium of exchange, the legal status of the medium of exchange plays an important role in discharging the obligations of parties to a contract. Such a medium should desirably have two important features. First, it should be immediately available for onward transfers in future transactions. Second, it should be free from any adverse claims, which is a prerequisite for the first feature. In other words, the payment should be made with freely transferable funds.[59]

Payments in currency (ie, legal tender) satisfy both conditions of having immediate availability and of being freely transferable funds. This is because there are well-established and clear rules regarding the moment at which the legal tender settles the obligations.[60] This clear legal regime rests on three sets of rules: take-free rule, the shelter rule, and the defences such as good faith and the purchase for value rule. However, such a determination, ie, whether the medium of exchange can be deemed to be immediately available and free of any adverse claims, is not straightforward in the case of the transactions in which cryptocurrencies are intended to function as a medium of payment in discharge of obligations. In addition to the concerns about fungibility, this is partly because the finality in the Bitcoin Blockchain cannot be operationally ensured. Seen through this lens, the probabilistic finality in the Bitcoin Blockchain can hardly meet the first criterion, ie, the immediate availability for onward transfers.

Regarding the second criterion (ie, the take-free rule), due to the uncertainty about the legal nature of bitcoin, especially, whether it can be recognised as property or could benefit from a more precise recognition as money, it is not obvious whether, which, and to what extent the adverse claims of third parties to a given bitcoin, which is used as a medium of exchange, can travel with it. Therefore, there is considerable uncertainty as to whether the freely transferable funds condition can be met. This means that, from a private law perspective, Bitcoin may not be a suitable candidate for becoming a medium of exchange.

Despite Bitcoin's legal handicap, parties may still choose to use it as a medium of exchange according to the above-mentioned freedom that allows the parties to contractually agree on the moment of finality. When bitcoin is contractually used as a medium of exchange, and not the object of exchange, a great number of private law rules traditionally applied to money, such as the take-free rule, shelter

the intention of the parties (when the parties intend it to pass). ibid [78] 'If the goods are ascertained, under an f.o.b. contract, property in them passes when they are shipped unless the passing of title is postponed by express or implied stipulation; thus, the seller may have reserved the right of disposal of the goods until the contract terms of payment have been complied with.' ibid [30].

[59] 'In the case where payment must be made "in freely transferable funds" the payment will normally be made when the funds are freely available in the hands of the recipient, and this will not normally be the case until the funds have been credited to the account specified for receiving payment so that the payee has control over the money following payment.' Beale (n 57) 1617.

[60] The moment of finality is not an independent topic in the private law. Finality is largely a regulatory concept, which is mainly discussed and studied in relation to SIPS. See Regulation (EU) No 795/2014 as amended by Regulation (EU) 2017/2094 (n 5), Art 10 para 1. However, the basic concepts rely on private law concepts of passing the property or proprietary interests from one party to his counterparty.

rules, as well as the defences such as good faith and purchase for value, may be applicable to such a transaction. This means that private ordering can effectively make the traditional defences, which are available to money, applicable to Bitcoin as well. In this case, for example, if defences such as good faith and purchase for value are defeated, there would be a need for requiring a party to a transaction to send bitcoins or their equivalent value off-chain back to his counterparty, because it may not be practically feasible to technically unwind the transaction. As such contractual agreements could be cumbersome for the parties to cryptocurrency transactions, especially if such currencies gain considerable adoption, the way forward may be through giving legal effect and recognition – either judicially or by legislation – to the industry standards by developing a legal or regulatory concept of settlement finality in blockchains relying on probabilistic settlement finality.

A. The Private Law Origins of Legal Finality

One of the main concerns in private law is the potential impact of the insolvency of a party to a transaction on settlement finality. The insolvency concern has been of great significance in all areas of business law, however, it is of special importance to the settlement finality and the time at which the property passes unconditionally and irrevocably from one party to another, because the party making an advance payment may find himself in a precarious position if the seller becomes insolvent before the passing of property in the goods sold under the contract.[61] Determining the moment of finality in private law, where the obligations of parties to a trade are discharged could increase legal certainty in trade and could function as a circuit breaker of potential chain reactions that unwinding of a single transaction in a chain of transactions could create. In the next section, the paper first analyses the origins of the concept of finality in private law and then it investigates the regulatory concept of finality before venturing into its extension to cryptocurrencies with PoW blockchains.

i. Passing of Proprietary Interests under Private Law

In private law, the transaction finality depends on the type and the terms of the contract as well as the nature of the medium of payment. In contract law, one of the most important moments in a transaction is the moment at which the property or proprietary interest passes from one party to another. This moment determines the rights and obligations as well as potential liabilities of the parties to a transaction, which is of great importance in case of insolvency of one party to a transaction. The general principle under the private and commercial law of many jurisdictions, such as the US, the UK, and certain civil law countries, is that the property (or the

[61] See Murray, Holloway and Timson-Hunt (n 45) 80.

proprietary interest in goods) passes when the parties intend it to pass, irrespective of the actual delivery of the physical goods.[62]

This means that in commercial law, the passing of proprietary interests to goods sold may often be separate from the actual delivery of those goods. The traditional decoupling of the finality of transfer of ownership in commercial law from the physical possession and delivery or transfer of the goods is rooted deep in the foundations of property law where, due to exigencies of commerce, such a separation had to be recognised.[63] Documentary sales in international sales of goods present an interesting case where the decoupling of the delivery of physical goods and the legal passing of property reaches its pinnacle. In the law of documentary credits, the property only passes when the bill (of lading) is delivered to the buyer, irrespective of the actual delivery of the goods.[64] This decoupling presents many benefits, such as allowing the buyer to resell the goods that are in transit, practically functioning as a source of funding and liquidity in international trade.[65]

The decoupling of the legal treatment of the moment of the passing of proprietary interests from the moment of the delivery of physical goods (akin to operational finality) has wider implications in legal and financial systems. The entire apparatus of title(-based) finance including seller finance, buyer finance, and lessor finance are directly or indirectly built on the concept of separation of the (physical) possession of goods from the property rights to goods.[66]

[62] See ibid 78–79.

[63] ibid 81; see also H Hansmann and R Kraakman, 'Organizational law as asset partitioning' [2000] *European Economic Review* 807. The separation of physical goods from the rights attached to the goods has manifestations in all areas of law from property to contracts, and from company to financial law. For example, stock ownership, contrary to popular belief, does not indicate that the owner of the stock actually owns part of the premises of the company, it only means that the owner has a bundle of rights regarding the legal entity that is called a company. See generally Dignam and Lowry (n 44). In addition, in modern securities law and regulation, the concept of separation of the legal ownership from the beneficial ownership is based on such a decoupling. In property law, and in secured transactions, the floating charge (where a charge is placed on a floating/changing inventory of goods), is a manifestation of this phenomenon. The decoupling of physical possession and transfer of goods from their legal construct of passing of property or being subject to a security interest is what has allowed the development of the effective markets in such property and has been a great impetus for growth. See H De Soto, *The mystery of capital: Why capitalism triumphs in the West and fails everywhere else* (New York, Basic Books, 2000).

[64] This is applicable to the situations in which it is the seller's duty to deliver the bill. If no such duty exists, such as in Ex Works or Free on Board (where the buyer contracts with the carrier) or free delivered contracts, the physical delivery of the goods to the buyer or to the carriers is presumed to be the time at which the property passes to the buyer. See Murray, Holloway and Timson-Hunt (n 45) 81.

[65] As it is well known in international trade, the banks do not deal with the goods, they only deal with the documents (containing certain rights to goods). This means that such decoupling of right to the goods from the goods themselves allows banks to extend credit to the buyer (by opening a line of credit in his favour). This also happens in many secured transactions where the secured party's rights to the personal or real property is detached from the owner of the real property allowing the items of which the security is created to be used by the owner (obligor) while a security interest in favour of an oblige (secured party) is created. The big chunk of expansion and contraction of credit relies upon the secured financing, facilitated by the developments in property and contract laws.

[66] PR Wood, *Law and practice of international finance* (London, Sweet & Maxwell, 2008) 292 (explaining title financing). In the modern securities markets with immobilised and dematerialised securities,

For example, in the retention of title, the English law allows a clause providing that the seller retains the property in the goods sold until he receives the purchase price in cash. Such a clause is deemed to be effective and defeats the general presumption that the property in the goods sold passes when the bill of lading passes from the seller to the buyer. In this respect, such a clause is believed to make the passing of property conditional upon a specified event.[67]

This section briefly discussed how property passes from the buyer to the seller – which is akin to the transaction finality in our discussion – in transactions the object of which is goods (sale of goods). The objective of the section is to demonstrate that even where the transaction involves physical goods, due to commercial reasons, certain legal constructs have been designed to decouple the moment of the finality of a transaction (passing of proprietary interests) from the actual delivery of the goods. The next sections study the transactions, in which either negotiable instruments or cash (funds or money) is the medium of exchange in a trade and where the finality of payments is determined not by the actual transfer of funds, but by the legal constructs such as the delivery of a payment instrument.

ii. Private Law and Negotiable Instruments

Although the initial forms of money that seemed to function as the settlement layer for trades were in the form of commodity money (ie, precious metals), the exigencies of (international) trade and recurring ebbs and flows in the supply of the medium of settlement (ie, gold and silver) gave rise to the creation of (debt) instruments as a medium of exchange that largely came to replace the settlement asset in routine trade transactions. The passing of such instruments from one party to another established a presumption that the proprietary interests in goods subject to trade settled the obligations with finality. Negotiable instruments are a case in point. A common feature of all negotiable instruments is that they are concerned with a promise to pay in the ultimate medium of exchange, clearing, and settlement in the underlying layer of a centralised payment system wherein tendering the medium of exchange immediately discharges all the obligations of the parties to a transaction.[68]

the concept of control is taken to be equivalent of the concept of possession, especially for the purposes of creation and perfection of security interests. See Directive 2002/47/EC of the European Parliament and of the Council of 6 June 2002 on financial collateral arrangements [2002] OJ L168/43, Arts 1 para 5, 2 para 2; see also Case C-156/15 *Private Equity Insurance Group v Swedbank* ECLI:EU:C:2016:851 [2015] 36–37, 44.

[67] See Murray, Holloway and Timson-Hunt (n 45) 83.

[68] This is why the creditor has no obligation to accept a negotiable instrument (bill, note, or check) in payment of a debt, unless he has expressly or impliedly agreed to do so. See Beale (n 57) 1433. In addition, where an agent is authorised to receive payment, he has the authority to receive the payment only in cash. The principal cannot be bound by the agent accepting a bill of exchange without the principal's express authority. ibid 1427.

But what makes some instruments act as negotiable instruments is a legal construct called the concept of negotiability. Under English law, a payment medium should have at least three characteristic features to be considered negotiable:

1. If made payable to the bearer, it is transferable by delivery; and if made payable to order by endorsement and delivery enabling the transferee to sue upon it in his own name;
2. There is a presumption of consideration; and
3. Good title is acquired by the transferee who takes the instrument in good faith and for value, even though the transferor did not have a good title or did not have the title at all.[69]

The third feature of negotiable instruments is the most important feature of such instruments for the purpose of this study. This feature means that the classic doctrine of *nemo dat quod non habet*[70] is not applicable to such negotiable instruments if the good faith purchase-for-value conditions are met.[71] When it comes to cash, ie, notes and coins, the *nemo dat* doctrine has never applied. Notes and coins pass by delivery and are not recoverable from a person who obtains possession in good faith.[72] The disapplication of this principle is mainly due to commercial reasons because money is the medium by which all other forms of value change hands.[73] The disapplication of the *nemo dat* doctrine to cash makes it the most efficient medium of exchange in the economy.[74] Based on this principle, stolen money cannot be recovered if it is paid for a valuable consideration to a bona fide third party.[75] This rule is also applicable to banknotes, as they are considered cash

[69] JS Rogers, *The Early History of the Law of Bills and Notes: A Study of the Origins of Anglo-American Commercial Law* (Cambridge, Cambridge University Press, 2004) 3 (quoting WS Holdsworth, A History of English Law [first published 1909–1952, FB&c 2023] 113–14). Despite this, money could be recovered from a bad faith payee or a payee who received it for no consideration. Money cannot be recovered by means of an action for wrongful interference with goods unless the specific notes and coins can be identified. See C Proctor, *Mann on the Legal aspect of money*, 7th edn (Oxford, Oxford University Press, 2012) 44.

[70] Latin phrase meaning 'No one can give what he has not got.'

[71] In other words, an important exception to the generally applicable rules of derivative transfer of title is the defence of good faith purchase for value, recognised both in common law and equity. D Fox, 'Cryptocurrencies in the Common Law of Property' in D Fox and S Green (eds), *Cryptocurrencies in Public and Private Law* (Oxford, Oxford University Press, 2019) 159.

[72] See C Proctor, *Mann on the Legal aspect of money* (Oxford, Oxford University Press, 2012) 43–44 citing *Higgs v Holiday* [1600] Cro. Eliz. 746; *Miller v Race* [1758] 97 Eng. Rep. 398, 401; *Wookey v Poole* [1820] 106 ER 839; *but compare* German Civil Code BGB s 935, 2.

[73] ibid 43–44.

[74] Because it removes the uncertainty regarding potential third party rights as well as liquidity and counterparty risks. In other words, such mechanism essentially transforms money into an information-insensitive asset. *See* Nabilou and Prüm (n 8); TV Dang, G Gorton and B Holmström, 'Ignorance, debt and financial crises' (2012) www.columbia.edu/~td2332/Presentation_Ignorance.pdf; G Gorton, 'The development of opacity in U.S. banking' [2013] *Yale Journal on Regulation* 825; G Gorton, S Lewellen and A Metrick, 'The Safe-Asset Share' [2012] *The American Economic Review* 101.

[75] C Proctor (n 72) 44 citing *Miller v Race* [1758] 97 Eng. Rep. 398, 401.

and not goods or securities.[76] Therefore, the banknotes and coins are essentially negotiable chattels if received in good faith and for valuable consideration. This means that the transferee acquires good property (good title), even though the transferor did not have a good title or property.

As there are only two conditions for the disapplication of the *nemo dat* doctrine (ie, good faith and valuable consideration),[77] when money or banknotes are offered in the discharge of a debt, the payee is not required to inquire about the title as the recognition as a currency of such chattels and changing of hands of such currency not only passes the possession but also the property.[78] In addition, payment in cash enables the payee to use it immediately. In other words, the transferee has the unrestricted right to immediate use of the transferred funds.[79] This feature of cash is what differentiates it from negotiable instruments, such as bills of exchange, checks (and drafts), notes, and negotiable letters of credit, which are built upon the underlying payment layer, and consist in promises to pay in the ultimate medium of clearing and settlement (ie, cash or CeBM).

iii. Private Law and Finality in Cryptocurrencies

Given the above description, the legal treatment of finality in transactions involving PoW cryptocurrencies ultimately depends on the legal categorisation of the cryptocurrency in question. In the context of private law under the common law regimes, if bitcoin is recognised as a type of intangible property (a type of personal property),[80] its transfer would be subject to the rules of derivative transfer of title. This would mean that the *nemo dat* doctrine would apply. Suppose that A passes 5 bitcoins to B, B will only get an indefeasible right to ownership in coins if A was the rightful owner of the 5 bitcoins and the transaction was valid. Under this rule, A cannot give a better title to B than A has originally had.[81] The law of tracing allows the defects in A's title to be traced back to B's title.

As explained in the previous sections, in common law, an equitable title to personal property is extinguished against the purchaser if the latter purchases for value (valuable consideration) and without notice of the competing equitable title. This defence seems to be applicable to cryptocurrency transactions, regardless

[76] ibid 44. The same rule was developed in the US See *Newco Rand Co. v Martin*, 213 S.W.2d 504, 509 (1948) (stating '[m]oney is currency, is not earmarked and passes from hand to hand [...] One may give a bona fide transferee for value a better title to money than he himself has.').

[77] *See Banque Belge pour L'Etranger v Hambrouck* [1921] 1 KB 321, 329; see also *R. v Curtis* [2010] EWCA Crim 123, exp A-G (1988) 1 Qd R 546, 548; *Grant v The Queen* (1981) 147 CLR 503, 506; *Sinclair v Brougham* [1914] AC 398, 418.

[78] See ibid.

[79] See Beale (n 57) para 279.

[80] See D Carr, 'Cryptocurrencies as property in civilian and mixed legal systems' in D Fox and S Green (n 71) 179 (discussing the treatment of cryptocurrencies as property in civilian and mixed systems).

[81] See Fox in D Fox and S Green (n 71) 139, 156.

of their characterisation as money or some other type of property or interest.[82] Under this rule, if B is a good faith purchaser for value of the cryptocurrency that he has received from A, who has stolen the cryptocurrency from C, then B defeats proprietary claims by C to recover the cryptocurrency or their traceable proceeds.[83] However, this defence has been traditionally only available to money and negotiable instruments such as bills of exchange and promissory notes.[84] This means that the common law rules of good faith and purchase for value only apply if the cryptocurrencies are characterised as money for the purpose of the rule and if the parties choose to treat them as money exempting them from the full application of the *nemo dat* doctrine.[85] If this rule is applied, an indefeasible legal title in a transferee who has received the money in good faith and for value is created.[86]

To summarise, the moment of the finality of a transaction or payment is significant in private law because, unless otherwise indicated or required, it can determine who owns what at a particular moment in time. In a commercial transaction, the passing of the physical possession of goods does not necessarily signify the passing of title to those goods. The opposite is also true; the passing of title may not necessarily signify the passing of possession of the goods. For example, in documentary credits, the passing of title happens when the documents of shipment (bills of lading) are passed from the seller to the buyer. And there is no need for taking the actual possession of goods by the buyer. It is a legal construct that decouples the actual possession and control (physical) of an asset from its legal concept for the facilitation of trade between two parties. The same principle can apply to the cryptocurrencies with PoW blockchains, meaning that the passing of proprietary interest or title to cryptocurrencies could be independent of the passing of the cryptocurrency on the blockchain (constructive transfer).

Despite being problematic, the probabilistic finality may not be a huge cause for concern in the contractual and non-systemically important retail payment settings. However, uncertainty about the finality of transactions may eventually halt trades in cryptocurrencies or even may create systemic risks if such cryptocurrencies are used for wholesale payments. As in the context of wholesale payments where funds are constantly and immediately reused and reinvested, the absence of deterministic finality – be it legal or operational – would introduce new risks in the financial system stemming from the linked exposures of counterparties and potential unwind of all linked transactions.[87] This may mean that the private law alone may not be able to provide a bullet-proof deterministic legal finality. Therefore, if, for some legal reason such as the absence of valuable consideration or good faith, the transaction could be voided, such transaction cannot

[82] ibid 159.
[83] ibid 160.
[84] ibid 160.
[85] ibid 160.
[86] ibid 160.
[87] Bank for International Settlements (n 10).

be considered final. Therefore, given the systemic implications of certain systems (eg, FMIs), there has been a need for additional regulatory measures that have aimed to achieve finality by creating certain legal presumptions for the moment of finality. In such systems, a transaction would be final according to the rules of the system even if there might be legal grounds to revoke the transactions. As will be seen shortly, the residual remaining legal risks to the finality of transactions in the conventional FMIs have been managed by additional institutional mechanisms such as liquidity facilities, the introduction of central clearing counterparties (CCPs), and the mandatory buy-in tool in securities settlement systems.

B. Transaction Finality in Payment and Securities Settlement Systems: Legal Framework

The concept of transaction finality in the context of financial instruments, money, and fund transfers[88] is slightly different from the concept of transaction finality in the context of the sale of goods. To say the least, money constitutes one leg of any trade other than countertrades (eg, barter) and its prevalence as a medium of exchange in commercial transactions has necessitated a special legal treatment, which has led to special judicial and legal protections regarding its settlement finality. As previously mentioned, one such special protection is the disapplication of *nemo dat* doctrine in private law.

However, given the commercial and systemic importance of payment and settlement systems, the lawmaker has taken an extra step forward and has required the operators of the payment and settlement systems to define certain moments in the life of a transaction for the purposes of finality of transactions by clearly defining a point in time where transactions become final and by outlining the legal implications of finality.[89] The reason behind the special legal protections for transfer orders is not very different from the finality concept in the sale of goods discussed in previous sections. This has been very well explained by the European Central Bank (ECB), '[b]etween the time a transfer order is accepted for settlement by the payment operator and the time the order is actually settled [in the

[88] For a definition of the concept of funds under the European Union law, see Nabilou, 'The dark side of licensing cryptocurrency exchanges as payment institutions' (n 8).

[89] In the context of FMIs, including payment and securities settlement systems, finality denotes the moment in time when the transfer order or the transfer itself becomes unconditional and irrevocable. In this context, finality can be used both in the legal and technical sense. When used in its legal sense, it means that the transfer discharges the obligations, and it cannot be revoked by the counterparties or other third parties. When it is used in its technical sense, it refers to the making of entries in accounts. See European Central Bank, *The Payment System: Payments, Securities and Derivatives, and the Role of the Eurosystem* (Frankfurt am Main, European Central Bank, 2010) 145 www.ecb.europa.eu/pub/pdf/other/paymentsystem201009en.pdf. Although making debit or credit entries in the accounts triggers the settlement finality, it is not the crediting or debiting of the accounts that are irrevocable as the financial intermediary has the power to change the ledger, but making such a debit or credit entry makes the transactions final in the eyes of the law.

books], participants are subject to credit or liquidity risks, as the transfer order can be revoked or a participant could become insolvent.'[90]

In addition to special protections to the transfer orders, to increase the certainty about the finality of transactions in a payment system, the legal systems in major jurisdictions, such as in the EU, have slightly diverged from the private law concept of finality. They take a different approach to determining the moment of finality. Under the current payments and securities settlement systems, a final settlement is only possible under the settlements conducted by the payment and securities settlement systems. This means that such settlements should be conducted within a securities settlement system that is designated by a Member State under the Settlement Finality Directive (SFD).[91] Only in this case will the parties be protected against insolvency proceedings initiated by other participants.

Under such regulatory frameworks, the settlement finality concept in payment and settlement systems has taken a more granular shape, and a fine distinction between the settlement finality concept applicable to 'transfer orders' (or settlement instructions) and the one applicable to actual 'transfers' (ie, entries in securities and cash accounts) has emerged.[92] Accordingly, the SFD is mainly about the 'moment of entry' and the 'moment of irrevocability' of transfer orders and not the actual transfer of assets.[93] In the EU, Article 3(1) of the SFD, states that even in the event of insolvency proceedings against a participant, transfer orders and netting shall be legally enforceable and binding on third parties if they were entered into a system before the moment of opening of such insolvency proceedings.[94]

Under European regulations, a securities settlement system, such as a central securities depository (CSD) is required by the Central Securities Depository Regulation (CSDR)[95] to define three distinct definitions of settlement finality that grant protection against insolvency proceedings of other participants in the securities settlement system. Settlement Finality I occurs at the exact moment of the entry of a transfer order into the system. If a transfer order is entered into the system before the opening of an insolvency proceeding, it is protected against insolvency proceedings.[96] Article 3 of the SFD stipulates that the moment of entry of a transfer order into a system should be defined by the rules of that system.[97] Settlement Finality II is the moment after which the transfer order becomes irrevocable and neither a participant of the system, nor a third party can revoke it.

[90] ibid.

[91] Directive 98/26/EC (n 45).

[92] ibid.

[93] European Post Trade Forum, *EPTF Report – Annex 3: Detailed Analysis of the European Post Trade Landscape* (2017) 73 finance.ec.europa.eu/document/download/0481b029-e716-4474-9ac1-9b5819d7e26e_en?filename=170515-eptf-report-annex-3_en.pdf.

[94] Directive 98/26/EC (n 45).

[95] Regulation (EU) No 909/2014 of the European Parliament and of the Council of 23 July 2014 on improving securities settlement in the European Union and on central securities depositories and amending Directives 98/26/EC and 2014/65/EU and Regulation (EU) No 236/2012 [2014] OJ L257/1.

[96] ibid.

[97] Directive 98/26/EC (n 45).

Settlement Finality III is the moment after which the transfer orders are binding and enforceable against third parties, even in case of opening of an insolvency proceeding.[98]

Similarly, and in compliance with the SFD, under the TARGET2-Securities (T2S) operational framework, Settlement Finality I (moment of entry) is achieved at the moment of validation of the settlement instruction on the T2S platform. Settlement Finality II (irrevocability) is achieved at the matching of the instruction on the T2S platform, and finally, Settlement Finality III (finality of transfer) is achieved at the moment at which the cash account is credited if the transfer concerns cash, or when the securities account is credited or debited if the instruction relates to a securities transfer.[99]

It is important to note that such a moment of finality, despite being recorded and operationalised in the books and records of the intermediaries and the parties, should essentially be characterised as legal finality as it is the rules applicable to the system or the operator define the moment of finality. Overall, the payment and settlement finality even in the centralised FMIs remain operationally probabilistic, but it is the touch of the law that attempts to transform the probabilistic operational finality to a deterministic legal finality.

However, to say that the law provides for a completely deterministic finality would be inaccurate, in particular if we adopt a definition of finality based on the irrevocability of the transaction (or transfer order) even in cases of bankruptcy. This is because even the transactions that are deemed to be final in a legal sense could be unwound in exceptional circumstances. For example, in the EU, Article 3 para 1 of the SFD states that even in the event of insolvency proceedings against a participant, transfer orders and netting shall be legally enforceable and binding on third parties if they were entered into a system before the moment of opening of such insolvency proceedings.[100] *However*, if transfer orders are entered into a system *after* the commencement of the insolvency proceeding and are carried out on the day of the opening of such proceedings, they will be enforceable and

[98] European Post Trade Forum (n 93). Furthermore, tools such as the buy-in tool have been introduced to deal with potential settlement failures. See Regulation (EU) No 909/2014 (n 95), Art 7 para 3; Commission Delegated Regulation (EU) 2018/1229 of 25 May 2018 supplementing Regulation (EU) No 909/2014 of the European Parliament and of the Council with regard to regulatory technical standards on settlement discipline [2018] OJ L230/1, Art 16; see also E Wymeersch, 'Central securities depositories and reform of the settlement process' [2021] *Journal of Securities Operations & Custody* 13; International Capital Market Association (ICMA), 'How to survive in a mandatory buy-in world: A discussion paper by the ICMA Secondary Market Practices Committee' (June 2018) 4 www.icmagroup.org/assets/documents/Regulatory/Secondary-markets/How-to-Survive-in-a-Mandatory-Buy-in-World---June-2018-260618.pdf.

[99] European Post Trade Forum (n 93).

[100] This provision effectively disapplies the 'zero-hour' rule (ZHR) or midnight hour rule. The ZHR entails the retroactive application of the insolvency proceedings from 00:00 hours of the day when the insolvency is declared, or the insolvency proceedings are commenced. See also Regulation (EU) No 909/2014 (n 95), Arts 6 and 7; Directive 2002/47/EC (n 66), Art 8 (stating it also disapplies the ZHR for financial collateral). For more details, *see* M Haentjens, *Financial Collateral: Law and Practice* (Oxford, Oxford University Press, 2020) 289.

binding on third parties *only if* 'after the time of settlement, the settlement agent, the central counterparty or the clearing house can prove that they were not aware, nor should have been aware, of the opening of such proceedings'.[101] This means that under such circumstances if the settlement agent was aware or should have been aware of the opening of such proceedings, the transaction could be challenged and eventually unwound. To ensure that remaining risks would not threaten the safety and soundness of the overall settlement system, institutional arrangements have emerged that are to be briefly discussed in the next section.

i. Institutional Arrangements and the Settlement Discipline Regimes

A judicial stamp of approval on the current practices, or a legislative or regulatory measure protecting the settlement finality on PoW blockchains, may be seen as an easy solution for the problem of settlement finality, however, merely introducing the concept of legal finality would be hollow if it is not supported by the mechanisms and institutional arrangement that would credibly enable the participants in the network to ensure the finality of payments and settlements. In the conventional FMIs, complex mechanisms have emerged to prevent settlement fails, protect settlement finality, and in case of settlement fails, remedy them. Such measures – constituting the settlement discipline regime – consist of a set of rules and mitigation techniques aimed at preventing fails and protecting the settlement layer of a payment and settlement system.[102] These mechanisms include market rules, regulations, and best practices at the trading level, or pre-settlement level as well as the institutions and mechanisms to ensure settlement finality, including the following non-exhaustive list:[103]

1. Fail monitoring and reporting mechanisms;
2. Technical pre-settlement measures;
3. Hold-release mechanism encouraging early matching and allowing for matching to be separated from the availability of cash or securities;
4. Other technical measures for facilitating settlement and reducing liquidity risks and securities needs, such as queue management facilities, settlement optimisation techniques, and multiple settlement cycles during the day;

[101] Article 3 para 2 of the SFD pre-empts the law and regulations of member states that are related to the transactions concluded before the moment of opening of insolvency proceedings that would otherwise lead to the unwinding of a netting. See Directive 98/26/EC (n 45); see generally D Devos, *Legal Protection of Payment and Securities Settlement Systems and of Collateral Transactions in European Union Legislation* (2006) www.imf.org/external/np/seminars/eng/2006/mfl/dd.pdf.

[102] See generally D Russo and S Rosati, 'Chapter 9 – Short Selling, Clearing, and Settlement in Europe: Relations and Implications' in GN Gregoriou (ed), *Handbook of Short Selling* (Waltham, Academic Press, 2012) 159.

[103] European Central Bank, 'Settlement fails – Report on securities settlement systems (SSS) measures to ensure timely settlement' (April 2011) www.ecb.europa.eu/pub/pdf/other/settlementfails042011en.pdf.

5. Existence of central clearing counterparties (CCPs) and the methods they use to avoid settlement fails, including stringent membership requirements;[104]
6. Arrangements for reducing liquidity risks such as access to credit and liquidity facilities (of central banks), securities lending arrangements,[105] transaction shaping mechanisms and partial delivery solutions; and
7. Mechanisms similar to a mandatory buy-in tool.[106]

From among the above-mentioned arrangements, CCPs occupy a relatively *sui generis* position within FMIs. CCPs mitigate systemic risk by acting as a circuit breaker when risks of defaults leading to settlement fails tend to propagate from one counterparty to another. This is made possible through either novation or open offer.[107] By standing in between counterparties, CCPs reduce the risk of a panic reaction to solvency problems of a single counterparty and decrease the likelihood of a sudden failure of chains of counterparties. Additionally, they enhance transparency regarding counterparty credit risk, which enables both market participants and regulators to have a better assessment of counterparty risks in the financial system.[108] CCPs also monitor and ensure the uniform application of collateral requirements on all clearing members.[109] Furthermore, central clearing with fewer CCPs lowers the average counterparty risk through netting.[110]

Given CCPs' role in the financial markets, they are considered too big, too interconnected, or too important to fail. In addition, their incentives would not be aligned with those of society due to the moral hazards arising from being recognised as such.[111] This is why CCPs are subject to strong and harmonised regulatory

[104] ibid; H Nabilou and I Asimakopoulos, 'In CCP We Trust … Or Do We? Assessing the Regulation of Central Clearing Counterparties in Europe' (2020) *Capital Markets Law Journal* 70.

[105] Financial Stability Board, 'Securities Lending and Repos: Market Overview and Financial Stability Issues: Interim Report of the FSB Workstream on Securities Lending and Repos' (April 2012) www.fsb.org/wp-content/uploads/r_120427.pdf; Russo and Rosati (n 102); J Benjamin, G Morton and M Raffan, 'The future of securities financing' [2013] *Law and Financial Markets Review* 4.

[106] For a definition of mandatory buy-in, *see* International Capital Market Association, 'CSDR Settlement Discipline, Mandatory buy-ins: European settlement regulation with global trading level implicaitons' (August 2019) www.icmagroup.org/assets/documents/Regulatory/Secondary-markets/CSDR-Settlement-Regulation/CSDR-Brochure-August-2019-190819.pdf.

[107] Committee on Payment and Settlement Systems and Technical Committee of the International Organization of Securities Commissions, 'Recommendations for Central Counterparties: Consultative Report' (March 2004) 13 www.iosco.org/library/pubdocs/pdf/IOSCOPD176.pdf. See generally J Braithwaite and D Murphy, 'Central Counterparties (CCPs) and the law of default management' [2017] *Journal of Corporate Law Studies* 1.

[108] Committee on Payment and Settlement Systems and Technical Committee of the International Organization of Securities Commissions (n 107).

[109] D Duffie, 'Replumbing our financial system: uneven progress' [2013] *International Journal of Central Banking* 251.

[110] D Duffie and H Zhu, 'Does a Central Clearing Counterparty Reduce Counterparty Risk?' [2011] *The Review of Asset Pricing Studies* 74.

[111] H Nabilou and A Pacces, 'The Law and Economics of Shadow Banking' in IH Chiu and IG MacNeil (eds), *Research Handbook on Shadow Banking: Legal and Regulatory Aspects* (Cheltenham, Edward Elgar Publishing, 2018).

minimum margin standards.[112] In addition, systemic liquidity events necessitate extending central bank liquidity facilities to CCPs, and in many jurisdictions, such a liquidity backstop has been made available to CCPs. In Europe, Article 85 para 1 lit a of EMIR opens up the possibility for CCPs to have access to central bank liquidity facilities by mandating the European Commission to assess, in cooperation with the members of the European System of Central Banks (ESCB), the need for any measure to facilitate the CCPs' access to central bank liquidity facilities.[113] In some jurisdictions, such as the US, banks used to have almost exclusive access to central bank liquidity facilities, with limited opportunities for non-bank financial institutions.[114] Although the Dodd-Frank Act does not expressly allow access to the Federal Reserve liquidity facilities to CCPs, currently in the US (and likewise in the UK), such access is granted.[115]

The reason for highlighting the importance of institutional arrangements that help ensure the settlement finality is mainly because the law is unable to provide for 100 per cent bulletproof settlement finality. In other words, technical limitations and the requisites of justice and fairness in the traditional FMIs do not allow for a deterministic finality in its strictest sense. Therefore, to remedy such a shortcoming, a whole host of institutional arrangements to ensure settlement finality in conventional FMIs have emerged, without which the legal as well as operational risks in the payment and settlement systems could destabilise the financial markets.

The same line of reasoning could apply to the PoW blockchains. As such networks cannot provide for the deterministic finality of the transactions, it is imperative to have legal mechanisms in place to provide for a moment of finality in such transactions if such networks ever want to be used as a reliable medium of exchange or a settlement layer for upper layers of a payment network (as is the case with the Lightning Network). For example, various moments could be defined as the moment of settlement finality. One way of defining such a moment is to defer to the long-established tendency in the law to be reliant on the practice of merchants (eg, a law merchant).[116]

Currently, on the Bitcoin Blockchain, a number of confirmations are required by industry practices to deem a bitcoin transaction final. These numbers vary from zero to six.[117] On the extreme low, traders and merchants accepting unconfirmed

[112] Duffie (n 109).

[113] European Market Infrastructure Regulation (EMIR), Art 85(1)(a).

[114] Duffie (n 109).

[115] M Dobler et al, 'IMF Working Paper WP/16/10: The lender of last resort function after the global financial crisis' (2016) www.imf.org/external/pubs/ft/wp/2016/wp1610.pdf.

[116] Indeed, one of the well-established conceptions of the common law has been the fact that the judges find the law rather than make it. See RD Cooter, 'Decentralized Law for a Complex Economy: The Structural Approach to Adjudicating the New Law Merchant' [1996] *University of Pennsylvania Law Review* 1643. In the spirit of this tradition, it would be reasonable for legal systems, at least for private law purposes, to presume settlement finality after 5 blocks are built on the block containing the transaction.

[117] Since an unconfirmed transaction could be reversed, accepting an unconfirmed transaction as payment is a very risky practice.

transactions is not unheard of, however, the most conservative approach seems to be accepting a transaction as final when that transaction has had six confirmations. This is because undoing six blocks requires a very high investment in energy.[118] To reduce the uncertainty about the settlement finality especially within the first 60 minutes, the industry has developed its own commercial customs. Depending on the wallet used, as soon as a transaction is broadcast to the Bitcoin Blockchain, the receiving wallet receives a notification confirming the receipt of payment, but the payment is only considered final after six confirmations. However, even such legislation or regulation will, at best, import the two most important traditional exceptions to the generally applicable rules of derivative transfer of title, ie, the defences of good faith and purchase for value, eventually making 100 per cent deterministic finality impossible. Even in the unlikely scenario that the laws and regulations would adopt the most accommodating approach to cryptocurrencies by offering the strongest protections to cryptocurrency transactions akin to the regime applicable to fund transfers, such a law would not be able to guarantee a deterministic finality.

In the absence of such a deterministic finality, the role of institutional arrangements akin to the settlement discipline regime becomes important. However, such institutional arrangements can hardly be applied or imposed on PoW cryptocurrencies. Given the anti-institutional and libertarian ethos of PoW blockchains, adapting the technology to the established institutional constraints of settlement regimes would go deeply against the raison d'être and the main value proposition of such cryptocurrencies. As it is highly improbable that such institutional arrangements could be transplanted in the PoW blockchains, the use of such blockchains for payment purposes will inevitably carry certain levels of finality risk. Thus far, there has been no system-wide realisation of such risks, and only the future will tell how finality risks in PoW blockchains will be dealt with if such cryptocurrencies gain wider acceptance.

V. Conclusion

The settlement finality has been one of the most controversial aspects of the cryptocurrencies that rely on PoW consensus algorithms for their transaction confirmations. The main critique is that since the PoW blockchains rely on probabilistic finality, they would be unsuitable for payment processing. However, it seems that the critiques of the probabilistic finality on PoW blockchains often confuse *operational* finality with *legal* finality. The main contribution of this chapter is to identify the real source of concern about the probabilistic finality in the

[118] This is not to say that it amounts to complete immutability. Theoretically complete immutability cannot be achieved.

PoW blockchains. As it turns out, the real cause of concern has little to do with the operational or even legal finality but originates from the incompatibility of PoW blockchains with the institutional arrangements (akin to the settlement discipline regime) that deal with the remaining risks that neither legal nor operational finality can address.

To identify the root of the problem, this chapter highlighted the key distinctions between legal finality and operational finality. It argued that since operational finality cannot be realistically ensured in any payment and settlement system, ultimately it is the law that should intervene and fill the gap by devising the concept of *de jure* or legal finality as opposed to operational finality.[119] However, after studying the concept of legal finality in conventional trade of goods (tangible goods) and payment and settlement systems, this chapter argues that the concept of settlement finality in law is, at best, a non-deterministic concept, and neither the law nor technology can provide a bulletproof 100 per cent deterministic finality. Even in the most systemically important FMIs, the law may not provide for complete certainty and finality as the exigencies of certainty, finality, efficiency, and financial stability may give way to the requisites of justice and fairness ingrained in the insolvency laws.[120] Accordingly, legal systems have gone as far as the law can go to provide for as much finality as possible through using legal presumptions and rules to provide certainty to the parties to a transaction and to avoid potential systemic implications of settlement fails in the payment and securities settlement systems.

Therefore, rather than taking a strong position to provide completely deterministic finality, in the case of the most systemically important FMIs, the law aims to provide the maximum achievable degree of finality. To manage the risks stemming from the remaining degree of uncertainty, the law requires alternative institutional mechanisms that could mitigate the risks that would emanate from the potential unravelling of transactions. These mechanisms include those employed by the CCPs or other systems and operators of the payment and settlement systems, such as having access to central bank liquidity facilities, stringent membership

[119] For example, the draft UNIDROIT principles on digital assets states that 'The law should specify the requirements for a transferee to qualify as an innocent acquirer (IA) of digital assets and derivative digital assets and the rights obtained by an IA (e.g., requirements and rights akin to those found in good faith purchase, finality, and take-free rules).' UNIDROIT, 'Digital Assets and Private Law Working Group Issues Paper, Study LXXXII' (June 2021) 18 www.unidroit.org/english/documents/2021/study82/wg03/s-82-wg03-02-rev01-e.pdf. Although this is a first step toward recognising legal finality, it is far from ensuring the complete finality of the transactions as it may require various other regulatory actions.

[120] The level of optimal certainty and precisions of law have been subject to a great scholarly debate under the rubric of the debate on the rules versus standards. See I Ehrlich and RA Posner, 'An economic analysis of legal rulemaking' [1974] *The Journal of Legal Studies* 257; L Kaplow, 'Rules Versus Standards: An Economic Analysis' [1992] *Duke Law Journal* 557; HB Schaefer, 'Legal Rule and Standards' in CK Rowley and F Schneider (eds), *The Encyclopedia of Public Choice, Volume I* (Dordrecht, Kluwer Academic Publishers, 2004) 347; CR Sunstein, 'Problems with Rules' [1995] *California Law Review* 953; P Schlag, 'Rules and Standards' [1985] *UCLA Law Review* 379.

requirements, and the buy-in tool in case of settlement failure in CCPs and central securities depositories (CSDs).[121]

This chapter argues that this institutional backstop for the finality of transactions is what differentiates the PoW blockchains from the conventional financial systems. As the law may be unable to provide a deterministic finality, it resorts to alternative mechanisms to require the participants to remedy the issue by establishing arrangements that could minimise the instances of settlement fails, and in case of settlement fails, such fails could be remedied as soon as practicable. However, establishing such institutional mechanisms to deal with the remaining risks of settlement finality requires a certain level of centralisation in the PoW blockchains. In the absence of such mechanisms, and centralised control, the law may be unable or unwilling to extend its traditional protections for the settlement finality in PoW blockchains, and such PoW networks may continue to suffer from the finality issues in the absence of any market-driven mechanisms to remedy the potential settlement fails. Along with other reasons,[122] this may be a legitimate reason for pessimism about the potential use-cases of decentralised PoW blockchains in traditional post-trade processes.

[121] Such a requirement is introduced in the EU in its short selling regulation as well as the CSDR. See Regulation (EU) No 236/2012 of the European Parliament and of the Council of 14 March 2012 on short selling and certain aspects of credit default swaps [2012] OJ L86/1; Regulation (EU) No 909/2014 (n 95).

[122] See Advisory Groups on Market Infrastructures for Securities and Collateral and for Payments (n 12).

16

Finality, Rights *in Rem*, and the Blockchain: Can Transactions in Crypto Assets be Set Aside?

AMY HELD

I. Crypto Assets, Insolvency, and Finality on a Blockchain

Since the original case of *Mt Gox* captured the attention of the crypto-legal sphere in 2014, there has continued to be a steady stream of insolvency proceedings featuring crypto assets in various jurisdictions around the world. The circumstances of the debtor have differed from case to case, but the existence – or purported existence – of crypto assets in the debtor's estate or patrimony has consistently given rise to novel legal issues. Many of these have essentially been matters of private law, ranging from: whether cryptocurrencies may form part of a debtor's insolvency estate at all;[1] whether a claim in cryptocurrency against a debtor entitles the holder to present a petition for winding up;[2] the correct property law classification of cryptocurrencies and the resulting priority between the accountholders of and unsecured creditors of a crypto exchange;[3] and, of course, the question of whether cryptocurrencies can be the object of ownership or comparable property rights.[4]

Whilst insolvency law and general private law remain distinct legal disciplines that pursue different policies, crypto assets as a contemporary feature of insolvency proceedings illustrate the extent to which these two disciplines nevertheless remain closely intertwined. On the one hand, many of the issues arising in insolvency proceedings are often readily resolved by simple recourse to the existing definitions and classifications in private law. On the other hand, where these existing definitions and classifications prove unable to accommodate new forms

[1] *Re Tsarkov*, Case No A40-124668/17, Moscow Arbitrazh Court, 9th Arbitrazh Appellate Court (Civil Division).

[2] *Re Koinz Trading*, Rb. Amsterdam 14 February 2018, ECLI:NL:RBAM:2018:869.

[3] *Ruscoe v Cryptopia Ltd (In Liquidation)* [2020] NZHC 728.

[4] Mt Gox Co Ltd, Case claiming the Bitcoin transfer, *Tokyo District Court*, Judgment of 5 Aug 2015, Ref 25541521.

of economic value, the immediacy of the interests at stake may find insolvency cases spurring on the development of private law. This quasi-symbiotic relationship between insolvency law and private law is well illustrated by an issue unique to the insolvency context, but which has not yet (to the author's knowledge) been considered in any crypto insolvency proceedings to date: the interplay between the entitlement of the insolvency practitioner to set aside or avoid qualifying transactions in the interests of the general body of creditors; and the entitlements of those who assert a right *in rem* in the subject matter of such transactions.

Admittedly, consideration of this issue may well be premature insofar as it remains premised on the due recognition in private law of crypto assets as objects of rights *in rem*. Nevertheless, the issue merits serious attention; and not only because such recognition in private law seems imminent.[5] In addition, and perhaps more critically, reforms to property law to this extent will not necessarily provide a complete answer to the question of whether the asserted right *in rem*, whilst recognised in private law, will nevertheless prevail when subjected to the insolvency policy of maximising value in the interest of the general body of creditors. The proof for this particular question will most likely be an action by an insolvency practitioner to set aside the relevant transaction, where a range of further legal issues consequent to the recognition of these assets as objects of rights *in rem* will require further resolution. Such further legal issues will, moreover, be significantly complicated by issues of fact arising from the underlying decentralised ledger technology itself. Any attempt by an insolvency practitioner to set aside a transaction and claw back the associated asset will, in the blockchain context, engage at least in principle an issue that has already received independent attention in the wider crypto asset discourse:[6] the extent to which settlement on a blockchain can ever be final.

To explore all of these issues, this chapter is structured in the following way. Part II elucidates the basic issues that arise in striking the balance between the interests of the general body of unsecured creditors and those who assert rights *in rem* to assets in or removed from the insolvency estate by contextualising them in the framework of the EU Insolvency Regulation Recast. It will then narrow the scope of the present discussion to one discrete issue of property law that is of particular significance in the insolvency context, but which does not generally receive specialised treatment in the property law discourse itself. Part III then sets

[5] Notably, following the findings of the Japanese courts in the *Mt Gox* case that bitcoin cannot be the object of property rights, the legislator introduced in 2017 amendments to the Payment Services Act that expressly recognise that cryptocurrencies can be owned; see T Morishita, ch 14 in this volume. Similarly, Principle 3 of the Draft UNIDROIT Principles provides that 'digital assets can be the subject of proprietary rights'. In England and Wales, following a consistent trend in the courts recognising bitcoin and other crypto assets as property for certain purposes, the Law Commission has recommended that a third category of personal property be recognised for digital assets. The draft for this chapter was finalised in August 2023.

[6] International Securities Services Association (ISSA), 'Infrastructure for Crypto-Assets: A Review for Infrastructure Providers' (October 2018) 19.

out a proposed approach to resolving this discrete issue, before Part IV explores its application in full to reach a range of possible solutions. Part V returns to the broader question of whether transactions on the blockchain can be set aside in insolvency proceedings and offers insights into the core considerations to be addressed when formulating any legal rules in this context. Part VI closes with a general summary and conclusions.

II. Actions to Set Aside vs Rights *in Rem* under EU Law

The EU Insolvency Regulation Recast[7] is broadly concerned with the efficient and effective operation of cross-border insolvency proceedings and the coordination of measures to be taken in respect of the insolvent debtor's assets within the EU. As such, it is primarily an instrument of private international law and procedural law that lays down general rules of jurisdiction, of applicable law, and for the recognition of judgments for both primary and secondary insolvency proceedings opened in the EU Member States.

Notwithstanding this primary focus, the Regulation is further concerned, albeit to a lesser degree, with other various policy objectives. At the forefront of these more secondary concerns are rights *in rem*, which are accorded special protections owing to their 'considerable importance for the granting of credit'.[8] Accordingly, the competing interests of the general body of unsecured creditors and those who assert rights *in rem* to assets *prima facie* belonging to the insolvency estate find a delicate balance in the overall framework of the Regulation. This provides for the situation where the main insolvency proceedings have been opened in one Member State pursuant to the general rule of jurisdiction set out in Article 3, but the debtor allegedly owns assets situate in another Member State to which third parties assert a right *in rem*.

In these circumstances, two legal provisions, each expressing a different policy objective pursued by the Regulation, come into play. Article 7 para 2 lit m supports the broad policies of efficiency, effectiveness, coordination, and disincentivising forum shopping pursued by Article 3; and provides that the *lex fori concursus* governs the actions for voidness, voidability, or unenforceability of legal acts detrimental to the general body of creditors. On the other hand, Article 8 gives effect to the policy of facilitating the granting of credit by providing that the rights *in rem* of creditors and third parties in assets of the debtor situate in another Member State 'shall not be affected' by the opening of insolvency proceedings. These rights should continue to be governed by (normally) the *lex situs*.[9]

[7] Regulation (EU) 2015/848 of the European Parliament and of the Council of 20 May 2015 on insolvency proceedings (recast) [2015] OJ L141/19 ('IRR').

[8] IRR, Recital 68.

[9] IRR, Recital 68.

Whilst Recital 68 makes clear that a proprietor of a right *in rem* should be able to continue to assert his right to segregation or separate settlement of the collateral security, this entitlement is not intended as being absolute. Recital 68 further provides that an insolvency practitioner appointed in the main proceedings may open secondary proceedings in the Member State in which the asset is situate. In the same vein, Article 8 para 4 expressly provides that the application of the *lex situs* to rights *in rem* does not preclude actions for voidness, voidability, or unenforceability pursuant to Article 7 para 2 lit m. Article 16, nevertheless, entitles the creditor or third party asserting the right *in rem* to raise a defence under the *lex situs* to any such action to set aside.

The interplay between these provisions came to the fore in *Lutz v Bäuerle*,[10] which concerned insolvency proceedings opened in Germany. In sum, the insolvency practitioner appointed by the German courts brought an action to claw back a sum of money paid out to an Austrian creditor. The payment had been disbursed, however, from the German debtor's Austrian bank accounts pursuant to an attachment order granted by the Austrian courts in respect of a contract for the sale of a car concluded by the creditor and the debtor's Austrian subsidiary. The primary legal question referred to the CJEU arose from the particular chronology of relevant events before and after insolvency proceedings had been opened, as follows.

On 17 March 2008, the Defendant Austrian creditor obtained an enforceable payment order from the Austrian courts against the debtor for the reimbursement of the purchase price paid for the car, which had not then been duly delivered under the contract of sale. About a month later, on 13 April 2008, the debtor filed an application to open insolvency proceedings in the German courts. On 20 May 2008, certain Austrian bank accounts of the debtor were attached pursuant to leave by the Austrian courts to enforce the payment order of 17 March 2008. On 4 August 2008, the German courts opened insolvency proceedings against the debtor. Over six months later, on 17 March 2009, the Austrian bank disbursed a sum of €11,778.48 to the Defendant pursuant to the attachment order granted some 10 months earlier in March 2008. The Claimant German liquidator subsequently informed the Defendant of the intention to challenge both the attachment and the disbursement, before bringing an action before the German courts on 23 October 2009 to set aside the transactions and claw back the sums paid out to the Defendant.

In these circumstances, if German law applied, both the Defendant's right to attach and subsequent payment itself would have been invalid. Pursuant to section 88 para 1 of the German Insolvency Code, the attachment order would have automatically become invalid upon the subsequent opening of insolvency proceedings as an execution of a security interest by way of attachment within the prescribed one-month suspect period prior to the request to open proceedings. The subsequent payment would also have been invalid as a disposition made

[10] Case C-557/13 *Hermann Lutz v Elke Bäuerle* ECLI:EU:C:2015:227 [2015].

after insolvency proceedings were opened under section 81 of the same Code. By contrast, if Austrian law applied, the liquidator's challenge would have been time-barred by section 43 paras 1 and 2 of the Austrian Insolvency Code, which provide that actions to set aside transactions must be brought within a year of opening insolvency proceedings, failing which they become time-barred. The German court, however, considered that the Defendant would only have been entitled to raise this defence if the payment of 17 March 2009 fell within the scope of what is now Article 16 of the Insolvency Regulation Recast. Accordingly, the German *Bundesgerichtshof* requested a preliminary ruling on, *inter alia*, the question of whether an Article 16 defence may be raised in respect of an act that occurred after the opening of insolvency proceedings.

The CJEU answered this question in the negative. However, the CJEU continued that, in the present case, whilst the payment itself had been made *after* the opening of insolvency proceedings, thereby precluding a defence based on Article 16; the basis of the payment could also have been the right to attach, which had accrued *prior* to the opening of insolvency proceedings. If, under the *lex situs*, a right to attach the credit standing to a bank account were in essence an exclusive right as against the other creditors to have a claim met by the object of attachment, such right could constitute a right *in rem* within the scope of what is now Article 8 para 1. From this, the CJEU further ruled that such right to attach could, in principle, benefit from the protections conferred by Article 8 and, therefore, Article 16.

Thus, on the assumption that the right to attach was indeed a right *in rem*, the CJEU referred to what is now Recital 68 and Article 8 to note that the Regulation 'shall not affect' rights *in rem* already accrued before the opening of insolvency proceedings. As such, a creditor relying on Article 8 would be entitled to do so, both before and after insolvency proceedings have been opened, to protect a right *in rem* established before the opening of insolvency proceedings. Accordingly, the CJEU held that Article 16 must be interpreted as 'applying to a situation in which a payment, challenged by an insolvency administrator, of a sum of money attached before the opening of the insolvency proceedings was made only after the opening of those proceedings'.

Insofar as *Lutz v Bäuerle* concerned the credit standing to a bank account, it remains unexceptional as a matter of property law. It is hardly contentious that attachment orders over such bank accounts may have an effect *in rem* and, as such, engage Article 8. Nor is it controversial that, pursuant to Article 2 para 9 (iii) of the Insolvency Regulation Recast, the credit standing to a bank account is situate in the Member State 'indicated in the account's IBAN, in which the credit institution holding the account has its central administration, or in which the branch, agency, or other establishment with which the account is held is located'. Accordingly, apart from the temporal aspects of the facts, there is little that is remarkable in itself about an Austrian creditor raising an Article 16 defence in asserting a right *in rem* to the credit standing to a bank account situate in Austria under Article 8, where primary insolvency proceedings had been opened in Germany.

By contrast, the same factual matrix with the single substitution of a quantity of bitcoin held directly for the bank account immediately calls into question whether Article 8, and by extension Article 16, is engaged at all. The most immediate and obvious question, which continues to divide jurisdictions around the world, is whether bitcoin can be the object of an attachment or other rights *in rem*. Even if, however, that question were answered in the affirmative, it leads immediately to the equally difficult question of where the bitcoin is then situate such that it is without the scope of the primary proceedings opened in Germany and subject to the law of another EU Member State.

Although these two issues are of considerable significance, this contribution will not address them in any depth. As private law matters that engage policy considerations at the most fundamental level in both property law and private international law, they are well beyond the scope of insolvency law, which, moreover, has its own unique set of policy objectives with which it is concerned. In this respect, it cannot be said that insolvency law has any more a pressing need than private law has itself for clarity on the property status of bitcoin and the situation of bitcoin for the purpose of those rules of private international law that refer to the *situs*.

As such, this chapter leaves these two matters to the on-going debates in their respective fields of law;[11] and focusses instead on an equally important and technical point of property law that tends not to receive much independent treatment in property law itself, has neither received any attention in the crypto-private law discourse, but is of unique significance in the insolvency context. It is in this respect that *Lutz v Bäuerle* is noteworthy in highlighting an important issue of private law that will be of particular concern for insolvency practitioners engaged in crypto insolvencies. As the Schmidt Report makes clear, the protections conferred by Article 8, both before and during the insolvency proceedings, are limited to rights *in rem* that existed prior to the opening of such proceedings.[12] This, in turn, raises a critical question: when does a person acquire a right *in rem* in bitcoin such that it may be said to have accrued before insolvency proceedings were opened, or better yet, before any relevant suspect period began?

[11] See, eg, A Held, 'The modern property situationship: Is bitcoin better off (left) alone? (2024) 20(2) *Journal of Private International Law* 391–436' and A Held, '(Digital) Things as Objects of Property Rights: What Can Crypto Learn from Comparative Law?' (2024) *Oxford Journal of Legal Studies*, gqae034, https://doi.org/10.1093/ojls/gqae034. See also n 15.

[12] Schmit Report to the Insolvency Convention Para 103:

> In order to facilitate the application of the Convention and avoid doubts Article 5(2) provides a list of types of rights that are normally considered by national laws as rights in rem. This list is inspired in two main considerations. The first, that a right which exists only after insolvency proceedings have been opened, but not before, is not a right in rem for the purposes of Article 5 (which protect pre-existing rights).

Note that Article 5 of the Convention is Article 8 of the Regulation Recast.

III. The Approach to the Question

As already intimated, the question of *when* a right *in rem* is validly transferred, created, or acquired does not generally attract much specialised attention in the broader property law discourse. In civilian jurisdictions, it is often overshadowed by or subsumed under the broader question of *how* ownership is transferred; whereas, in common law jurisdictions, it tends to feature indirectly as an incidental question preliminary to ascertaining the order of priority as between competing interests in the asset in dispute, or to the question of the passing of risk as between a buyer and seller in a contract for the sale of goods. The issue is also somewhat protean in both civilian and common law systems of property law in that it takes on slightly different guises of terminology, depending on the specific context and object of the right in question.

Superimposed upon these complexities at the national level are the difficulties that arise when the question is considered in the international or cross-border context. Here, the analysis will rarely proceed without at least some presumptions and premises rooted in specific traditions of property law. The present discussion is no exception, suffering as it does at the most basic level of terminology for the object of its inquiry; with the use of 'rights *in rem*' thus far distinctly prejudicial to common law systems of property law in favour of their civilian counterparts. Such biases are all the more problematic in the present context where, as noted, there remain equally unresolved problems of private international law as to what law, as identified by the *situs*, even governs the question of whether bitcoin may be the object of 'rights *in rem*'.[13]

Whilst the substantive private law applicable to crypto assets remains, thus, significantly underdeveloped, for present purposes, the general trend towards recognising such assets as objects of rights *in rem* suffices as a premise from which an analysis of *when* such a right *in rem* is acquired in respect of bitcoin need not necessarily be left at an impasse. As already intimated, this contribution does not seek to pre-empt the development of specific substantive rules of law applicable to property disputes concerning bitcoin, but has a rather more modest objective of setting out an approach according to which such rules might be best developed. Nevertheless, to avoid framing the discussion in terms that may – however inadvertently – presume the application of certain principles of property law or favour one legal system over the other, this contribution proceeds using a two-stage methodology, as follows.

The first stage involves reframing the basic question of 'had the right *in rem* accrued before insolvency proceedings were opened?' as it arises in the insolvency

[13] In cross-border property disputes, courts consistently depart from the general rule that the *lex fori* governs issues of characterisation, and apply the *lex situs* instead. See A Held, 'Cryptoassets and Decentralised Ledgers: Does Situs Actually Matter?' in M Lehmann, A Bonomi and S Lalani (eds), *Blockchain and Private International Law* (Leiden, Brill, 2023), fns 2 and 3.

context into more the neutral terms of '*when* – if ever – does the acquisition of a right relating to bitcoin become valid against persons generally?'

Such reframing is advantageous for two main reasons. First, it retains the essential characteristic of property law, consistent across jurisdictions, as a legal discipline concerned with rights in relation to objects that are valid against persons generally rather than against a specific person.[14] Second, such phrasing does not presume legal context, jurisdiction, nor classification within the property or private law taxonomies. This helpfully circumvents the unresolved fundamental question as to whether bitcoin is an object in which rights *in rem* may subsist; and instead facilitates a more focused consideration on the 'when' aspect of the alleged rights such that they are effective on insolvency, without undue distraction by the 'what' aspect per se.

The second stage involves then addressing this reframed question through substantive comparison with other asset types to ascertain what relevant principles may be extrapolated from the existing rules to inform potential solutions by analogy.

Before embarking on the analysis thus, it is worth clarifying that the question is examined in the context of direct node-to-node transactions in the native crypto asset of a public decentralised ledger network; with no crypto intermediaries, such as exchanges or custodians, involved. Hence, the paradigm facts under consideration are a challenge to a bitcoin transaction recorded directly on the blockchain as a redistribution of unspent transaction outputs ('UTXO') amongst the public addresses of the bitcoin network in circumstances where the transferring node has become insolvent and the claim for claw back is made directly against the recipient node.

IV. When Does the Acquisition of a Right in Bitcoin Become Valid against Persons Generally?

Four precedents are offered for examining the question of when, if ever, the acquisition of a right in bitcoin might be said to become valid against persons generally,

[14] Whilst the common law and civilian law systems reach this conclusion in slightly different ways, it is common amongst comparatists that the hallmark of private property law is the right valid, not against a specific person or specific class of persons, but against persons generally. In civilian jurisdictions, the preferred expression tends to be 'rights valid *erga omnes*' which is implicit in the nature of rights *in rem*: given that these subsist in the object as it moves from hand to hand, the holder of the right is entitled to assert it against anyone into whose hands the object goes. See, eg, the Schlosser Report to the Brussels Convention, para 166; and the Schmit Report to the Insolvency Convention, para 103. In common law systems, the principle is expressly part of the definition of property law as concerned with 'rights binding third parties to its creation'. Hence, the property right at common law is binding against 'all the world', whereas property rights in equity are binding only 'against all the world, except the *bona fide* purchaser for value without notice'. To accommodate both the civilian and common law positions, the expression 'valid against persons generally' is here preferred.

such that it gives rise to a right to segregation effective in insolvency: (1) what are called 'things in action' in common law jurisdictions and 'claims' in civilian jurisdictions; (2) what are called 'things in possession' in common law jurisdictions and 'corporeal movables' in civilian jurisdictions; (3) registered assets; and (4) book-entry securities. These do not mirror strictly the existing taxonomies of private property law nor classifications used in other legal contexts but are focussed on the substantive features of the assets themselves as legal objects. At this stage, the focus remains on elucidating potential rules, rather than weighing their relative merits.

A. Things in Action/Claims

Things in action/claims are the most complex of the precedents here examined, insofar as they attract considerably different treatment across legal systems. Approaches to fundamental issues such as basic classification within the overarching scheme of private law vary considerably, with a marked divergence on the specific question of whether things in action/claims may in themselves be objects of property rights. Here, the ontological difference between common law and civilian law systems of property comes to the fore.[15]

Nevertheless, to the extent that property law is concerned with rights in relation to an object that is valid against persons generally, there is a broad consensus amongst jurisdictions that where there is a contract between an assignor and assignee to transfer the benefit of performance, such agreement may become valid and enforceable directly as against the obligor, a third party to that contract, upon notice to him. Prior to such notification, the assignment remains valid only as between assignor and assignee[16] at least insofar as the obligor may continue to be validly discharged by performance to the assignor as the original obligee. Thus, the general rule for things in action/claims is that the acquisition of rights in relation to these objects becomes valid against persons generally by 'perfecting' the right by notice.[17] Where there are competing claims for performance against the obligor, such as in the case of multiple assignments, the first to give notice tends to prevail.[18]

Prima facie, things in action/claims merit special attention; not only because these objects are also intangible/incorporeal as a matter of fact, but also because the mechanism for the 'transfer and acquisition' of these objects tends to be consistently recognised, even in those jurisdictions that deny recognition of the

[15] See section V below. See further/generally A Held, '(Digital) Things as Objects of Property Rights: What Can Crypto Learn from Comparative Law?' [2024] *Oxford Journal of Legal Studies*, gqae034, https://doi.org/10.1093/ojls/gqae034.

[16] In some jurisdictions, this may well have real effects, but this remains conceptualised under civilian concepts of property law as a body of law concerned with the relationship between a person and a *res*.

[17] Sections 398, 407, 409 *Bürgerliches Gesetzbuch* (Germany); Arts 1690 and 1691 *Code Civil* (France); s 136 para 1 Law of Property Act 1925 (England and Wales).

[18] See, eg, in England and Wales, *Dearle v Hall* (1828) 3 Russ 1.

underlying objects themselves as objects of property rights.[19] Nevertheless, the utility of things in action/claims as a precedent from which rules for crypto assets may be developed is limited, owing to the extent that assignment remains a *sui generis* solution to the *sui generis* problems that arise from the fundamental nature of things in action/claims as a legal object.

For most of western legal history, it was not possible for the obligee of a personal obligation to transfer unilaterally the benefit of performance to a stranger to that obligation; a 'personal' obligation to repay a sum of money was strictly personal as between the original creditor and the original debtor[20] in exactly the same way that marital obligations are – and today remain – personal as between spouses.[21] The only way to effect a result comparable to the transfer of a freely alienable object was for the obligor to be released from the original obligation owed to the original obligee and undertake a new obligation to the intended transferee.[22] Given, however, that the relative complexities of novation rendered it a cumbersome procedure, the modern technique of assignment developed as a more streamlined means to achieve the same economic result in support of an emerging capitalist economy.[23]

As such, the rules of assignment are very much tailored to these specific circumstances of facilitating a legally effective transfer, directly from a transferor to a transferee, of an object that, by law, could not be transferred thus beyond the original two parties to its creation at all. Accordingly, the rule that the transfer and acquisition of rights relating to things in action/claims become valid against

[19] This is usually on the basis that claims are intangible/incorporeal. The German Civil Code remains the paradigm example of a system of property rights strictly limited to corporeal objects; see ss 90 and 903 *Bürgerliches Gesetzbuch* and the accompanying commentary, eg, B Brückner, 's 903' in FJ Säcker et al, *Münchener Kommentar zum Bürgerlichen Gesetzbuch*, 9th edn (Munich, CH Beck, 2023). Nevertheless, German law does recognise the assignment of claims under ss 398, 407, 409 BGB; a right of pledge in incorporeal objects under s 1068 BGB; and a right of usufruct in respect of claims under s 1273 BGB.

[20] This position dates from Roman law, see C Lebon, 'Property Rights in Respect of Claims' in S van Erp and B Akkermans (eds) *Cases, Materials, and Text on Property Law* (London, Hart Publishing, 2012) II.B.2.a, 398, fn 39 and text.

[21] This very proposition featured and was indirectly considered at the highest level in England and Wales in *National Provincial Bank v Ainsworth* [1965] 1 AC 1175. For a concise summary of the case and its implications for English property law, see A Held, 'Cryptoassets as Property Under English Law: Surveying the Present Lie of the Land' [2022] *Journal of International Banking & Financial Law* 538.

[22] Gai Inst II, ss 38–39. Gaius further notes that obligations are not susceptible to the modes of transfer used for the *res corporales* and *res incorporales*, the latter referring to rights *in rem* such as servitudes and usufruct, not things in action/claims.

[23] In England, at least, the prototypes of the modern technique of assignment were apparent in commercial practice by the 15th century but remained effective at law only by means of a judicial fiction even at the time of Blackstone. It would not be until the late 19th century that s 25 para 6 of the Judicature Act 1873, now s 136 of the Law of Property Act 1925 (UK), prescribed a statutory method of assigning debts. See further A Held, 'Crypto-Financial Assets in a DLT-Based Market Infrastructure: Legal Principles of Ownership and Obligation' (2019) MLS Law Library, 3–4, fns 4–7 hdl.handle.net/11343/274809. For the role of contract in supporting the capitalist economy, see generally PS Atiyah, *The Rise and Fall of Freedom of Contract* (Oxford, Clarendon Press, 1979, 1986 [printing]); and J Commons: 'Modern capitalism begins with the assignment and negotiability of contracts' J Commons (ed), *The Legal Foundations of Capitalism* (London, The Macmillan Company, 1924) 253.

persons generally upon notice to the original obligor is not helpful for the present analysis; which simply is not concerned with an object grounded in the relationship between two identified persons and which cannot, therefore, be removed from this specific personal context without the assistance of special legal provisions. Put another way, the rule cannot be applied to the acquisition of rights in bitcoin because there is no 'original obligor' to whom such notice should or could be given. Nor does bitcoin, as an object that effectively moves from one public address to another as a matter of fact, require any legal means to facilitate transfer and acquisition at the most basic level of what happens 'on the ground'. This fundamental difference in the empirical nature of the object goes a long way to rationalise why the rules applicable to things in action/claims, including those of private international law applicable to the corresponding category of intangibles/incorporeal movables, find no logical application to crypto assets.[24] In both private law and private international law, mere incorporeality or intangibility as a similarity in fact emerges as an insufficient basis from which legal analogies to things in action/claims may be drawn.

Things in action/claims do not, therefore, serve as a useful precedent from which substantive principles may be extrapolated and applied to the question under present consideration. Nevertheless, things in action/claims do serve an equally valuable function in highlighting the importance of looking beyond formal categories and rather focussing on substance to determine the extent to which a precedent is useful when developing a legal framework for new and novel economic objects. As such, whilst there has sometimes been significant recourse in the contemporary crypto-legal discourse to things in action/claims and the parallel categories of intangibles/incorporeal movables as the appropriate property classification for bitcoin and other digital assets more broadly, these are rather useful reminders against such mechanistic recourse to form over substance.

B. Things in Possession/Corporeal Movables

Things in possession/corporeal movables prove to be a more promising precedent in that crypto assets effectively move from one public address to another through use of the private key with almost the same ease with which things in possession/corporeal movables pass from one hand to another. Thus, it is no coincidence that, in the technology sphere, it is said that the private keys lie 'at the root of all ownership in the Bitcoin system'.[25] Nor is it surprising that the initiatives on the private law of digital assets to date tend to proceed on the assumption that the person who has lawfully acquired control over a crypto asset, usually by knowledge of the

[24] For a discussion, see Held (n 13).

[25] AM Antonopoulos, *Mastering Bitcoin: Programming the Open Blockchain*, 2nd edn (California, O'Reilly Media, 2017) 58.

private key, is its 'owner'.[26] Implicit in both propositions is an identification with the general rule for things in possession/corporeal movables, largely consistent across jurisdictions, that possession conveys at least a presumption of title, if not conferring an absolute title outright.[27]

As a legal precedent for the present inquiry, however, things in possession/corporeal movables are not entirely straightforward, as the question of when the acquisition of a right in respect of these objects becomes valid against persons generally is answered differently across legal systems. The approaches taken, however, may be categorised into three main types of transfer systems that are used for things in possession/corporeal movables: causal consensual systems; casual tradition/delivery systems; and abstract delivery systems. These systems are plotted across two broad axes: casual systems stand in contrast to abstract systems; and consensual systems stand in contrast to tradition/delivery systems. Of these, only the distinction between consensual and tradition/delivery systems is of present relevance.[28]

In sum, tradition/delivery systems require that possession of the object be delivered to effect the valid acquisition of property rights.[29] Consensual systems, on the other hand, do not require such delivery; the acquisition of property rights is effected through the conclusion of the *causa traditionis*, or 'legal cause' for the acquisition itself. Thus, under Austrian law, a causal tradition system, a contract for the sale of a corporeal movable, such as a car, requires both a valid contract of sale[30] plus delivery of the car sold[31] before ownership in the car passes from seller to buyer.[32] Thus, in *Lutz v Baüerle*, the Defendant did not acquire ownership in

[26] See, eg, UK Jurisdiction Taskforce, 'Legal Statement on Cryptoassets and Smart Contracts', (November 2019) 43 technation.io/lawtech-uk- resources/#cryptoassets. The Draft UNIDROIT Principles on Digital Assets and Private Law is less explicit in this respect, but strongly presumes that control, as a functional equivalent of possession, gives rise to proprietary rights in itself, particularly in Principle 8 and its rule on innocent acquisition. See www.unidroit.org/wp-content/uploads/2023/01/Draft-Principles-and-Commentary-Public-Consultation.pdf.

[27] French law notably takes the strictest position in this respect; Art 2276 of the French *Code Civil* provides that, for movables, possession confers title. In England and Wales, possession of an object in itself vests in the possessor a (relative) possessory title good against persons generally, with the exception of those who claim under a better title, see *Costello v Chief Constable of Derbyshire Constabulary* [2001] EWCA Civ 338.

[28] In abstract systems of transfer, the juridical act establishing the *causa traditionis*/legal cause for the transfer (eg, gift, contract of sale, etc) is wholly distinct from the juridical act that transfers property rights, whereas in causal systems the two are linked. The key difference that arises between the two systems is seen where the causal act is found to be invalid (eg, the contract is void for formal reasons) after the property right has been transferred. In abstract systems, the invalidity of the cause does not invalidate the transfer of property rights; whereas, in causal systems, the invalidity of the cause also invalidates its property effects. For a good account of the various systems from a comparative perspective, see L van Vliet, 'Transfer of Movable Property' in JM Smits (ed), *Elgar Encyclopaedia of Comparative Law*, 2nd edn (Cheltenham, Edward Elgar Publishing, 2012).

[29] This delivery of possession remains valid generally only for corporeal movables; for immovables, the second act of transferring/acquiring property has been largely transposed to the act of registration.

[30] *Allgemeines Bürgerliches Gesetzbuch* (Austria), s 380.

[31] *Allgemeines Bürgerliches Gesetzbuch* (Austria), s 426.

[32] *Allgemeines Bürgerliches Gesetzbuch* (Austria), s 1053 restates the principles set out in ss 380 and 426 in the context of sales contracts specifically.

the car, notwithstanding a valid contract of sale and due payment of the purchase price. By contrast, under French law, a *solo consensu* or 'consensus alone' system,[33] a contract of sale validly concluded suffices in itself for ownership of the object being sold to vest in the buyer.[34] These rules on transfer determine the rights and remedies of the buyer and seller, as well as those of third parties to the contract of sale, should either buyer or seller become insolvent before the object of sale has been delivered or purchase price paid.

Hence, the relevant rules for the purpose of the present inquiry are that the acquisition of rights in things in possession/corporeal movables becomes valid against persons generally when (1) possession is delivered (tradition/delivery transfer systems); or (2) when the cause for the acquisition of rights becomes legally effective (consensus transfer systems). Neither the consensual nor tradition/delivery system, however, transposes easily into the crypto asset context.

The obvious difficulty with applying the principles underpinning the tradition/delivery system is the requirement that possession of the object be delivered to the transferee. If this is taken literally, bitcoin, nor any other digital asset, could never be accommodated within a tradition/delivery system of transfer for the simple reason that, as incorporeal objects, they are not amenable to a physical transfer of possession. A more nuanced understanding of possession as a legal construct, however, demonstrates that this need not necessarily prove fatal. It is, for example, largely uncontroversial in the contemporary digital assets discourse that, whilst it is difficult to reconcile the concept of possession as rooted in corporeal fact with the incorporeal nature of digital assets; an analogous concept of control might be applied to this new class of incorporeal objects.[35]

Such concession is, however, by no means novel, and simply reiterates the traditional understanding of possession as ultimately, notwithstanding its empirical dimension, a legal construct relative to its object. This is reflected in the various circumstances, recognised as early as Roman law, in which the requirement of physical delivery for the vesting of property rights is attenuated in line with the empirical features of the object in question. Thus, for immovables and other objects not amenable to total manual control, such as land or the textbook pile of logs, pointing out the object from the top of the nearby tower constitutes a long-handed delivery/*traditio longa manu* that suffices for the delivery of possession. Similarly, a symbolic delivery/*traditio symbolica* of all the goods stored in a warehouse might entail the delivery of the keys, whereas the transfer of clumps of

[33] The principle is stated in general terms in Arts 1138 and 711 of the French *Code Civil*. It is reiterated in relation to specific legal causes for the transfer, eg, Art 1583 for contracts of sale; Art 938 for gifts; Art 1703 for barter.

[34] Article 1583 *Code Civil* (France).

[35] See Section III of the Draft UNIDROIT Principles and its focus on the control, in particular, Paragraph 1 of the Commentary to Principle 6. See also Legal Statement UK Jurisdiction Taskforce, 'Legal Statement on Cryptoassets and Smart Contracts' (November 2019) 43.

earth would suffice for a symbolic delivery of land.[36] Such principles remain today features of the civilian codes and the English common law.[37]

Hence, if it is accepted that control of certain bitcoin via knowledge of the relevant private key is sufficiently comparable to possession of a corporeal movable, an application of the rules underpinning tradition/delivery systems of transfer leads to the conclusion that the acquisition of rights in bitcoin become effective against persons generally when the relevant control is delivered or conceded by arrangements relating to the corresponding private keys. The consensual system of transfer, on the other hand, lends itself to a more straightforward application in the bitcoin context: the acquisition of rights would simply become effective against persons generally upon the valid conclusion of a legal cause by the parties to create or transfer the right in question.

C. Registered Assets

'Registered assets' is not a category recognised in any property taxonomy but is offered here for those objects in respect of which the question of legal entitlements is answered by reference to registration in a definitive register constitutive, as opposed to merely declaratory, of legal rights. Assets in this category therefore include land/immovables in most jurisdictions, ships, aircraft, registered shares in companies, patents, registered trade-marks, and increasingly, security interests in non-land assets.[38]

To these, we might add bitcoin. By focussing the emphasis on the blockchain as a definitive ledger of transaction histories and recording the consequent distribution of unspent transaction outputs (UTXO) across all nodes, bitcoin is amenable to characterisation as a registered asset in respect of which the blockchain operates as the register definitively recording the 'spend entitlements' of each participating node. In this conceptualisation of the legal object, the private key does not hold the same overriding importance as it does for the things in possession/corporeal movables form as the indicia of possession/control. Rather, in the registered asset form, use of the private key functions as the means of registration, akin to the process of executing a share transfer form and delivering it to the company

[36] For an account of the medieval ceremony of livery of seisin in England, see K Gray and SF Gray, *Elements of Land Law*, 5th edn (Oxford, Oxford University Press, 2009) 2.1.5 and especially fn 2. The concept, as a right to possession, shares a common history with the French *saisine* and Germanic *Gewere*.

[37] See generally M Hinteregger and L van Vliet, 'Transfer' in S van Erp and B Akkermans (eds), *Cases, Materials and Text on Property Law* (London, Hart Publishing, 2012) I.D 813 et seq.

[38] It has been recognised for some decades already that there is a general trend of moving away from delivery of possession to fulfil the traditional publicity requirements and towards a system whereby security interests are perfected by registration. See EM Kieninger, 'Evaluation: A Common Core?' in EM Kieninger (ed), *Security Rights In Moveable Property in European Private Law* (Cambridge, Cambridge University Press, 2004) 652.

registrar in a transfer of registered shares, or an application to the land register in respect of interests in land.

Although this makeshift category comprises thus a range of seemingly miscellaneous asset types spanning all three familiar categories of the property taxonomies, the relevant legal rule they have in common is prima facie simple: acquisition of the relevant rights in these objects becomes effective against persons generally when the right is constituted by due registration.[39] This simple formulation of the rule, however, belies the nuances and legal artifice involved in defining the moment when a right is deemed 'duly registered'.

For example, in England and Wales, the Land Registration Act 2002 provides that the registrable disposition of a registered estate in land must be completed by entry of the disponee in the Land Register as the new proprietor of the relevant interest.[40] The transfer is, thus, not final and effective at law until the registrar has entered the name of the disponee in the register as the new proprietor.[41] This, however, is not taken literally as the moment in fact when the register is updated; entries are dated retrospectively with an effective date of registration, which is defined as the time of application[42] (ie, the time at which the application for registration is lodged at the Land Register). Rounding off these provisions at law lies the position in equity. Generally, in a sale of title to land, a vendor-purchaser constructive trust is imposed upon the valid exchange of contracts, which creates an obligation on the vendor to transfer title that is specifically enforceable in equity.[43] The effect is that the purchaser acquires rights in the land that are enforceable against persons generally upon the exchange of contracts of sale,[44] albeit within the more limited scope of equity.[45]

Thus, defining the moment at which the acquisition of right is 'duly registered' for the purposes of the law is open to myriad possibilities, most of which will not reflect the chronology of events surrounding entry on the register as a matter of sheer empirical fact. Keeping this firmly in mind, the next question in the present analysis is to define the precise moment when a bitcoin transaction is 'entered on the blockchain register' such that the transferee's spend entitlement to the sum of the quantum transferred is effective against persons generally.

[39] Registers that are merely declaratory operate, of course, differently.

[40] Land Registration Act 2002 (England and Wales), s 27(1)–(2) and Sch 2.

[41] Land Registration Act 2002 (England and Wales), para 2(1), Sch 2.

[42] Land Registration Act 2002 (England and Wales), s 74.

[43] *Lysaght v Edwards* (1876) 2 Ch D 499, 506.

[44] Although this rule of equity is valid only for those objects in respect of which specific performance of the contract is available (ie, objects of sale for which damages would not be an adequate remedy on breach), the general principle is in line with the consensual systems of transfer for corporeal movables. However, the general class of persons against whom the right is valid differs in equity; see n 45 below.

[45] The general rule is that equitable rights are exigible against persons generally, but with the exception of the bona fide purchaser for value of a legal estate without actual, constructive, or imputed notice of the equitable right. The position is substantively similar to the 'good faith purchaser/acquirer' defence recognised in many civilian jurisdictions in respect of corporeal movables; by contrast, English law applies a strict *nemo dat* rule at law to things in possession.

Whilst it might be intuitive to consider that a spend entitlement should be recognised as 'duly registered' on the blockchain once the corresponding transaction is successfully included in a block, the conventions recognised in various crypto asset communities suggest otherwise. Taking into account the idiosyncrasies of the underlying technologies, such as simple forks,[46] these conventions generally refer to the number of confirmations a transaction must have, ie, the number of successive blocks on which a particular transaction is included on the blockchain, before the recipient's entitlement to spend the amount received is deemed secure. For bitcoin, six confirmations are the general standard for a transaction to be considered secure,[47] although many exchanges require only three.[48] By contrast, the Ethereum Whitepaper suggests that seven confirmations are sufficient before a recipient may spend a transfer of ether, although miners are required to confirm the parameters of the previous 250 blocks when propagating a new block.[49]

Accordingly, a proposed rule based on registered assets might be that the acquisition of rights in bitcoin becomes effective against persons generally upon the requisite number of confirmations, in accordance with the applicable convention for blockchain finality, of the transaction in question.

D. Book-Entry Securities

Book-entry securities 'held' in the securities settlement systems fall under the broader category of 'registered asset' above yet warrant separate consideration given that they are often subject to a distinct legal regime. In the EU, the Settlement Finality Directive[50] provides that the acquisition of rights in book-entry securities have effect against persons generally in the specific sense of being insolvency-proof when the relevant transfer order is entered into the settlement system.[51] This point in time is left to be defined by the rules of the settlement system itself;[52] as is the point at which a transfer order can no longer be revoked by a participant of the system nor by third parties.[53] Mirror provisions are found in the Central Securities

[46] Simple forks typically occur when two winning blocks are near-simultaneously propagated when extending the blockchain, and are relatively common and unproblematic: the fork is typically resolved within one block, with any transactions on the orphan block released into the mempool to be included in the next block. See further Antonopoulos (n 25) 468.

[47] Antonopoulos (n 25) 28.

[48] buybitcoinworldwide.com/confirmations/.

[49] ethereum.stackexchange.com/questions/319/what-number-of-confirmations-is-considered-secure-in-ethereum.

[50] Directive 98/26/EC of the European Parliament and of the Council of 19 May 1998 on settlement finality in payment and securities settlement systems [1998] OJ L166/45 ('SFD').

[51] SFD, Art 3 para 1.

[52] SFD, Art 3 para 3.

[53] SFD, Art 5.

Depositories Regulation,[54] which further provides that issuers established in the EU must arrange for securities admitted to trading venues to be represented in book-entry form.[55]

Hence, whilst a book-entry security is broadly a registered asset as defined above, the rules differ in that the EU regime focuses – at least as a matter of law – on a sightly prior moment in time to many registration models: the point at which the transfer order is entered into the system, rather than the slightly later moment in time when the register itself is updated accordingly. Just as, however, the factually 'later' moment of 'entry into the register' may well, for legal purposes, be retrospectively dated to the moment when the application for entry is lodged or received by the registrar; the factually 'prior' moment of in time relevant for book-entry securities is just as open to legal artifice for the purposes of the law. However, book-entry securities warrant separate consideration in that they give rise to a further criterion relevant to the formulation of a legal rule: the Settlement Finality Directive leaves it to the rules of the settlement system to define, not only when a transfer order is 'entered into the settlement system,' but also when a transfer order can no longer be revoked. The considerations surrounding revocation are apparent also in English equity: in *Re Rose*,[56] the court held that a gift of registrable shares imposes a constructive trust in favour of the donee once the donor has done all that is necessary on his part to effect the transfer of property at law. On the facts of the case, this was held to be the moment in time when the donor duly completed the share transfer form and arranged for them to be sent to the company for registration, and could no longer revoke or cancel the transfer.

Applying these concepts in the bitcoin context, one clear event in the idiosyncratic process of effecting a bitcoin transaction emerges as a contender for the point at which it is no longer possible for a transferor to revoke a 'transfer order' once it is 'entered into' the blockchain 'settlement system'. All on-chain transfers of bitcoin begin with a transfer message duly signed with the private key that is broadcast to the entire network of nodes for initial validation. If the message passes this first cryptographic test, it will then await in the mempool as an unconfirmed transaction for further processing by a miner. If it does not, it will automatically be rejected. Hence, if passing this first stage of cryptographic validation by the network is accepted as the analogous point at which a 'transfer order' is 'entered into' the bitcoin system, it may technically be revoked at any time during which the unconfirmed transaction awaits in the mempool for processing by a miner, but before the first confirmation of the transaction on the blockchain.[57] Thus, a

[54] Regulation (EU) No 909/2014 of the European Parliament and of the Council of 23 July 2014 on improving securities settlement in the European Union and on central securities depositories and amending Directives 98/26/EC and 2014/65/EU and Regulation (EU) No 236/2012 [2014] OJ L257/1 ('CSDR'), Art 39 paras 2 and 3.

[55] CSDR, Art 3.

[56] [1952] EWCA Civ 4.

[57] See, eg, buybitcoinworldwide.com/confirmations/ and bitcoinist.com/can-you-cancel-unconfirmed-bitcoin-transactions-yes-heres-how/.

rule based on an analogy to book-entry securities would be that the acquisition of rights in bitcoin becomes valid against persons generally upon the first confirmation of the transaction on the blockchain.

V. The Core Legal Challenge

Four possible rules thus emerge for answering the question of when the acquisition of a right in bitcoin becomes valid against persons generally:

1. When control over the relevant bitcoin is delivered or conceded by arrangements relating to the corresponding private keys (analogy to the tradition/delivery system for things in possession/corporeal movables).
2. Upon the valid conclusion of a legal cause by the parties to create or transfer the right in the relevant bitcoin (analogy to the consensual system for things in possession/corporeal movables).
3. Upon the requisite number of confirmations on the blockchain, in accordance with the applicable convention for blockchain finality, of the transaction (analogy to registered assets).
4. Upon the first confirmation of the transaction on the blockchain (analogy to book-entry securities).

At this point, it is worth the reminder that this chapter does not intend to weigh the relative merits of these possible solutions for the purpose of recommendation. This brief survey of just four precedents illustrates why it would be premature at this stage to go further than propose an approach to be taken: each of the potential legal rules proposed in Part IV are premised upon taking up particular positions in the on-going debates on more fundamental property law issues.

Of these, one core outstanding legal issue is abstracting from the relevant empirical features a definitive legal form for the object. Is bitcoin, as a legal as opposed to factual object, a new intangible type of thing in possession/incorporeal movable through a focus on the private key as signifying control/possession? Or is bitcoin a registered asset in law, on the basis that the blockchain record is the more significant of its technical features? If it is an intangible thing in possession/incorporeal movable, what is the precise relationship between control and 'ownership', and what is the role of the blockchain record? If it is a registered asset, which of the two models for registered assets considered is the more apposite? In this respect, the author has previously said that the critical consideration will be to strike the right balance between the private key and blockchain as two constituent and intertwined components of the underlying decentralised ledger technology; which is particularly challenging insofar as they refer to different precedents in property law.[58] Such challenge is apparent in the foregoing analysis: whilst there

[58] See A Held, 'Private Keys v Blockchains: What *is* a Cryptoasset in Law?' [2020] *Journal of International Banking and Finance Law* 247.

are compelling arguments for each of the possible proposed rules, none are wholly satisfactory.

For example, recourse to the tradition/delivery systems for things in possession/corporeal movables through an analogy with knowledge of the private key is highly intuitive. It is also easily applied to certain types of transactions, such as secured transactions effected by multi-sig arrangements. Nevertheless, it is difficult to apply the precedent consistently across all use cases of bitcoin; in particular, its logic applies slightly differently in the most basic transaction of an on-chain transfer from one public address to another. In this context, 'delivery' is not effected by the transferor conceding to the transferee the requisite knowledge of the private key that controls the 'transferor' public address; rather, the transferor, by using that private key, causes the transferee's public address, controlled by its own private key, to be registered with a higher spend entitlement. Accordingly, the question of when the transferee acquires control over the sum transferred through attribution to the corresponding public address cannot be answered other than by reference to the blockchain. If this is so, it is open to question whether an analogy to possession and things in possession/corporeal movables remains the preferable approach.

Applying the precedent of registered assets by favouring an emphasis on the blockchain is equally intuitive. It is also easily applied to the basic on-chain transfer of bitcoin from one public address to another, as well as to more sophisticated transactions, such as secured transactions implemented on the blockchain through the use of coloured coins or escrow public addresses. Nevertheless, the precedent is also equally not without significant difficulty.

It is worth immediately clarifying that the difficulty is not, as the argument often goes, that finality can never be achieved on a public blockchain because, in this context, 'settlement is not final but probabilistic: it simply becomes more final the more times the transaction is committed to the ledger'.[59] The foregoing analyses of registered assets succinctly illustrates that the point at which an entry in the register becomes 'duly registered' in law is often divorced from the moment when the registrar updates the register in fact. Thus, the point at which a registered right thus becomes legally effective against persons generally is and will always remain a legal construct for the courts or legislator to define.

In this respect, book-entry securities provide a particularly instructive example. Unlike decentralised ledgers, the transaction records of the settlement systems are not designed to be technically immutable. As such, transactions in book-entry securities, once entered into the records of the settlement systems, are technically reversible at any point as a matter of fact. Nevertheless, the legal effect of the Settlement Finality Directive is that transactions entered into the relevant system are *de jure* finally binding on persons generally after a defined point in time. Accordingly, whilst the underlying records may well be *de facto* reversible,

[59] International Securities Services Association (ISSA), 'Infrastructure for Crypto-Assets: A Review for Infrastructure Providers' (October 2018) 19.

the legal position is such that the records of the settlement systems as a matter of law might as well be as immutable as a decentralised ledger is as a matter of fact. Hence, by parity of reasoning, that settlement on a decentralised ledger can only ever be probabilistic only as a matter of fact, does not necessarily mean settlement on a decentralised ledger can never be final as a matter of law.

Hence, the core difficulty with applying the rules for registered assets by analogy to bitcoin lies not in the fact of probabilistic settlement; but in the inverse problem of the blockchain being rather too final as an 'entitlement register', insofar as it is designed to be immutable. This is particularly problematic in the present context of an action by an insolvency practitioner to set aside a transaction, where the objective ultimately is to claw back the asset *in specie*: if the purported secured creditor or third party asserting the right *in rem* is determined to retain the bitcoin to which the transaction under challenge relates, there is very little a court order setting aside the transaction can achieve. Whilst coercive measures, such as contempt of court, are often effective, they do have their limits;[60] and, in the most extreme case, a particularly recalcitrant respondent may well destroy the private keys or send the bitcoin in question to a burn address.

These considerations, arising in the insolvency context of claw back, draw attention to the wider issue of ensuring that any private law regime for crypto assets is supported by an effective scheme of remedies, tailored to the particular challenges crypto assets pose in this respect. Upon closer examination, the same issues of an effective remedy arise in the application of the consensual system of transfer to the crypto context: if the civilian ownership right in bitcoin becomes effective against persons generally simply upon the valid conclusion of a *causa traditionis* and does not require a delivery from transferor to transferee, the corresponding right of the *rei vindicatio* vested in the transferee may prove difficult, if not impossible, to enforce should the transferor refuse to cooperate. In these circumstances, a legal right of ownership would be largely devoid of any practical meaning, at least insofar as recovery of the object is sought.

The question of effective remedies thus leads to a pressing consideration for property law more broadly. Whilst useful analogies have been drawn with various different asset types, it remains the case that property law knows no precedent for an object of rights that resists legal methods of enforcement insofar as it depends entirely on the voluntary cooperation of the present holder to surrender the asset. Bitcoin held directly is not amenable to the traditional methods of execution: lawful force cannot be applied for the purpose of a self-help remedy; judicial processes sanctioned by contempt of court may prove ineffective; and there are no third parties, such as banks, title registrars, or crypto intermediaries, amenable to the jurisdiction of the court who may assist in enforcement. This has given rise to

[60] *Lakatamia Shipping Co Limited v Nobu Su* [2021] EWHC 1907 (Comm). The Respondent in this case has been described as the worst contemnor of court seen by the English courts in his persistent defiance of *in personam* orders over several years.

considerable concern as to effective enforcement over crypto assets, both in the simple debt and insolvency contexts.[61]

Here, the common law system of property law provides a noteworthy precedent. The traditional structure of the common law property taxonomy fundamentally differs from civilian systems in that objects are not grouped according to their empirical features, but rather by reference to the remedies they attract. Hence, real property, or 'realty', as a class of objects does not align with the civilian category of immovables; but rather refers to objects in respect of which a right to recover the asset *in specie* is available. Similarly, personal property, or 'personalty', as a class of objects does not align with civilian movables; rather, it is reserved for objects in respect of which a right to recovery is not admitted but to which property rights are vindicated by the personal remedy of damages.

It is critical that these concepts of remedies are not conflated with the definitive feature of property law itself, namely, effectiveness against persons generally rather than against a specific person alone. Unlike in civilian systems, property law in common law systems is not defined as a relationship between a person and a *res*, with the result that property rights subsist in specific objects that are, as such, valid *erga omnes*. Rather, in common law systems, property rights are expressly defined by reference to their sphere of exigibilty. Thus, property rights, as distinct from personal rights, are variously defined as rights that 'bind third parties to their creation' or are binding 'against all the world'. This, however, says nothing on the question of available remedies. It may well be that a property right in, for example, a car, is valid against persons generally as opposed to a specific wrongdoer; but gives rise only to a remedy of damages to the value of the car with no inherent right to reclaim the car itself.[62] The position is, thus, the inverse of the civilian notion of the *rei vindicatio*, where recovery *in specie* remains the default remedy with damages as a secondary remedy should recovery prove not possible.[63]

Whilst a personal remedy in damages only to vindicate a property right may seem, at least on a theoretical level, somewhat inadequate when compared to civilian notions of ownership, Blackstone's justification for the common law position is particularly instructive as what might be the closest precedent for the challenges bitcoin poses to the law of remedies:

> … in replevin and detinue [the only actions for recovering the specific possession of personal chattels] *if the wrong-doer be very perverse, he cannot be compelled to a restitution of the identical thing taken or detained*; but he still has his election, to deliver the goods, or their value: an imperfection in the law, that results from the nature of personal

[61] See, eg, the work of the UNIDROIT Working Group on Effective Enforcement.

[62] Torts (Interference with Goods) Act 1977 (UK), s 3(3) and 3(4). This is a semi-codification of the common law position.

[63] The Schlosser Report to the Brussels Convention illustrates the emphasis on specific recovery. Paragraph 166 states:

> The most important legal consequence flowing from the nature of a right *in rem* is that its owner is entitled to demand that the thing in which it exists be given up by anyone not enjoying a prior right.

> property, *which is easily concealed or conveyed out of the reach of justice, and not always amenable to the magistrate.*[64]

Applying this logic to an object even less amenable to legal process gives serious cause to consider whether any further efforts aimed at ensuring the cooperation of a 'very perverse' debtor in respect of direct crypto asset holdings are warranted; and whether instead the issue of effective enforcement might be more fruitfully addressed by reference to alternative remedies. In this respect, it is worth noting that English law has further remedial devices that lend significant practical support to a system of property law that theoretically limits rights to recovery of the object itself.

For example, the techniques of following an asset and tracing its value through transactions[65] enable a claimant to recover a substitute asset in the hands of a complete stranger for that of which it was unlawfully deprived to an extent well beyond that permitted by the civilian technique of real subrogation.[66] Critically, however, for present purposes, such techniques of tracing and following are available for claims where the transaction in question was effected by a company director for wrongful and fraudulent trading.[67] Further possibilities in insolvency lie in personal claims against the directors personally to compensate for the value unlawfully transferred away to the detriment of the company's creditors.[68]

Many of these common law techniques, thus, may prove to be far more potent in practice than the absolute rights of an owner in civilian jurisdictions; thereby illustrating the relative limits of a property system based on rights subsisting in a particular object, as compared to a property system in which the identity of the Defendant is rather more the pertinent question. In certain contexts, including claw back upon the setting aside of a transaction in insolvency, the latter approach may well prove to be of significant practical value.

Part IV set out to formulate potential rules as to when a right *in rem* to crypto assets accrues relative to the events of insolvency proceedings to determine whether an action by an insolvency practitioner to set aside a transaction in the interest of the general creditors might succeed. What emerged from this analysis is, however, a more general question regarding the standard remedy of claw back in this context, that drew attention to a broader issue of property law. Thus, a serious question arose as to the utility of recognising bitcoin as an object of rights *in*

[64] 3 Bl 413. Emphasis added.

[65] See *Foskett v McKeown* [2001] 1 AC 102 (HL).

[66] Real subrogation is typically far more limited than tracing and following in equity. See in particular B Häcker, *Consequences of Impaired Consent Transfers: A Structural Comparison of English and German Law* (London, Hart Publishing, 2013), particularly at 297 and 313. In any event, real subrogation is generally the exception rather than the rule, and in any event, the German provisions for title retention agreements on insolvency tend to be the most generous of all civilian jurisdictions; see also V Sagaert, 'Cour de cassation française, 26 Avril 2000 – priority conflict between the seller under title retention and the assignee of the resale claim' [2002] *European Review of Private Law* 823–835.

[67] Insolvency Act 1986 (UK), ss 213, 214, 238.

[68] Insolvency Act 1986 (UK), ss 212(3) and 214.

rem at all, insofar as such rights are conceptualised as subsisting in a specific object and thereby giving rise to a right to vindicate *in specie*. It was, therefore, suggested that it may well be worth considering whether an alternate system of legal protections comprising robust personal remedies and substitution techniques might prove more effective in protecting the interests of those who transact in bitcoin.

Hence, the core legal challenge in developing a system of rights in respect of crypto assets, whether they apply in civil or insolvency proceedings, will be ensuring that legal, factual, technical, and commercial realities are sufficiently aligned; such that legal rights are more than empty theoretical propositions, but have real value as rights fully supported by an effective system of remedies in line with the features of the asset itself.

VI. So … Can Transactions in Crypto Assets be Set Aside?

Drawing together all these threads, the short answer to the title question of this chapter is that there is no reason in principle why, as a matter of law, transactions in crypto assets recorded on a public blockchain cannot be set aside by an insolvency practitioner. As this chapter has sought to demonstrate, however, the long answer is somewhat more complex and takes into account a wide range of considerations.

Part II drew attention to Articles 8 and 16 of the Insolvency Regulation Recast as a firm reminder that, in any action by an insolvency practitioner to set aside a transaction, the interests of the unsecured creditors must be carefully balanced against those of secured creditors and other third parties who assert a right *in rem* to the object of the transaction under challenge. In this respect, *Lutz v Bäuerle* was a further reminder of the temporal limitations on the interests of each of these parties. In this context, the question of *when* an asserted right *in rem* accrued relative to the various events in the procedural history of the insolvency proceedings emerged as the critical issue. This specific question was then identified as a technical issue of property law that has not yet received any attention in the crypto-legal discourse, but is of unique significance in the insolvency context.

Accordingly, Part III set out a proposed two-step approach to this discrete question of when a person acquires a right *in rem* in bitcoin such that it may be said to have accrued before or after the relevant events in the procedural chronology of the insolvency proceedings. The first step of the proposed approach involved reframing the question away from the insolvency context and into the more context-, asset-, and jurisdiction-neutral terms of when, if ever, the acquisition of a right in bitcoin becomes valid against persons generally.

Part IV then explored the second step of the proposed approach by answering the question reframed thus by reference to four precedents drawn from other areas of property law. Following a warning against uncritical recourse to precedents due to formal similarity rather than to substance, four possible solutions to the question were set out.

Part V analysed the relative merits and demerits of these solutions to identify the core legal challenges in developing the most appropriate rule. Here it was suggested that a key consideration for legislators and courts should be ensuring that any private law framework for crypto assets sufficiently reflects factual, technical, and commercial realities. Drawing upon the court order typically sought upon a successful action by an insolvency practitioner to set aside a transaction, attention was drawn to the question of appropriate remedies in respect of blockchain transactions; which are immutable as a matter of technical design, and might be also effectively immutable as a matter of law. Given that any right to recover a bitcoin *in specie* relies wholly on the voluntary cooperation of the present holder, it was suggested that a focus on personal remedies and extended techniques of following and tracing value may well prove more effective than traditional remedies such as claw back. Such considerations were shown to be equally relevant for the wider law of property, notably in concepts such as remedies *in specie* and the *rei vindicatio*, insofar as this is generally used to seek recovery of the relevant asset in which the right *in rem* is said to subsist.

Accordingly, the full answer to the title question is as follows. There is no reason in principle why, as a matter of law, transactions in crypto assets recorded on a public blockchain cannot be set aside by an insolvency practitioner. The first consideration will, however, be to determine whether, pursuant to the relevant provisions of insolvency law, the rights of the general creditors prevail over those of whom assert a right *in rem* to the crypto asset in question. Even if, however, the insolvency practitioner is entitled to set aside the relevant blockchain transaction, it cannot be assumed that any consequent court order for claw back will not be without significant practical difficulty.

Hence, as a general conclusion, this chapter identifies two key points for legislators and courts to consider when developing an insolvency law to accommodate transactions in crypto assets. First, attention should be given to defining, as a matter of law, the point at which the acquisition of a right in a crypto asset becomes binding on persons generally, such that the crypto asset is removed from the insolvency estate for distribution amongst the general creditors. Such point in time should ideally reflect factual and technical realities to a certain extent, but need not be slavishly bound by them. Second, consideration should be given to whether traditional remedies consequent to an order setting aside a transaction, such as claw back, will be adequate in the blockchain context. It was suggested that it may be more fruitful to develop a system of personal remedies aimed primarily at recovering the value of the voided transaction, rather than the subject of the transaction itself. Ideally, all of these issues should be considered in conjunction with developments in the general private property law to ensure optimal consistency between these two, ever closely linked areas of the law.

17

Property Rights in Digital Assets under Uniform State Laws in the United States

BENJAMIN GEVA

I. Introduction

The emergence of digital assets, facilitated by new technologies, has posed a challenge to both commercial and insolvency laws. Specifically, ascertaining property rights in such assets has become necessary to enhance their economic value and their use in finance, as well as in order to determine existing rights in an insolvency. In the latter context, one issue between parties to a commercial transaction relating to a digital asset is to whom the asset or any right therein belongs. Another issue relates to the legal underpinning of holding digital assets for customers. In this context, generally speaking, the question is whether third-party exchanges hold digital assets for customers as 'virtual bailees' or as debtors. If the former, the digital assets belong to the customers and title thereto does not vest in the trustee in bankruptcy for the benefit of the exchanger's creditors. If the latter, the digital assets belong to the exchanger, who, similarly to a banker, merely owes their value to the customer. In this case, title thereto vests in the exchanger's trustee in bankruptcy for the benefit of the trustee's creditors.

This chapter presents, discusses, and analyses statutory developments in the United States (US) designed to meet the challenge posed by the evolution of digital assets as products of emerging technologies. The chapter focusses on the recently approved Uniform Commercial Code (UCC) Article 12 with reference to other statutes in the US, particularly the Uniform Regulation of the Virtual-Currency Businesses Act (URVCBA) and international proposals particularly UNCITRAL Model Law on Electronic Transferable Records (MLETR). The chapter concludes that UCC Article 12 is a leap forward in the effort to address legal issues stemming from the proliferation of emerging technologies. Even as it stands to be improved, Article 12 is a beacon, and not only a starting point, for jurisdictions seeking to have their laws keeping up with progress.

II. UCC Article 12

A. Controllable Electronic Records (CER)

UCC Article 12, which deals with controllable electronic records (CERs), 'often … referred to as digital assets',[1] is a major part of an effort to adapt the UCC to emerging technologies, as they might affect electronic commerce. It was introduced in 2022 after being drafted by the Uniform Law Commission in partnership with the American Law Institute. The Uniform Law Commission then approved and recommended it for enactment in all the States at its 131st annual meeting in Philadelphia on July 8–13, 2022.[2]

Under Section 12-102(a)(1), 'Controllable electronic record ("CER") means a record stored in an electronic medium that can be subjected to control under Section 12-105 …'.[3]

This definition becomes clearer, when looking at further sub-definitions contained in the UCC: 'Electronic', in turn, is defined in UCC Section 1-201(b)(16A) to mean 'relating to technology having electrical, digital, magnetic, wireless, optical, electromagnetic, or similar capabilities'. For its part, 'Record' is defined in UCC Section 1-201(b)(31) to mean 'information that is inscribed on a tangible medium or that is stored in an electronic or other medium and is retrievable in perceivable form'. It has to be noted that this definition in Article 12 is therefore technology neutral; as such it will cover both technologies that are presently known and those that will be invented in the future.

B. Control of CERs

According to the Preface, the following general functions, all of which have been established after experience with 'record-management systems,' form the basis of the control[4] concept. This is supposed to facilitate the use of electronic records as effective and reliable means of transferring economic value.

1. The electronic record must have some … benefit that one person can enjoy and can exclude all others from enjoying, ….

[1] Prefatory note to Article 12.

[2] By October 14, 2023, it was enacted in 11 jurisdictions and introduced in 17. For a full list see www.uniformlaws.org/committees/community-home?communitykey=1457c422-ddb7-40b0-8c76-39a1991651ac. Wide adoption is anticipated. The author was an observer in the drafting process and yet all views and errors are his.

[3] Along the same lines Draft Unidroit Principles on Digital Assets And Private Law, Principle 2(1) defines 'digital asset' to mean 'electronic record which is capable of being subject to control'. UNIDROIT, 'Digital Assets and Private Law Public Consultation, Study LXXXII' (January 2023), hereafter: UNIDROIT Draft Principles.

[4] According to the Prefatory Note to Article 12,

2. A person must be able to transfer to another person this exclusive power to use and the exclusive power to transfer the electronic record. To remain exclusive, the transfer must divest the transferor of the power to use the electronic record.
3. A person must be able to demonstrate to others that the person has the power to use and transfer control of the electronic record.

To that end, under Section 12-105(a), for the purposes of UCC Article 12,

> A person has control of a controllable electronic record if the electronic record, a record attached to or logically associated with the electronic record, or a system in which the electronic record is recorded:
>
> (1) gives the person:
>
> (A) power to avail itself of substantially all the benefit from the electronic record; and
>
> (B) exclusive power,[5] subject to subsection (b), to:
>
> (i) prevent others from availing themselves of substantially all the benefit from the electronic record; and
>
> (ii) transfer control of the electronic record to another person or cause another person to obtain control of another controllable electronic record as a result of the transfer of the electronic record; and
>
> (2) enables the person readily to identify itself in any way, including by name, identifying number, cryptographic key, [public][6] office, or account number, as having the powers specified in paragraph (1).[7]

According to Official Comment (7) to the section, subsection (a)(2), which requires 'control' to enable 'a person to identify itself in any way, including by … cryptographic key', does not oblige a person to identify itself as having control. 'However, to prove that it has control, a person would need to prove that the relevant records or any system in which the controllable electronic record is recorded readily identifies the person as such.' Put differently, relevant records or the system – rather than the person itself – ought to identify the person in control. For its part, 'control' under UCC Section 12-105(e) can also be exercised indirectly,

The meaning of control in the UCC depends on the type of property involved. See Sections 7-106 (electronic documents of title): 8-106 (four different types of investment property, each with a different definition of 'control'): 9-104 (deposit accounts): 9-105 (chattel paper): 9-105A (electronic money). The Comments to Section 12-105 explain the requirements for obtaining control of a controllable electronic record. For present purposes of exposition, it is sufficient to think of bitcoin and other virtual currencies as prototypical controllable electronic records. The provisions under other law that govern control and other matters for other types of electronic records (some of which are modified by these amendments) are not addressed by Article 12.

[5] Under UCC s 12-105(b), power is exclusive even if: (i) the electronic record or its system 'limits the use of the electronic record or has a protocol programmed to cause a change'; or (ii) 'the power is shared with another person', except that under UCC s 12-105(c), each one of them is authorised to exercise the power alone.

[6] See Official Comment 7 referring to 'Section 3-110, Comment 3.'

[7] UNIDROIT Draft Principles, n 3 Principle 6(1) is to a similar effect. For the identification of a person in control see also Principle 7.

that is, through another person (other than the transferor) who has actual control. It does not matter whether this person acts with or without an acknowledgement of the agency.

C. Rights to the CER Acquired by Control

Under Section 12-104(c), 'law other than [Article 12] determines whether a person acquires a right in a controllable electronic record and the right the person acquires'. This appears to suggest that Article 12 governs neither rights in 'controllable electronic records', nor the rights that such records confer. Indeed, the UCC does not purport to harmonise the property laws of the various states. Rather, it is designed to secure that rights in electronic assets are recognised in each adopting jurisdiction.

To that end, under the shelter principle of Section 12-104(d),[8] a 'purchaser of a controllable electronic record acquires all rights in the controllable electronic record that the transferor had or had power to transfer'. 'Purchaser' is broadly defined as a person that is at the receiving end of 'any … voluntary transaction creating an interest in property' and thus includes buyers, secured parties or even recipients of a gift;[9] hence, to benefit from the shelter principle a 'purchaser' is not even required to take control of the CER.

Under certain circumstances, a bona fide purchaser under a non-gratuitous transaction might even be in a better situation: The purchaser obtains better title than that of the transferor.[10] Thus, under UCC Section 12-104(e), a 'qualifying purchaser acquires its rights in the controllable electronic record free of a claim of a property right in the controllable electronic record'. For its part, under UCC Section 12-102(a)(2), a 'qualified purchaser' must have obtained control of the CER in return for remuneration, in good faith, and without notice of a claim of a property right in it.

'Value' is defined in Section 3-303(a), to which UCC Section 12-102(a)(4) directs. It refers to the following: the issuance or transfer for a promise of performance, to the extent the promise has been performed; the acquisition of a security interest or lien otherwise than that obtained by judicial proceedings; payment of or a security for an antecedent debt; an exchange for another CER, or an exchange for an irrevocable obligation to a third party.

D. The CER 'Qualifying Purchaser'

Overall, the 'qualifying purchaser' of a controllable account, CER, or controllable payment intangible, is required to acquire the record under conditions

[8] The corresponding principle in UNIDROIT Draft Principles, n 3 is Principle 9.
[9] UCC s 1-201(30) and (31).
[10] The corresponding principle in UNIDROIT Draft Principles, n 3 is Principle 8.

corresponding to those under which a holder in due course of a negotiable instrument is required to meet under UCC Section 3-302. However, the latter requires a holder in due course to accept the instrument without knowledge of claims and defences. They then acquire it free from contract defences[11] and property claims.[12] In contrast, the qualifying purchaser of the CER is required under UCC Section 12-102(a)(2) to accept it without knowledge of property claims; under UCC Section 12-104(c) they then acquire the CER only free from property claims. Freedom from (contract) defences is not mentioned in these provisions. The Official Comment to UCC Section 12-104 explains this discrepancy by stating that a CER is 'information' to which there are no parties. This reasoning is, however, unconvincing. As will be seen below, it is effectively repudiated or at least qualified by the drafters in connection with controllable accounts and payment intangibles.

Either way, as a rule, the acquisition of rights in a CER, whether or not as a qualifying purchaser, may turn out to be a Pyrrhic victory. This is so because, in principle, Section 12-104(d) governs rights *to* the CER, not *on* the CER. In turn, rights *on* the CER, that is, rights in the asset evidenced by the CER, are governed by law other than Article 12. Accordingly, for example, the acquisition of a CER evidencing a contract for the purchase of land will give the purchaser no more than what would have been given to that party through the acquisition of a written contract for the purchase of land. This is regardless of whether the former is a qualifying purchaser or otherwise in control of the CER. In each case, the acquisition will confer rights to the record (a piece of paper in the case of the written contract, the CER in the case of the electronic contract), but not to the land that is being sold. It is other legal provisions than Article 12 that will determine whether the right to the CER as a record of information also affects the right specified on the record. In the example, that would be how one acquires rights under a contract for the purchase of land.[13] Indeed, this is very much alike to the fact that a right to the piece of paper containing a written contract is not necessarily a right to enforce the right on the written contract. This might, for example, be different if the written contract is a negotiable instrument. Accordingly, under the same analysis but with the opposite result, control of an electronic negotiable instrument made out to the bearer will in principle give the party in control also the power to sue on it. It thus works exactly like the right of a claimant to a written bearer instrument in the holder's hands.[14]

E. Rights on a CER Acquired by Control

There are, however, exceptions to the inapplicability of Article 12 to the acquisition of rights on the CER by virtue of the acquisition of the CER itself. These

[11] UCC s 3-305.
[12] UCC s 3-306.
[13] UCC Art 12 Preface.
[14] UCC s 3-301.

exceptions are stated in Article 12 as part of the exceptions to its scope provided in Section 12-102(a) (1). The contents of each of these exceptions are addressed elsewhere, mostly under UCC Article 9.[15] These exceptions to the scope of Article 12 are stated in Section 12-102(a)(1) to be a 'controllable account',[16] a 'controllable payment intangible';[17] a 'deposit account',[18] 'electronic copy of a record evidencing chattel paper',[19] an 'electronic document of title',[20] 'electronic money',[21] 'investment property',[22] or a 'transferable record'.[23] Under Section 12-102(a) (1), Article 12

[15] For the incorporation of definitions from Articles 1 and 9 see UCC s 12-102(c). Note also that in case of conflict between Article 12 and Article 9-provisions, the latter prevail. See UCC, s 12-103(a). The precedence of consumer law is addressed in UCC s 12-103(b).

[16] Defined in UCC s 9-102(a) (27A) to mean 'an account evidenced by a controllable electronic record that provides that the account debtor undertakes to pay the person that has control under Section 12-105 of the controllable electronic record'. Subject to specified exceptions, 'account' is defined in s 9-102(a)(2) to mean 'a right to payment of a monetary obligation, whether or not earned by performance …' of listed types of contract, such as for the purchase of property, service, guarantee, and energy.

[17] Defined in UCC s 9-102(a) (27B) to mean 'a payment intangible evidenced by a controllable electronic record that provides that the account debtor undertakes to pay the person that has control under Section 12-105 of the controllable electronic record'. Under UCC s 9-102(a) (61) 'Payment intangible' is defined to mean a 'general intangible under which the account debtor's principal obligation is a monetary obligation' Generally speaking, 'general intangible' is defined in s 9-102(a)(42) to mean a chose in action.

[18] Subject to specified exception, defined in s 9-102(a)(29) to mean 'a demand, time, savings, passbook, or similar account maintained with a bank …'.

[19] 'Chattel paper' is defined in s 9-102(a)(11) to mean:

(A) a right to payment of a monetary obligation secured by specific goods, if the right to payment and security agreement are evidenced by a record; or
(B) a right to payment of a monetary obligation owed by a lessee under a lease agreement with respect to specific goods and a monetary obligation owed by the lessee in connection with the transaction giving rise to the lease, if:

(i) the right to payment and lease agreement are evidenced by a record; and
(ii) the predominant purpose of the transaction giving rise to the lease was to give the lessee the right to possession and use of the goods.

For 'control of electronic copy of a record evidencing chattel paper' see UCC s 9-105.

[20] Electronic documents of title are documents that are stored in an electronic medium instead of in tangible form. See Official Comment to UCC s 1-201. 'Document of title' is defined in UCC, s 1-201(b)(16) to be a bill of lading, warehouse receipt, or a similar document. Under the UCC documents of title are governed by Article 7.

[21] UCC s 9-102(a)(31A) defines 'electronic money' to mean 'money in an electronic form'. Under UCC s 1-204(a)(24) 'Money' means a medium of exchange currently authorised or adopted by a domestic or foreign government. The term includes a monetary unit of account established by an intergovernmental or-organisation or by agreement between two or more countries.

[22] Defined in UCC s 9-102(a)(49) to mean 'a security, whether certificated or uncertificated, security entitlement, securities account, commodity contract, or commodity account' and is governed by UCC Art 8.

[23] See UCC s 12-102(3). Fundamentally this is an electronic promissory note, governed by either s 201(a)(1) of the Electronic Signatures in Global and National Commerce Act, 15 USC s 7021(a)(1) [as amended] [ESGNCA] or s 16 of the Uniform Electronic Transactions Act 1999 [UETA], National Conference of Commissioners on Uniform State Laws (NCCUSL), Annual Conference Meeting in its 108th Year in Denver, Colorado, July 23–30. Both statutes are discussed at length in Part III of this chapter.

does not apply to such categories which means that the rule under which right to a CER does not automatically include the right on the CER does not apply to them.

Nonetheless, two categories are partly excluded from the exceptions to the scope of UCC Article 12. As such, these two excepted categories are effectively returned, albeit partly, into the scope of Article 12. Thus, under UCC Section 12-104 (a), the provisions of UCC Section 12-104 apply to controllable accounts and controllable payment intangibles. Effectively, this means that UCC Section 12-105, which deals with control over CERs, applies also to controllable accounts and controllable payment intangibles.

Nothing in Article 12 turns on the distinction between controllable accounts and controllable payment intangibles. Jointly, they make up controllable electronic records embodying unsecured monetary debts. They will thus be addressed here as one category of controlled unsecured monetary debts (CUMDs), governed by UCC Sections 12-104 (the acquisition and purchase of rights in CUMDs) and 12-105 (control of CER).

A return to Article 12, could have meant a return to its inapplicability to the right on the CER except that on this point, Article 12 takes the opposite position with regard to CUMD. Thus, under UCC Section 12-106, an account debtor on a CUMD, that is, the party liable on it,[24] may discharge its obligation by paying the person having control of the CER that evidences the CUMD.[25] This rule hinges on proper notification of the transfer of control. Effectively, *it provides that the one in control of a CUMD is entitled to enforce the right it evidences*. As Official Comment 6 to UCC Section 12-104 explains,

> Even though a controllable electronic record evidences a controllable account or controllable payment intangible, the controllable electronic record is distinct from the account or payment intangible that it evidences. The account or payment intangible is connected with (or 'tethered' to) the electronic record by virtue of the relevant account debtor's obligation to pay the person in control of the controllable electronic record [under Section 12-106]. Moreover, *control of the controllable account or payment intangible is achieved only by obtaining control of the controllable electronic record that evidences the account or payment intangible*. (Emphasis added)

For its part, as indicated for CERs in general, under UCC Section 12-104(e) a qualifying purchaser 'acquires its rights in the controllable electronic record free of a claim of a property right in the controllable electronic record'. With regard to the fact that the UCC deliberately does not grant a qualifying purchaser freedom from (contractual) defences under Section 12-104(e), as discussed above, the Official Comment fills in by pointing to UCC Sections 9-403 and 9-404. While the former provides for the assignee's subjection to the account-debtor's contractual defences, the latter validates an agreement not to assert them. Such agreements are effective in the hands of an assignee who takes the assignment

[24] See UCC s 9-102(a)(3).

[25] In UCC ss 9-106 CER ought to be taken to cover a CUMD.

under holding in due course requirements. Accordingly, the position of a 'qualifying purchaser' beneficiary of such an agreement who takes the assignment in compliance with holding in due course requirements is that of a holder in due course of a negotiable instrument.[26]

F. Applicable Law

UCC Section 12-107 addresses the applicable law. It distinguishes between: (i) controllable accounts and controllable payment intangibles, namely CUMDs, on one hand, and (ii) CERs, from which CUMDs are excluded under UCC Section 12-102(a) (1), on the other hand.[27] For each of these two categories, the key concept is 'the local law of a controllable electronic record's jurisdiction' ('the local CER law'). For CERs, this law 'governs a matter covered by this article'.[28] For CUMDs, the local CER law governs a matter covered by Section 12-106 [discharge], 'unless an effective agreement determines that the local law of another jurisdiction governs'.[29] The exclusion of matters other than the discharge on the CUMD from the application of the local CER law to CUMDs is explained in Official Comment 4 to Section 12-107. The explanation is on the fact that 'an account debtor's rights and duties are generally governed by the law applicable to the underlying obligation of the account debtor, and not by the law applicable to the [security] agreement between the assignor (debtor) and the assignee (secured party)'.

Under Section 12-107 (c), the local CER law may be provided in the CER or otherwise by the rules of the system in which the CER is recorded. Either the agreement or the rule must designate the jurisdiction 'for purposes of this article or [the Uniform Commercial Code]'. In the absence of such an agreement or rule, the local CER law must be the one designated by agreement. If there is no such agreement, it is determined by the system rules, as the one governing the CER in general. In each of these cases, the agreement or rules must be express and 'readily available'. In the absence of such an agreement or rule, the local CER law is that of the District of Columbia (Washington DC).[30] Under Section 12-107(e), the selected local CER law applies even 'if the [specific] matter or [...] transaction to which the matter relates does not bear any relation to the controllable electronic record's jurisdiction'. Finally, UCC Section 12-107(f) also provides for the rights acquired under Section 12-104 by a purchaser or qualifying purchaser and states

[26] Indeed, a 'qualifying purchaser' who takes a controllable account or controllable payment intangible with knowledge of a defence – takes it subject to the defence but free of the claim. At the same time, in connection with a negotiable instrument, knowledge of defence disqualifies the holder from becoming a holder in due course. They thus take the negotiable instrument subject to both the defence and the property claim.

[27] See text at n 23.

[28] UCC s 12-107(a).

[29] UCC s 12-107(b).

[30] For the latter point see UCC s 12-107(c).

that such rights 'are governed by the law applicable under [UCC Section 12-107] at the time of purchase'.

III. Uniform Electronic Transactions Act – UETA §16 & Electronic Signatures in Global and National Commerce Act – ESGNCA §7021(A)(1)

As discussed, the definition of a CER under UCC Section 12-102(a)(1) is subject to enumerated exceptions,[31] one of which is a 'transferable record' as defined in UETA Section 16(a) or ESGNCA Section 7021(a)(1).[32] Under each of these provisions, 'transferable record' is defined to mean an electronic record[33] that 'would be a note under [UCC Article 3] … if the electronic record were in writing'.[34] Such an electronic record is referred to below as an 'electronic note'.

UCC Article 3 governs negotiable instruments, one of which is the promissory note ('note'). Under UCC Section 3-104, the note is a negotiable instrument in the form of an unconditional written and signed[35] promise[36] to pay to bearer or to order a fixed amount of money payable on demand or at a definite time. A note that does not state a payee is payable to bearer.[37] To be a 'note' under UETA or ESGNCA, a 'transferable record' must contain this information in an electronic record as well as be electronically signed.[38]

Each statute contains its own qualification to the basic definition of a 'transferable record' as an electronic note. Under ESGNCA Section 7021(a)(1)(C), only an electronic note relating 'to a loan secured by real property' is a 'transferable record'. For its part, UETA Section 16(a)(2) provides that an electronic note is covered by

[31] See text at nn 16–23.

[32] Cited in n 23.

[33] 'Electronic record' is defined in UETA (n 23) s 2(7) to mean 'a record created, generated, sent, communicated, received, or stored by electronic means'. For its part, 'Record' is defined in UETA s 2(13) to mean 'information that is inscribed on a tangible medium or that is stored in an electronic or other medium and is retrievable in perceivable form.' Finally, 'Electronic' is defined in UETA (n 23) s 2(5) to mean 'relating to technology having electrical, digital, magnetic, wireless, optical, electromagnetic, or similar capabilities'.

[34] Under UCC s 1-201(b)(43), 'writing' requires the reduction to tangible form. Information inscribed on a tangible medium (ie, written information) is distinguished from information stored in an electronic medium which is retrievable in a perceivable form in UCC Section 1-201(b)(31). Hence, under the UCC, an electronic record is not written.

[35] Under UCC s 1-201(b)(37) 'Signed' includes using any symbol executed or adopted with present intention to adopt or accept a writing.

[36] UCC s 3-103(12). For its part, the promise to pay may be implicit. *cf. Banco de Portugal v Waterlow and Sons, Ltd* [1932] AC 452 (HL) 483, 487, a non-UCC case addressing the issuer's implicit promise to pay the sum appearing on a banknote.

[37] UCC s 3-109(a).

[38] Under UETA s 2(8) as well ESGNCA s 7006(5) (made applicable under s 7021(2)) (n 23) 'electronic signature' is defined to mean 'an electronic sound, symbol, or process, attached to or logically associated with a contract or other record and executed or adopted by a person with the intent to sign the record'.

UETA only where 'the issuer of the electronic record expressly has agreed [that it] is a transferable record'.[39] Arguably, where the respective qualification does not exist, the electronic note remains covered under UCC Article 12 as a CUMD.

As a matter of policy, no justification for the proliferation of statutes can be identified. Stated otherwise, there is no apparent justification for not including the electronic version of the 'note' in UCC Article 12. While it is true that, historically, legislation addressing the electronic version of the 'note' preceded UCC Article 12, this does not justify the choice not to include it into UCC Article 12 once the latter was promulgated.

Be it as it may, where it is excluded from UCC Article 12, the electronic version of the 'note' is governed by the UETA or ESGNCA.[40] Under UCC Article 3, a written note is transferable from hand to hand by delivery (plus endorsement, as may be required) so as to facilitate the right to enforce obligations embodied therein.[41] In turn, UETA Section 16(d) (as well as ESGNCA Section 7021[d]) provides a functional equivalent for the transferability of the electronic note (governed by UETA or ESGNCA) with that of the written note (governed by UCC Article 3). Accordingly, unless otherwise agreed, notwithstanding the absence of delivery, physical possession, and endorsement, a person in control[42] of an electronic note is to be treated as its 'holder'.[43] They are in the same legal position as a holder of a written negotiable instrument, who, upon compliance with the required statutory conditions,[44] may qualify as a holder in due course[45] or purchaser.[46] Possession and delivery are replaced by their functional equivalents; that is, control and transfer of control. Endorsement has its functional equivalent in the form of an electronic signature and hence it is not clear why it has been dispensed with.

UETA's Section 16(e) (as well as ESGNCA Section 7021(e)) complements the respective subsection (d). It provides that unless otherwise agreed, an obligor on a transferable record is in the same legal position as an obligor on an equivalent record or writing under the UCC.

[39] Query why the mere issuance of the 'transferable record' should not suffice to signal the issuer's agreement.

[40] I take this to mean that it is up to the jurisdictions that adopt UCC Article 12 to make this choice.

[41] UCC s 3-201 in conjunction with s 3-301.

[42] Under para (f) of both UETA s 16 and ESGNCA s 7021, 'the person seeking to enforce the transferable record shall provide reasonable proof that the person is in control of the transferable record. Proof may include access to the authoritative copy of the transferable record and related business records sufficient to review the terms of the transferable record and to establish the identity of the person having control of the transferable record.'

[43] Under the relevant part of UCC s 1-201(b) (210) 'Holder' is defined to mean 'the person in possession of a negotiable instrument that is payable either to bearer or to an identified person that is the person in possession …'.

[44] Under the relevant part of s 3-302(a) 'Holder' is defined to mean 'the person in possession of a negotiable instrument that is payable either to bearer or to an identified person that is the person in possession …'.

[45] The holder in due course's freedom from claims are provided for in UCC s 3-306. Defences available against a holder in due course are addressed in UCC s 3-305(b).

[46] See, eg, UCC s 3-203 (rights acquired by transfer).

As under UCC Article 12, the key to having and exercising rights on a transferable record is control, UETA Section 16(b) (as well as ESGNCA Section 7021(b)) requires 'control' to be evidenced by a reliable system establishing an issuance or transfer to the claimant. Generally speaking, UETA Section 16(c) (as well as ESGNCA Section 7021(c)) goes on to require such a system to be premised on a uniquely identifiable, unalterable single authoritative copy of the transferable record. According to the Comment, the control requirements may be satisfied by the use of a trusted third-party registry system, such as those existing for the transfer of securities entitlements under UCC Article 8 and for the transfer of cotton warehouse receipts.

IV. UNCITRAL Model Law on Electronic Transferable Records – MLETR

This functional equivalence principle also guided the drafters of the *UNCITRAL Model Law on Electronic Transferable Records* (2017)[47] (MLETR). The MLETR addresses the digitisation of those paper documents or instruments that entitle their holder to claim the performance of the obligation indicated in the document or instrument and to transfer the right to its performance through the transfer of the containing document or instrument. Such digitised documents or instruments are referred to as electronic transferrable records. Purporting to set international standards for rights to and on such electronic transferrable records, the MLETR is addressed here by way of comparison to the American legislation discussed in the earlier parts of this contribution.

Under the MLETR, similarly to UCC Article 12 and UETA, the key to acquiring rights in an electronic record is control. Specifically, Article 11 of the MLETR treats 'exclusive control of [an] electronic transferable record' as a functional equivalent of 'the possession of a transferable document or instrument'. 'Transferable document or instrument' is then defined in Article 2 of the MLETR as follows:

> a document or instrument issued on paper that entitles the holder to claim the performance of the obligation indicated in the document or instrument and to transfer the right to performance of the obligation indicated in the document or instrument through the transfer of that document or instrument.

In turn, Article 2 of the MLETR defines 'electronic record' as 'information generated, communicated, received or stored by electronic means'.[48]

[47] United Nations, *UNCITRAL Model Law on Electronic Transferable Records* (United Nations 2017). Available online at uncitral.un.org/sites/uncitral.un.org/files/media-documents/uncitral/en/mletr_ebook_e.pdf.

[48] For when an electronic record becomes an 'electronic transferable record', see MLETR (n 47) Art 10(1).

In the footsteps of UETA and unlike UCC Article 12, insofar as it governs the digitisation of 'a [transferable] document or instrument issued on paper that entitles the holder to claim the performance of the obligation indicated [therein]',[49] the MLETR appears to exclude electronic transferable records existing only in electronic form. However, this view is not shared by its own drafters who state that if an adopting jurisdiction wants to exclude from the scope of the MLETR electronic transferable records that exist only in an electronic environment, it ought to specifically do so.[50] This means that both the MLETR and UCC Article 12, but not UETA, cover electronic records with no corresponding paper-based document. At the same time, the MLETR and UETA, but not UCC Article 12, cover electronic versions of existing paper-based instruments and documents. In addition to that, UCC Article 12 even reaches records whose transfer does not lead to a transfer of the right on them, something which exists neither under UETA nor the MLETR. Yet, this is merely an unnecessary exercise of hair splitting.[51]

Article 8 of the MLETR renders information that is 'accessible so as to be usable for subsequent reference' the functional equivalent of 'writing'. Similarly, the MLETR's Article 9 provides that where 'a reliable method is used to identify [a] person and to indicate that person's intention in respect of the information contained in [an] electronic transferable record', a legal signature requirement of that person is satisfied.

Article 11(1) of the MLETR goes on to state that the exclusive control over an electronic transferable record established by a reliable method, which also identifies the person in control, meets the legal requirement for 'the possession of a transferable document or instrument'. For its part, under Article 11(2) of the MLETR, the transfer of control over an electronic transferable record is the equivalent to the transfer of possession of a transferable document or instrument.[52] 'The requirement to identify the person in control … demands that the method or system employed to establish control as a whole should perform the identification function with respect to all concerned parties.'[53] In fact, identification may occur by means of 'pseudonyms rather than … real names' where the possibility of linking pseudonym and real name, if need be, is available.[54] Being the functional equivalent of 'possession', which 'in turn, may vary in each jurisdiction', the notion of 'control' is not defined in the MLETR.[55]

[49] MLETR (n 47) Art 2.
[50] MLETR (n 47) para 7 n 1; see also para 28.
[51] See paragraph containing n 13.
[52] In this context, ibid Article 15 provides the following:

> Where the law requires or permits the endorsement in any form of a transferable document or instrument, that requirement is met with respect to an electronic transferable record if the information required for the endorsement is included in the electronic transferable record and that information is compliant with the requirements set forth in Articles 8 and 9.

[53] Explanatory Note to the UNCITRAL (n 47) para 116.
[54] ibid para 117.
[55] ibid para 106.

MLETR Article 1(3) provides that the statute 'does not apply to securities, such as shares and bonds, and other investment instruments'. As long as they are not investment instruments, bills of exchange, promissory notes and cheques are not excluded, other than at the discretion of an adopting jurisdiction.[56] The rationale provided for the permissible exclusion of bills, notes, and cheques addresses the formalism of the law of negotiable instruments. To fill in the vacuum created by such an exclusion, the rationale also points at the option of creating alternative electronic instruments to fulfil the function of negotiable instruments.[57] In my view, neither the rationale nor the proposed solution is convincing. Formalism can be transported to an electronic format and digital alternatives to every paper document can be created. Yet, there is no point for re-inventing the wheel. Rather, even if a few specific provisions may need to be added to address requirements of the law of negotiable instruments, as done eg, in UETA and ESGNCA,[58] negotiable instruments appear to be the 'transferable records' par excellence of which digitisation will benefit from the MLETR.

V. Holding Virtual Currencies

A. Introduction

CERs and CUMDs may be held in a deposit account. Thereunder, the depositary is a mere debtor of the depositor, owing the depositor the amount on deposit, as if it were a bank owing a customer on a bank account.[59] Alternatively, either specific digital assets or, more likely, an undivided share in a stock of digital assets of the same type may be held with a depositary acting as a custodian or bailee of intangible assets. For its part, the depositary could be a financial institution such as a bank of an exchange.

UCC Article 12 does not address the holding of CERs and CUMDs by a third party. This is in contrast with the UNIDROIT Draft Principles.[60] Principle 10 speaks of a custodian maintaining a digital asset[61] for a client by *controlling* the digital asset in a way that 'the client does not have the exclusive ability to change the control of the digital asset'. Control lies with the custodian, yet it exercises it for the client. This sounds like a quasi-bailment[62] arrangement and not like a deposit account. By way of further elaboration, under Principle 11(2), '[u]nless prohibited

[56] MLETR (n 47) para 7 n 1.
[57] ibid paras 28(b), 30–33.
[58] n 23.
[59] *Foley v Hill* (1848) 2 HLC 28; 9 ER 1002 (HL).
[60] n 3.
[61] For the interchangeability between 'CER' and digital asset see text at n 1.
[62] It is a quasi-bailment and not strictly a bailment only because traditionally bailment is associated with chattels and not intangibles.

by the custody agreement or by other law, a custodian may maintain fungible digital assets of two or more of its clients in an undivided pool'. In this case, each client holds an undivided share in a stock of digital assets.

B. URVCBA: Scope and Core Concepts

In US jurisdictions, virtual currency business activity may be regulated under the Uniform Regulation of the Virtual-Currency Businesses Act (URVCBA), which so far has been adopted only in Rhode Island and is being considered in California, Nevada and Illinois.[63] Under URVCBA Section 102(23), virtual currency is defined to mean the digital representation of value used as a medium of exchange, unit of account or store of value, and is not legal tender,[64] even if so denominated. This definition is flawed, as it does not clarify what 'digital representation' means and yet it covers CERs and CUMDs. Under Section 102(25), 'Virtual-currency business activity' is defined primarily to mean either the exchange, transfer, or storage of virtual currency, or an engagement in virtual currency administration,[65] whether directly or through an agreement with a virtual currency control-service vendor.[66]

According to the Comment, 'Exchange, Transfer, and Store – cover the core concepts animating what constitutes "virtual-currency business activity"'. URCVB Section 102(5), (20), and (21) explain the meaning of these 'core concepts'.

C. URVCBA: Control

For its part, the term 'control' is central to the definitions of each of the three 'core concepts animating what constitutes "virtual-currency business activity"'

[63] URVCBA was drafted by the National Conference of Commissioners on Uniform State Law (NCCUSL) and approved and recommended by it for enactment in all the states in the United States at its Annual Conference Meeting in its 126th year in San Diego, California on July 14–20, 2017. For its disappointing degree of adoption see www.uniformlaws.org/committees/community-home?CommunityKey=e104aaa8-c10f-45a7-a34a-0423c2106778. Commercial law rules for transactions covered by URVCBA are provided by the Uniform Supplemental Commercial Law for the Uniform Regulation of Virtual Currency Business Act, drafted by the National Conference of Commissioners on Uniform State Laws and by it approved and recommended for enactment in all the states in its Annual Conference Meeting in Its one-hundred-and-twenty-seventy seventh year, in Louisville, Kentucky, July 20–26. So far it has only been adopted in Rhode Island and is being considered in Nevada: www.uniformlaws.org/committees/community-home?CommunityKey=fc398fb5-2885-4efb-a3bb-508650106f95.

[64] For its part, 'legal tender' is defined in URVCBA s 102(8) to mean 'a medium of exchange or unit of value, including the coin or paper money of the United States, issued by the United States or by another government'.

[65] Defined in URVCBA s 102(24) to mean the issuance of virtual currency with the authority to redeem it for legal tender, credit to a bank account, or another digital currency.

[66] Defined in URVCBA s 102(26) to refer to a person in control of virtual currency exclusively under an agreement with one who is in control of virtual currency on behalf of another person.

under paragraphs 5, 20 and 21 as well as that of a 'virtual-currency control-service provider' under paragraph 26. URCVB Section 20(3) defines 'control' by reference to the power to unilaterally execute or prevent a virtual-currency transaction, as well as to direct management, operations or policies.

In relation to 'Store', the Comment is confusing. It states that the term 'is analogous to deposit-taking and holding or to safe deposit business' – just as if these two activities were the same. It goes on to explain that 'storage is similar to placing a deposit of funds with a bank' or else 'on an "electronic wallet"'. It is thus not clear whether for the storage activity, the URVCBA envisages 'custody', namely bailment, or whether it envisages ownership passing to the storer, so that it owes a debt. Even if the latter, it is not clear whether the debt is under a fractional reserve, like that of a commercial bank on a bank deposit, or under what is known under Roman law as 'irregular deposit' which requires a 100 per cent (non-fractional) reserve.[67]

The issue is, however, resolved by URVCBA Section 502, providing for the position of a virtual-currency business that has control of virtual currency for another person. For its part, as indicated in the language quoted above, 'control' may be acquired in any virtual-currency business activity, *viz.* an exchange, transfer, and storage transaction, as well as by a virtual-currency administration and virtual-currency control-services vendor.[68] Effectively, URVCBA Section 502 confers on the one for whom control on virtual currency is held by a virtual currency business an '*entitlement to virtual currency*'. This right is modelled on Part V of UCC Article 8 (to which Ontario Securities Transfer Act (OSTA)[69] Part VI corresponds). It governs 'indirect holding' of securities and provides an investor with a 'security entitlement' to securities held by the securities intermediary for that investor. The investor's claim is thus fully backed by securities held by the securities intermediary, which are beyond the reach of the latter's creditors.

Under URVCBA Section 407(2), breach of URVCBA Section 502 entitles the injured party to sue the breaching party. This is stated to be the only private right of action under the URVCBA.

[67] R Mangano, 'The Insolvency of Cryptocurrency Exchanges: Lessons from the *BitGrail* Case – Reification of Coins, *Pari Passu* Ranking, and Nominalism' [2019] *Banking and Finance Law Review* 197. In general, for the irregular deposit, see RW Lee, *The Elements of Roman Law with a Translation of the Institutes of Justinian*, 4th edn (London, Sweet & Maxwell, 1956) 295 and R Zimmermann, *The Law of Obligations-Roman Foundations of the Civilian Tradition* (Munich, Juta, 1990) 215–19.

[68] 'A virtual-currency administration' is defined in URVCBA s 102(24) to mean 'issuing virtual currency with the authority to redeem the currency for legal tender, bank credit, or other virtual currency'. In turn, 'a virtual-currency control-services vendor' is defined in URVCBA s 102(26) to mean 'a person that has control of virtual currency solely under an agreement with a person that, on behalf of another person, assumes control of virtual currency'.

[69] Securities Transfer Act, 2006, SO 2006, c 8. This is also the approach of UNIDROIT Convention (Geneva Convention), www.unidroit.org/instruments/capital-markets/geneva-convention/. For its part, Wyoming deviated from the URVCBA characterised the investor's right as full ownership. See M Lehmann, 'National Blockchain Laws as a Threat to Capital Markets Integration' [2021] *Uniform Law Review* 148, text that follows fn 109 academic.oup.com/ulr/issue/26/1.

According to the Comment to URVCBA Section 502, the provision is based on UCC Section 8-503 and 8-504 (to which OSTA Sections 97 and 98 correspond). Thereunder, the virtual currency under the control of a licensee or registrant is placed off the balance sheet of the virtual currency business which cannot deal with it as its own property.

Comment (1) refers to the one who relinquishes control of virtual currency to a virtual-currency business as 'the owner of virtual currency'. However, in fact, by giving control, this person's ownership of the virtual currency is replaced by an 'entitlement to virtual currency'. This is in effect a personal claim against the virtual-currency business in control, albeit fully backed by the virtual-currency, now owned by that business, and subject to the claim of that person. Terminology is thus imprecise and yet the drafters' intention is clear.

D. URVCBA: Concluding Remarks

The obligatory application of the UCC Article 8 regime to virtual-currency businesses is quite controversial. In Coinbase's view, 'a simpler full-backing, permissible investment obligations regime is preferable'. It argues that incorporating UCC Article 8 would invoke 'a distinct body of law not well-developed in our field, will complicate future application of prevailing consumer financial protection laws that may come to bear on retail virtual currency businesses and does not appear to enhance the fundamental obligations Coinbase and similar licensees already owe to their customers'.[70]

In the final analysis, whether the UCC Article 8 route is selected or not, the nature of the obligations of one in 'control' of a virtual currency to a participant in a transaction involving virtual currency is a matter of commercial or private – and not regulatory – law. In principle, it would thus be welcome to include the passage of a detailed statute specifically addressing the holding of and the transaction with virtual currencies, as well as CERs, as a matter of commercial law.

VI. Conclusion

The determination of proprietary rights in digital assets is crucial to their distribution in case of insolvency. First, between buyer and seller, the transfer of control appears to be a critical element in the acquisition of a proprietary right in a digital asset under all discussed legislative acts. Accordingly, where one of the parties to a sales transaction becomes insolvent, the transfer of control denotes the tipping

[70] As quoted by K Cooper, 'Uniform Regulation for Virtual Currency Business: Coming to a State Near You' (*coindesk*, 2 July 2017) www.coindesk.com/uniform-regulation-virtual-currency-businesses-coming-state-near/.

point as to the estate into which the asset will fall. Second, between a depositor-customer and a depositary-exchanger of digital assets, the terms of the deposit will determine whether upon the insolvency of the depositary, the asset will fall into the hands of its creditors or be taken by the depositor. For its part, the URVCBA regime protects the depositor upon the insolvency of the depositary by treating the depositor's right as an entitlement to virtual currency.

More generally, the CER alongside with the CUMD and the 'transferable record', which have all been created by emerging technologies, are new types of assets. To that end, UCC Article 12 provides a basis for commercial law transactions in CERs and CUMDs. It is a more than welcome clarification of the legal situation. And yet, as this paper has demonstrated, several issues arise in the way the subject is treated.

First, there is no point in addressing CERs and transferable records in separate pieces of legislation. Rather, the transferable record, effectively being an electronic note, should have been brought into the ambit of UCC Article 12.

Second, the relationship between the CER and the transferable record is addressed in a very confusing manner. Thus, the transferable record is excluded from the CER,[71] brought to be covered in part by UCC Article 12,[72] and then treated as if it were a CER.[73] Clarity could have been gained by a more coherent approach.

Third, it is also confusing that UCC Article 12 states that the control over CERs does not confer rights to enforce obligations thereon.[74] It might have been wiser to follow the footsteps of the MLETR also for UCC Article 12 and address only records in which control is the key to the enforcement of the rights thereon, while still explicitly extending coverage to electronic records with no parallel paper-documents.[75]

Fourth, some negotiability issues ought to be further examined. For example, the automatic protection that a 'qualifying purchaser' is given upon good faith acquisition for value[76] may go too far. Nothing of that sort exists under the MLETR. On the other hand, the notice requirement as a condition for discharge[77] and the indirect way to accomplish freedom from contract defences[78] are not in line with full negotiability. A broad scope of the acquisition of negotiability (upon a mere good faith acquisition) and yet in a limited form (requiring notice to be given) is not a self-explanatory or obvious policy choice and is something to be further explored.

[71] Text at n 23.
[72] Text that follows paragraph containing n 23.
[73] n 25.
[74] Text at paragraphs containing nn 13–14.
[75] See Part IV.
[76] Text that follows n 10.
[77] Text at n 25.
[78] Text around n 12 and between nn 25–26.

Fifth, storage regimes ought not to be dealt with separately, as it is now done under the URVCBA.[79] Rather, rules for the storage regime should have been integrated into UCC Article 12. Whether or not to adopt the specific URVCBA regime remains to be further explored.

In the final analysis, UCC Article 12 is a leap forward in the effort to address legal issues stemming from the proliferation of emerging technologies. Even as it stands to be improved, it is a beacon, and not only starting point, for jurisdictions seeking to keep up with progress in their laws.

[79] See Part V.

INDEX

www.ingramcontent.com/pod-product-compliance
Lightning Source LLC
LaVergne TN
LVHW021259080425
808019LV00003B/62
* 9 7 8 1 5 0 9 9 7 6 7 5 1 *